Applied Anthropology

Domains of Application

Edited by

Satish Kedia and John van Willigen

Westport, Connecticut
London

Library of Congress Cataloging-in-Publication Data

Applied anthropology : domains of application / edited by Satish Kedia
and John van Willigen.
    p. cm.
    Includes bibliographical references and index.
    ISBN 0–275–97841–9 ((cloth) : alk. paper) — ISBN 0–275–97842–7 ((pbk) : alk.
    paper)   1. Applied anthropology. I. Kedia, Satish. II. Van Willigen, John.
  GN397.5.A657   2005
  301–dc22   2005017486

British Library Cataloguing-in-Publication Data is available.

Library of Congress Catalog Card Number: 2005017486
ISBN: 0–275–97841–9
    0–275–97842–7(pbk.)

First published in 2005

Praeger Publishers, 88 Post Road West, Westport, CT 06881
An imprint of the Greenwood Publishing Group, Inc.
www.praeger.com

Printed in the United States of America

∞

The paper used in this book complies with the
Permanent Paper Standard issued by the National
Information Standards Organization (Z39.48–1984).

10 9 8 7 6 5 4 3 2 1

Contents

Acknowledgments

The seeds for this book project were sown a number of years ago during a series of conversations we had about the lack of a resource book in applied anthropology that presented an overview of the important domains of application. It was clear to us that students and practitioners alike could benefit from such a resource. In 2001, we contacted several of our colleagues across the United States—some of the well-known authorities on various domains of applied anthropology—to contribute to such a volume. We asked them to consider the topic from the perspective of their academic and applied experience and provide a state-of-the-art discussion and analysis on their areas of expertise. Although the scope of the collection prevented us from including many other domains, the ones covered here represent the most important. We would like to express our deepest thanks to the contributors—Marietta Baba, Linda Bennett, Deborah Crooks, Nancy Greenman, Bob Harman, David Himmelgreen, Peter Little, Thomas McGuire, Anthony Oliver-Smith, Robert Rhoades, and Linda Whiteford—for their hard work, tenacity, and patience, as well as for being so generous and responsive to editorial comments. We believe that this volume belongs to them and is a tribute to their extensive knowledge and lifetime service to applied anthropology.

Throughout the process of compiling this book, several scholars provided invaluable comments on various portions of the text, including Melissa Checker, Margaret Kedia, Heidi Kenaga, Sunil Khanna, Jackson Montgomery Roper, Hillary Sasse, and a number of anonymous reviewers. Great appreciation is due Linda Sadler for her editorial prowess in helping to create a uniform style across all of the contributions. We would also like to thank Sharese Willis and Julie Grady for their assistance at various stages of this project. We are grateful to Mary Campbell, Sarah Frith, and Jennifer

Kadrovich for checking the references and for performing other tasks during the volume's long gestational period. We are also thankful to the hardworking staff at Praeger Publishers for their help in facilitating the publication of this book, especially Assistant Editor Elizabeth Potenza and Production Manager Bridget Austiguy-Preschel. The manuscript tremendously benefited from the expertise of the staff at Publication Services, Inc., including Project Manager Susan Yates, Production Manager Foti Kutil, and Production Coordinator Sarah Lee.

In addition to the contributors of this volume, many teachers, colleagues, and friends have played a significant role in shaping our views on applied anthropology and have directly or indirectly influenced the publication of this book. We would like to thank Susan Abbott-Jamieson, Tom Arcury, Carol Bryant, Michael Cernea, Erve Chambers, Bill DeWalt, Kathleen DeWalt, Bill Dressler, Ruthbeth Finerman, Shirley Fiske, Art Gallaher Jr., Tom Greider, Stan Hyland, Indrajit Marwah, Juliana McDonald, Steve Morin, Chad Morris, Kathy Oths, Flor Palis, Steve Pavey, Sara Quandt, Barbara Rylko-Bauer, Jean Schensul, Steve Schensul, Nancy Schoenberg, and Vinay Srivastava.

Finally, we appreciate the encouragement and support from our families during this endeavor. For this, Satish Kedia thanks his wife, Margaret; daughters, Sapna and Reeva; and parents, Sitaram and Saraswati Kedia. John van Willigen thanks his wife, Jacqueline, and daughters Anne and Juliana.

Satish Kedia and John van Willigen

1 Applied Anthropology: Context for Domains of Application

Satish Kedia and John van Willigen

Applied anthropology is conceived as the application of anthropological knowledge, methodology, and theoretical approaches to address societal problems and issues. The focus of this book is on how anthropologists put their skills to work in a variety of settings or domains to inform policy and to initiate action that alleviates some of the most pressing social, economic, health, and technological problems facing communities and organizations. Committed to protecting the diversity and vitality of human lifeways around the world, applied anthropologists play a central role in developing programs and projects that have a lasting impact on the lives of individuals and communities. The scope and variety of their research challenges prevalent stereotypes about anthropologists in popular cinema and culture, such as the adventurer Indiana Jones and the lone excavator wearing a pith helmet. Increasingly, many of those with postgraduate training in anthropology pursue careers in government, nongovernmental organizations (NGOs), or business rather than teaching at a university. According to a recent study, from 1977 to 1997 roughly one third of new PhD graduates worked outside academia, often in applied domains, and in some years the figure was as high as 42 percent (Price 2001).

The work of applied anthropologists is interdisciplinary and involves a variety of stakeholders, including decision makers in government or corporations, NGOs, and other interest groups; scientific or technical experts; and leaders and members of communities and organizations. This intrinsic collaboration in the field requires that applied anthropologists be skilled in working with others and be conversant in the specific technical languages of related fields for effective communication with other experts. In addition, anthropologists must have a firm grasp of the research methodologies and communication practices specific to a particular domain in order to produce the desired information efficiently. Although the foundation of effective practice in a domain of application is mastery over a broadly diverse set of research and communication skills, advocacy is an important aspect of achieving the desired outcome. It is through advocacy that anthropologists build long-term, collaborative relationships with communities. Effective advocacy entails being a consistent proponent of a particular set of goals in the public life of a domain. Many applied anthropologists have had a significant impact on important issues through their advocacy, advancing the interests not of the discipline but of the public beneficiaries of their work.

The domains where applied anthropologists might find themselves employed are quite diverse, and the number continues to increase. They can be defined narrowly or broadly. In *Applied Anthropology: An Introduction,* van Willigen (2002, 8) provides a list of common domains, though not exhaustive, including.

Agriculture	Human Rights, Racism, and Genocide
Alcohol and Drug Use	Industry and Business
Community Action	Land Use and Land Claims
Criminal Justice and Law Enforcement	Language and Action
Cultural Resource Management	Media and Broadcasting
Design and Architecture	Military
Development Policies and Practices	Missions
Disaster Research	Nutrition
Economic Development	Policy Making
Education and Schools	Population and Demography
Employment and Labor	Recreation
Energy Extraction	Religious Expression
Environment	Resettlement
Evaluation	Social Impact Assessment
Fisheries Research	Training Programs
Forestry and Forests	Urban Development
Geriatric Services	Water Resources Development
Government and Administration	Wildlife Management
Health and Medicine	Women in Development
Housing	

The primary goal of this anthology is to discuss important domains of application in anthropology where knowledge, methodologies, and theories relevant to a particular setting for applied work are employed to connect research, policy, and action. The domains of application discussed in this volume include development, agriculture, environment, health and medicine, nutrition, resettlement, business and industry, education, and aging. Applied anthropologists working in these domains have amassed knowledge through their own research and from relevant literature in anthropology and cognate disciplines, agencies, professional organizations, networks of colleagues, legal and regulatory frameworks, and projects and programs that utilize best practices. There are many other settings where anthropologists are honing their skills while meaningfully contributing to the domain in which they are working. In this chapter, we provide a contextual background to anthropology, including the history, methodologies, roles, and ethics of applied anthropology. In the latter part of the chapter, we briefly introduce the domains of application as elaborated upon in this volume.

Historical Context of Applied Anthropology

The beginning of applied anthropology is truly the beginning of anthropology. Some scholars trace the foundation of applied anthropology as far back as the classical age. Herodotus (circa 485–325 BCE) gathered data for his government about the neighboring peoples in the Mediterranean Sea basin to inform Greek foreign policy (van Willigen 2002). In fact, most work of an anthropological nature during this period had a practical impetus: to acquire data on enemies or subjects that could be used to maintain power. This is true throughout the time of the Persian dominance, the Roman Empire, and the Crusades (Gwynne 2003).

As imperialism spread in the 1700s and 1800s, Western countries realized the value of applying their studies of remote subjects to developing strategies of domination and economic exploitation. Eventually, studies of other cultures for such purposes became a regular activity. An important early applied scholar in North America was Father Joseph Lafitau, who arrived in New France in 1711 as a missionary to the Iroquois Indians and became thoroughly familiar with their culture (Marthaler 2002). His experiences were published in an ethnography, *Customs of American Indians Compared with the Customs of Primitive Times* (1724). Scholars from other sciences also influenced the burgeoning field. Lending scientific credence to the methodology, famous botanist Carolus Linnaeus used ethnographic approaches in developing his revolutionary system for classifying and naming plants that was published in *Systema Naturae* in 1735. François Péron, a zoologist, was asked to accompany the 1801–04 Baudin French scientific expedition to New Holland (southern and western Australia), where his responsibilities included gathering ethnographic information that later yielded extensive contributions to the growing fields of natural history and anthropology (Adams 1998).

Applied anthropological work heightened in the 1800s in both government and industry. In 1807, the East India Company appointed Francis Buchanan to study the people of Bengal in India after earlier company governance of the natives had led to disaster and to the British Parliament's taking control of the territory (Vidyarthi 1984). In the United States, Congress hired Henry R. Schoolcraft, one of the founders of the American Ethnological Society, to compile his studies of Native American tribes. His six-volume ethnology, *Information Respecting the History, Condition and Prospects of the Indian Tribes of the United States,* produced from 1851 to 1857, served to inform U.S. policy on the indigenous population. In Europe, anthropology initially grew out of a split among British ethnographical societies dealing with humanitarian issues in the early and mid-1800s resulting from a growing desire by one faction to no longer be caught up in discussions but to *apply* their knowledge by taking an active role in the abolition of slavery and in securing better treatment of aborigines (Reining 1962).

At the turn of the twentieth century, the divergent strands of applied anthropology began to coalesce, and the field of anthropology formed those institutional apparatuses that give a discipline legitimacy: academic departments, degree programs, and professional associations. Researchers in the United States, Great Britain, and Mexico conducted national and regional ethnographic surveys, single-culture focused ethnographies, and topic-specific ethnographies. Though most of the anthropological research of this era was government sponsored, there were privately funded projects as well, including the Women's Anthropological Society of Washington's 1896 study of housing conditions for the poor in the nation's capital (van Willigen 2002). Publications of problem-oriented research conducted on behalf of the government or private organizations contributed greatly to a growing body of anthropological literature.

The first university courses in anthropology, conducted at Oxford in the 1880s, were designed to train administrators for colonial work; the first use of the term applied anthropology occurred in a description of the Oxford program (Fortes 1953; van Willigen 2002). Applied work undertaken by the Ethnological Society of London and later the Anthropological Society of London, founded in 1843 and 1863 respectively, provided the field with much of its disciplinary infrastructure (Reining 1962). The *American Anthropologist* journal was begun in 1888 by the Anthropological Society of Washington (ASW) and came under the auspices of the American Anthropological Association (AAA) when it was founded in 1902. At the time, there were many other anthropological societies, but the AAA was able to bring these professional organizations together nationally as never before.

Anthropology in the United States was considered synonymous with the government's Bureau of American Ethnology (BAE), which was created in 1879 by a congressional act to gather data to assist the federal government in the area of Indian affairs. It was for a BAE report in 1902 that James Mooney coined the term "applied ethnology" (Hinsley 1976; van Willigen 2002). A similar institute was established by the U.S. government in the Philippines in 1901, initially as a museum, although it became the Division of Ethnology of the Bureau of Science in 1906. In 1899, Franz Boas, the father of American anthropology, became the first professor of anthropology at Columbia University. The United States Immigration Commission sponsored Boas's 1907 research on European immigrant children, which countered existing eugenic and racist views of the effects of immigration on the American population by examining race, culture, and language separately. This later became the basis for cultural relativism and deeply influenced several of his famous students, including Alfred Kroeber, Ralph Linton, Margaret Mead, and Ruth Benedict.

Then, as now, research in anthropology was primarily empirical, comprising the collection and analysis of data about a specific culture or community in order to contribute to what we know about the origin and great diversity of human organization and adaptation. Still, the Darwinian evolutionary paradigm, dominant in the natural sciences, was equally influential in anthropology, which meant that during the applied ethnology era, 1860–1930 according to van Willigen (2002), practitioners trained in the West held a teleological view of human culture. Fieldwork was primarily devoted to documenting the lifeways of the indigenous populations of the Western hemisphere and the so-called less developed societies in Africa, Asia, and the Pacific Rim. This view was commonly held by many cultural anthropologists from Europe affiliated with governments that had colonial interests and by administrators being trained in ethnology in preparation for work in the colonies. Study in ethnology had been part of foreign service training in the Netherlands since 1864 (Held 1953; Kennedy 1944), the Union of South Africa since 1905 (Forde 1953), the Anglo-Egyptian Sudan since 1908 (Myres 1928), Belgian territories since 1920 (Nicaise 1960), and Australian New Guinea since 1925 (van Willigen 2002).

Many governments were supportive of anthropologists and their work for a variety of reasons. Great Britain hired anthropologists for their unique research abilities to work in the colonial empire, which encompassed several territories by the late 1800s and early 1900s, including Ireland, India, the Sudan, Uganda, Zimbabwe, Iraq, and Guyana. These anthropologists served as representatives or facilitators, acquainted administrators with the subjects of their jurisdictions, and informed colonial policy (Chambers

1989). In 1909 the Sudanese government appointed C. G. Seligman to conduct an ethnographic survey of the region. Later, as a professor, he prompted the research of other anthropologists, including E. E. Evans-Pritchard, who wrote one of the best-known ethnographies of his time *The Nuer* (1940), and S. F. Nadel, whose studies of the Nigerian Nupe state and the Nuba of Sudan were published in 1947.

World War I diminished this focus on ethnographies by thrusting populations into harsher realities and by leaving in its wake a generation of survivors searching for greater freedom and social justice. This soon proved to become a basis for the transformation of applied anthropology, as seen in the work of A. R. Radcliffe-Brown, an early supporter of applied work. Appointed as a professor of social anthropology at the University of Cape Town in South Africa from 1920 to 1925, he championed anthropology as a means to help quell the caustic racial environment in the region. Radcliffe-Brown's work established a functional theoretical framework that sparked other interest in applied anthropology and government sponsorship of such research. E. W. P. Chinnery, an anthropologist trained at Cambridge University, served as labor advisor to New Guinea Copper Mines Ltd. in 1924 before accepting a post as Government Anthropologist in New Guinea (1924–32). He later developed an anthropological training program at the University of Sydney (1957), subsequently making a practice of sending students to the New Guinea post for two years of practical anthropological training, after which the graduates received permanent appointments in administration.

Still, this type of research—although providing the discipline with invaluable case studies—implicitly sanctioned the hegemony of a Eurocentric perspective and colonial power. Moreover, it was largely unconcerned with how such communities themselves might effectively use this knowledge to meet the challenges of everyday life and ensure their cultural survival. Prior to 1945, when anthropologists worked in an applied capacity, they approached their research from a value-implicit perspective, devoted to principles of positivism (van Willigen 2002). Although some applied anthropologists felt that such an approach was unnecessarily restrictive, others argued persuasively that it was central to their work. Likewise, the role of the applied anthropologist was to remain as a consultant because it was largely believed during this period that extending beyond this role would overstep the expertise and function of an applied anthropologist.

In the United States, the onset of the Great Depression during the 1930s provided an opportunity for the field of anthropology to establish itself as instrumental in addressing practical societal problems. Although there were few anthropological academic positions available before World War II, work for the federal government and private business increased. As a result of President Franklin D. Roosevelt's New Deal, trained social scientists who could provide the information needed for policy development and implementation of government programs were in demand, particularly those with anthropological expertise in land tenure, migration, nutrition, education, and economic/resource development for Native Americans and rural America. Several applied research organizations arose during this time, including the Applied Anthropology Unit of the Bureau of Indian Affairs (BIA), created by John Collier in the mid-1930s. Under his leadership, the unit published several reports regarding settlement patterns and informed policy related to education and economic development.

Although the research and resulting reports were intended to impact policy, they actually had little influence on the process. Nevertheless, Collier's promotion of anthropology as a practical endeavor helped to further increase federal employment opportunities for anthropologists. In a 1935 program called Technical Cooperation—Bureau of Indian Affairs (TC-BIA), anthropologists worked with the U.S. Department of Agriculture to carry out projects related to economic and resource development on various Indian reservations (van Willigen 2002). These anthropologists also worked on a large-scale research project in the Rio Grande basin on land use effects caused by cultural factors within ethnic communities of the Southwest. Meanwhile, anthropologists working in private industry were especially interested in the link between the work environment and productivity, the well-known example being W. Lloyd Warner's ethnographic observations of work cultures at Western Electric during the Hawthorne Experiments of 1924–32, which eventually gave birth to industrial and business applied anthropology. Policy development and business projects of this era led to an expanded use of applied anthropology and applied methodologies such as action research, exemplifying the changes leading up to and through the crisis of World War II.

In 1941, the American Anthropological Association offered its firm support of the United States' participation in World War II, with anthropologists assisting in the country's war efforts. In fact, as van Willigen stated, "[Margaret] Mead (1977) estimate[d] that over 95 percent of American anthropologists were involved with work in support of the war effort during the 1940s" (2002, 28). The war attracted many anthropologists to federal employment, some on behalf of the War Relocation Authority, which managed the Japanese-American internment camps and used anthropologists as liaisons. Just as Britain had turned to Cambridge and Oxford for personnel trained in anthropology to assist those serving in the colonies, during World War II the United States turned to its universities to create institutes for educating government workers and the military on how to treat Germans and Japanese in recaptured areas.

In response to the growth of applied anthropology, in 1941 Margaret Mead, Ruth Benedict, and others established the Society for Applied Anthropology (SfAA), a professional organization coexisting with the AAA, which at that time had no applied division. About the same time, the Smithsonian Institute of Social Anthropology, founded in 1943, initiated several research projects, some of which employed methods under the leadership of George Foster that would later help shape applied medical anthropology (van Willigen 2002). The types of employment taken by applied anthropologists—researcher, instructor, consultant—remained relatively unchanged until around 1945. Many anthropologists were reticent about identifying themselves primarily as applied anthropologists. Consequently, they maintained a careful balance between academic and applied work, or they left federal jobs for employment in academia. In post–World War II America, the patriotic fervor that had driven support of the war waned, and anthropologists began to look critically upon their discipline's involvement in war efforts, particularly those assisting in Japanese-American internment camps. Because of this, and the government's declining need for anthropologists, government work opportunities for anthropologists all but evaporated. However, any job crisis in the discipline was averted because of an increased demand for college professors as university enrollment began to swell after the 1944 GI Bill began providing subsidies to returning veterans.

Applied anthropology did not fade away; postwar political and social upheavals and the waning of European colonial domination across the world were fomenting changes in the Western worldview and generating a new need for anthropologists. Some anthropologists actively sought positions of advocacy for marginalized cultures and communities, providing them with empirical information in the interests of self-determination and autonomy and to secure resource allocation or political representation. They thus ventured into decision making instead of merely providing the data that would inform such decisions. This transformation reflected the field's growing rejection of the value-implicit approach, which portrayed an impossible standard of objectivity that did not reflect the real world, and it became the basis for innovative applied anthropology methods that allowed for more direct involvement with study subjects and more efficient means to positively transform communities, such as action anthropology of the 1950s. Some practitioners implemented methods directed toward changes in behavior through interactive planning for the betterment of the community. The Fox Project, affiliated with a University of Chicago field school, was established by Sol Tax in the late 1940s to assist the Fox tribe in Iowa in developing greater community self-determination through a dual action and research project approach. From this first action-involved, value-explicit application ensued research and development anthropology, community development, collaborative research anthropology, and culture brokerage (van Willigen 2002; Tax 1958). With this change in perspective, however, a number of problematic ethical issues emerged.

These concerns were epitomized in the Vicos Project, headed by Allen Holmberg, an anthropologist at Cornell. In the 1950s, Holmberg and his associates contended that anthropology inherently affected studied communities and could not avoid this influence. In Vicos, Holmberg directly acted to alter the established hacienda hierarchy in Peru by purchasing and running a hacienda, then empowering the Indian laborers, through research and community development led by the anthropologists, to own and run it themselves. Although the goals of the project were indeed largely achieved and spawned other development and action projects, it raised serious questions about the ethics of such intervention and the role of the anthropologist (Chambers 1989; van Willigen 2002; Holmberg 1958).

Ethical issues continued to be a concern as anthropologists increasingly asserted their voices in criticism of the conflict in Vietnam and shunned federal employment in protest. The increasing politicization of the discipline at that time is best illustrated by the controversy over Project Camelot, a well-known case in the history of anthropological ethics. Sponsored by the U.S. Army in 1964, the project was purported to be one in which anthropologists and other social scientists were enlisted to help Latin American governments abate civil war in their countries, but it was summarily condemned by much of the anthropological community for its interference in the politics of other countries and its possible reinforcement of class divisions. Ultimately, Project Camelot was cancelled after the scientists involved discovered that their participation entailed conducting intelligence activities for the U.S. Army Special Operations Research Office.

During the latter part of the twentieth century, the rise of multinational corporations and global economies created a greater demand for utilizing anthropologists' expertise as a means to understand workplace or labor operations and to gain access to markets and consumers. During this period, more anthropologists began to use their knowledge instrumentally, serving the needs of specific client groups rather than studying particular cultures. In this vein, practicing anthropologists working for international agencies made tremendous contributions to the growth of applied anthropology. Over the last three decades, much of this impetus came from social scientists in the World Bank, the US Agency for International Development (USAID), the Food and Agriculture Organization (FAO), the World Health Organization (WHO), and other international organizations.

Especially noteworthy is the role played by anthropologists and sociologists at the World Bank in setting socially conscious policy and program guidelines using innovative methodologies with "competence, moral responsibility, and increased applicability" (Cernea 1994, 2). These social scientists contributed a significant amount to the literature in a variety of domains while promoting applied theory and methods, evaluation and impact assessment, and ethical practices in development projects through interdisciplinary and collaborative research.

In the United States, two additional factors helped foster the employment and research trends in this time: the reduction in the number of academic positions in the late 1970s through the present (Balderston and Radner 1971; Cartter 1974; D'Andrade et al. 1975) and the expansion in federal regulation, which mandated policy research. With recent concerns for accountability and cost-effectiveness, most federal grants for the provision of services require that a certain proportion of the budget be allocated toward program evaluation, an arena in which contemporary anthropologists effectively use their research expertise (Ervin 2000). Today, rather than working exclusively in universities as teachers or scholars, anthropologists work in a variety of settings. The majority are employed by government, state, or municipal agencies; international groups or policy institutes; nonprofit or charitable groups; and sometimes private research and consulting firms or corporations. Correspondingly, there has been a proliferation of new domains in which anthropologists may apply their skills, leading to additional meaningful roles for applied work.

Typical Settings and Roles for Applied Anthropologists

Currently, applied anthropologists have a variety of potential roles and domains of application from which to select. As Trotter and Schensul noted, in selecting a particular area of practice applied anthropologists must decide "with whom they wish to work, whether they have the skills or experience to conduct research and engage in practice, what their personal and professional values are, to what degree these values are rooted in particular theoretical frameworks, what position they [wish to] occupy in the structure of the research setting, and where they wish to place themselves on the continuum from critical outsider to activist insider" (2000, 694).

In their overview, Trotter and Schensul outlined five general areas of practice, delineated according to the anthropologist's level of involvement in programs and activities (2000). She or he may (1) generate research to be used in policy development at the local, state, or federal level, while not being actively involved in the process of implementation or (2) participate in project evaluation or monitoring, assessing its efficacy and identifying areas of improvement rather than developing models anew (692). The three remaining areas generally diverge from this perspective, in that the anthropologist takes a more active role. She or he may (3) develop "culturally based, theory-driven" interventions, for example, a public health campaign specifically directed at young HIV-positive Hispanic males in urban areas who reject condom use (693); (4) pursue advocacy or action work that attacks inequities in power and resource allocation in both local and global settings by assisting underrepresented groups in removing barriers to equity and social justice; or (5) undertake participatory action research (PAR), which entails long-term, joint partnerships with local communities to implement programs that are socially beneficial and impart residents with a sense of self-determination and empowerment (693). PAR is based on three important assumptions: that all people have the capacity to think and work together for a better life; that current and future knowledge, skills, and resources are to be shared in equitable ways that deliberately support fair distributions and structures; and that authentic commitment is required from participants (Fals-Borda and Rahman 1991).

Within a particular domain of application, applied anthropologists might operate in one role exclusively or combine multiple roles. All of these roles can be subdivided into five general categories: policy researcher or research analyst; evaluator, impact assessor, or needs assessor; culture broker; public participation specialist; and administrator or manager. The generic title anthropologist is not commonly used when discussing these roles, in part because most of these jobs are also available to other types of social scientists. Still, the foundation of anthropological work is its unique research repertoire, which is common to all of these positions.

Many applied practitioners' prime function is as policy researcher; as such, they provide data to those who make decisions based on the information. A 2000 National Association for the Practice of Anthropology (NAPA) survey of those who have master's level training in applied anthropology showed that more than 30 percent of respondents have researcher occupational roles and 22 percent required data collection skills on the job (Harman, Hess, and Shafe 2005). Thus, a solid background in research and data collection and assessment is necessary for successfully performing applied work. Applied anthropologists not only collect and provide data; they are often called upon to analyze that data, thereby functioning as research analysts, a role for which applied anthropologists are well suited, given their empirical background in ethnographic methods. The 2000 NAPA survey also showed that more than 20 percent of positions required quantitative data analysis skills and about 18 percent required ethnographic skills (Harman, Hess, and Shafe 2005). In addition, these research and analysis competencies have the potential to lead to policy development and implementation with the power of information control. When applied anthropologists become a part of the whole process, they allow themselves more input in the decisions that are made on the basis of their work (Chambers 1989).

The role of the evaluator also calls upon the research skills of anthropologists and may involve program monitoring and outcomes or social impact assessment. An evaluator's work begins after the implementation of a project, program, or policy in order to gauge its success, or lack thereof. When this work entails impact assessment, the evaluator conducts research on how communities will be affected by certain physical changes in their environments, such as new reservoirs, airports, or highway construction. Some anthropologists step in early as planners designing programs and projects or as needs assessors gathering information relevant to the design of programs in terms of social, economic health, and education requirements.

Cultural brokers liaise between programs or organizations and communities. In this role, many anthropologists serve as advocates for people unfamiliar with the entities that usually have some power over them. To bridge the gap that may exist between those in power and the people of a community, the applied anthropologist can facilitate achieving the goals of the community by empowering its individual members through education and organization. The belief is that with members who can more accurately represent their interests, the community is more likely to take action. In this way, anthropologists are able to more ethically serve as advocates, supporting the work of communities and other individuals (Chambers 1989). Cultural brokering always involves two-way communication and is rarely an anthropologist's primary role, but it may be applied functionally to other roles such as that of the public participation specialist, who is sometimes called upon for expert input in the planning process. Serving in this capacity, the applied anthropologist might organize public education using media and public meetings. This is a relatively new role for applied anthropologists, but more and more practitioners are being called upon to disseminate their knowledge and expertise in the public sphere. In the 2000 NAPA survey, 15 percent of respondents listed "planner" as their occupational role, whereas 8 percent listed "program services" (Harman, Hess, and Shafe 2005).

As the employment of applied anthropologists in new work settings increased during the early 1970s, anthropologists came to occupy positions of authority, including some high-ranking positions as key decision makers.

In the 2000 NAPA survey, about 10 percent of respondents identified "administrator" and 22 percent of respondents identified "manager" as their current roles (Harman, Hess, and Shafe 2005). In many instances, applied anthropologists advance in a natural progression from their research and policy roles to such positions, which reflects the success of anthropological training and the effectiveness of its methods.

Methodological Approaches

The nature of applied anthropological work is such that it is usually conducted at the request of an agent or an agency that needs answers to questions in order to make important decisions about programs and program funding. Therefore, it is unlike most academic inquiry in which the researcher decides the course, including the scope and length of the study. Applied anthropologists often work within the time constraints set by others and therefore must be equipped with a variety of methodological tools conducive to the nature of the work.

The general methodological framework most associated with anthropology is ethnography, an approach that can be defined as the systematic documentation and interpretation of human cultures in action. Although not exclusive to anthropology, this method is an especially valuable tool in the discipline. Interviewing skills, direct or participant observation, learning the local language, data recording and coding, and other aspects of qualitative research are the foundations of all ethnographic work. In addition, as Plattner and his colleagues (1989) assert, quantitative data collection and analysis should be equally familiar to cultural anthropologists, and graduate anthropology education should develop skills in research design that quantitatively tests a given hypothesis.

Traditionally, anthropologists have known ethnography as a research process that takes months or years of observation and data collection. However, because of the time sensitivity of applied work, a faster turnaround is often necessary. Since the 1970s, a series of more rapid research procedures have emerged. These are called by various names; the most common are rapid anthropological assessment or rapid assessment procedures (RAP), following Scrimshaw and Hurtado (1987). The techniques involved in these swifter, issue-focused ethnographic assessments include

novel forms of direct observation and participant observation; researcher's participation in the studied activity; semi-structured interviews; group interviews; focus groups; mapping; aerial photographs; group walks; diagramming; quantifications; ranking; group reading of satellite imagery; simulation games and role playing; sondeo techniques and small team investigations; imaginative selection of key information as in chain-interviews; procedures for eliciting the subject's assessments; self-definition. (Cernea 1992, under "Twin changes" in Section I: 1) [an unpaginated electronic publication]

Though seemingly efficient, RAP is not without critics. Its techniques do not use random sampling to yield statistically significant quantitative data; therefore, results cannot be used to make generalizations about a given population. Further, some practicing anthropologists do not feel it necessary to be trained in RAP because of its similarities to traditional methods, but, as with any research technique, for the methodology to work properly the researcher must be trained in proper usage. This is particularly true with RAP because it often involves practices of and collaboration with other fields. In order to conduct fieldwork using RAP methods, a triangulation of techniques such as easy-to-analyze sampling techniques, focus groups, and streamlined surveys can be employed to enhance reliability. Often RAP is simply used as a basis for long-term research or as pilot research in program development. It can also be specific to a subdiscipline, as with anthropologists working in agriculture who use rapid rural appraisal (RRA) (Rhoades 1982). RRA relies on obtaining information from insiders through rapid but reliable methods derived from ethnographical practices and survey methodologies, including collection of secondary data like maps and articles, and less formal, selective-sample, dynamic and iterative interviews, the results of which may possibly be used as a basis for a more elaborate survey (van Willigen 2002).

For gathering data quickly, focus group interviewing is frequently used in applied research in place of in-depth interviewing. In-depth interviewing is one of the most common methods of data collection in anthropology, but in the applied setting, it takes too much time to prepare and set up each interview, perform multiple interviews, and transcribe all. Although focus groups have not replaced in-depth interviewing for applied anthropologists, they are used in specific situations where the practitioner wants input from a number of people on the same topic or responses to the same questions from a number of stakeholders in a short period of time. In focus group interviewing, a facilitator asks participating members a set of open-ended questions prepared at the beginning of the session. Specific individuals are asked to attend because they have some significance or interest related to the main research topic and the researcher wants to get their perspective. Focus groups typically include a small number of participants (from six to ten) who form a mostly homogeneous group, unless the research specifically involves studying the dynamics of heterogeneous social mixtures with a common interest in the topic (e.g., staff of one company with differing ranks, like managers and warehouse personnel). Focus groups are helpful in forming hypotheses based on informant feedback, evaluating various research settings and subjects, developing questions for later surveys or interviews, and obtaining feedback on findings from previous studies (Morgan 1988). However attractive focus groups are for their efficiency in revealing detailed information about a certain population, they also have disadvantages. Their responses are influenced by the social context of a public group setting and other factors that can alter results, such as mixed gender or education levels among participants, or physical settings and times of sessions. The abilities of the facilitator can also affect responses, since it is his or her responsibility to keep conversations lively and on-topic enough to answer the research questions, while not avoiding those responses not directly on topic that could still be significant to the research.

Another important applied method is participatory action research (PAR), which requires collaboration from the community or group with a commitment to change in order to lead to a collective action benefiting the members of that community or group. Fals-Borda refers to effective PAR practices as those that "convert cultural elements into political and economic actions" (2000, 632). As described by Smith, Pyrch, and Ornelas Lizardo, "[t]he essence of the PAR approach is dynamic engagement in collective reflection and action" (1993, 320). As a group working together, people engaged in PAR fluctuate between analyzing or educating and investigating to bring about action and transformation (Smith, Pyrch, and Ornelas Lizardo 1993).

An approach used less often by applied anthropologists is social network analysis, which involves both formal and informal data collection "identify[ing] the structure and meaning of relationships, explain[ing] their impact, and predict[ing] how they will affect the future of individuals, organizations, and societies" (Trotter 2000, 210). Such networks might be ego-centered (comprise the connections between one person and the population being researched), full/relational (all individuals belonging to a general group or network within a culture), or partial/specialized (those individuals who share specific beliefs or behaviors). This visualization of social networks can result in significant observations of groups by displaying common interactions and relationships that may not be evident in hierarchical or organizational charts.

In addition to these techniques, applied anthropologists may be more likely than other anthropologists to use quantitative and technologically advanced data collection techniques. They may administer quantitative surveys and use cognitive methods such as free listing, pile sorts, triad tests, or decision-making modeling. Some rely on Geographic Information Systems (GIS) as a way of mapping the local terrain, or spatial mapping to study human perceptions of space. As societies and technologies change, so do the research methodologies employed by applied anthropologists. Participatory research, for example, continues to be demanded more and more often, coinciding with the shift in all types of development (program, policy, product, marketing, business) toward a more user-focused approach. Increasingly, various fields cross over and mesh, as do cultures and communities; therefore, applied anthropologists have to continue to develop more sophisticated means to exact useful and precise data. Much more so than in the past, they need to communicate their results to increasingly diverse audiences (clientele and study participants) who may have different competencies. This means that applied anthropologists should have well-developed written and oral communication skills and that such expertise should be cultivated in graduate school to better prepare students for professional life. Much of the writing that students currently perform comprises variations on the term paper, which can serve as a framework. Writing requirements need to be expanded, however, to include more accessible exposition, such as brochures, monographs, policy reports, press releases, formal letters, persuasive reports, and other media forms such as Web sites, radio, and film. Also, most graduate training at U.S. universities entails teaching, which can foster oral communication skills; however, students should be encouraged to make presentations in conferences and participate in workshops to enhance these skills. All of the methodologies mentioned here are representative of the most commonly used and the most recent additions to the applied toolbox and should be considered mandatory in training future practitioners.

Ethical Issues

Ethics—the discernment of moral duty and obligation given a particular situation and setting—is very important, if not absolutely central, to applied anthropological work. The very reputation of the field depends on adherence to a strong ethical policy (Chambers 1989). The ethical requirements of applied anthropology are especially challenging since the practitioner must negotiate an intricate balance between the interests of the clients who commission the work and those of the community being studied. Adding to the complexity of a situation's ethics is that the perceptions and goals of those involved can be quite varied.

Applied work can involve many stakeholders because it often depends on collaboration with various communities or organizations, governments, and professionals from other fields. Applied anthropologists must consider the ethics of relevant parties—including their own—and of major actions to be taken as well as minor utterances. In addition, the ethical issues of applied anthropology are as varied as the subdisciplines within the field. For instance, in business anthropology researchers must consider whether reported findings to managers in a corporation may lead to worse working conditions or streamlining and the elimination of jobs (Baba 1998).

The guidelines of ethical conduct, now prevalent in applied anthropology, have been developed over time, unfortunately largely as a result of mistreatment of or disregard for study populations or unintended harm that ensued after applied anthropological research was conducted. As early as 1919, ethics had become a concern in applied anthropology. About a year after World War I ended, Franz Boas instigated much discussion by exacting bitter criticism in a letter to *The Nation* titled "Scientists as Spies" about four anthropologists who conducted covert spying operations under the pretext of doing anthropological research (Weaver 1973). Two decades later, an unintentional ethical breach occurred in the aftermath of Cora Du Bois's fieldwork among the people of Alor, who reside in what is now Indonesia. They had never heard of America before Du Bois's time among them, which was cut short by the onset of World War II. When the Japanese later occupied the region, some of the Alorese said that America would win the war, and as a consequence Japanese officials beheaded the alleged U.S. supporters in public to dissuade anyone else from being sympathetic to the Allied cause (van Willigen 2002).

In the post–World War II era, the U.S. military was prevented from funding many of the anthropology projects that dealt with issues such as culture and political stability. Simultaneously, the Nuremberg trials of 1945–1949 caused a backlash in the biological sciences with regard to the ethical treatment of human subjects and the moral responsibilities of the individual despite the dictates of those in power. Increasingly, during this period the social sciences were accused of naiveté or of being a tool of imperialism (Wax 1987). In response to these developments, in 1949 the SfAA developed the first professional code of ethics in anthropology (Mead, Chapple, and Brown 1949). On the international front, the World Medical Assembly adopted the Declaration of Helsinki in 1964 to address the ethical treatment of human subjects. Further safeguards were developed for national adoption: Institutional Review Boards (IRBs) were initiated and the National Research Act was passed in 1974 to help ensure protection of study populations in biomedical or behavioral research. Still, even more alarming breaches in ethical behavior among applied anthropologists emerged.

Those social scientists involved in the 1964 Project Camelot were misled to believe that it was designed to study political effects of social change in developing nations, but they were, in fact, meant to spy for the U.S. government. The project in Chile was actually a military counterinsurgency effort to discover a social systems model for predicting and affecting social changes that would influence Third World politics (Horowitz 1967). Many social scientists felt disdain for Project Camelot because they thought their disciplines ill-fitted to an endeavor designed to interfere with the concerns of other nations, especially situations in which research would be used to reinforce deep class divisions and not eradicate them. The controversy sparked by Project Camelot and other similar situations led to the formation of the American Anthropological Association's Committee on Ethics in 1970.

Concerns about ethical behavior again came to bear in a project in Thailand. Opium trade was increasingly becoming a global problem, and the hill tribes in the northern part of the country were a major source of poppies for this trade (van Willigen 2002). Social scientists studied the hill tribes under the guise of informing policy for dealing with the trade, while fighting in Vietnam escalated. Agencies within the U.S. government, such as the Advanced Research Projects Agency (ARPA) of the Department of Defense, were major backers of the research. Interested in maintaining the status quo, they saw the utility of descriptive cultural data in securing a government in a country whose proximity to the spread of communism rendered it potentially unstable. An investigation later revealed that some of the anthropologists involved knew of the government's intended use of the data from the beginning (Chambers 1989). The maelstrom precipitated in the discipline by this event and others related to the Vietnam conflict resulted in more frequent and, often, heated discussions about the ethical responsibilities of applied anthropologists.

One of the ongoing problems with ethics in applied anthropology is how to deal with the issue of privacy. Realizing that the potential for abusing the researcher-informant relationship is high, the anthropologist must always be on guard for any hint of infringement. Unfortunately, researchers have not always honored this relationship. Only with the increasing focus on modern societies, shadowing the attention given to Third World communities in years past, have social scientists begun to insist on more stringent protection of informants, mostly because subjects in modern societies would be more likely to have access to published research findings (Chambers 1989). Because study results in anthropology are now largely out of the control of the researcher and are subject to public purview, ethical research must begin with informed consent. This is not always easy, since the scope of the proposed research may not be immediately apparent. Inductive research, the kind most often conducted by anthropologists, creates multiple possibilities and a host of ideas that might be investigated. Given the breadth of the issues that surface in such work, it is difficult to determine just what the researcher should ask the subject to agree to. Should general consent be sought only at the beginning of the work, or should consent be sought for a second time once the researcher has discovered an interesting aspect of the findings to pursue further? Also, if a researcher knows from the start that a research request will be denied, should she or he obtain a general consent and then pursue the desired work once rapport is developed with the subject?

Any clear sense of proper ethics may become mired in the many documents produced in the process of applied anthropological research. For instance, fieldnotes are required to conduct thorough research, but the question remains as to who actually owns them: the researcher or the client? In the past, fieldnotes were considered the personal domain of the researcher, but this assumption is tenuous today. The client may demand their return, or worse, law enforcement officials may subpoena them in cases in which illegal activity, such as drug use or domestic violence, has been under study.

One notable case on the issue of informed consent was brought out by Patrick Tierney in his book, *Darkness in El Dorado: How Scientists and Journalists Devastated the Amazon* (2000), in which he levied a series of allegations against James V. Neel and his team for their research on the Yanomami of the Amazon. According to Tierney, Neel's research team took biological samples from the Yanomami under the pretense of looking for infectious diseases, while the primary goal was actually to observe patterns of genetic change between individuals and groups in a village and beyond—a goal left unexpressed to the Yanomami. Tierney claimed that though Neel's group did test for intestinal parasites, hepatitis B, and other health-related matters and provided medical treatment for some time, there was, in fact, no intended health benefit to the study population. Tierney's accusations were so injurious to Neel's reputation and ultimately to the field of anthropology that in 2001 the AAA appointed an El Dorado Task Force to investigate the charges. The crux of the problem was Neel's alleged failure to fully inform the subjects about the goals of the study. The Task Force, however, cautioned that the AAA not view the findings as a trial of a specific anthropologist but as an opportunity for anthropologists to reflect on the ethics of all dimensions of research conducted (AAA 2003).

Knowledge control is at the root of informed consent and is the basis for many ethical questions that may arise concerning the use of applied research, particularly fieldwork. Information so obtained can be used for political purposes and may be implicated in the psychological, political, or economic control of human beings. As van Willigen has noted, "Just how anthropological data plays into the hands of an exploitive, multinational corporation, an oppressive, totalitarian organization, or a secret intelligence agency is not clear" (2002, 52). Seemingly, the only protection is the establishment and maintenance of an honest, open, and respectful relationship between the researcher and all participants, which can aid in obtaining ongoing consent, fruitful participation, and productive conversation about research goals and possible implications of the work. It is critical that applied anthropologists be familiar with and carefully employ in their research and practice the current ethical guidelines developed by professional organizations such as the AAA (2005), the SfAA (2005), and NAPA (2005).

Domains Discussed in This Anthology

As discussed previously, the domains of application for applied anthropology are quite varied and have led to a growing number of subdisciplines. This text explores some of the dominant subdisciplines emergent at the turn of the twenty-first century, including development, agriculture, environment, health and medicine, nutrition, involuntary resettlement, business and industry, education, and aging.

Development

Peter D. Little describes development anthropology as the application of anthropological knowledge to the solution of problems that are endemic in developing countries, such as poverty, hunger, and environmental degradation. Development anthropology began in the 1970s, accompanying changes in governmental policies, international and local employment opportunities for anthropologists, and a growing literature base. Throughout his exposition, Little offers supportive historical context and examples of anthropological studies.

Crossing into discussions on recent training, careers, theory, and methods, Little establishes the important functional and economic relationships between development anthropologists and an array of state and privately funded organizations, from large, wealthy development bureaucracies and NGOs to small university institutes and grassroots and indigenous groups. He also describes development anthropology practices as interdisciplinary collaborations with other social scientists, economists, ecologists, and agriculturalists. Little notes the benefits of this collaborative effort on substantiating methods like PAR but also stresses that development anthropologists should build upon those particular skills that distinguish them from other anthropologists and social scientists and work toward an integration of theory, method, and practice to elevate the field into a noted subdiscipline.

Little argues in particular that those theories (e.g., populist-inspired, dependency theory, or Marxist-derived) grounding empirical work need to be brought to the fore in order to highlight the innovative contributions of development anthropologists to the field and to international policy debates. He details a few examples of how development anthropologists' key theoretical contributions have led to program modifications. To further demonstrate the importance of integrating theory, method, and practice, Little offers a case study of his work with the Kenya Wildlife Services to establish a project monitoring their initiative to protect the pastoral tradition in East Africa. He suggests that since development anthropologists are knowledgeable about indigenous peoples' use of natural resources in key wildlife regions, environmental organizations will continue to solicit their expertise on potential outcomes at the local level.

Agriculture

Robert E. Rhoades explains just how significant agriculture is to all humans—it affects culture, technology, economics, societies, and religions. He defines the domain of agricultural anthropology as concerned with the "human element in the total agrarian system," from production to consumption and symbolic systems of culture, from the origins of agriculture to future developments. Rhoades states that agricultural anthropologists strive to translate their knowledge of agriculture as a social and cultural practice into "technical and policy advances," some working in academia and many more employed by international institutes, NGOs, and governmental agencies.

Agricultural anthropology is a relatively young subdiscipline, and Rhoades argues that agriculture was kept distanced from the intellectual work of early anthropologists, though it was often a part of ethnographies and a source of employment, with practitioners serving as liaisons among governments, colonies, and peasants. He points to the New Deal's Soil Conservation Service of the 1930s as the first time anthropologists worked in agriculture. Though applied and theoretical studies of agricultural practices published in other fields (such as sociology and economics) used anthropological field research, agriculture and anthropology failed to synthesize until the 1970s, when new PhDs began to seek work as professional anthropologists in private and nonprofit sectors.

Rhoades details stereotypes that have held back the profession and outlines strategies for developing a better model to secure employment: develop good communication; have basic familiarity with bioscientific terminology; demonstrate clearly how anthropological methods can make a difference in terms of production, income, or nutrition; show how farmers are "expert ethnobotanists" with indigenous knowledge that is very useful to project goals; negotiate an integral place for themselves and their contribution early in the research process; and ensure that their professional status is perceived as commensurate with the other affiliated scientists. He then describes three case studies in which agricultural anthropologists at the International Potato Center in Lima, Peru, initiated key technological and policy changes.

Rhoades concludes his chapter by urging agricultural anthropologists to develop a professional relationship with a public constituency, to the extent seen in other fields, such as economics, law, or education, as a means "to declare its relevance through action." This will entail the communication of agricultural anthropology skills and ideas to an audience wider than the narrow community of practitioners, as well as a modification of university training to incorporate coursework on application and policy, the material base of agriculture, and the languages of agricultural sciences.

Environment

Thomas R. McGuire describes a variety of settings for applied anthropological work concerning humans and the environment. For example, practitioners specializing in this domain might conduct research on the management of renewable resources and the people dependent upon them or on how local knowledge can be used to build ecologically sustainable communities or even on environmentalism as a social movement. He stresses the importance of theoretical foundations in all such work and discusses those key conceptual "building blocks" of environmental anthropology research: cultural ecology, political economy, and political ecology. He maps these concepts according to a chronology of theoretical shifts in the field from the post–World War II era to the present.

McGuire characterizes the 1950s as a time when researchers in environmental anthropology were primarily interested in human ecosystems. Key questions addressed how individuals rather than market forces could be empowered to access and control resources in their region. He notes that during the 1980s and 1990s environmental anthropologists increasingly employed political ecology to bring these two levels together, "how political and ecological forces interact to cause social and environmental change." Other environmental anthropologists have found such research too politicized in assuming that external forces should take priority, and they in turn substituted event ecology, focusing on the history of a significant environmental change in order to offer policymakers more workable solutions. Still others, having found the field insufficiently political, are committed to liberation ecology and strive to promote alternative development strategies using community knowledge.

McGuire encourages practitioners to pay attention to "both of its [environment anthropology's] theoretical roots," addressing both the specific, local ways in which human activity transforms the environment and the broader political economy that shapes and potentially constrains how that activity will take place. To detail how concepts and applications play out in the field of environmental anthropology, he examines the effects of local and state policies on communities of fisheries. Whatever the approach and subfield of environmental anthropology, he notes that practitioners should always endeavor to supplement cultural knowledge at the local level with the specific political economy of regions. Some are applying their skills and methods, including mapping systems, to address the potential transformation of habitats and those populations dependent on them. Others have been working with indigenous communities to construct countermaps that communicate their knowledge of key topological features and to use ethnocartography as a political tool for gaining state recognition of indigenous rights and for protecting biodiversity.

McGuire acknowledges that, in the late 1990s, backyard anthropology emerged as an opportunity "for asserting anthropological methods and engagement in community-based environmental protection efforts," a fertile area for the employment of those with a particular expertise in and commitment to environmental justice. In fact, he argues that anthropologists with substantive expertise in ethnographic technique and a thorough understanding of the geopolitical dimensions of environmental change are increasingly being called upon to ensure that a "healthy and productive life in harmony with nature is indeed a human entitlement."

Health and Medicine

Linda M. Whiteford and Linda A. Bennett define medical anthropology as the domain that explores how cultural belief systems shape humans' experience of health and illness. The application of a biocultural synthesis is where anthropology goes beyond traditional medical social science, situating an individual's physical or mental status within a network of practices that recognize the "co-primacy and power of both biology and culture" in the maintenance of health. This relationship is subject to theorization, but for Whiteford and Bennett nearly all research in medical anthropology has an applied dimension. Contemporary practitioners are employed not just in academia but also in medical, social work, and public health fields, where their research has immediate implications for policies and programs.

Contemporary medical anthropologists apply their training in cultural analysis to a variety of medical or health care systems. They examine differences in birth practices, exploring how gender, socioeconomic status, class, and ethnicity impact health status and the public health. Whiteford and Bennett detail possible approaches, such as employing a political economy of health care, the ecological/evolutionary approach, and the interpretive approach, which argues that human experiences of illness and health are essentially cultural constructs. Consensus and cultural modeling examines the relationship between cognitive models of disease and the health status of those afflicted.

Whiteford and Bennett stress that ethical considerations are a constant theme in medical anthropology, since research so often deals with serious health conditions or biological materials. Whatever the circumstances, applied medical anthropologists conduct research to make a difference, to benefit not just the sponsoring agency but also the community involved. Anthropologists working in medical settings use traditional modes of data gathering (participant observation, in-depth interviews, surveys, and epidemiological methods) and also newer strategies like rapid appraisals. Whiteford and Bennett offer a detailed case study of how medical anthropology's biocultural perspective "offers significant advances over less inclusive analysis of health" via its interdisciplinary, collaborative approach that applies ethnographic techniques to understanding medical systems. The authors conclude by reemphasizing the importance of the combined humanistic and social science traditions mobilized by applied medical anthropology to solve real-world problems, such as the HIV/AIDS pandemic. For Whiteford and Bennett, understanding cultural conditions, the biological bases of disease, and especially how unequal distribution of resources can impact epidemiological patterns is crucial for effective public health campaigns.

Nutrition

David A. Himmelgreen and Deborah L. Crooks note that although practitioners with diverse theoretical perspectives, from varied anthropological subdisciplines and other fields, comprise nutritional anthropology, they are united in their desire to understand and improve the nutritional status of populations. The authors emphasize that, since biological and sociocultural factors influence food selection and consumption in human societies, anthropologists' expertise in both areas makes them uniquely valuable to public health officials, who require culturally specific, reliable research data to inform policy regarding a particular nutritional problem. Himmelgreen and Crooks describe nutritional anthropology as a relatively new subdiscipline, with an official history beginning in the 1970s, although important research on food practices was conducted by British social anthropologists prior to World War II.

According to the authors, in the 1940s Margaret Mead was the first to use anthropological methods for applied nutritional research performed on behalf of the Committee on Food Habits of the National Academy of Scientists, which brought together nutritionists, sociologists, and behaviorists. Following World War II, nutritional anthropological work turned to symbolic/semiotic research for cultural studies, as Himmelgreen and Crooks evidence through reference to Levi-Strauss, Fero-Luzzi, Harper, and Douglas. The authors also describe nutritional work resulting from the influence of the social consciousness movement of the 1960s and that of biological anthropologists since the 1980s. Himmelgreen and Crooks suggest that nutritional anthropology is currently expanding in new directions but with the common thread of engaging holistic approaches that focus on "cultural ideologies that underlie social aspects of food organization and distribution, which shape food consumption behaviors and . . . nutritional status."

The authors provide an overview of the three best-known theoretical models (ecological, adaptation, and political economy) used in the domain and assert that qualitative and quantitative techniques, ranging from anthropometry to data surveys and from ethnographic observation to health assessments, are the primary tools of nutritional anthropologists, who must also concern themselves with techniques of other fields such as development, agriculture, and geography. In fact, Himmelgreen and Crooks note that today many nutritional anthropologists are involved in multidisciplinary research, reflecting practitioners' overlapping interests in culture, socioeconomics, development, program policy, and evaluation. The authors also mention areas of growing concern and elaborate on malnutrition/child survival in developing countries, food insecurity, and global obesity.

Involuntary Resettlement

Around the globe, millions of people are permanently relocated from their homelands and, subsequently, disempowered and left destitute as the result of development-induced displacement and resettlement (DIDR). Anthony Oliver-Smith explores the key role played by applied anthropologists, since the mid-twentieth century, in mitigating the severe impact of DIDR upon communities deprived of both livelihood and human rights. He suggests that in the future the field will continue to "address the challenges presented by DIDR at the local community and project level, in national and international political discourse, and in the policy frameworks of multilateral institutions."

As Oliver-Smith details, development projects are carried out to enhance the well-being of local populations and state economies by increasing the flow of productive power and thus increasing the consumption by inhabitants in the region. However, whether DIDR can be accomplished in an ethical and democratic way is subject to contention. He states that anthropologists have challenged national development ideologies that place entire communities at risk for the political and economic gains of those in power. The author discusses a controversial DIDR case with poor results and another that exemplifies a practical and democratic resettlement program through the active participation of anthropologists and other social scientists. Oliver-Smith notes that, although the roots of DIDR research extend back to the politically forced relocations of World War II, empirical and theoretical work in the domain began to flourish in the 1980s, spurred in part by the dire consequences of many large infrastructure projects around the world and by Scudder and Colson's (1982) influential work, which explored predictive models of DIDR process and impact. The author also describes other influential research and related DIDR models, including Cernea's Impoverishment Risks and Reconstruction (IRR) model, which tries to reduce the risks of environmental degradation and economic decline by ensuring that "political commitment, appropriate legal protections, and adequate resource allocations" are part of DIDR.

Drawing upon a recent analysis of directions in DIDR research today, Oliver-Smith outlines three broad perspectives of contemporary practitioners: advocacy anthropology, stakeholder analysis, and political ecology ethnography. He concludes by stressing the ongoing need for critiques of development models that assume the necessity of relocation without questioning the scope of initiatives causing such disruption in individuals' lives and their environment. As Oliver-Smith contends, the specific knowledge and analytical skills of applied anthropologists will be crucial in such interventions.

Business and Industry

Marietta L. Baba demonstrates how anthropologists' skills in understanding and interpreting cultures, particularly those subcultures manifest in consumer behavior and corporate work organizations, can be invaluable assets in a competitive marketplace. These skills are especially useful in a transnational economy that requires contemporary business professionals to have cross-cultural competency. Baba begins with a concise discussion of the historical foundations of applied anthropological work in industry, focusing on the famous Hawthorne Experiments conducted during the late 1920s and 1930s for which anthropologist W. Lloyd Warner was enlisted to understand work groups holistically as a social system. Baba describes the 1940s and

1950s as a period of expansion for industrial anthropology, when a number of anthropologists and significant studies rose to prominence. She then details a period of sharp decline and, eventually, disuse from 1960 to 1980, resulting from theoretical shifts, heightened needs for anthropology professors, and political and ethical tensions.

At the same time, Baba elaborates, fertile developments in anthropological theory set into motion those frameworks used by practitioners today, including the documentation in the 1970s of "informal working knowledge," later used in the 1990s to argue that workforce knowledge is a valuable economic asset. In addition, she describes how work among a variety of professional and occupational groups was studied using descriptive methods and ethnographic techniques to establish a high degree of worker control over labor and product, providing a basis crucial to developments in organizational theory in subsequent decades. With the United States' postwar dominance of global markets beginning to be challenged by businesses elsewhere, Baba states that, starting in the 1980s, consumer markets were fragmented into subspecialties associated with population segments having unique characteristic consumption patterns. This, according to the author, led to the need for new kinds of knowledge not accessible by traditional means, an increased need for ethnographically trained evaluators, and a way for businesses to shift their corporate culture from being less producer-driven to more market- and consumer-oriented. Baba offers two case studies to demonstrate how anthropologists' knowledge of cultural formation and ethnographic method can be put into action in the corporate world.

She concludes by summarizing aspects of anthropologists' expertise that add value to modern business, particularly the ability to integrate a large range of social and behavioral phenomena to explain culture, cultural changes, and the roots of cultural patterns, even when the researcher may not have knowledge of that particular setting. Baba argues that anthropologists' facility in simply knowing how to learn about other cultures is a great asset. Further, she states, it is anthropologists' grasp of best practices in ethnographic research, ability to depict human experience in nuanced and innovative ways, and commitment to protecting the individuals being studied that make anthropologists uniquely suited to enhance productive activities and bring humane approaches to the corporate work environment.

Education

Nancy P. Greenman addresses education as a domain of application in which anthropological concepts and perspectives are employed to understand how humans acquire knowledge deemed important in their respective cultures. She notes that educational anthropologists also study those informal means by which children and youth acquire knowledge beyond the boundaries of school. As such, an educational anthropologist studies "the lifelong acquisition of knowledge, skills, insights, attitudes and experiences accumulated through a person's interaction with personal, social, cultural, and physical environments."

Greenman presents a brief historical overview, noting that the origin of educational anthropology came about at the turn of the nineteenth century in a push by sociologists to link anthropology and education. She mentions anthropologist Maria Montessori's promotion of the influence of culture on learning styles, the impact of educational psychology, and the eugenicist-inspired views of educational sociologists and others who perpetuated racial bias by solely advocating "industrial and vocational training" for people of color, both at home and abroad. The importance of a more culturally sensitive approach came to the fore during the post–World War II era, epitomized by the 1954 Stanford-Carmel Valley Conference, which established the domain professionally.

For Greenman, the 1968 establishment of the Council on Anthropology and Education (CAE) and the subsequent growth of its newsletter into a scholarly journal gave educational anthropology credibility. The politicized approach of much academic work during the 1960s and 1970s, according to the author, emerged in educational anthropology as researchers adopted positions of advocacy, promoting a particular perspective over others to achieve a desirable outcome. The case studies Greenman describes address transformation in educational practices to foster greater equity, empowerment, and social justice for students and families alike. Greenman expands on the subfields of educational anthropology by listing the standing committees of CAE, which reflect the varied interests of members. She also includes extensive testimonies from researchers who have worked or are working to bring about changes in education, detailing their goals, challenges, and accomplishments in different areas: culturally diverse parents, school systems and communities, and multicultural programs. Educational anthropologists, Greenman notes, are "best known for their work with culturally diverse and indigenous groups." Ethnographic information might be used to "create culturally relevant educational structure and pedagogy."

Greenman states that the most traditional methodologies used in educational anthropology—ethnographic and qualitative research designs—are currently being supplemented with participant engagement, discourse analysis, rapid assessment, and especially action research, which is described by Geoffrey E. Mills as "any systematic inquiry [using qualitative methods] . . . to gather information about the ways that their particular schools operate." Outcomes evaluation is increasingly prevalent, as with David Fetterman's empowerment evaluation strategy by which participant-insiders actively engage in the process of program assessment. Greenman concludes by noting that educational anthropology provides multiple tools and approaches for understanding changes in a complex multicultural society.

Aging

Robert C. Harman notes that rapid improvements in health care and living conditions during the twentieth century resulted in significant increases in human longevity. He charts the role anthropologists play in creating a better quality of life for older persons, which involves working in tandem with physicians, social workers, psychologists, and others who currently dominate the "aging enterprise." Harman argues that anthropologists bring a broad perspective and wealth of skills that make them best suited to study the needs of the elderly.

Anthropologists have long relied upon elders as cultural informants, since traditionally they were rich repositories of community knowledge. Still, says Harman, substantive research on the aged did not appear until the mid-twentieth century, involving first quantitative then qualitative methods and later combining the two with context-specific and culturally sensitive approaches to build programs that benefit older persons. For the author, anthropologists assess age-related biological factors or sociocultural issues through empirical research. As exemplars, Harman refers to Margaret Clark's studies in the late 1960s on the aged in San Francisco and Christine Fry's cross-cultural comparisons of aging published in the early 1980s. He discusses those areas related to aging and elderly populations in which applied anthropologists have contributed significant insights through their research. These settings include advocating on behalf of nursing home residents, supporting legislation to mandate changes in institutional living, encouraging alternative perspectives on home care, addressing caregiver needs, alleviating strained relationships between older immigrants/refugees and their younger American-born family members, and providing legal support/guardianship for older individuals experiencing interfamilial conflict. As an example, Harman refers to anthropologist Patricia Slorah, who was instrumental in securing Florida legislation to guarantee visitation rights for those concerned about grandchildren at risk and who has been key in the Grandparents' Rights Advocacy Movement.

Anthropologists working with the aged predominantly use a combination of quantitative and qualitative methods. Harman notes that these require more than the usual confidentiality, respect, and care because the older informant may have physical or mental disabilities that can impede the research process. Because public policy is often involved, research may mean dealing with media sources, but practitioners have to consider the effect of public disclosure in helping or harming subjects. As researchers begin to organize seemingly disparate data, Harman suggests finding a theme that specifies a culture's particular way of viewing the aging process that has meaning for subjects as they articulate life experiences.

Harman concludes with three case studies detailing how anthropologists have had an impact on policies affecting the aged. He then returns to his key point that anthropologists are best equipped to serve the growing population of older individuals. He cites anthropologists' familiarity with ethnographic practices and qualitative methods requiring long-term commitment and close rapport with informants as ideal for positions of advocacy. He further contends that anthropologists' facility in matters related to community and family and their knowledge of diverse cultures and kinship patterns in addressing specific subpopulations of the elderly, such as immigrants and refugees, are critical for delivering culturally appropriate services for the aged, given the recent shift from federally supported institutions to local and home care settings involving family members.

References

Adams, William. 1998. *Philosophical roots of anthropology.* Lecture notes. Stanford, Calif.: Center for the Study of Language and Information.

American Anthropological Association (AAA). 2005. *Code of ethics of the American Anthropological Association.* Retrieved January 21, 2005, from http://www.aaanet.org/committees/ethics/ethicscode.pdf

American Anthropological Association (AAA). 2003. *Final report of the AAA El Dorado Task Force.* Retrieved January 21, 2005, from http://www.aaanet.org/edtf/index.htm

Baba, Marietta L. 1998. Anthropologists in corporate America: Knowledge management and ethical angst. *Chronicle of Higher Education* (May 8): B4–B5.

Balderston, F. E., and Roy Radner. 1971. Academic demand for new Ph.D.s 1970–90: Its sensitivity to alternate policies. Paper P-26. Berkeley: Ford Foundation Program in University Administration, University of California, Berkeley.

Cartter, Alan M. 1974. The academic labor market. In *Higher education and the labor market,* edited by M. S. Gordon. New York: McGraw-Hill.

Cernea, Michael M. 1992. Re-tooling in applied social investigation for development planning: Some methodological issues. In *Rapid assessment procedures—Qualitative methodologies for planning and evaluation of health related programmes,* edited by Nevin S. Scrimshaw and Gary R. Gleason. Boston: International Foundation for Developing Countries (INFDC). Retrieved January 21, 2005, from http://www.unu.edu/unupress/food2/UIN08E/uin08e00.htm

Cernea, Michael M., with April Adams. 1994. Sociology, anthropology, and development: An annotated bibliography of World Bank publications, 1975-1993 (Environmentally Sustainable Development Series and Monographs Series, Paper No.3). Washington, D.C.: The World Bank. Retrieved January 21, 2005, from

http://www.wds.worldbank.org/servlet/WDS_IBank_Servlet?pcont=details&eid
=000009265_3970311123104

Chambers, Erve. 1989. *Applied anthropology: A practical guide.* Prospect Heights, Ill.:
Waveland Press.

D'Andrade, R. G., E. A. Hammel, D. L. Adkins, and C. K. McDaniel. 1975. Academic
opportunity in anthropology, 1974–90. *American Anthropologist* 77 (4): 753–73.

Ervin, Alexander M. 2000. *Applied anthropology: Tools and perspectives for contemporary
practice.* Boston: Allyn and Bacon.

Fals-Borda, Orlando. 2000. Peoples' space times in global processes: The response of the
local. *Special Issue: Festchrift for Immanuel Wallerstein–Part II, Journal of World-Systems
Research* 6 (3): 624–34. Retrieved January 21, 2005, from http://jwsr.ucr.edu/
archive/vol6/number3/pdf/jwsr-v6n3-falsborda.pdf

Fals-Borda, Orlando, and Mohammad Anisur Rahman. 1991. *Action and knowledge:
Breaking the monopoly with participatory action-research.* New York: Apex Press.

Forde, Daryll. 1953. Applied anthropology in government: British Africa. In *Anthropology today,* edited by A. L. Kroeber. Chicago: University of Chicago Press.

Fortes, Meyer. 1953. *Social anthropology at Cambridge since 1900, an inaugural lecture.*
Cambridge: Cambridge University Press.

Gwynne, Margaret A. 2003. *Applied anthropology: A career-oriented approach.* Boston:
Allyn and Bacon.

Harman, Robert C., Jim Hess, and Amir Shafe. 2005. Report on survey of alumni of master's level applied anthropology training programs. Retrieved February 2005 from
http://www.practicinganthropology.org/docs/surveys/masters_survey_results_
2005.pdf

Held, Jan G. 1953. Applied anthropology in government: The Netherlands. In
Anthropology today, edited by A. L. Kroeber. Chicago: University of Chicago Press.

Hinsley, Curtis M. 1976. Amateurs and professionals in Washington anthropology,
1879 to 1903. In *American anthropology, the early years,* edited by John V. Murra
(1974 Proceedings of the American Ethnological Society). New York: West
Publishing.

Holmberg, Allen R. 1958. The research and development approach to the study of
change. *Human Organization* 17: 12–16.

Horowitz, Irving Louis, ed. 1967. *The rise and fall of Project Camelot: Studies in the relationship between social science and practical politics.* Cambridge, Mass.: MIT Press.

Johannsen, Agneta M. 1992. Applied anthropology and post-modernist ethnography.
Human Organization 51 (1): 71–81.

Kennedy, Raymond. 1944. Applied anthropology in the Dutch East Indies. *Transactions of the New York Academy of Sciences,* series 2 (6): 157–62.

Marthaler, Berard L., executive ed. 2002. *New Catholic encyclopedia.* 2nd ed. Farmington
Hills, Mich.: Thomson Gale.

Mead, Margaret. 1977. Applied anthropology: The state of the art. In *Perspectives on
anthropology, 1976,* edited by A. F. C. Wallace. Washington, D.C.: American
Anthropological Association.

Mead, Margaret, Eliot D. Chapple, and G. Gordon Brown. 1949. Report of the Committee on Ethics. *Human Organization* 8 (2): 20–1.

Morgan, David L. 1988. *Focus groups as qualitative research.* Newbury Park, Calif.: Sage
Publications.

Myres, John L. 1928. The science of man in the service of the state. *Journal of the Royal Anthropological Institute of Great Britain and Ireland* 59: 19–52.

National Association for the Practice of Anthropology (NAPA). 2005. NAPA Ethical Guidelines. Retrieved January 21, 2005, from http://www.practicinganthropology .org/about/?section=ethical_guidelines

Nicaise, Joseph. 1960. Applied anthropology in the Congo and Ruanda-Urandi. *Human Organization* 19: 112–17.

Plattner, Stuart et al. 1989. Commentary: Ethnographic method. *Anthropology Newsletter* (January): 32.

Price, Laurie J. 2001. The mismatch between anthropology graduate training and the work lives of graduates. *Practicing Anthropology* 23 (1): 55–7.

Reining, Conrad C. 1962. A lost period of applied anthropology. *American Anthropologist* 64 (3): 593–600.

Rhoades, Robert E. 1982. The art of the informal agricultural survey. Social science department training document 1982-2. Lima: International Potato Center (CIP).

Scrimshaw, Susan C. M., and Elena Hurtado. 1987. *Rapid assessment procedures for nutrition and primary health care: Anthropological approaches to improving programme effectiveness.* Tokyo: United Nations University; Los Angeles: UCLA Latin American Center Publications.

Scudder, Thayer, and Elizabeth Colson. 1982. From welfare to development: A conceptual framework for the analysis of dislocated people. In *Involuntary migration and resettlement,* edited by Art Hansen and Anthony Oliver-Smith. Boulder: Westview Press.

Society for Applied Anthropology (SfAA). 2005. *Ethical and professional responsibilities.* Retrieved January 21, 2005, from http://www.sfaa.net/sfaaethic.html

Smith, Susan, Timothy Pyrch, and Arturo Ornelas Lizardo. 1993. Participatory action-research for health. *World Health Forum* 14 (3): 319–24. Also available at http://whqlibdoc.who.int/whf/1993/vol14-no3/WHF_1993_14(3)_p319-324.pdf

Tax, Sol. 1958. The Fox Project. *Human Organization* 17: 17–19.

Tierney, Patrick. 2000. *Darkness in El Dorado: How scientists and journalists devastated the Amazon.* New York: Norton.

Trotter, Robert T. 2000. Ethnography and network analysis: The study of social context in cultures and societies. In *The handbook of social studies in health and medicine,* edited by Gary Albrecht, Ray Fitzpatrick, and Susan C. Scrimshaw. Thousand Oaks, Calif.: Sage Publications.

Trotter, Robert T., and Jean J. Schensul. 2000. Methods in applied anthropology. In *Handbook of methods in cultural anthropology,* edited by H. Russell Bernard. Walnut Creek, Calif.: AltaMira Press.

van Willigen, John. 2002. *Applied anthropology: An introduction.* 3rd ed. Westport, Conn.: Bergin and Garvey.

Vidyarthi, L. P. 1984. *Applied anthropology in India (principles, problems and case studies).* New Delhi: Kitab Mahal.

Wax, Murray L. 1987. Some issues and sources on ethics in anthropology. In *Handbook on ethical issues in anthropology,* AAA Special Publications 23, edited by Joan Cassell and Sue-Ellen Jacobs. Washington, D.C.: American Anthropological Association.

Weaver, Thomas, ed. 1973. *To see ourselves: Anthropology and modern social issues.* Glenview, Ill.: Scott, Foresman.

2 Anthropology and Development

Peter D. Little

Introduction

Development anthropology emerged in the 1970s as a recognized area of concentration within social anthropology, although its legacy can be traced to the 1940s or even earlier (Gardner and Lewis 1996; Nolan 2002). Defined by this author as the study of development problems (e.g., poverty, environmental degradation, and hunger) and the application of anthropological knowledge toward their solution; it is a field of both study and application, but it is not a subdiscipline with a distinct arsenal of theory (Hoben 1982). In the international arena its establishment was spurred by the increased concern among major development institutions, such as the United States Agency for International Development (USAID) and the United Nations Development Programme (UNDP), to incorporate social and equity issues in their policies and programs and to rely less on development indicators measured mainly by economic gains in a nation's gross national product (GNP). Part of the rationale for this shift was the recognition that global poverty and inequity were actually on the rise in the 1970s, even in those countries that had witnessed relatively strong gains in economic growth. And it was spurred by a realization that programs focused on large infrastructure, technology transfer, and urban investment could actually marginalize rather than help the poor and the vulnerable, such as children and minorities. The idea that the benefits of large-scale projects and investments would eventually trickle down to local communities and the rural poor was simply not supported by the evidence. In the 1970s the new emphasis in U.S. foreign aid programs on addressing the social and eco-nomic concerns of the poor rural majority was called "New Directions." Similar reorientations occurred in other major development agencies, where the emphasis was said to be on the "poor majority" and the "poorest of the poor."

At approximately the same time that these changes were taking place in development programs and policies, opportunities for anthropologists to engage—and even be employed—in international development programs grew. In a matter of a very short period of time in the late 1970s and 1980s, a variety of development organizations began to seek anthropological exper-tise and advice on development. In part, the attraction to anthropology was its considerable experience in living and studying in poor, underdeveloped regions of the world. When international development agencies turned toward local development and programs that targeted the rural poor, they found anthropologists there, often advocating for the communities that they studied. This period of growth, both in employment and anthropological research funded by international development programs, correlated with a time of declining academic opportunities for professional anthropologists; thus, the increased engagement also had a very pragmatic outcome: a job! The opportunism associated with the 1970s and the growth in consulting opportunities and employment has not been without its major critics in the discipline, some of whom view this era as a period when development anthropology sold itself out to the mandates of large development agencies (Escobar 1991). This contentious point will be addressed later in the chapter.

In addition to the increased number of practicing development anthro-pologists, there was the emergence of an expanding body of scholarship associated with the field. The first institute dedicated solely to research and application in development anthropology was the Institute for Development Anthropology, Binghamton, New York, formed in 1976 by three senior anthropologists (Michael Horowitz, David Brokensha, and Thayer Scudder). In Europe development groups were established, such as the Overseas Development Institute (UK), the Institute for Development Studies (UK), the Centre for Development Research (Denmark), and the Office de la Recherche Scientifique et Technique Outre-Mer (France), that began to employ anthropologists but had no counterpart units solely for development anthropology. Other research institutes from around the world, including the Pakistan Institute for Development Economics and the Institute for Development Studies (Kenya), which had not traditionally hired anthropol-ogists, had them among their staff by the 1980s. At the time it was not uncommon (nor is it unusual today) for development research institutes to be dedicated solely to economic research.

In principle, however, development anthropology is as much about the projects of financially strapped institutes, grassroots groups, and indigenous organizations who bitterly oppose large-scale development schemes as it is about the activities of wealthy development bureaucracies, consulting firms, and nongovernmental organizations (NGOs) that wield considerable clout in international development. There is plenty of room in development anthropology for different types of practitioner groups, theoretical approaches, and political perspectives, and, in fact, it is a healthy indicator for the field that it began to generate so much heated debate and differing viewpoints as early as the 1980s (Escobar 1991).

At this point let me acknowledge the distinction that is commonly made between development anthropology (the practice of development) and the anthropology of development (the study of development). I opt for the simpler term development anthropology, which for me includes both the study and practice of development, and I find a dichotomy between scholarship and application not to be particularly useful. I will return to this issue later in the chapter.

Along the lines discussed above, this chapter summarizes the different dimensions of development anthropology. It restricts itself to the arena of international development, the main concern of the great majority of development anthropologists, and, for example, it does not address community development in the United States. The latter has played an important role in the development of applied anthropology in this country (United States), and some of its methods and models have obvious similarities. Some development practitioners work in both settings (van Willigen 2002).

The chapter starts with a brief history of development anthropology in the post–World War II era. Some of the larger historical and intellectual forces that have shaped it are highlighted in this part. The discussion then turns to training and career paths in development anthropology, followed by a discussion of theoretical and methodological issues. The latter section suggests that many of its practitioners insulated themselves from recent works in anthropological theory and method and from the very local communities with whom they often said they represented, which hampered the recognition of the field's legitimacy within the discipline. However, this does not mean that the field has not made an important methodological contribution, particularly in areas like participatory research (Chambers 1997). By working in interdisciplinary settings where methods are heavily scrutinized by other social scientists, development anthropology actually has strengthened anthropological research techniques (and, indirectly, theory), but these achievements are rarely acknowledged. With the increased demand in many parts of the world for social science to show its relevance, development anthropologists have benefited from research opportunities and access to research locations that have not been afforded other anthropologists. In doing so, the field has generated considerable contemporary research materials of unique value to the discipline as a whole. However, because many of these anthropologists do not have access to the discipline's more prestigious journals, much of the information remains in unpublished reports and papers (which is often called gray literature). The latter may include research findings that remain as local working papers and publications at local research institutes and universities, often to be exploited by visiting Western researchers.

The next three sections of the chapter deal, respectively, with training and employment trends in development anthropology, theory and methods, and a case study from the author's own research. In the final part of the chapter, future directions in development anthropology are discussed, highlighting the field's need to strengthen its theoretical and methodological links to anthropology while maintaining its unique commitment to the study of development problems and applications. In the conclusion it is argued that development anthropology must still collaborate with other disciplines (for example, economics, ecology, and agricultural science) that figure prominently in development studies and programs. In doing so, however, it should avoid the tendency of anthropologists in interdisciplinary work to isolate themselves from their home discipline, a pattern that retarded theoretical growth in development anthropology in the 1970s and 1980s.

Early Origins of Development Anthropology

A number of publications trace the origins of anthropology's involvement with social and economic development programs to the 1930s and 1940s or, in some cases, to a much earlier period (1900s) (Ferguson 1997; Hoben 1982). While recognizing these early linkages, it is best to situate the establishment of development anthropology as a field in the post–World War II era. As noted earlier, I would place its distinct emergence in the 1970s, but it is important to recognize earlier legacies. For example, in the 1950s and 1960s, anthropologists made frequent contributions to the premier international development journal of the time, *Economic Development and Cultural Change (EDCC)*. This journal was (is) the forum where social scientists from different disciplines debated the best ways to transform "traditional" societies and rarely questioned the benefits of Western market- and technology-driven development. Modernization, a paradigm that espoused the benefits of Western technology and education in bringing development to the non-West, mistakenly believed that societies had to be transformed (modernized) to develop socially and economically. And the *EDCC* is where these ideas were most prominent. As Little and Painter pointed out, "anthropologists and sociologists, many of whom were based at the University of Chicago, figure prominently among the contributors to the journal, and anthropologist Manning Nash served as editor between 1958 and 1964" (1995, 604). Even Clifford Geertz, in his *EDCC* article on rotating credit associations in Indonesia, argued for modernizing traditional (or static) economies through increased savings and consumption, in order to deliver the benefits of development to middle-income groups (1962, 242).

Anthropologists at the time may have been unaware of their influence on modernization theory, a particularly ethnocentric and dated theory, but their role was important if not troublesome. They often provided the empirical grist for the economist's models, including the well-known work of Nobel laureates W. A. Lewis and Theodore Schultz (Lewis 1970; Schultz 1964; also see Adams et al. 1960), who suggested that development problems among the poor stemmed from "non-modern" values, livelihoods, and lifestyles. Oscar Lewis's work in rural Mexico on what he called the "culture of poverty" was an obvious early case in anthropology (Lewis 1960). The general premise in his work is that people were poor because of cultural values and customs that inhibited economic and social improvement. Remnants of his misplaced ideas are still occasionally echoed in explanations of why most of the world's populations remain poor (Huntington and Harrison 2000).

Although a stark contrast to one of the discipline's most cherished premises, cultural relativism, anthropological studies of development in the immediate post–World War II years did little to counter the basic premises of modernization theory. For example, in writing about development in rural Brazil, noted anthropologist Charles Wagley remarked that rural communities "provided little basis for the development of a dynamic new society" (1960, 230). Again, the essence of this position is that indigenous culture was a constraint to the emergence of "modern" economies and, therefore, could not be the basis for a modern society without major changes.

Later on in the 1960s, many of the anthropologists involved with the early years of the *EDCC*, such as Manning Nash, retreated back into the mainstream of the discipline or into the growing field of economic anthropology. Overall, the controversy over U.S. involvement in the Vietnam War and the association of U.S. foreign assistance programs with human rights violations and questionable practices in Southeast Asia instigated a further retreat from the modernization paradigm and from general engagement in international development activities during the 1960s.

Certain events of the mid-1970s helped overcome this legacy and establish development anthropology, including:

- The end of the Vietnam War and the emergence of legislation that mandated the separation of any intelligence (espionage) activities of the U.S. government from official international development assistance.
- The strong involvement of anthropologists in the humanitarian efforts associated with the Sahelian drought and famine of the early 1970s. When development agencies sought expertise for this part of the world, anthropologists were strongly represented.
- As noted earlier, the initiation of new policies at large development agencies, many that seemed receptive to anthropological input. Most noteworthy were USAID's New Directions, which emphasized rural development, the "poor majority" orientation of the World Bank (the so-called McNamara Doctrine), and the UNDP's "basic human needs" approach.
- The initiation of social soundness analysis requirements at some large development organizations. USAID went furthest in its requirement that social soundness analyses had to be conducted during the design of development projects to show potential impacts on different social groups (women, poor, minority groups, etc.), a commitment that it unfortunately abandoned in the 1990s (Horowitz 1997).
- The establishment of the Institute for Development Anthropology (IDA) in 1976.
- The publication of articles and books that highlighted development anthropology (e.g., Cochrane 1971).

Many of the early development anthropologists, especially those associated with IDA, were significant anthropologists in their own right. Such well-known scholars as T. Scarlet Epstein, Michael Horowitz, Elizabeth Colson, Thayer Scudder, and David Brokensha had published in many of the discipline's most prestigious outlets and were associated with the fields of economic or ecological anthropology. Unlike some applied anthropologists, the scholars associated with IDA were accepted as anthropologists in their own right, and most had been trained as social and cultural anthropologists and had strong research reputations. They became involved with development through their long-term research projects, some of which identified widespread poverty, social injustices, and food insecurity as critical research and development problems. With the exception of David Brokensha, who served as a social development officer during the British colonial period, these anthropologists became involved in international development through research rather than development projects. Importantly, they often were called on by development organizations as much for their topical expertise (for example, on resettlement or pastoralism) as for their anthropological training. The central point is that not only were the institutional and policy environments at this time favorable for development anthropology but also that the emergence of certain individuals with strong topical and disciplinary credentials, posts at major universities, and good international linkages aided the legitimacy of the field. That the field needed to be legitimized probably is an unfortunate indictment of the elitism of anthropology in the 1970s, an attribute that some development anthropologists might argue continues to characterize large parts of the discipline.

At the same time that development anthropology was emerging as a field, ecological and economic anthropology were growing and the latter subdisciplines established strong synergies with development anthropology. Many noted economic anthropologists, such as Harold Schneider and Frank Cancian, and ecological anthropologists, such as Robert Netting and Emilio Moran, wrote about economic and social development in their regions of study. These subdisciplines were clearly more receptive to the study and practice of development than other parts of the discipline, in part because of their common bases in materialist-oriented theories and empirically based research. At least two of the annual conferences and monographs of the Society for Economic Anthropology in the past two decades have been devoted to economic development issues (Bennett and Bowen 1988; Cohen and Dannhaeuser 2002).

The field of development anthropology has clearly matured since the 1970s, even while the major international actors have waffled in—or even reversed—their commitment to alleviating rural poverty and injustices (Horowitz 1994). In some cases, official development assistance at the onset of the twenty-first century has regressed to the old style economic aid programs focused on export promotion and economic growth rather than human welfare. Although there was a modicum of serious scholarship on development anthropology published in the 1970s and 1980s, it has exploded in the past 15 years, with dozens of new books appearing annually. The field also has become better integrated within the broader discipline of anthropology (Ferguson 1997; Horowitz 1998; Little 2000; Gardner and Lewis 1996). Once considered a peculiar specialty of applied anthropology, in many cases disdained by anthropologists, the study of development has received increased attention among those who clearly would not classify themselves as applied anthropologists and who are leaders in the discipline (Barth 1997; Herzfeld 2001). Here I would argue that development anthropology is closely tied to applied anthropology in its concern with the application of anthropological knowledge, but the former increasingly encompasses more than application. By recognizing that the study of development and its multifarious dimensions is both an intellectually and morally acceptable endeavor (Gow 2002), development anthropology in the United States has begun to mirror its counterpart fields in Europe, where the distinction between applied and mainstream anthropology is not as marked (Gardner and Lewis 1996). This transition has been achieved in part by anthropologists who believe that development anthropology should not only involve a concern with the applied projects and policies of large development agencies, such as the World Bank and USAID, but also be a serious field of study that generates more than just employment and incorporates organizations at the smallest level (Gardner and Lewis 1996; Little 2000).

The number of anthropologists who studied or were employed in the field of development grew considerably in the 1980s and 1990s, even at a time when development agencies retreated from social and equity mandates. Many of these anthropologists took on employment as project managers and administrators where their anthropological training was underutilized, and few held positions identified with anthropology. Horowitz makes this same point in noting that anthropologists are employed throughout development organizations, but "rarely are any of these people identified by their disciplinary training" (1997, 28). In these positions not only do they commonly lose touch with their discipline but also, more tragically, their links to the local communities whose interests they purport to represent are greatly diminished.

By the early 1990s, the gains in legitimizing development anthropology as a serious intellectual endeavor within the discipline had waned, and attacks about the field's opportunism, ethics, and lack of scholarly rigor became numerous (Escobar 1991, 1995; Ferguson 1997; Grillo and Stirrat 1997). Although some may have taken these attacks personally, others welcomed them as a means to revitalize the intellectual agenda of the field and establish new ideas and ways of thinking about and doing development work (Horowitz 1998; Little 2000). Clearly some healthy reflection about where the field was headed at the time was warranted because many individuals involved with development had uncritically accepted the assumptions and discourses of their employers—some of which ran strongly counter to their own discipline and training. Consequently, they had isolated themselves from new ideas and concepts within the discipline and, as mentioned above, the very communities that they studied. Unfortunately, some of the important research and policy work that development anthropologists were conducting at the time was not acknowledged in these critiques; and, ironically, other disciplines and social scientists praised the important roles (actual and potential) of anthropology in development studies and programs (Bardhan 1989; Chambers 1984, 1997). Moreover, much of the work of development anthropologists in Africa, Asia, and Latin America was not recognized because many of these individuals did not publish in English-language journals in the United States and Europe (Little and Painter 1995; Mathur 1989).

Training and Careers

The discipline of anthropology was not prepared in the 1980s and 1990s for the growth in the number of graduate students with interests in development-related careers. Only a handful of U.S. departments of anthropology, like those at the University of Kentucky, State University of New York-Binghamton, and the University of Florida, and European departments, such as those at the University of Sussex (UK), the University of Copenhagen, and Wageningen University (the Netherlands), had PhD tracks that combined interests in development and anthropology (Brokensha 1992). On a much smaller scale, development anthropology was receiving increased attention from a few Japanese universities (*Development Anthropologist* 1995). In the United States, the most receptive departments to the training needs of development students were those that already had a strong tradition of applied anthropology, especially those programs at the University of Arizona and University of Kentucky, which also boasted strengths in economic and ecological anthropology. The best departments in applied anthropology were able to integrate interests in development with basic training in anthropological theory and methods and thus allow their PhD graduates the option of either academic or nonacademic careers. By the 1990s most major graduate departments of anthropology in the United States and Europe taught at least one course related to development anthropology, but few had well-defined training tracks.

In anthropology departments based in developing countries, courses and training related to development proliferated in the 1980s and 1990s. In Eastern Africa, for example, where problems of poverty, food security, and political violence are widespread, whole graduate programs in development anthropology emerged. At Moi University (Kenya), the department of anthropology had particularly close ties to development studies, in part due to the leadership of Professor Joshua Akong'a and the high demand for graduates who combined knowledge of development with social and cultural expertise (*Development Anthropology Network: Bulletin of the Institute for Development Anthropology* 1990). Similarly, at Addis Ababa University (AAU) in Ethiopia, the graduate program in anthropology had a direct emphasis on anthropological studies of development, and most of their faculty with recent PhDs had expertise in development-related issues (Pankhurst 2003; Amare et al. 2000; Abate 1998). A quick perusal of recent MA theses in anthropology at AAU reveals titles related to development, including work on food security, pastoral development, ethnic conflict, and resettlement. Finally, the department of anthropology at the University of Khartoum (Sudan), one of the oldest programs on the continent, had a strong concentration in development anthropology (Ahmed 2003). Many of its graduates and professors provided strong critiques of what was going on in their countries under the guise of "development" and did not merely sell out to the interests of the large Western development agencies. What they did acknowledge, however, is that their countries confronted serious equity and development problems and that to distance themselves and their work from them made little sense and was perhaps ethically questionable.

For many anthropologists from sub-Saharan Africa and Asia, development anthropology and development studies offered a break from the discipline's colonial past and a way to offer scholarship that was useful to their communities. For example, Abdallah Bujra, former director of the Council for the Development of Social Science Research in Africa (CODESRIA), argued that development anthropology could help African anthropologists to revive their discipline:

> Apart from the scale of research in development anthropology, it is in my opinion substantive, relevant, and more likely to yield theoretical tools useful for a better analysis and understanding of contemporary African societies. African anthropologists in the present search for a return or a new start in Anthropology should carefully consider development anthropology as an area of entre. (1991, 21)

Such strong advocacy statements required fairly major changes in the curriculum of anthropology departments in sub-Saharan Africa. According to Abdel Ghaffar M. Ahmed, one of Africa's best-known anthropologists and the executive secretary of the Organization of Social Science Research in Eastern and Southern Africa (OSSREA), the department of anthropology at the University of Khartoum did just this and moved away from its early colonial curriculum by promoting courses with an "orientation towards development issues" (2003, 34).

Similar patterns occurred in development anthropology in Latin America and South Asia, and they were in some cases motivated by factors similar to those that have already been mentioned. In countries like Mexico, Peru, Ecuador, and Brazil, the number of anthropologists at universities and elsewhere who were concerned with development issues grew considerably in the 1980s and 1990s. In Asia, India has probably led the way in the number of anthropologists involved with development-related research and activities, either as researchers, practitioners, or both (Mathur 1989). In neighboring Pakistan, there was growth in the number of anthropology students and faculty interested in development studies. In writing about the anthropology program at Quaid-i-Azam University (Islamabad, Pakistan), Rauf remarks that:

> Questions were raised concerning the appropriateness of anthropology as a field of study in Pakistan's educational system, the benefit of anthropological knowledge to society, and, on a more mundane level, the career opportunities in Pakistan for anthropology graduates. Responding to these concerns, the anthropology department designed its program to combine extensive field research on applied topics with intensive course work on problems of development in Third World countries. . . . As a result of this approach, the anthropology department has completed five studies on topics of major significance for the development of the country. . . . (1984, 19)

In Asia, rallying cries against inappropriate development interventions, such as large dams (Fisher 1999), and in Latin America, campaigns against the destruction of indigenous lands occurring under the guise of development instigated local anthropologists to be concerned about development issues in their own countries (Macdonald 1997; Fox, Stephen, and Rivera 1999). Indeed, the number of anthropologists in developing countries who hold expertise and interests in development anthropology, including those who are strongly antidevelopment in their orientation, probably has grown faster in the past 15 years than elsewhere in the world.

The 1990s marked a phenomenal growth in the role of NGOs, both Western and non-Western, in development activities. The shift in funding priorities stemmed from a number of factors, but it generally resulted from an ideologically based premise that anything associated with the private sector (including NGOs) had to be better than government initiatives. The structural adjustment programs of the International Monetary Fund (IMF) and World Bank, which slashed government budgets and bureaucracies in developing countries, is probably the best-known example of these antistatist campaigns. Thus, although official employment data are not available, based on my own observations I would estimate that more anthropologists have been employed by NGO development organizations and research organizations (both large and small ones) in the past 15 years than by large development agencies and consulting firms. In part, this has been a consequence of the large amounts of official development resources that have been redirected to the NGO sector, as well as a recognition by NGOs (including those focused on international agricultural research) of the skills that anthropology can bring to local development work. Many anthropology graduates from Asian, Latin American, and African universities are working for these organizations, and the same is true for American and European-trained anthropologists. Many of these graduates gain employment with MA degrees only, and they opt not to go on for the PhD. The larger NGOs that deal with disasters and development work, including CARE International, Oxfam UK and Oxfam America, Save the Children-United Kingdom (SCF-UK), and World Vision International, employ anthropologists both at their headquarters and on field projects.

Additionally, the growing interest in social development issues by environmental NGOs, such as World Conservation International (WCI), International Union for the Conservation of Nature (IUCN), and the World Wide Fund for Nature (WWF), also has resulted in employment opportunities, for both Western and non-Western anthropologists. In acknowledging that successful environmental programs need to benefit local communities, many environmental organizations have hired anthropologists at all levels, including upper-level management positions. As might be expected, the involvement of anthropologists in some environmental programs has not been without controversy because social goals often have taken a distant backseat to strong environmental agendas, some of which have hurt local populations (Hitchcock 1999; Peluso and Watts 2001). Later in the chapter I deal with one environmental program—that of a community-based wildlife conservation in Kenya—that has tried to integrate local development concerns with conservation goals.

Theory and Method

Development anthropologists today need to better acknowledge the importance of theory to their work. All development policies and programs are informed, implicitly or explicitly, by theoretical assumptions about how economies and societies develop, who benefits from development, what the main constraints to development are, and what the main causes of underdevelopment ("lack of development") are. I have already mentioned how modernization theory affected the types of development programs funded in the 1950s and 1960s. The ways that anthropologists think about development or underdevelopment also have been strongly influenced by dependency theory. The latter highlights how peripheral communities can easily be exploited by international capital (the core) and, in the extreme, suggests that local development can only be achieved by eliminating market relations with the global capitalist system. Marxist theory, in turn, cautions against the tendency of development in which most benefits are captured by small groups of capitalist elites, hence exaggerating inequities. Finally, populist-inspired theories, which privilege local knowledge and practice and programs based on these, inspire anthropological notions of development, whereas ideas derived from neoclassical economic theory are reflected in market-based programs to improve local welfare. Thus, regardless of whether theory is acknowledged by development practitioners or even by critics of development, their actions and ideas always have theoretical underpinnings. Although there has been a considerable amount written on development theory by economists and other social scientists (Corbridge 1995; Leys 1996; Peet and Hartwick 1999), few anthropologists have explicitly addressed the theoretical bases of development and underdevelopment (for exceptions, see Escobar 1995; Long and Long 1992).

It is equally important for anthropologists not to confuse development approaches and theory. For example, the study of resettlement, women and development, or social forestry offers useful approaches or strategies for addressing a range of problems, but it should not be mistaken for theory (Cernea 1991; Pottier 1993). A model of how a successful social forestry or gender-based development program can operate is an important contribution but not necessarily a theoretical contribution (cf. Cernea 1991). As I indicated earlier in the chapter, development anthropology is not a distinct subdiscipline with a coherent body of theory of its own. Indeed, most of the "theorizing" about development has been done by other disciplines.

Development anthropologists need to build on the methodological and analytical strengths that distinguish them from other anthropologists and social scientists. Anthropologists already are doing important research along these lines, some working in the context of development and some outside it. Their work is helping to overcome the theoretical impasse in development studies that has marked the start of the new millennium (Little 2000) by critically reexamining key concepts and assumptions about the nature of development, avoiding broad theoretical categorization (or castigation), and highlighting the important contribution of anthropology to theoretical and policy debates (Fairhead and Leach 1996; Moore and Vaughan 1994; Peters 1994). Thus, in many cases, current research on key development issues, like persistent poverty, inequality, and environmental degradation, represents cutting-edge theoretical topics within the discipline of anthropology itself (see also Wedel and Borofsky 1997).

Two substantive areas where recent theoretical contributions and development applications have been made by anthropologists are in the study of intrahousehold relations and common property systems. For example, considerable research during the past two decades has reshaped the ways that household and intrahousehold relations are perceived. No longer the dark box of undifferentiated relationships headed by a husband, the household as reflected in the work of Hart (1992) and Guyer (1981, 1986) comprises different sets of actors with their own independent interests and activities. Internal negotiation and bargaining by household members, often differentiated by gender and age, characterize the new household model. Recent excellent studies by Astone (1996), Carney (1994), and Dolan (1997) highlight the ways in which a unified household model can distort planned development and exacerbate gender-based inequities. These are studies that have importance both for theory and application.

These new insights, based on better understandings of intrahousehold relations, have informed development practice in a positive way by allowing nutritional and agricultural programs to be directed at vulnerable segments of the household: women and children. Anne Fleuret's work on food-aid programming in Kenya shows how feeding programs targeted directly at intrahousehold units of mothers and children rather than at households generally improve the nutritional impact of food-aid programs (Fleuret 1988). A similar study by Kennedy and Peters (1992) shows how development programs aimed at agricultural crops for which women control the income has a positive impact on children's nutrition. Based on data from Malawi and Kenya, they note that "Not only is household food security influenced by total household income but the proportion of income controlled by women has a positive and significant influence on household caloric intake" (1992, 1077). Both of these examples of applied research build on new and sophisticated understandings of intrahousehold dynamics, as well as nicely indicate how development practice is informed by theory.

A second area of anthropological research and practice that has greatly benefited from recent field studies associated with development is the study of common property systems. Perhaps the most influential early publication that contributed to the common property debate was a report by Michael Horowitz in a USAID publication series (1979). Ironically, the report actually castigates USAID and other donor agencies whose programs are based on flawed assumptions about local tenure systems. Drawing on his long-term field research among West African pastoralists, Horowitz convincingly demonstrates that communal tenure systems are not inherently destructive of the environment as suggested in Garrett Hardin's popular idea of a "tragedy of a commons" (1968). He goes on to show that development failures in Africa's livestock sector often are closely tied to misunderstandings about common property systems that were informed by Hardin's original argument. Since that time, there has been an explosion in anthropological research on common property systems, some of it done within the context of development programs and most of it confirming what Horowitz pointed out about these systems almost 20 years ago (McCay and Acheson 1987; Peters 1994).

Although a silver stake has yet to completely kill the tragedy of the commons argument—its flawed ideas still emerge in development policies and programs—there are cases where development practice has been changed by new understandings of common property systems. Examples that come to mind include agricultural policies in West African countries that now acknowledge the importance of communal tenure systems, conservation programs in Southern Africa and in South Asia based on common property institutions, and programs in Burkina Faso that reinforce communal rather than private ownership of natural resources. Powerful, outside private interests clearly are threatened by the maintenance of common property systems, and they will continue to lobby for privatization (as in the case of Mexico), but there is at least some recognition by policymakers that past theories of land tenure were flawed.

Improved understandings of households and common property systems are greatly enhanced by methodological advances in field research. In fact, each of these concepts benefited from improved research methods, while they were strengthened in turn through the testing of these two concepts. Long is correct that theoretical discussions in development anthropology should incorporate "appropriate research methodology that can facilitate the analysis of social action and interpretation" (1992, 268). Without effective methods—and here I include more than narrow concerns with the mechanics of data collection but broader issues related to fieldwork generally—knowledge of the theories and concepts discussed earlier would have been limited. Unlike other disciplines involved with development studies, in anthropology, research methods, data, and analysis are scrutinized almost as much as theory. In short, theory and concepts inform methods and vice versa.

As noted earlier, practice is intricately related to theory and method, and efforts to dichotomize them are misplaced, particularly in development. The two examples discussed earlier in this chapter demonstrate the important linkages between theory, method, and practice. Popular development concepts like participation and empowerment have important theoretical and methodological implications. Grassroots groups and NGOs currently invoke both in local development work because meaningful development cannot really occur without them. Evidence shows that equitable development is more likely to occur when communities and households participate in project planning and decisions and when community members (including women) are empowered to manage and control their own resources and futures. Through research efforts and practical experiences, anthropologists know much more about the theory, method, and practice of local participation and empowerment. Disciplinary knowledge of how communities are organized, differentiated, and affected by unequal power relations has been significantly enhanced through applied community development work (Korten 1990; for U.S. work, see van Willigen 2002).

Case Study: Community-Based Conservation among Kenyan Pastoralists

To better illustrate this point, an actual project example is presented in this section of the chapter. I was invited by the Kenya Wildlife Services (KWS) to help establish a socioeconomic monitoring unit to look at project impacts and to gather ongoing data in a community-based conservation project.

Background

The role that pastoral livelihoods in East Africa play in the shaping of savanna landscapes and their biodiversity cannot be understated. East Africa possesses a rich historical and archaeological record documenting the significant influences of pastoral land use on savanna habitats and the significant wildlife herds that inhabit them (Gifford-Gonzalez 1994; Robertshaw 1990). This evidence strongly suggests that the savanna ecosystems of East Africa, which support the richest variety and density of large mammals in the world, were shaped by human activity and were not the "wilderness" areas so often considered by early explorers and naturalists (Thompson 1885). Nonetheless, beyond the spectacular vistas of the East African savanna and the proliferation of expensive conservation programs lay a starker reality of poverty and injustice. Current communities of herders, who played such important roles, are increasingly impoverished by the expansion of national parks and game reserves, as they have lost access to large tracts of valuable rangelands and critical water points. At least 20 percent of critical Maasai grazing lands have been taken over by wildlife reserves and parks since the 1940s (Little 1994).

Recent events in Kenya have resulted in some healthy—if not contradictory—rethinking of pastoral land use and its effects on savanna landscapes. Anthropologists have been heavily involved in these debates. Confronted with the prospects of large-scale subdivision and capital-intensive agriculture near some of Kenya's most important wildlife areas, international conservation groups and the government now embrace pastoral land use for its positive benefits to wildlife conservation. Indeed, Maasai herders, who have inhabited the Rift Valley area of Tanzania and Kenya since at least the 1600s, are actually being compensated near key animal dispersal areas south of Nairobi National Park just to keep their areas in open range rather than farm and fence them (for historical and ethnographic information on the Maasai, see Spears and Waller 1993). As one young herder remarked to me, "people are earning money just by keeping cattle and not fencing" (author's fieldnotes, November 2001). The rationale behind this change in policy is that open rangelands and mobile pastoralism are more conducive to wildlife populations than are sedentary agriculture and permanent villages.

Thus, although governments in East Africa during the past 100 years have done their best to discourage pastoralism—often in brutally forceful terms—they now are in the paradoxical position of actually encouraging it in key biodiversity areas outside parks and protected areas. Richard Leakey, an anthropologist and the former head of the KWS, remarked that Maasai pastoralists are "par excellence conservationists . . . if the Maasai had not been so tolerant, we wouldn't have any wildlife in the Maasai Mara today" (cited in Horgan 1989, 42). This new shift in thinking has not been without major critics, most of whom are environmentalists who still feel local populations are the cause of the region's declining wildlife populations and that both herders and farmers should be removed from critical wildlife management zones.

Policy Changes, New Programs

This new attitude toward pastoral land use has contributed to a healthy rethinking of conservation policies in the region. The Kenyan government's current wildlife policy states that "the conservation of biodiversity is best achieved by perpetuating open space and . . . the center-piece of the conservation policy will therefore revolve around averting the fragmentation of natural habitats" (Kenya 1996, 11). Although the reality on the ground may be quite different, this text supports the maintenance of pastoralism around parks' borders and discourages large-scale cultivation in these buffer areas. The openness and "natural" flavor of unfenced rangelands also complements the cultural values of European conservationists and urban-based tourists who wish to view Kenya's "undisturbed wilderness" rather than land uses that reek of human influence. Such depictions are consistent with Lusigi's (1984) position that the European infatuation with wildlife conservation was very difficult for East Africans to understand. Regardless of its ideological overtones, the new policy thinking could help, in theory, to maintain extensive land use systems like pastoralism that are consistent with biodiversity conservation but are threatened by agricultural encroachment and external forces (e.g., unregulated investments in tourism infrastructure).

The association of pastoralism with nature and hence biodiversity conservation has not gone unnoticed; a range of actors, including local communities and politicians, have linked the two ideas. For example:

- International NGOs and development agencies are supporting "partnerships" between national parks and pastoral communities in eastern and southern Africa;
- Pastoral communities themselves are forming wildlife associations and organizations, and in some cases establishing their own ecotourism facilities;
- Pastoral politicians are forming their own NGOs to work on wildlife and pastoralism programs, and they are voicing their political agendas in increasingly environmental terms. (Hodgson 2002)

Not surprisingly, the number of local pastoral NGOs has grown considerably during the past decade, as have the number of proposals from pastoral communities seeking funds from international conservation bodies and government agencies (Hodgson 2002). The reality that biodiversity conservation programs must look beyond parks and protected areas provoked a concern with community-based conservation, and thus a proliferation of new activities were initiated in the 1990s by many of the international environmental organizations (e.g., the World Wide Fund for Nature and the International Union for the Conservation of Nature). Indeed, the issue of wildlife conservation in the region, ironically, seems to be closely tied to perceptions of cultural survival and the maintenance of indigenous identities. In short, the cultural survival of indigenous groups like the Maasai and the survival of the environment and wildlife are closely interlinked and, according to some, can result in new types of tourist activities (including ecotourism) that benefit local development. As one senior KWS official remarked to me, "our surveys in the Maasai Mara show that a majority of tourists want to see traditional Maasai as well as wildlife" (author's fieldnotes, June 1997). The association between the persistence of indigenous cultures and the conservation of critical environmental resources also is echoed in conservation and development programs of the Amazon region of South America (Bray and Irvine 1993). In East Africa it raises particularly thorny issues about the rights of outsiders to influence—even determine—rates of social and cultural change among indigenous groups (Neumann 2000).

Dissatisfaction on the part both of government and NGOs with restrictive conservation policies and programs dating to the colonial period (1940s and

1950s) opened the way for more participatory environmental programs in Kenya. Until recently, national park officials were perceived as another type of police force that punished and intimidated local communities who resided near important zones of biodiversity (some would argue that this local perception still exists in some parts of East Africa). The new initiatives that called for more local participation and benefits had conservation as well as development objectives. The KWS, for example, developed a program in the early 1990s that was to build partnerships with local communities and to generate local benefits by sharing park revenues and conservation-related activities (KWS 1997a). To quote a popular KWS document, the principle is simple: "Give people an economic return from the wildlife living on their land and the wildlife will thereby assume a value in the community's eyes and encourage the application of sensible conservation practices" (1997b, 9).

The purpose of the Community Wildlife Services (CWS) of the KWS, which received a bulk of its initial funds from USAID, was to increase the flow of socioeconomic benefits to communities who bear the high costs of wildlife on their lands. Note that up to 85 percent of wildlife populations in Kenya alone roam and feed outside of designated parks and reserves for at least part of the year. In turn, they frequently invade farms and consume large areas of pasture. The KWS, however, insisted that the system of parks and game reserves remain off-limits for human occupation, and it prohibits use of its natural resources other than for tourism. This position was maintained even though some park officials recognized that environmental damage in certain wildlife areas, such as the proliferation of unpalatable species and bush encroachment, resulted from the removal of local human populations and use. At least one park official acknowledged to me in 1997 that increased unpalatable plant species in the Samburu National Game Reserve, a popular tourist destination carved from the grazing lands of a Maasai-related group (Samburu), might have resulted from the ban on customary bush burning by local herders. Nonetheless, officials there and elsewhere in East Africa refuse to adjust their policies to allow some limited grazing rights and use of controlled burns.

A second assumption of the KWS is that local benefits and development can accrue to local communities (and households and individuals within them) through the establishment of a separate unit, CWS, to work with local populations. Activities were implemented by the CWS in an attempt to improve opportunities for local communities to benefit directly from wildlife-related activities. These include small-enterprise development projects around parks and tourist facilities, ecotourism activities, and wildlife utilization projects (which allow some limited commercial culling of certain species of wildlife). It is still too early to evaluate how much of a positive impact—if any—these initiatives have had on the welfare of households and communities, but

there is little question that they have heightened local conservation awareness and the formation of local environmental groups in the area.

The government also is providing incentives (for example, cash payments) that discourage intensive cultivation in certain wildlife corridors
because of its potential for disrupting animal migration patterns and instigat-
ing wildlife-human conflicts. This policy acknowledges that certain types of
local land use activities (including sedentary agriculture) pose a greater
threat to wildlife than others. Unlike a sustainable agriculture program
where improved practices should reap indirect income benefits through
increased crop sales, community wildlife programs have to make direct
income payouts and grants to households and communities. The justification is that this may be the only way to encourage certain management and
production activities and ensure that local communities benefit from investments in tourist facilities and other projects.

Those local anthropologists who have been involved with community-
based conservation programs have usually done so under the auspices of an
NGO; unfortunately most university-based institutions and anthropologists in
the region have had little opportunity to work on these programs. Like other
community-based conservation programs in Botswana (Tropical Research
and Development 1993), Zimbabwe (Metcalfe 1994), and elsewhere in
Africa (Western et al. 1994), the community-based wildlife program in
Kenya was based on the assumption that communities will better manage
their wildlife resources and habitats if they receive direct economic benefits
from them (KWS 1993). It wants to encourage communities and landowners
to derive some economic benefits from wildlife (KWS 1993, iii). Even though
there is little evidence to show whether the community-based conservation
approach has made any positive impact on conservation of biodiversity, the
emphasis continues. There is at least some indication that communities have
received increased amounts of funds generated from national parks and wildlife tourism, although as noted earlier it is unclear what kinds of social and economic benefits these have generated (author's fieldnotes, January 1996).

The community-based wildlife efforts in Kenya and neighboring countries continue to engage anthropologists in their research and development
projects. In Zimbabwe, Botswana, and South Africa, the same is true and
reflects certain trends in the establishment of development anthropology
that were noted earlier. For example, when environmental and development
organizations began to include (or at least attempt to include) local communities in their conservation programs, they found anthropologists working in
these areas. Moreover, anthropologists knew the most about local populations and their use of local natural resources in the critical wildlife corridors,
which strengthened their value to environmental organizations. Recall this

chapter's earlier discussion of the 1970s, when anthropologists were strongly represented in regions and on topics that suddenly were of concern to international development groups. The proliferation of NGOs (both external and indigenous) in the wildlife sector meant that many development anthropologists worked with these organizations, a trend that increasingly characterizes general employment patterns in development anthropology.

Future Directions and Conclusions

The previous section highlighted one kind of global issue—biodiversity conservation—that development anthropologists increasingly are likely to address in their work. Over the past decade it has become commonplace for development anthropologists to look at the local and regional impacts of global processes, such as increased global markets, structural adjustment programs of the IMF and the World Bank, and global environmental movements (Little 2000). The larger economic and political forces that shape development programs and policies require anthropologists to look beyond local communities and to do what Laura Nader recommended more than a decade ago, which is to "study up and look at larger organizations, processes, and policies" (Nader 1996). This tendency is occurring not just in development anthropology but also in the discipline as a whole (Appadurai 1996; Friedman 2002).

Development anthropologists are challenged to learn the languages of policymakers and macroeconomists, whose economic reform and investment programs are having far-reaching impacts in many of the areas where we work and study. Theoretical advances in political ecology and political economy are useful in equipping the development anthropologist with insightful concepts and tools for assessing how global forces are affecting local communities and development programs. To be blind to these larger development forces would isolate anthropology from the real world, as well as from important research and theoretical advancements occurring elsewhere in the discipline.

Yet development anthropology needs to remain committed to its traditional strengths: (1) an insistence on sound research methods and (2) a capacity to work in interdisciplinary settings and learn from other disciplines. Anthropologists who have had an impact on development policies and programs that benefit the rural poor will still be among those who have strong topical expertise. Because local welfare and livelihoods are dependent on how data are collected and then incorporated in the design of development initiatives, development anthropologists should continue to improve data collection techniques, whether participatory or standard case study and survey techniques. Although methods often are treated as a pedestrian, uninteresting topic by much of the discipline, development anthropologists often are challenged to justify and improve their research techniques, in many cases under very demanding field and political situations. They can continue to make important methodological advances with both practical and scholarly implications. By the very nature of their work, development anthropologists will continue to work in interdisciplinary settings, and they could reinvigorate the discipline with insights from other disciplines.

In closing, development anthropology must better reflect the concerns of anthropologists in developing countries. This position has always received lip service in the academy, but it rarely receives active endorsement by Western-based universities and development organizations. Whether intentionally or not, it meets strong institutional resistance in some quarters of the discipline, where research careers are advanced by individual, not collaborative, work and where the shield of "objective science" is raised against anything with a hint of application. Nonetheless, like the indigenous populations that we study and attempt to empower, the community of Third World scholars and practitioners must be invited to participate in a meaningful fashion. Important roles by non-Western anthropologists in defining training, research, and policy agendas of development anthropology are the types of participatory collaboration that should be advocated. Too much of the development debate, including poststructuralist and postdevelopment critiques, reflect intellectual concerns of northern scholars who can comfortably distance themselves from practice and policy, a reality that often is not available in developing countries. As Appadurai aptly queries: "Is there a principled way to close the gap between U.S. social scientists, who are suspicious of any form of applied or policy-driven research and social scientists from many other parts of the world who see themselves as profoundly involved in the social transformations sweeping their own societies?" (1997, 59). In short, "selective distancing is not . . . an option for . . . social scientists who are, with rare exceptions, immersed in the popular struggles of their countries whether they wish to be or not" (Little and Painter 1995, 606).

Anthropologists who have taught at universities in poor countries or collaborated with grassroots organizations quickly learned how problematic the distinction is between theory and practice. There is much about the study and practice of development anthropology that American- and European-based anthropologists can learn from our colleagues in Africa, Asia, and Latin America, who, because of funding and resource constraints, often succumb to training, research, and project activities designed from the outside. Development anthropologists should make strong efforts to ensure that participation and collaboration include the intended beneficiaries of development projects and policies, as well as the professionals who live in these regions.

References

Abate, Teferi. 1998. *Land, capital and labour in the social organization of farmers: A study of household dynamics in Southwestern Wollo, 1974–1993.* Social Anthropology Dissertation Series. Ethiopia: Addis Ababa University.

Adams, R., J. Gillin, A. Holmberg, O. Lewis, R. Patch, and C. Wagley. 1960. *Social change in Latin America: Its implications for United States policy.* New York: Harper and Brothers, for the Council on Foreign Relations.

Ahmed, Abdel Ghaffar M. 2003. *Anthropology in the Sudan: Reflections by a Sudanese anthropologist.* Utrecht, The Netherlands: International Books.

Amare, Yared, Yigremew Adal, Degafa Tolossa, Alfonso Peter Castro, and Peter D. Little. 2000. *Food security and resource access: A final report on the community assessments in South Wello and Oromiya zones of Amhara Region, Ethiopia.* Madison, Wisc.: Broadening Access and Strengthening Input Market Systems Collaborative Research Support Program, University of Wisconsin.

Appadurai, Arjun. 1997. The research ethic and the spirit of internationalism. *Items* 51 (4): 55–60.

———. 1996. *Modernity at large: Cultural dimensions of globalization.* Minneapolis, Minn.: University of Minnesota Press.

Astone, Jennifer. 1996. Negotiating work burdens: Women's home gardens in Fuuta Jalon, Guinea, 1930–1995. PhD thesis, Department of Anthropology, State University of New York-Binghamton, Binghamton, New York.

Bardhan, Pranab. 1989. *Conversations between economists and anthropologists: Methodological issues in measuring economic change in Rural India.* Delhi, India: Oxford University Press.

Barth, Fredrik. 1997. Economy, agency, and ordinary lives. *Social Anthropology* 5 (3): 233–42.

Bennett, John W., and John R. Bowen, eds. 1988. *Production and autonomy: Anthropological studies and critiques of development.* Lanham, Md.: University Press of America.

Bray, David Barton, and Dominique Irvine. 1993. Resource and sanctuary: Indigenous peoples, ancestral rights, and the forests of the Americas. *Cultural Survival Quarterly* 17 (1).

Brokensha, David, ed. 1992. Development anthropology in Europe. A special issue of *Development Anthropology Network: Bulletin of the Institute for Development Anthropology* 10 (1).

Bujra, Abdallah S. 1991. Anthropology and the African crises: Challenging the dilemma. Paper presented at the workshop on "Anthropology in Africa: Past, present, and emerging visions," CODESRIA, Dakar, Senegal. November 11–13.

Carney, Judith. 1994. Contracting a food staple in the Gambia. In *Living under contract: Contract farming and Agrarian transformation in Sub-Saharan Africa,* edited by Peter D. Little and M. Watts. Madison, Wisc.: University of Wisconsin Press.

Cernea, Michael. 1991. *Putting people first: Sociological variables in rural development.* New York: Oxford University Press.

Chambers, Robert. 1997. *Whose reality counts? Putting the first last.* London: Intermediate Technology Development Group.

———. 1984. *Rural development: Putting the last first.* London: Longman.

Cochrane, Glynn. 1971. *Development anthropology.* New York: Oxford University Press.

Cohen, Jeffrey, and Norbert Dannhaeuser, eds. 2002. *Economic development: An anthropological approach.* Walnut Creek, Calif.: Rowman & Littlefield.

Corbridge, Stuart, ed. 1995. *Development studies: A reader.* London: E. Arnold.

Development anthropologist. 1995. Development anthropology in Japan. 13 (1 & 2): 34.

Development anthropology network: Bulletin of the Institute for Development Anthropology. 1990. Department of Anthropology/Sociology, Moi University, Eldoret, Kenya. 8 (1): 21–22.

Dolan, Catherine. 1997. Contested terrain: Gender and labor dynamics in horticultural exporting, Meru District, Kenya. PhD thesis, Department of Anthropology, SUNY, Binghamton.

Escobar, Arturo. 1995. *Encountering development: The making and unmaking of the Third World.* Princeton, N.J.: Princeton University Press.

———. 1991. Anthropology and development: The making and marketing of development anthropology. *American Ethnologist* 18 (4): 658–82.

Fairhead, J., and M. Leach. 1996. *Misreading the African landscape: Society and ecology in a forest-savanna mosaic.* Cambridge: Cambridge University Press.

Ferguson, James. 1997. Anthropology and its evil twin: "Development" in the constitution of a discipline. In *International development and the social sciences: Essays on the history and politics of knowledge,* edited by Frederick Cooper and Randall Packard. Berkeley: University of California Press.

Fisher, William F. 1999. Going under: Indigenous peoples and the struggle against large dams. *Cultural Survival Quarterly* 23 (3).

Fleuret, Anne. 1988. Food aid and development in rural Kenya. In *The anthropology of development and change in East Africa,* edited by David Brokensha and Peter D. Little. Boulder, Colo.: Westview Press.

Friedman, Jonathan. 2002. *Globalization, the state, and violence.* Walnut Creek, Calif.: AltaMira.

Fox, Jonathan, Lynn Stephen, and Gaspar Rivera. 1999. Indigenous rights and self-determination in Mexico. *Cultural Survival Quarterly* 23 (1).

Gardner, K., and D. Lewis. 1996. *Anthropology, development and the post-modern challenge.* London: Pluto Press.

Geertz, C. 1962. The rotating credit association: A "middle rung" in development. *Economic Development and Cultural Change* 10: 241–63.

Gibson, Clark C. 1999. *Politicians and poachers: The political economy of wildlife policy in Africa.* Cambridge: Cambridge University Press.

Gifford-Gonzalez, Diane. 1994. Position Paper: Biodiversity in Africa's Human Landscapes. Paper presented at the SSRC/African Academy of Sciences/Smithsonian Institute Workshop on "Biodiversity in Africa's Human Landscapes," Nairobi, Kenya. July 21–23.

Gow, David D. 2002. Anthropology and development: Evil twin or moral narrative? *Human Organization* 61 (4): 299–313.

Grillo, Ralph D., and R. L. Stirrat, eds. 1997. *Discourses of development: Anthropological perspectives.* Oxford, UK: Berg.

Guyer, J. 1986. Intra-household processes and farming systems research. In *Understanding Africa's rural households and farming systems,* edited by J. Moock. Boulder, Colo.: Westview Press.

————. 1981. Household and community in African studies. *African Studies Review* 23: 87–137.

Hardin, Garrett. 1968. The tragedy of the commons. *Science* 162: 1243–48.

Hart, G. 1992. Household production reconsidered: Production, patronage, and gender politics in rural Malaysia. *World Development* 20 (6): 809–23.

Herzfeld, Michael. 2001. *Anthropology: Theoretical practice in culture and society.* Oxford, UK: Blackwell.

Hitchcock, Robert. 1999. Resource rights and resettlement among the San of Botswana. *Cultural Survival Quarterly* 22 (4): 51–55.

Hoben, Allan. 1982. Anthropologists and development. *Annual Review of Anthropology* 11: 349–75.

Hodgson, Dorothy. 2002. Precarious alliances: The cultural politics and structural predicaments of the Indigenous Rights Movement in Tanzania. *American Anthropologist* 104 (4): 1086–97.

Horgan, John. 1989. The Masai: These pastoralists are key to the future of Kenya's wildlife. *Scientific American* (September): 38–44.

Horowitz, Michael M. 1998. Introduction: Development and the anthropological encounter in the 21st century. *Development Anthropologist* 16 (1–2): 1–6.

————. 1997. Notes on Social Science and the U.S. Agency for International Development. *Development Anthropology Network: Bulletin of the Institute for Development Anthropology* 15 (1–2): 23–29.

————. 1994. Development anthropology in the mid-1990s. *Development Anthropology Network: Bulletin of the Institute for Development Anthropology* 12 (1–2): 1–14.

————. 1979. *The sociology of pastoralism and African livestock development.* AID Program Evaluation Discussion Paper No. 6. Washington, D.C.: AID.

Huntington, Samuel, and L. E. Harrison. 2000. *Culture matters: How values shape human progress.* New York: Basic Books.

Kennedy, E., and P. Peters. 1992. Household food security and child nutrition: The interaction of income and gender of household head. *World Development* 20: 1077–85.

Kenya, Government of. 1996. *Wildlife policy.* Nairobi: Government Printer.

Kenya Wildlife Services (KWS). 1997a. *Parks beyond parks: Celebrating 50 years of national parks in Kenya, 1946–1996: Annual report.* Nairobi, Kenya: KWS.

————. 1997b. *Partnership news* 1: A newsletter of the Partnership Department of the Kenya Wildlife Services. Nairobi, Kenya: KWS.

————. 1993. A policy framework and development programme, 1991–1996: Annex 6. In *Community conservation and wildlife management outside parks and reserves.* Nairobi, Kenya: KWS.

Korten, David. 1990. *Getting to the 21st century: Voluntary action and the global agenda.* West Hartford, Conn.: Kumarian.

Lewis, Oscar. 1960. *Tepoztlán, village in Mexico.* New York: Holt.

Lewis, W. A. 1970. *Tropical development.* Evanston, Ill.: Northwestern University Press.

Leys, Colin. 1996. *The rise and fall of development theory.* Bloomington: Indiana University Press.

Little, Peter D. 2000. Recasting the debate: Development theory and anthropological practice. In *The unity of theory and practice in anthropology: Rebuilding a fractured synthesis*, edited by Carole E. Hill and Marietta L. Baba. NAPA Bulletin 18. Washington, D.C.: American Anthropological Association.

———. 1994. The link between local participation and improved conservation: A review of issues and experiences. In *Natural connections: Perspectives in community-based conservation*, edited by D. Western and M. Wright. Washington, D.C.: Island Press.

Little, Peter D., and Catherine Dolan. 2000. What it means to be restructured: "Nontraditional" commodities and structural adjustment in sub-Saharan Africa. In *Commodities and globalization: Anthropological perspectives*, edited by A. Haugerud, P. Stone, and P. Little. Monographs in Economic Anthropology Series. Boulder, Colo., and London: Rowman and Littlefield.

Little, Peter D., and Michael Painter. 1995. Discourse, politics, and development: A response to the "making of development anthropology." *American Ethnologist* 22 (3): 602–609.

Long, Norman. 1992. Conclusion. In *Battlefields of knowledge: The interlocking of theory and practice in social research and development*, edited by N. Long and A. Long. London: Routledge.

Long, Norman, and Ann Long, eds. *Battlefields of knowledge: The interlocking of theory and practice in social research and development*. London: Routledge.

Lusigi, Walter. 1984. Future directions for the Afrotropical realm. In *National parks, conservation and development*, edited by J. McNeely and K. Miller. Washington, D.C.: Smithsonian Institution Press.

Macdonald, Theodore, Jr. 1997. Introduction: 25 years of the indigenous movement in the Americas and Australia. *Cultural Survival Quarterly* 21(2).

McCay, Bonnie J., and James M. Acheson, eds. 1987. *The question of the commons.* Tucson: University of Arizona Press.

Mathur, Hari M. 1989. *Anthropology and development in traditional societies.* New Delhi, India: Vikas Publishing House.

Metcalf, Simon. 1994. The Zimbabwe Communal Areas Management Programme for Indigenous Resources (CAMPFIRE). In *Natural connections*, edited by David Western, R. Michael McWright, and Shirley C. Strum. Washington, D.C., Island Press.

Moore, H., and M. Vaughan. 1994. *Cutting down trees: Gender, nutrition, and agricultural change in the Northern Province of Zambia, 1890–1990.* London: James Currey.

Nader, Laura, ed. 1996. Naked science: Anthropological inquiry into boundaries, power, and knowledge. London: Routledge.

Neumann, Roderick P. 2000. Primitive ideas: Protected area buffer zones and the politics of land in Africa. In *Producing nature and poverty in Africa*, edited by Vigdis Broch-Due and R. Schroeder. Uppsala, Sweden: Nordiska Afrikainstitutet.

Nolan, Riall. 2002. *Development anthropology: Encounters in the real world.* Boulder, Colo.: Westview Press.

Pankhurst, Alula. 2003. Conflict management over contested natural resources: A case study of pasture, forest and irrigation in South Wello, Ethiopia. In *Natural resource conflict management case studies: An analysis of power, participation and protected areas*, edited by A. Peter Castro and Erik Nielsen. Rome, Italy: UN Food and Agriculture Organization.

Peet, Richard, and E. Hartwick. 1999. *Theories of development.* New York: Guilford Press.

Peluso, Nancy L., and Michael Watts, eds. 2001. *Violent environments.* Ithaca, N.Y.: Cornell University Press.

Peters, Pauline. 1994. *Dividing the commons: Politics, policy, and culture in Botswana.* Charlottesville: University Press of Virginia.

Pottier, Johan, ed. 1993. *Practicing development: Social science perspectives.* London: Routledge.

Rauf, Mohammed A. 1984. Anthropology program, Quaid-i-Azam University, Islamabad, Pakistan. *Development Anthropology Network: Bulletin of the Institute for Development Anthropology* 2 (1–2): 19.

Robertshaw, Peter. 1990. *Early pastoralists of south-western Kenya.* Nairobi: British Institute in Eastern Africa.

Schultz, Theodore W. 1964. *Transforming traditional agriculture.* New Haven, Conn.: Yale University Press.

Spears, Thomas, and R. Waller, eds. 1993. *Being Maasai: Ethnicity and identity in East Africa.* Oxford, UK: James Currey.

Thomson, Joseph. 1885. *Through Masai land.* London: Cass.

Tropical Research and Development. 1993. Midterm evaluation of the Botswana Natural Resources Management Project. Washington, D.C.: USAID.

Wagley, Charles. 1960. The Brazilian Revolution: Social change since 1930. In *Social change in Latin America: Its implications for United States policy,* edited by Richard N. Adams, J. Gillin, A. Holmberg, O. Lewis, R. Patch, and C. Wagley. New York: Harper and Brothers, for the Council on Foreign Relations.

Wedel, J., and R. Borofsky. 1997. How others see us: An interview with Fredrik Barth. *Anthropology Newsletter of the American Anthropological Association* 38 (2): 58, 60.

Western, David, Michael Wright, and Shirley Strum, eds. 1994. *Natural connections: Perspectives in community-based conservation.* Washington, D.C.: Island Press.

van Willigen, John. 2002. *Applied anthropology: An introduction.* 3rd ed. Westport, Conn.: Bergin and Garvey.

3 Agricultural Anthropology

Robert E. Rhoades

Introduction

The term agriculture refers to the intentional cultivation of plants and tending of domesticated animal species for human benefit. Agriculture has been the dominant human economy since cultivation originated independently three to ten millennia ago in several different Old World and New World regions (MacNeish 1992; Mannion 1999). Food surpluses produced from farming and herding formed the basis of urban civilization, with its expanding populations, widespread trade networks, and modern complex society. Roughly half of contemporary humanity is directly engaged in some form of food or fiber production. In poor countries, 70 percent of people depend on the land for their livelihood. Even in modern industrial and postindustrial nations, such as the United States and Japan, where less than 10 percent of the population is directly engaged in farming, agriculture remains the "primary" industry due to its fundamental economic and nutritional role in sustaining society.

Few realms of human life touch more components of culture—technological, economic, social, and religious—than agriculture and its products. On the one hand, agriculture functions to satisfy biological needs; on the other, it embodies powerful cultural symbolism in all its physical, natural, and organizational aspects. Agriculture is the primary way human beings satisfy basic requirements (food, shelter, and clothing) for nourishment and protection from the elements. It also provides luxuries such as sugar, coffee, cocoa, spices, and condiments, which are not essential for human survival but certainly make our lives more enjoyable.

The word agriculture is derived from two Latin roots: *agri*, which means "field," and *culture*, which carries a double meaning in English of both "to cultivate" and "a way of life." This original dual meaning of culture provides a special historical linkage between agricultural sciences and anthropology. Because cultivation defined the way of life of most preindustrial peoples, the modern distinction between the two meanings of culture would have been redundant for these societies. In the mid-nineteenth century, European intellectuals recrafted the word culture as a separate key concept of the young field of anthropology, which has nothing less than the ambition of becoming the science of all cultures, not just cultivators. Unfortunately, for more than a century, this separation had the effect of isolating two academic fields—anthropology and agriculture—that should have been intellectually and institutionally aligned in solving food and fiber problems.

The purpose of this chapter is to tell the story of how the subdiscipline of agricultural anthropology was established in the latter half of the twentieth century, thus returning anthropology to one of its basic roots. Agricultural anthropology is an interesting case because, starting from a limited base, in less than 25 years it has become a highly valued specialty. Applied anthropologists can draw inspiration from this success because it is a story of anthropologists overcoming a suspicious clientele—agricultural scientists and rural communities—by translating anthropological concepts and methods into useful tools for technical and policy advances. To explore the agricultural domain of anthropology, I will (1) define agricultural anthropology, (2) trace early anthropological contributions to agricultural research, (3) present case studies where anthropology is applied to contemporary agricultural issues, and (4) discuss new directions for agricultural anthropology. This chapter draws heavily on my own experience in numerous research and development contexts ranging from agricultural extension in Nepal in the early 1960s, to the Green Revolution in the late 1960s and mid-1970s, to Farming Systems Research in the 1980s, and, finally, down to natural resource management and sustainable agriculture from the 1990s until the present.

Agricultural Anthropology: Definition of the Domain

Agricultural anthropology is the comparative, holistic, and temporal study of the human element in agricultural activity, focusing on the interactions of environment, technology, and culture within local and global food systems, and it has the practical goal of responsibly applying this knowledge to improve the efficiency and sustainability of food and fiber production (Rhoades 1984a). Agricultural anthropologists are concerned with the human element in the total agrarian system, from production to preparation, distribution, consumption, and storage, along with cultural meanings and practices associated with these activities. With interests ranging from archaeological studies of the origin of agriculture to ethnographies of modern industrial farming, anthropologists have left few agrarian thematic stones unturned (Rhoades 1980). Despite this long engagement with agricultural issues, however, a subfield within anthropology called "agricultural anthropology" emerged only 25 years ago as more and more anthropologists specializing in agrarian issues realized the importance of application, interdisciplinarity, and employment outside the academy. Most agricultural anthropologists today carry out their research and application in international institutes, governmental agencies, nongovernmental organizations (NGOs), or nonprofits, but even those anthropologists affiliated with universities conduct research that aims to improve our understanding of the human food system. The viability of the Culture and Agriculture Group within the American Anthropological Association (AAA) testifies to the contemporary importance of agricultural anthropology to the discipline.

Culture in the anthropological sense remains a key—but neglected—part of agriculture in the diverse forms practiced throughout the world today. As long as humans modify and simplify landscapes for production and utilize the products of agriculture—such as food, clothing, and building material—agriculture will be culturally significant. Culture is embellished through the execution of farming and herding: food rituals, landscapes, symbols, ethnicity, and cultural memory. Particularly in societies that depend primarily on agriculture, the internal workings of social organization, ideology, and kinship are closely linked with the technical execution of planting, cultivating, harvesting, and preparing food. Food—the most critical product of agriculture for humans—is culturally central to all societies. For example, the modern Japanese depend on rice, which plays a role in every national dish, including sake and sushi, and is an industrial input into paper, mats, and baskets. Rice is also a key component in most religious ceremonies. In European "bread" societies, wheat is not only the staple crop but also serves as a cultural icon in many ways. English speakers, for example, refer to "breaking bread together" as a way to resolve conflicts or socialize. In Mesoamerica, maize serves this food-culture role; in the Andes, the potato functions in the same way.

Early Anthropological Contributions to the Agricultural Domain: Potential Unrealized

Although not historically recognized as an agricultural field, anthropology has focused on farming and herding as distinct human endeavors since the discipline was established in the nineteenth century. As the youngest social science, anthropology sought to establish a subject matter separate from the other Western disciplines like history, sociology, and economics (Wolf 1964). In using non-Western peoples as their topics, anthropologists found themselves studying the rural societies that constituted the mass of humanity living mainly in the colonized marginal areas of Africa, Asia, North America, and Latin America. These people were called uncivilized, savage, native, and exotic by the outside world until anthropologists discovered that these people hitherto described as "simple" in fact possessed complex cultures equal in many respects to the cultures found in Europe. Although many early anthropologists generated useful information on agriculture in the course of ethnographic fieldwork, their intellectual interests focused on less mundane aspects of culture such as kinship terminology, rituals, and marriage customs (Netting 1974). Also, many nineteenth-century anthropology pioneers, as well as the following generations in Europe and America, hailed from privileged urban families who looked upon farming as a low-status endeavor.

During the first half of the twentieth century, anthropology played a limited direct role in agricultural research despite rich ethnographic studies on farming and herding peoples (Evans-Pritchard and Fortes 1940; Forde 1934). Within colonial and neocolonial governments, anthropologists were called upon to serve as important informational links between the colonized, often tribal or peasant populations, and expatriate bureaucrats. Although most of the activities centered on the description of traditional ways and the impact of European contact, early anthropologists assisted in areas of public health, education, community development, and, in a few cases, agriculture (see Foster 1969, 181–217, for an early history of applied anthropology).

The first documented involvement of anthropologists in agriculture in the United States was during the 1930s New Deal era with the Soil Conservation Service, but, unfortunately, this effort was short-lived and left no institutional anchor (Foster 1969, 202). In the 1940s, a few anthropologists began to touch base with agricultural scientists. Among them was Charles Loomis (1943), one of the founders of the Society for Applied Anthropology, who spent half a year in Peru analyzing problems with establishing an agricultural extension service. He went on to help establish the social science department in the Instituto Interamericano de Ciencias Agricolas (IICA) in Costa Rica. During the same period, some of the biggest names in anthropology—such as Robert Redfield, Margaret Mead, and John Bennett—gave high priority to the study of foodways and nutritional studies (Montgomery and Bennett 1979). In 1947, Walter Goldschmidt published a well-known study on the effects of industrial agriculture on rural communities in California, in which he demonstrated that the type of community was directly linked with changes in agriculture (Goldschmidt 1947). Finally, in the 1950s, the famous Vicos Project in Peru led by Cornell anthropologists proved to have a major impact on our thinking about applied anthropology, especially about ethical issues in policy and planning (Holmberg et al. 1962; Holmberg et al. 1965). In this very controversial program, Cornell University actually assumed ownership of a hacienda and control over the Indians who had lived and worked as virtual serfs. Cornell's plan was to provide training to peasants and to ultimately turn over control and ownership of the hacienda to the Vicos indigenous community. Although many anthropologists, including others from Cornell, bitterly opposed the project on the ethical ground that U.S. universities should not become hacienda owners, the program has been hailed by many observers as a precursor and model for Peru's Agrarian Land Reform under the Velasco presidency. Mario Vasquez, a Peruvian anthropologist in the Vicos Project, served as director general of Peru's Agrarian Reform and Rural Settlement from 1973 to 1976 (Rhoades 1984a, 2).

Unfortunately, many early anthropological studies that contained invaluable insights for agricultural research and development were ignored or written off as irrelevant. For example, Harold Conklin's (1957) detailed study of Hanunoo agriculture—prepared as a major report to the UN Food and Agriculture Organization (FAO)—ultimately helped revolutionize conventional thinking about shifting cultivation, although it took science many years to recognize his contribution. Conklin demonstrated that shifting cultivation was not irrational, as most agricultural scientists argued, but was ecologically sensible and based on a complex folk-scientific knowledge of plants, soils, and ecological interactions (Conklin 1954).

The most interesting yet unrecognized impact of anthropology is found in the work of Theodore Schultz, who won the Nobel Prize for economics in 1979 for his insightful reanalysis of Third World agriculture. Although few people credit the influence of anthropology on Schultz's work, the Nobel Laureate himself gave due credit in the introduction to his book *Transforming Traditional Agriculture*, which ultimately became the theoretical basis of the Green Revolution.

> Agriculture economists have restricted their studies to farming in that small class of countries to which agriculture has been successful in contributing to national income . . . but they have neglected traditional agriculture, *leaving it to anthropologists who have made some useful studies as will become evident later.* (1964, iv, emphasis added)

What becomes evident later in Schultz's concise 200-page book is a global analysis of Third World agriculture, which starts and ends by drawing on two anthropologically grounded village studies: *Penny Capitalism*, Sol Tax's

1953 monograph on Panajachel, Guatemala, and W. David Hopper's 1957 Cornell dissertation on the village of Senapur, Uttar Pradesh, India. Schultz relied on these two studies to overturn the contemporary world view that Third World peasants were irrational, backward, lazy, resistant to change, and isolated from the world. Schultz's genius, however, did not stop with this anthropological insight—as policy-shy anthropologists might have done—but he argued that a program was needed to provide Third World farmers with the necessary seeds, irrigation, fertilizer, credit, and technical know-how. Farmers, as "rational decision makers," would make agriculture viable and productive for their national economies. In 1964, this was a paradigm-shifting argument inspired by anthropological field research. Although not all of his insights or data came from anthropology, there is no doubt that anthropological thinking had a powerful impact on Schultz, who started from the thesis that economic theory was bankrupt for addressing Third World agriculture (and, by admission, the reverse was true for anthropology). Although anthropologists later became some of the greatest critics of the Green Revolution, it is clear that anthropology's insights have power and will be used for policy formation, whether anthropologists guide the process or not (Netting 1993; Dahlberg 1979).

Unfortunately, neither the early applied efforts nor the theoretical breakthroughs by anthropologists guaranteed a lasting place for agricultural anthropology within the public or private sphere. Part of the blame lies with anthropology, which in the 1960s opted to turn inward to tribal ethnography and away from application and policy. As William Foote Whyte (1984) commented: "the prevailing orientation of many anthropologists in that era was self-defeating, insofar as their gaining partnership in these programs. Anthropologists were known to be arrogantly aloof, refusing often on moralistic grounds to apply their expertise to practical agriculture." In addition, anthropologists also framed agriculture in a cultural framework that saw tradition as cast in concrete rather than thinking of it as a creative, adaptive, flexible framework within which people solve food problems. Working with agriculturalists to understand and improve production was not considered legitimate anthropology, and few rewards and little space were given to the anthropologist so inclined (Whyte 1984). This situation was exaggerated by the fact that anthropology is not typically associated with land grant agricultural colleges in the United States. Even within a single university, anthropology departments tend to be located in liberal arts colleges, separate from agricultural science. Thus, anthropology—unlike rural sociology—was institutionally isolated from agriculture during the post–World War II national and international expansion of agricultural development. This condition did not apply only to the agricultural domain; in fact, throughout the immediate postwar period, few anthropologists entered development or applied work at all. At most, they were relegated to helping expatriates cope with culture shock, but they were not involved with planning, policy, or action (Hall 1961, 1966).

Crafting an Agricultural Anthropology

Overcoming Stereotypes and Creating Effective Roles

Two trends during the 1970s set the stage for formal recognition and acceptance of agricultural anthropology. The first was the rise of an ecologically informed anthropology with its emphasis on energy flows, technology, traditional knowledge, systems analysis, and human interaction with plants, animals, water, and soils. The influential writings of Marvin Harris (1965), Clifford Geertz (1963), Roy Rappaport (1968), and John Bennett (1969) were widely debated by agricultural scientists. In 1976, the first informal meeting of the future Culture and Anthropology Group of the AAA was held, and agricultural anthropology was discussed as an emerging subdiscipline. The second trend related to a unique combination of demographic and economic conditions affecting job opportunities for recent PhDs in anthropology. During the mid-1970s, the baby boom cohort of graduate students peaked, leading to record numbers of fresh PhDs who had no future in academics. Instead, many turned to the expanding applied job market as a way to simply survive. Faced with this uncertain future, a large number of young anthropologists had no choice but to cast their fate with employers outside the university setting with, for example, the FAO, the Consultative Group for International Agriculture Research (CGIAR), the United States Department of Agriculture (USDA), charitable foundations, and NGOs. After a difficult start in which they were largely isolated from their academic anthropological colleagues, these young anthropologists, who were ill-equipped for applied research, ultimately learned to blend and modify anthropological methods and skills to match the needs of interdisciplinary research agendas.

Among the numerous nonacademic agencies in which anthropologists have gained experience is CGIAR, a UN-affiliated network consisting of 16 member institutes. Although the CGIAR's greatest fame came from its plant-breeding role with the Green Revolution, the CGIAR today plays a number of diverse roles for Third World agriculture, ranging from biotechnology research to management training for agricultural administrators. In the wake of the criticism that Green Revolution technologies had profound and unintended socioeconomic consequences on small-scale farmers, the

CGIAR moved in the late 1970s to add social scientists to their interdisciplinary teams that looked at integrated farming and food systems instead of only food production. The first anthropologists were postdoctoral fellows of the Rockefeller Foundation, which paved the way by providing most of the fellows' funding. The biological scientists who dominated agricultural centers were not initially interested in using their own resources to involve anthropologists—members of a discipline considered largely irrelevant to the production tasks at hand. Since that time, well over 150 anthropologists have been employed in some capacity within the CGIAR; today some of them even fill top management roles. Examples of CGIAR centers (today called Future Harvest Centers) where anthropologists are employed include the International Rice Research Institute in the Philippines and the International Potato Center in Lima, Peru. In addition to the institutes focusing on major world crops, other centers use anthropologists to deal with policy, forestry, natural resources, and tropical or semiarid agroecosystems.

The CGIAR experience illustrates the dynamics and problems of integrating anthropology into a nonacademic interdisciplinary setting that focuses on technical or policy issues (Thiele, van de Fliert, and Campilan 2001). Performance in the CGIAR is evaluated in terms of how well an individual or team serves the clearly focused public-goods objectives of the organization, not on their contributions to their own disciplines. Given this emphasis on teamwork and impact, the first several years of anthropologists' efforts were far from successful. The high rate of failure—as measured by resignations, early release, and on-the-job resistance—was due to two factors: (1) administrators, biological scientists, and economists held stereotypical views of what they thought anthropologists should be doing (which rarely corresponded to what anthropologists thought they should be doing); and (2) anthropologists lacked experience in interdisciplinary research settings. Typically, anthropologists were assigned ex post facto service roles to biological scientists, such as studying adoption or diffusion of center-generated technologies or plant varieties.

The causes of difficulty in early experiences can be traced to poor training for applied research by the anthropologists' own academic departments and mentors. Anthropology did not have a "client relationship" with the domain of agriculture in the same way as biological science or economics did. Burton and colleagues contrasted anthropology with other social sciences such as agricultural economics, political science, or psychology: "These areas have clearly defined missions and methods and well-developed and stable relationships with institutional clients who provide employment. Practitioners of these fields are expected to know specific research skills which include procedure for measurement and evaluation" (1986, 21).

Anthropologists are often puzzled that others do not recognize the inherent value of their discipline. In fact, many agricultural scientists challenged anthropologists directly by asking what their field could possibly contribute to the problem of world hunger. In laboratories and experimental fields, jokes abounded about the esoteric anthropologist who behaved strangely. Often these stories were relayed third- or fourth-hand: a colleague elsewhere told a friend about the eccentric behavior of anthropologists. Seven common stereotypes of anthropologists circulated widely in international circles (Rhoades 1986).

1. The Loner. Anthropologists were not team players and typically shunned interdisciplinary research in favor of "Lone Ranger" research. Anthropologists were famous for setting up research projects to work alone in a single village with a few key informants. The research center's mandate, however, was to deal with millions of villagers in a major world agroecological zones (e.g., semiarid tropics or humid tropics).

2. The Soft Scientist. Anthropologists used methods and research styles that were vague, not replicable, time consuming, "soft," and costly. Anthropological research reports were said to be largely anecdotal in a research setting where empirical research was highly valued. How could qualitative results be used to extrapolate findings to large populations, such as rice or wheat growers in marginal areas?

3. The Tortoise. Long-term ethnography ("ten years to do fieldwork, ten years to write it up" was a common joke) was not easily blended into a time-pressure research strategy that required planning decisions in relation to the cropping calendar. Log frames and impact promises made it impossible to do in-depth research à la anthropology.

4. The Naysayer. Anthropologists were said to be guided by an antichange/ antidevelopment ideology. Considered incurably nostalgic about rural people by their team colleagues, anthropologists gave the impression that they identified more with preserving traditional culture than with improving food production or working on designing sustainable agricultural systems.

5. The Preacher. Although academic anthropologists hold negative views of agricultural scientists (seeing them as naive and techno-obsessed), agricultural scientists saw their hunger-fighting efforts as ethical and noble, and many believed that anthropologists had few legitimate claims to ethical superiority. At least "aggies" were producing more food for people while anthropologists were producing little more than words. Agricultural scientists were shocked at emotional outbreaks from frustrated anthropology colleagues who would publicly berate technical scientists for "techno-scientific salvationism" and Green Revolution fiascoes. Ripping apart technical projects was a favorite pastime of anthropologists,

who saw themselves as advocates for local communities. Female anthropologists, facing a male-dominated agricultural establishment, were charged with carrying the "gender bandwagon" too far. Anthropologists who were generalists in terms of a region (Andeanist, Asianist, Africanist) or, worse yet, too theory oriented had difficulty explaining what they could contribute to world hunger in specific terms.

6. The Romantic Zealot. Anthropologists sometimes idealized and overdefended indigenous agriculture, lending the impression that they believed local practices were already perfect, so how could any change be good? Attacks against anthropologists for their defense of tradition remain very common today because the whole philosophy of agricultural research is that guided change is good.

7. The Replaceable. Anthropologists were superfluous and fully replaceable. Many scientists, especially economists, believed anthropologists made no unique contribution that could not be made as well by socially sensitive economists who spoke the local language. In the pecking order of agricultural research at the International Potato Center, for example, each discipline felt it could do the job of the discipline just under it in status. The plant breeder believed that a good variety would be adopted automatically, so why did one need agronomists to do field trials? The agronomist could do simple cost-benefit analyses, so why was an economist necessary? And the economist thought that with fluency in the local language, why was it necessary to have an anthropologist to explain commonsense cultural phenomenon? Unfortunately, in this "anything you can do, I can do better" environment, intensity of hostility against anthropology was more intense because it was at the very bottom of the pecking order (and significantly below our closest low-class brothers, the economists).

In some instances, criticisms of early anthropologists in the CGIAR had less to do with anthropological theory, methods, or philosophical stance than with the "new kid on the block" syndrome. As representatives of the newest agricultural perspective, anthropologists were vulnerable to special scrutiny, especially from economists, who felt the most threatened by the newcomers. Anthropologists had little experience in translating to others exactly what anthropologists did and how they did it. Such shortcomings in team communication were answered more effectively by those anthropologists who had received training in ecological anthropology and multidisciplinary programs with training in agriculture. Prior involvement with farmers or agricultural scientists, either through upbringing, Peace Corps, or similar experience, was also useful.

Against this backdrop of myth and reality, agricultural anthropologists had to find their own way, defend their new roles, and carve out a new turf.

The sole anthropologist in a center with 100 diverse scientists, most of whom were biologically trained, felt the burden of proof to explain what anthropology could contribute to the mission or institutional objectives. This principle applies not only to anthropology but to all scientists and sciences. Just being an anthropologist doing village studies was not enough. How was this perspective useful to global food security?

Agricultural anthropologists who successfully overcome common stereotypes to become functioning and effective team members follow five main strategies.

First, they clearly communicate what anthropology has to offer, not in jargon but in lay terms. What they communicate is only the tip of anthropology's theoretical and methodological iceberg. An interdisciplinary team cannot absorb all the nuances from any discipline, much less anthropology. Those anthropologists who approach their research with a systems analysis of the natural/biological system and its relation to the human populations tend to be better understood because this is a language in common with the biological sciences (Netting 1974). In agricultural contexts, this necessitates an understanding of agroecological zones, crops, animals, seasons, soils, markets, production technologies, and climate. Training in basic biological principles helps put ecological anthropologists on common ground with their biological science colleagues. The articulate agricultural anthropologist also connects "components" (e.g., seeds, pests, soils, markets) into a systems framework and traces the linkages among technology, subsistence, social organization, and knowledge systems. Such holistic thinking is helpful to the biological scientist, who generally looks only at components in isolation. Anthropologists able to use Latin names for plants, understand energy equations, trace nutrient flows, describe production systems, and explain the complex structure of intercropping simply make good interdisciplinary team members.

Second, successful agricultural anthropologists demonstrate how anthropological cultural perspectives and methods concerning time and place, cognition, food habits, gender roles, and household economics dovetail with pressing technological and policy problems. The key to success in agricultural research is to show how a given perspective can make a production, nutritional, or economic difference. By learning to modify and blend traditional ethnographic methods into the ecological perspective, a new set of research tools became available to the agricultural research establishment. Examples of these methods are (1) participatory research methods appropriate to local village conditions directly with farmers and technology generation (Chambers 1992), (2) methods that elucidate micro-macro food systems linkages reaching from the village to world economics

(Holtzman 1986; Babb 1998), and (3) comparative methods using an agro-ecological framework (Rhoades 1988). Today, many anthropological research methods are immensely popular in international development (Chambers 1992; Rhoades 1984b). The Participatory Research Appraisal (PRA) movement, which hit international development in the 1980s and 1990s and was even being adopted by mainstream organizations like the World Bank or USAID, draws its basic methodology from anthropology (Chambers, Pacey, and Thrupp 1989). Participatory methods aim to involve the local population in an engaged self-interested manner instead of making people an object of research in which the outcome is only of interest to scientists.

Third, they demonstrate how indigenous or local knowledge and theories of small-farmer behavior drawn from anthropology improves agriculture and is not something standing in contradiction to the basic philosophy of agricultural research (DeWalt 1994; Sillitoe 1998; Purcell 1998). Indigenous knowledge systems are place-based ways of perceiving and understanding the world that have evolved through time-tested experiences and day-to-day trial-and-error challenges of adapting to local conditions (DeWalt 1994). According to Paul Sillitoe, anthropology's main contribution has been through research that "sets out explicitly to make connections between local people's understandings and practices and those of outside researchers and development workers" (1998, 224). For example, anthropologists demonstrated that farmers are expert ethnobotanists, avid experimenters in their own right, and possess a great deal of indigenous knowledge that can guide scientific research or be transferred to other contexts (Posey et al. 1984). Successful agricultural anthropologists possess the skills to capture indigenous knowledge within the context of biophysical and technical problems of concern to scientists and translate it into information useful to the goals of local people.

Fourth, they negotiate a place of influence, not one of ex post facto evaluators, for anthropologists early in the research process. If anthropologists are always relegated to mop-up operations—and are all too often the bearer of bad news—their future in agricultural research will be bleak indeed.

Fifth, effective agricultural anthropologists secure a place for future anthropologists by leaving a valued legacy. This means addressing other scientists, not just talking to anthropologists, as is typical in academics, especially academic anthropology. Using the term agricultural anthropology makes the point clear from the outset that people with this professional label apply anthropology to agricultural issues, just as an agricultural engineer or an agricultural economist applies economics or engineering to the agricultural domain.

Applying Agricultural Anthropology: Case Studies

In this section, I will discuss three agricultural research case studies in which anthropologists played significant roles. They are drawn from my own experience at the International Potato Center (CIP; in Spanish, *Centro Internacional de la Papa*), where more anthropologists have been utilized than any other agricultural organization. Over a 25-year period (1975–2000), at least 25 anthropologists have been employed in some capacity. CIP, like all CGIAR centers, has five main objectives related to its specific crop or ecoregion: (1) increasing production, (2) protecting the environment, (3) saving biodiversity, (4) improving policies, and (5) strengthening national research. Anthropologists at CIP have effectively contributed to all of these areas.

The ground rules of CIP's research and training expect anthropologists to address the technical and policy needs of potato research by translating their anthropological research findings into concrete action. Within these ground rules, anthropologists are free to choose among a wide range of research topics and activities, from technical concerns to policy. In the 1980s and 1990s, this normally involved joining one of the eight interdisciplinary research teams working on key problems ranging from breeding for improved potatoes to postharvest technology. Some of the teams were more open to anthropological involvement than others. Regardless of research theme, however, anthropological methodology in these contexts has to be relevant and integrated into a larger framework of social and biological science methods of interdisciplinary teams. CIP anthropologists, therefore, in addition to doing what anthropologists traditionally do, need to have a fundamental understanding of formal questionnaires, experimental design, use of Geographic Information Systems (GIS) and remote sensing, and basic agronomic techniques. In finding their productive niche, CIP anthropologists often broaden the scope of relevant research themes, propose new ways of looking at problems, and convince their audience that this new role is useful, practical, and worth the cost.

Anthropologist as Cultural Broker in Appropriate Technology Generation: Postharvest Team Research

This case illustrates how anthropologists helped a team of postharvest technology scientists generate a new system of storing potatoes that was subsequently adopted by thousands of farmers in over 20 countries (Rhoades et al. 1985). Serving the team as cultural brokers, the anthropologists demonstrated why scientific preconceptions of farmer conditions were incorrect and then pointed to common ground upon which both scientist and farmer could communicate.

Throughout the developing world—including Peru where CIP's headquarters is located—the FAO, the USDA, and other government agencies
had decided significant food security could be achieved by designing
national storage systems to profitably channel food into the large cities.
Large storage buildings were built between the production zones and the
large cities. One typical location was in the high zone between the potato-
producing Mantaro Valley and Lima. The idea was that farmers would use
these government-operated storage systems until demand and prices offered
them a fair return. At a cost of millions, technically perfect storage facilities
were designed and built by national and international engineers backed up
with precise cost-benefit calculations by economic consultants. Much to the
puzzlement of the storage experts, however, farmers rejected the storage
buildings. The postharvest team of CIP called on the anthropologists to
explain this seemingly irrational behavior of Andean potato farmers. Why
did these storage facilities become failed large-scale projects that were never
used to benefit the local people?

The anthropologists began their research with a simple but novel
premise: ask farmers (both male and female) what their problems are and
how would they like them solved. By ethnographically placing farm-level
storage in a holistic and cultural perspective, CIP anthropologists provided a perspective distinct from those of the economists and technical
scientists. First, they showed that technical scientists had been working on
consumer potato storage, but the farmers perceived that the problem was
seed potato storage of recently introduced improved varieties. Furthermore, with the new varieties that the farmers wanted for commercial markets, the issue was not losses or rottage, as biological scientists and
economists assumed, but labor costs of women and children desprouting
the new seed. The concept of losses, it turns out, is alien to Andean farmers because all potatoes, even rotting ones, are used in some way (such as
animal feed). Second, the anthropologists showed that farmers thought of
their stored potatoes like "bank accounts" that should be safeguarded
inside the household compound. Theft was a major problem in the area.
The concept of a separate storage barn is a European and North American arrangement, not an Andean one (where the animals, crops, and tools
are all a part of the human living compound). The farmers also felt it was
important to protect their potato crops from nosey neighbors, theft, and
the evil eye (in many cultures, it is believed that when a possessed person
sees an object, potatoes in this case, it will become polluted). Women kept
potatoes close at hand to sell small amounts as needed for the household
coffers. Finally, farmers did not trust the government and its centralized
storage facilities.

Based on this dialogue between farmers, technical scientists, and anthropologists, a completely new system of rustic seed potato storage using diffused light—which functions like refrigeration—was developed, tested, and transferred to many cultures. This storage case became the empirical basis of a new approach to agricultural research and development called "Farmer-Back-to-Farmer," which posits that agricultural research must begin and end with the ultimate decision maker—the farmer (Rhoades and Booth 1982). The model, in turn, became a core thread in the participatory research movement that dominated much of agricultural development in the 1990s (Sillitoe 1998).

Agricultural Anthropology as Policy: Global Information System of Potatoes

This case illustrates how agricultural anthropology impacted specific policy and planning at various levels. The effort helped place root and tuber research in a worldwide agroecological context and delineated the types and importance of different potato farming and household systems in different countries. Prior to this project, very little systematic information was available on where potatoes were grown, who was growing them, and what they were doing with them after harvest. Using the comparative method of cultural ecology (studying geographically separate but similar environments and parallel levels of technology that give rise to analogous human adaptations) and the methodology of the Human Area Relations Files (HRAF), potato information from 132 countries of the world was collected by CIP anthropologists collaborating with regional scientists. In addition to generating basic thematic maps, researchers attempted to identify analogous production zones and types of farmers for the purposes of setting research priorities and measuring impact. The project was called "The World Geography of the Potato," but its approach and methodology was anthropological.

Anthropology's advantage in this kind of research was in its comparative methodology and ability to analyze whole systems, not just component parts. Other scientists in the center, such as breeders or agronomists, had a very precise but reductionist view of their subject crop. The anthropologist, on the other hand, was interested in how the farming system was adapted to the environment and in the role of human culture in this adaptation. By modifying the approach of George Peter Murdock, who had done similar study and mapping of indigenous root crops in Africa, a socioeconomic global overview of the crop was developed (Murdock 1960).

The findings attracted the attention of CIP research management and international policy boards, which determine priorities in research funding. The project showed that the bulk of potatoes produced in developing countries are not grown in the tropical highlands (where the center had targeted most of its field research and germplasm distribution) but in the lowland subtropical zones of densely populated Asia, where potatoes are typically rotated with rice or wheat. The center learned from this study that its own development projects in tropical hill areas (e.g., the Philippines, Indonesia, Thailand, Sri Lanka, Rwanda, Burundi) had degraded the environment because potatoes leave the slopes precariously exposed during periods of high rainfall. Furthermore, in many of these same contexts, potatoes are grown by well-off farmers for marketing in urban areas as a luxury vegetable (fast-food outlets, tourist hotels, airlines, etc.), not as a food for the poor. Normally such potatoes require a great deal of pesticides and fungicides that are now known to adversely affect locally hired and typically landless laborers.

The research had several direct policy implications. The International Potato Center shifted its emphasis from hill station settings in tropical countries to the huge rice and wheat belt stretching from Pakistan to China. Globally, the status of potatoes (and roots and tubers in general) was elevated in terms of research and development priority among international donors and agencies. "The World Geography of the Potato" project later served as a model for other crop-based centers and programs (e.g., for rice, maize, wheat, peanuts) to develop their own knowledge bases. Today, more than a decade after the idea was developed at CIP, the center maintains an up-to-date Web page.

Agricultural Anthropology as Advocacy: Farmers' Rights and Plant Genetic Resources

A third example illustrates how agricultural anthropology played an advocacy role for small farmers involved in the controversial issues surrounding indigenous crop agrobiodiversity and intellectual property rights. The primary objective of many international centers is the collection and maintenance of wild and landrace species of their mandated crop. This genetic material, or germplasm, is the raw material for improved breeding and biotechnology. In recent years, questions have arisen about the ownership of this genetic material. The CBD (Convention on Biodiversity) placed patrimony in the hands of the nation-state where the material is grown or found in a wild state. However, as the traditional curators of cultivated species and their landraces, indigenous people have become more aware of their own rights and their crucial role in conservation. This connection between indigenous cultures and crop diversity has increased the demand for anthropologists, especially ethnobotantists, in agricultural research.

A central organizing concept of modern plant genetic resources issues is Nikolai Vavilov's Centers of Crop Diversity (locations of international agricultural research centers [IARCs], collecting, and protection). Few people realize that Vavilov developed those centers by reading accounts of early ethnographers and drawing the link between cultural diversity and biological diversity. Ethnobotanists working in the 1950s and 1960s, such as Weston La Barre (1947) and Harold Conklin (1957), explicitly documented the link between plant diversity and linguistic diversity. This work was continued through the 1970s and 1980s by anthropologists associated with the IARCs who contributed key research and ideas about *in situ* (in farmers' fields) and *ex situ* (in gene banks) conservation as well as intellectual property regimes (Rhoades and Nazarea 1998).

Anthropology's venture into the study of crop diversity was not popular at first with biological scientists, who typically looked upon germplasm as a commodity to be collected in the field and stored in a gene bank awaiting its use by a breeder or biotechnologist. Plant breeders trained in population genetics and modeling were suspicious as to what anthropologists could contribute to their sophisticated science. Further, the topic of ownership of plant genetic resources is an international minefield of controversy because it concerns profits, power, and politics at the highest levels of international government.

Anthropological contribution to this area took place in several ways. First, field-level studies demonstrated that farmers possessed a complex folk nomenclature of native potatoes (Brush 1992). Ethnobotanical studies provided basic information on farmer selections to assist with the center's efforts at collection and maintenance of a world germplasm pool for utilization in developing countries. This research formed the basis of an effort to conserve *in situ* genetic resources and link them with *ex situ* resources, including return from the gene banks of germplasm (landraces, cultivars) that no longer exist in farmers' fields. An approach called "memory banking," pioneered by anthropologist Virginia Nazarea (1998), demonstrated how cultural knowledge should be conserved along with the conventional gene bank "passport" data (e.g., place and date of collection, collector, plant descriptors) on landraces or wild species. Anthropologists have served on panels and international commissions to encourage implementation of farmers' rights as a way to maintain germplasm diversity. An effort has been made to lobby legislative bodies and get the message about genetic erosion and indigenous cultures to the general public (Rhoades 1991). In one instance involving sweet potato germplasm, CIP anthropologists mobilized local farmers to pressure the experiment station to plant, maintain, and distribute sweet potato cultivars that might have been disappearing. Today, several international centers—including the Rome-based International Plant Genetic Resources Institute—employ anthropologists and ethnobotantists to help guide participatory plant breeding efforts involving both scientists and farmers (Eyzaguirre and Iwanaga 1996).

New Issues in Agricultural Anthropology

As the previous case studies demonstrate, anthropologists have been highly successful within agricultural research and development as interdisciplinary team members who are focused on food production and postharvest problems. The kinds of priorities addressed today in agricultural research reflect themes of anthropological origin and connection: participatory research, agroecosystems analysis, sustainable human ecosystems, indigenous knowledge, farmer experimentation, low input agriculture, household analysis, gender issues, natural resource management by local communities, and ethnobotany in genetic resources preservation, to mention but a few.

In the 1990s, a new challenge was presented to agricultural anthropologists. Following the 1992 Earth Summit held in Rio, the environment became increasingly a concern of academic and applied anthropology (UNCED 1992). Whereas previously the environment was little more than a backdrop to the seemingly more important activity of agricultural production, it then became a focus of attention in its own right, both as a determinant and interactive force shaping human behavior and cognition. The main proclamation and action plan of the Earth Summit, called Agenda 21, led to a number of new theoretical and methodological issues that challenge agricultural anthropology today.

Rethinking Time in the Agriculture-Environment Nexus

"Sustainability" became the 1990s mantra under which agriculture was to operate. Indeed, in many funding spheres, any emphasis on food production fell into disfavor to the point that increasing production was deemed acceptable only if it protected the environment (hence many land grant agricultural colleges during this period changed their names to "College of Agriculture and Environmental Sciences"). The concept of sustainability carried the strong message that time had to be factored into production and that it was not sufficient to think in the short term of an annual cycle or of even a few annual cycles. Instead, long-term environmental change (even beyond that perceived by local populations) as well as intergenerational issues (bequeath factors) emerged as central research topics of agricultural anthropology. Development thinking, which had been driven by short-run economics that discounted the future, was questioned for its failure to "cost" long-term consequences of annual production behavior (Pretty 1995). The upshot was that agricultural anthropologists found themselves no longer pursuing simply synchronic studies of a few years' duration but attempting to cope with research questions over decades, centuries, and millennia (Rhoades 2001; Fairhead and Leach 1996).

Likewise, agricultural anthropologists have needed to expand both the spatial and socioeconomic scales that frame research questions about farming and the food system. It became necessary to move beyond the village focus to multiple scales of upstream-downstream, landscapes, catchments, watersheds, river corridors, and even beyond to the global economy. Learning more about multiscalar research is obviously linked to connecting space with human organization-demographic scales.

An example of this kind of research is the SANREM (Sustainable Agriculture and Natural Resource Management) interdisciplinary project I led (Rhoades 2001). Working with biological scientists and hydrologists, anthropologists on the team paved the way for the realization that the hydrologist's assumption—that the watershed is a natural human management unit—is not necessarily the way local people view their environment. Inhabitants of the Nanegal region of Ecuador, where the project took place, do not manage resources; they simply follow how surface water flows, although it can sometimes influence their decisions. Over the course of time, the researchers came to understand that watersheds, as closed human management units, are external bureaucratic or researcher fantasies, not indigenous ones. Through a dialogue between researchers (both biological and social) and the local people, it was easier to arrive at a better understanding of how social and biophysical boundaries overlapped (Rhoades 1999).

Understanding the Environment as Both a Biological and Cultural Phenomenon

Agricultural anthropologists have a major contribution to make in informing scientists and policymakers that the environment is as much a medium of ideas and imagination of a local people as it is of material substance (Williams 2002). Landscape, for example, pervades almost every aspect of daily life and reflects in myriad ways how farmers have encountered, constructed, and represented the physical landscape over time. Landscapes are the result of inspired human effort and imagination, and they are not so much given in nature as they are produced and subject to human transformation. This is a powerful message to teams of scientists who would study the landscape objectively as some isolated artifact or abstract physical system separate from the people who have shaped it. Agricultural anthropology can offer a powerful counterpoint to viewpoints strictly from the outside by showing how local populations engage, shape, and envision the environment (Fairhead and Leach 1996; Williams 2002; Feld and Basso 1996).

Designing New Methods of Agricultural Anthropological Research and Interdisciplinary Engagement

The multiactor, multiscale, multiyear, and multiresource themes of environmental and natural resource research create a set of demands beyond the traditional methodological toolkit of anthropology. Tying together past and present biological and cultural representations of agricultural landscapes has not been common in anthropology, despite our claims of holism. The need to grapple with these new dimensions has brought anthropologists into the world of spatial analysis and other computer-driven approaches (e.g., GIS, remote sensing, expert knowledge systems, and simulation modeling). The need, however, is to show more effectively how these scientifically derived tools and methods mesh with indigenous knowledge and ethnogeometric approaches. Just as agricultural anthropologists had to learn to work with agronomists and economists, a new need has arisen to learn the language and ways of the natural resource sciences (ecology, forestry, hydrology). Progress has been made but more case studies are needed to determine how well our methods are working and how effective we are in dealing with our colleagues from other environmental and agricultural disciplines.

Anthropology is not the only discipline that has had to rethink its place in the study of agriculture and the environment. All disciplines concerned with food production and postharvest food systems have had to take into consideration the importance of the environment (Pretty 1995). The American land grant colleges were established in 1862 through the Morrill Act that gave federal lands for colleges that offered agriculture, engineering, and home economics in addition to traditional subjects. Today, these colleges, which have led American agriculture, are experiencing a crisis in their service and research roles. The issues are no longer, for example, how to produce a bigger, fatter pig (private industry does this better than college PhDs) but how to deal with the conflict over industrial pork production waste, its intrusion into human communities, and the social issues of labor (Stull, Broadway, and Griffith 1995). These are largely uncharted territories that reach beyond our conventional thinking about agriculture and the environment but that will be necessary to conquer if agricultural anthropology is to continue as a viable and effective field of anthropology.

Engaging Issues of the Global Restructuring of Agriculture and its Local Counterpoint

Globalization and the restructuring of agriculture from small-scale family farms to large-scale transnational, multinational companies pose new research challenges for anthropologists (Thu and Durrenberger 1998). Proponents of the shift toward "farming factories" connected to vertical integrated agriculture (i.e., one company handles all aspects from production through marketing) see this as better efficiency and economy of scale. Proponents of sustainable agriculture, organic farming, animal rights, and other alternative movements project a future in which a few transnational companies will control the integration of the entire human food chain (Adams 2003). Such transnational companies will produce in several locations a homogenized food product that will be marketed globally with little regard for local social, environmental, or economic consequences (Charles 2001). The dialectic between these two distinct food streams—global and local—is now being framed by anthropologists who are looking at a range of issues including health, immigration and labor, impact on family farms, environmental consequences, and other issues. In the future, agricultural anthropology will turn more and more of its resources in this direction.

Conclusion

This chapter has looked at the development of agricultural anthropology, a few case studies of its application, and some future trends. The study of agriculture is still not something that is accorded high prestige in anthropology. At present, agriculture has taken a backseat to issues like the environment, natural resources, and health. This is probably short-term. In the future, as the world faces food shortages, poor distribution, control over the food chain, and other key issues, agriculture will once again return to anthropology's main agenda. It is wise for anthropologists to keep moving forward with an awareness of and interest in all aspects of our food and fiber system. Some key steps required to generate a vibrant agricultural anthropology are the following.

First, anthropologists need to learn from agricultural economists like Nobel Prize winner Theodore Schultz and develop a "client relationship" with society. Some anthropologists continue to harbor elitist attitudes toward those anthropologists who work on practical human problems, especially agriculture. Also, we must not leave it to other disciplines—such as agricultural economics—to take our powerful ideas and refashion them, only to leave anthropology to mop up again as "bearers of bad news." To draw an analogy from farming, if we are the ones breaking our backs to prepare the soil, sow the seed, and tend the fields, then we should be harvesting our own crops and not leaving that to someone else. Now more than ever, disciplines like economics, law, policy studies, and education contest our claim to culture and cross-cultural studies. Anthropology needs to declare its relevance through action.

Second, anthropologists must learn from our forebears in anthropology—like Margaret Mead and Ruth Benedict—and effectively communicate beyond the narrow confines of the anthropological community. Anthropologists still spend too much time talking to each other about their own issues. On key agricultural issues, as one goes up the political decision scale, the message becomes more generalized and ideological. Anthropology's ideas will not reach higher policy and action applications unless anthropologists learn to communicate beyond their own discipline. On this score, agricultural anthropologists should strive to write so biological scientists or the public can understand, a skill not valued or promoted by anthropology. An anthropologist who writes for *National Geographic*, for example, receives little professional reward. Each issue of *National Geographic*, however, reaches over 120 million people and is read even in the White House. Expanding the audience of anthropology's insights can help guarantee broader success and impacts.

Third, the training of anthropologists for policy and practice must begin in more creative, relevant academic university settings. Those who have succeeded in the real world and made a spot for more anthropologists to come have done so by modifying—sometimes dramatically—their academic training to fit the needs of client-oriented research and policy on agriculture. Today, purely academic endeavors are giving way to themes of social relevance—top among them are environment, food, nutrition, natural resources, and sustainable development. Anthropology faces the choice of joining the game or sitting on the sidelines as distant critics.

Finally, anthropology must continue to build ties with agricultural organizations and scientists. This means we need to continue to learn the language of the agricultural sciences. Unfortunately, a trend has emerged in which anthropologists remove themselves from learning about the material base of agriculture. The tendency to show little interest in biological and ecological phenomena, preferring instead to critique words and text, will not be a very productive, long-term direction for agricultural anthropology. Frederick Buttel has noted:

> One of the contradictory achievements of modern social science applied to agro-food systems is that it has enabled the analyst to deploy powerful abstractions which permit one to ignore the infinite details of biota, soils, agro-ecosystem processes, physical labor, and so on. . . . Modern social science has accordingly tended to conjure up a highly dematerialized view of agro-food realities—a view that tends to regard the natural environment of agriculture as being essentially epiphenomenal. (1997, 347)

In the end, agricultural anthropology must be eclectic and draw its strengths from numerous sources while learning to communicate with its partners. The bridge between theoretical anthropology and applied anthropology in the agricultural domain needs to be strong. In the final analysis, however, the future role of anthropology in the most important human endeavor for human survival—agriculture—depends on concrete contributions to sustainable food and fiber production and security.

References

Adams, Jane, ed. 2003. *Fighting for the farm.* Philadelphia: University of Pennsylvania Press.

Babb, Florence. 1998. *Between field and cooking pot: The political economy of market-women in Peru.* Austin: University of Texas Press.

Bennett, John M. 1969. *Northern plainsmen.* Chicago: Aldine.

Brush, S. B. 1992. Ethnoecology, biodiversity, and modernization in Andean potato agriculture. *Journal of Ethnobiology* 12: 161–85.

Burton, M. L., G. Mark Schoepfle, and Marc L. Miller. 1986. Natural resource anthropology. *Human Organization* 45 (3): 261–69.

Buttel, Frederick. 1997. Some observations on agro-food change and the future of agricultural sustainability movements. In *Globalising food: Agrarian questions and global restructuring,* edited by D. Goodman and M. Watts. London: Routledge.

Chambers, Robert. 1992. Rapid but relaxed and participatory rural appraisal: Towards applications in health and nutrition. In *Rapid assessment procedures,* edited by N. Scrimshaw and G. Gleason. Boston: International Nutritional Foundation for Developing Countries.

Chambers, Robert, Arnold Pacey, and Lori Ann Thrupp. 1989. *Farmer first.* London: Intermediate Technology Publications.

Charles, Daniel. 2001. *Lords of the harvest.* Cambridge, Mass.: Perseus Publishing.

Conklin, H. C. 1957. Hanunoo agriculture in the Philippines. Forestry Development Paper 12. Rome: FAO.

———. 1954. An ethnobotanical approach to shifting agriculture. *Transactions of the New York Academy of Sciences,* series 2, 17: 133–42.

Dahlberg, K. A. 1979. *Beyond the Green Revolution: The ecology and politics of global agricultural development.* New York: Plenum.

DeWalt, Billie R. 1994. Using indigenous knowledge to improve agriculture and natural resource management. *Human Organization* 53 (2): 123–31.

Evans-Pritchard, E. E., and M. Fortes. 1940. *African political systems.* International African Institute. London: Oxford University Press.

Eyzaguirre, P., and M. Iwanaga, eds. 1996. Participatory plant breeding. *Proceedings of a workshop on participatory plant breeding.* July 26–29, 1995. Wageningen, The Netherlands. Rome: International Plant Genetic Resources Institute.

Fairhead, James, and Melissa Leach. 1996. *Misreading the African landscape: Society and ecology in a forest-savannah mosaic.* African Studies Series, 90. Cambridge: Cambridge University Press.

Feld, Steven, and Keith Basso. 1996. *Senses of place.* Santa Fe: School of American Research Press.

Forde, C. D. 1934. *Habitat, economy, and society.* London: Methuen.

Foster, G. 1969. *Applied anthropology.* Boston: Little, Brown and Company.

Geertz, Clifford. 1963. *Agricultural involution: The processes of ecological change in Indonesia.* Berkeley and Los Angeles: University of California Press.

Goldschmidt, Walter. 1947. *As you sow.* New York: Harcourt Brace.

Hall, Edward. 1966. *The hidden dimension.* Garden City, N.Y.: Doubleday.

————. 1961. *The silent language.* New York: Fawcett Publications.

Harris, Marvin. 1965. The myth of the sacred cow. In *Man, culture, and animals*, edited by Anthony Leeds and Andrew P. Vayda. Washington, D.C.: American Association for the Advancement of Science.

Holmberg, A., H. Dobyns, C. Monge, M. C. Vasquez, and H. D. Lasswell. 1962. Community and regional development: The joint Cornell-Peru experiment. *Human Organization* 21 (2): 107–24.

Holmberg, A., M. C. Vasquez, P. L. Doughty, J. O. Alers, H. G. Dobyns, and H. D. Lasswell. 1965. The Vicos case: Peasant society in transition. *American Behavioral Scientist* 8 (7): 3–33 (special issue).

Holtzman, J. S. 1986. Rapid reconnaissance guidelines for agricultural marketing and food systems research in developing countries. Working Paper 30. East Lansing: Michigan State University.

Hopper, W. David. 1957. The economic organization in the village of North Central India, PhD thesis. Ithaca, N.Y.: Cornell University.

La Barre, Weston. 1947. Potato taxonomy among the Aymara Indians of Bolivia. *Acta Americana* 5: 83–103.

Loomis, Charles. 1943. Applied anthropology in Latin America. *Applied Anthropology* 2 (2): 33–35.

MacNeish, R. 1992. *The origins of agriculture and settled life.* Norman: University of Oklahoma Press.

Mannion, A. M. 1999. Domestication and the origins of agriculture: An appraisal. *Progress in Physical Geography* 23 (1): 37–56.

Montgomery, Edward, and John W. Bennett. 1979. Anthropological studies of food and nutrition. The 1940s and the 1970s. In *The Uses of Anthropology*, edited by W. Goldschmidt. Washington, D.C.: American Anthropological Association.

Murdock, George Peter. 1960. Staple subsistence crops of Africa. *Geographic Review* (May): 523–40.

Nazarea, Virginia D. 1998. *Ethnoecology: Situated knowledge/located lives.* Tucson: University of Arizona Press.

Netting, Robert. 1993. *Smallholders, householders: Farm families and ecology of intensive, sustainable agriculture.* Stanford, Calif.: Stanford University Press.

————. 1974. Agrarian ecology. *Annual Review of Anthropology* 3: 21–56.

Posey, Darrell A., J. Frechione, J. Eddins, L. F. DaSilva, D. Meyers, and P. Macbeth. 1984. Ethnoecology as applied anthropology in Amazonian development. *Human Organization* 43: 95–107.

Pretty, Jules N. 1995. *Regenerating agriculture.* London: Earthscan Publications.

Purcell, Trevor W. 1998. Indigenous knowledge and applied anthropology: Questions of definition and direction. *Human Organization* 57 (3): 258–72.

Rappaport, Roy A. 1968. *Pigs for the ancestors: Ritual in the ecology of a New Guinea people.* New Haven, Conn., and London: Yale University Press.

Rhoades, R. E. 2001. *Bridging human and ecological landscapes.* Dubuque, Iowa: Kendall/Hunt Publishing Company.

————. 2000. Agricultural anthropology: New disciplinary blood in an international research organization. In *Classics of practicing anthropology 1978–1998*, edited by P. Higgins and J. A. Paredes. Oklahoma City: Society for Applied Anthropology.

————. 1999. Participatory watershed research and management: Where the shadow falls. Gatekeeper Series no. 81. London: International Institute for Environment and Development.

————. 1991. The world's food supply at risk. *National Geographic* 179 (4): 74–105.

————. 1988. The reference file method: An eclectic approach for improving agroecological and crop data for developing countries. In *Social science planning conference proceedings*, September 3–7, 1987, 118–33. Lima, Peru: International Potato Center.

————. 1986. Using anthropology in improving food production: Problems and prospects. *Agricultural Administration* 22: 57–78.

————. 1984a. *Breaking new ground: Agricultural anthropology.* Lima, Peru: International Potato Center.

————. 1984b. Informal survey methods for farming systems research. *Human Organization* 44 (3): 215–18.

————. 1980. Agricultural anthropology: A call for the establishment of a new professional specialty. *Practicing Anthropology* 2 (4): 10–12, 28.

Rhoades, R. E., and R. H. Booth. 1982. Farmer-back-to-farmer: A model for generating acceptable agricultural technology. *Agricultural Administration* 11: 127–37.

Rhoades, R. E., R. Booth, R. Shaw, and R. Werge. 1985. The role of anthropologists in developing improved technologies. *Appropriate Technology* 11 (4): 11–13.

Rhoades, R. E., and Virginia D. Nazarea. 1998. Local management of biodiversity in traditional ecosystems. In *Biodiversity in agroecosystems*, edited by W. Collins and C. Qualset. Boca Raton, Fla., New York, London: CRC Press.

Schultz, Theodore. 1964. *Transforming traditional agriculture.* New Haven, Conn.: Yale University Press.

Sillitoe, Paul. 1998. The development of indigenous knowledge: A new applied anthropology. *Current Anthropology* 39 (2): 223–52.

Stull, Donald, M. J. Broadway, and David Griffith, eds. 1995. *Any way you cut it.* Lawrence: University Press of Kansas.

Tax, Sol. 1953. *Penny capitalism.* Chicago: University of Chicago Press.

Thiele, G., E. van de Fliert, and Dindo Campilan. 2001. What happened to participatory research at the International Potato Center. *Agriculture and Human Value* 18: 429–46.

Thu, Kendall M., and E. Paul Durrenberger, eds. 1998. *Pigs, profits, and rural communities.* Albany: State University of New York Press.

United Nations Conference on Environment and Development (UNCED). 1992. Agenda 21: Programme of action for sustainable development. Rio Declaration on Environment and Development. United Nations Publication.

Whyte, William Foote. 1984. Personal communication.

Williams, Dee Mack. 2002. *Beyond great walls.* Stanford, Calif.: Stanford University Press.

Wolf, Eric. 1964. *Anthropology.* Englewood Cliffs, N.J.: Prentice Hall.

4 The Domain of the Environment

Thomas R. McGuire

Environmental anthropology is a tag for a complex set of issues surrounding the relation of humans to their environment. In particular, environmental anthropologists are concerned with how to comprehend, analyze, and ameliorate environmental degradation and destruction (Escobar 1998; Sillitoe 1998). A long-standing concern is the management of renewable and nonrenewable resources and the communities of users that depend on such resources (King and Durrenberger 2000; Ostrom 1990). Anthropologists analyze and empower local knowledge about the natural world and use that knowledge to foster ecologically and socially sustainable communities (Descola and Pálsson 1996; Orlove and Brush 1996). Another focus has been on the rights of minorities and the poor to a healthy environment—environmental justice in the wake of environmental racism (Bowen et al. 1995; Mohai and Bryant 1998). Climate change, climate vulnerability (Glantz 2001; Magistro and Roncoli 2001), socially constructed "acts of God," and genuine natural hazards (Oliver-Smith 1996; Oliver-Smith and Hoffman 1999; Steinberg 2000) are also on the research agendas of environmental anthropologists and their interdisciplinary colleagues. Environmentalism in its many variants, radical and mainstream, North and South, is a complex topic of interest, both as a social movement and as a voice against the ecological consequences of economic development (Brosius 1999; Bryant 1998; Hvalkof and Escobar 1998; Kempton, Boster, and Hartley 1995; Milton 1993).

Although these are contemporary and pressing concerns, anthropologists have had a long-standing interest in ecology, that is, the total relations of animals, including humans, to their environment. Reminiscing in *The People of Puerto Rico* (Steward et al. 1956), Eric Wolf recounted how he and a number of his fellow students were attracted to the discipline of anthropology and to Julian Steward's project of "cultural ecology":

> For some of us, who were going to school after World War II on public funds, anthropology offered a prospect of studying a "real" world of "real people." One had some hope then that knowledge could be linked to action and that better knowledge would yield better action. Julian Steward, who had then begun to teach at Columbia University, seemed to us to offer the kind of matter-of-fact materialism which, we hoped, would allow us to study real people and to build that better knowledge. (Wolf 2001, 39)

Eric Wolf, through much of his career, would derive more inspiration from a Marxian political economy than Steward's cultural ecology. Nevertheless, those promises of the Puerto Rico project would still motivate subsequent generations of anthropologists and other social scientists to engage in the study of human relationships to the natural environment.

Social movements of the 1960s and 1970s invigorated an interest in the environment and offered some blueprints for taking action. The civil rights movement would evolve from the civil disobedience of the early 1960s to urban riots at the end of the decade. The antiwar movement could then model its marches on the Pentagon after those on Selma. Earth Day of 1970 was a nationwide teach-in, and when the antienvironment policies of Ronald Reagan and James Watt superseded those of Jimmy Carter, ecoterrorist groups such as Earth First! could draw on some of the tactics of the antiwar movement to keep environmental issues on the political agenda. Diverse as these movements were, they shared a culture of activism that stimulated people to take steps to address society's ills. Finally, the Rio Summit of 1992 issued a concise and global declaration: Human beings are entitled to a productive and healthy life in harmony with nature (Tsing 2001, 3).

I begin this excursion into the domain of environmental anthropology with a look at theoretical building blocks. Two of these were already introduced: cultural ecology and political economy. A third, political ecology, is hotly contested now. Some scholars and practitioners are for it (Watts n.d.), some against it (Vayda and Walters 1999). I examine this endeavor to reconcile cultural ecology and political economy. I then evaluate one subfield, maritime anthropology, not as a proxy for the entire domain of environmental anthropology, but as an arena in which a number of key concepts in human-environment relations have been addressed. These include the nature of property rights, the role of science and scientists in resource management, the possibilities and limits of local control of resources, and the nature of nature itself. Maritime anthropology is also an arena in which anthropologists and other social scientists have entered into the policy process.

Many of the advances in maritime anthropology have come through traditional ethnographic studies of coastal fishing communities. Environmental anthropologists have also engaged actively in the process of "scaling up," of developing methodologies for examining issues that affect large regions and global environmental concerns. Some of the tools required for scaling up have come from outside the discipline—remote sensing, geographic information systems (GIS), and powerful ecosystem simulation packages. Some are largely homegrown, such as the efforts to enlist local resource users and managers in mapping biodiversity over regional landscapes.

Environmental anthropologists are "scaling down" as well, addressing issues framed by neighborhoods. Backyard anthropology, an array of projects in which anthropologists address the environmental concerns of communities throughout the United States, offers another template for an applied environmental anthropology. Under a cooperative agreement between the Society for Applied Anthropology (SfAA) and the U.S. Environmental Protection Agency (EPA), practicing anthropologists have brought their skills and methods to bear on public issues. Few local problems were solved during these relatively brief apprenticeships, but as one of the architects of the program observed, "I think the projects did demonstrate the potential for tangible results and the fact that paying attention to social processes is at least necessary, if not sufficient, for community-based, environmental problem solving" (Young 2001, 48).

These three templates—one where theoretical concerns central to anthropology are brought to bear on issues of public policy, the second where information-processing technologies have opened new lines of research and intervention, the third where the issues themselves are largely defined by local communities—do not exhaust the possibilities for an applied environmental anthropology. I conclude this selective survey of the domain with some brief observations on the opportunities for the engagement of anthropologists in environmental affairs.

Theory and Practice in Environmental Anthropology

Julian Steward's cultural ecology, which he applied to the complex society of Puerto Rico, was born on a simpler landscape, the Great Basin of Nevada, Utah, and California. Steward documented that the institutions of the region's aboriginal inhabitants were "most extensively patterned by subsistence activities," hunting and gathering. His cultural ecology, as a research method, posed a straightforward question: "whether the adjustments of human societies to their environments require particular modes of behavior or whether they permit latitude for a certain range of possible behavior patterns" (Steward 1955, 36). The analytic strategy was three-pronged, requiring examination first of the natural landscape, then of the cultural or behavioral devices employed to exploit that environment, and finally of the institutional adaptations resulting from those behaviors (Steward 1938, 2).

This strategy would yield, for Steward, a "culture core," the "constellation of features which are most closely related to subsistence activities and economic arrangements" (1955, 40). This core thus encompasses the social, political, and religious institutions involved in making a living from the environment. Secondary or peripheral features of a culture, acquired by diffusion or random variation, give distinctive shapes to cultures with similar cores.

Eric Wolf, in his reassessment of cultural ecology as elaborated in *The People of Puerto Rico* (2001), drew strategically on a commentary on Steward's Great Basin work by Robert Murphy (1970). Murphy, a student (though not a disciple) of Steward's at Columbia in the late 1940s, observed that Steward's project was less about the grand relation between environment and culture and more about the (implicitly more mundane) process of "work," the employment of tools and technologies to transform nature. Wolf put Murphy's observations in a Marxian frame. What Steward was concerned with was the "labor process," the ways people use tools to transform nature (Wolf 2001, 40). Steward neglected to analyze, in *People* and in his earlier work in the Great Basin, what Marxists call the "social relations of production." These are concerned with the allocation of resources and the means to exploit them, questions that turn on differences in wealth and power (44).

In retrospect, then, Wolf was differentiating two strains of inquiry that would occupy anthropologists and other social sciences for several generations: political economy and cultural ecology. They are connected through a common concern for the material bases of human existence. Cultural ecology, in its several reconfigurations, would remain focused on the interactions of people and their local environments. Political economy would seek to tie those people to the world system of capitalism. The emergent political ecology, in turn, attempts to bring these levels of analysis, the local and the global, together. It seeks to understand how political and ecological forces interact to cause social and environmental change.

Cultural Ecology

Steward codified his approach to culture and the environment in his *Theory of Culture Change* (1955). In the 30 years that followed, Steward's students and their students actively worked to reconfigure cultural ecology. The first modification was to focus on populations as the unit of analysis, rather than Steward's culture core. This enabled anthropology to appropriate some powerful concepts and models from biology, primarily ecosystems, energy flows, and adaptation. Inspired heavily by Eugene Odum's *Fundamentals of Ecology* (1953), ecosystem ecology (some labeled this transformation as "human ecology," "systems ecology," or "neofunctionalism" [cf. Biersack 1999; Kottak 1999]) built on the definition of ecosystem, the "structural and functional interrelationships among living organisms and the physical environment within which they exist" (Moran 1990, 3). Emilio Moran, a leading practitioner, suggested that the ecosystem approach attracted anthropologists because it promoted holistic studies of human populations in their physical environment and because it could foster the development of a set of common principles in biology and anthropology. Moreover, with the growing concerns in the 1960s for the environment and the fate of nonindustrial societies, ecosystem ecology could turn the tools of science to the advocacy of habitat and species preservation (11).

The exemplar of the ecosystems approach was *Pigs for the Ancestors* (Rappaport 1968). Roy Rappaport measured energy flows through a New Guinea ecosystem, including its human component, the Tsembaga, based on the prevailing assumption that energy was the only measurable common denominator that structured ecosystems and that could serve to define their function (Moran 1990, 17). He concluded that one Tsembaga ritual, which culminates in the *kaiko*, the slaughter and distribution of pigs to allies in warfare, performed the function of adapting local population sizes—of humans and pigs—to the environment's carrying capacity, that is, the level of human activity that can be sustained through time without degrading the environment. Rappaport's analysis encompassed the nutritional requirements of pigs and people, the availability of land for cultivation, the energy expended in productive activities, and the relations of war and peace among neighbors (Rappaport 1968).

Anthropologists refined a systems ecology through the 1970s (cf. Orlove 1980), but fundamental rethinking in the mother sciences of biology and ecology generated a significant revisionist trend in the ecological anthropology of the 1980s. A "new ecology" developed in the 1970s and 1980s, and it challenged the basic understanding of ecosystems, that they contained mechanisms for self-regulation—for adjusting populations to the carrying capacity of the environment (Botkin 1990). Disapprovingly, Rappaport characterized this movement as follows: "whereas the older ecology was concerned with revealing nature's order and regularity, the newer ecology is concerned not only to discover disorder, disturbance and randomness but to

replace conceptions of order with them" (1990, 44). In the face of these challenges, Rappaport argued that it would be politically and socially absurd to
abandon the ecosystem concept altogether. At the very least, it is "good to
think" in ecosystemic terms when addressing contemporary environmental
problem such as ozone depletion, greenhouse warming, deforestation, and
acid rain—many of them systemically linked. Others, however, took up the
challenges of studying nonequilibrating ecosystems and nonsystemic environments. Some of these forays would feature individual decision makers
rather than populations and social groups.

John Bennett brought people to the fore in *Northern Plainsmen* (1969). His
central concern was adaptation, the "process of coping with resources in
order to realize goals—and by so coping, creating new goals or problems to
solve" (1969, 14). Bonnie McCay took up Bennett's charge by calling for a
"people ecology" in 1978, partly to critique the extant systems ecology. In
that frame, "What the analyst postulates as structure and function, or self-
regulation and system goal, may be the outcome of the diverse strategies of
multiple actors in complex interaction" (McCay 1978, 403).

As something of an aside, McCay acknowledged that "social relations of
production" ought to be incorporated into the analysis because these may
affect the ability of individuals and communities to control aspects of their
relations to their resources. This is what readers of Marx have sought to do
(Orlove 1980, 250; cf. Ortner 1984; Roseberry 1988).

Political Economy and Political Ecology

Marxist-inspired dependency theory was underdeveloped at the time of
Julian Steward's Puerto Rico project, and Eric Wolf acknowledged that the
work failed to adequately conceptualize local communities within states, and
states within larger systems. Andre Gunder Frank published *Capitalism and
Underdevelopment in Latin America* in 1967, giving academic legitimacy to the
long history of Marxist critiques of imperialism. The toolkit of dependency
theory evolved rapidly in the radicalized social and academic environment
of the late 1960s and 1970s, and Wolf drew upon this to restate the Puerto
Rico problem: Both Puerto Rico and the United States were enmeshed in
the world system, dominated by capitalist relations of production. In this
system, Wolf observed, "capital flows towards these segments, withdraws
from them, or avoids them altogether, depending on the ability of capital to
obtain above-average profits" (2001, 46–7). Through his prolific career, Wolf
would endeavor to understand real people within the world system. But
such people were not simply engaged in the "work process" of applying
technology to nature; rather, they were people caught up in struggles to
obtain and retain access to resources, to resist or manipulate the "penetra-

tion of capital" into the countryside, to fight peasant wars when the opportunities arose—real people enmeshed in relations of power.

In 1972, Eric Wolf sketched a political ecology that had roots in political economic approaches. He called for putting local rules of inheritance in a wider political and historical frame. The papers in the symposium he was introducing on the anthropology of the Alps, however, were still largely in the tradition of cultural ecology. Several documented the significance of environmental variations "on the distribution of men, animals, and plants over the landscape, and on the specification and scheduling of work sites and work tasks" (Wolf 1972, 201). Geographers would take the lead in fashioning a political ecology out of political economy. The driving force was a growing awareness in the 1980s of widespread land and resource degradation throughout the Third World, such as soil erosion, water pollution, and deforestation. Causes were to be found in the social relations of production and the macro-level politics of states and larger systems.

The defining text for political ecology was *Land Degradation and Society* (1987) by geographers Piers Blaikie and Harold Brookfield. Understandings of environmental change must address the political, economic, and historical context of the "land manager." Anthropologists Peter Little and Michael Horowitz published a collection the same year on *Lands at Risk in the Third World: Local-Level Perspectives* (1987). In that volume, Marianne Schmink and Charles Wood laid out a succinct agenda examining the environmental destruction in lowland Amazonia. As summarized in a subsequent volume, *The Social Causes of Environmental Destruction in Latin America* (Painter and Durham 1995), the elements to be researched included the following: the nature of production, whether precapitalist or capitalist, in a specific region; the class structure of the region and the patterns of conflict over access to resources; the nature of market relations and means through which surpluses are accumulated; the policies of the state that work to the benefit of certain classes over others; the role of international agencies and corporations in local resource use; and, finally, "the ideology that orients resource use—for example, the position that rapid economic growth is the best way to address social and environmental problems—and what groups benefit from that ideology" (Painter and Durham 1995, 8). This agenda for political ecology stimulated a large body of work by anthropologists and geographers through the 1990s (e.g., Bebbington and Batterbury 2001; Peluso 1992; Schroeder 1993; Zimmerer 1991).

Susan Stonich's (1995) research along the Pacific coast of Honduras followed this formula. After decades of economic stagnation and mounting foreign debt, the Honduran government embarked on an aggressive program to expand shrimp aquaculture along the country's coastlines. Concessions of land were granted to Honduran investors, including government officials, urban elites, and military leaders. Incentives were offered to transnational corporations. The U.S. Agency for International Development (USAID) loaned substantial funds for the establishment of large-scale shrimp farms. Under these stimuli, total production of cultivated shrimp grew 1,611 percent from 1978 to 1988; in a three-year period from 1986 to 1989, shrimp ponds expanded from 1,450 to 5,500 hectares. In Stonich's analysis, this export-driven expansion had severe social and environmental consequences. Small landowners have been removed from land needed for shrimp ponds; wetlands, once utilized by local residents for fishing, shellfish harvesting, and firewood, have been converted to private ownership; few new jobs have been generated by the aquaculture operations for displaced residents; the resource base of coastal fishers deteriorated as the construction of shrimp farms destroyed habitat, blocked estuaries, and rechanneled rivers. Stonich concluded that ignoring the environmental and social effects of development for export "may cause ecosystems to exceed their limits and precipitate a permanent human and ecological crisis in the region" (1995, 90).

This is vintage political ecology. Two critiques emerged, however. The first contended that political ecology contained too much politics and too little ecology. The second contended that it did not contain enough politics. Andrew Vayda and several of his colleagues and students are against political ecology to the extent that it gives priority—a priori—to politics. Michael Watts, Arturo Escobar, and others are for a "politicized" political ecology that attends to the struggles of peasants and other land managers to protest against the nexus of power they find themselves in—to employ environmental discourse to invigorate social movements (cf. Escobar 1999; Hvalkof and Escobar 1998).

Vayda is a veteran of the skirmishes within cultural ecology, urging as early as 1968 that populations, not Steward's culture core, be the object of analysis (Vayda and Rappaport 1968), then rejecting the equilibrium assumptions of a systems ecology (Vayda and McCay 1975), then promoting an actor-oriented approach to the study of environmental events and changes. Vayda's salvo against political ecology, published with co-combatant Bradley Walters, was aimed at the insistence of "self-styled political ecologists" that political influences—especially political influences from the outside, from the so-called wider political system—are *always* important, arguably more important than anything else, and should accordingly be given priority in research (Vayda and Walters 1999, 168).

In place of such "politics without ecology," they proposed an "event ecology," in which research begins with an environmental event or change and then proceeds "to work backward in time and outward in space so as to enable us to construct chains of causes and effects leading to those events or changes" (Vayda and Walters 1999, 169). In an earlier discussion of this method of progressive contextualization, Vayda highlighted its potential utility to policymakers, concerned with broad questions such as deforestation and how to arrest it. Researchers can thus break such broad questions down into more specific activities such as timber harvesting. These then become the objects for progressive contextualization. As Vayda contended, progressive contextualization "leads to concrete findings about who is doing what, why they are doing it, and with what effects, and the very concreteness of the findings means that the policy implications are quite concrete too and readily communicable to policy makers" (Vayda 1983, 276).

Politicized political ecologists are less concerned with applying knowledge to problems (especially when those problems are defined, top-down, by policymakers) than they are with the liberation of dominated peoples. Liberation ecology, as defined by geographers Richard Peet and Michael Watts (Peet and Watts 1996), starts with the proposition voiced by a Mexican activist: "You must be either very dumb or very rich if you fail to notice that 'development' stinks" (quoted in Peet and Watts 1993, 238). It incorporates a postmodern conception of "truths" as "statements within socially produced discourses, rather than 'facts' about reality" (228). Liberation ecology employs discourse analysis and examines local knowledge to comprehend sustainability and promote alternative development strategies. It seeks to "uncover the discourses of resistance" to development and to "put them into wider circulation" (Peet and Watts 1993, 247; cf. Escobar 1998).

Practitioners working in the developing arena of political ecology disagree on a number of issues, and a unified frame is perhaps as unlikely as it is unnecessary (cf. Paulson, Gezon, and Watts 2003). Nonetheless, to be a viable approach to the analysis of human-environment interactions, it cannot afford to ignore either its politics or its ecology. It should attend to the processes of "work" that Julian Steward was concerned with, the application of tools and technologies to the transformation of the environment. At the same time, it should attend to the larger political economy within which real people, doing real things, are often constrained in the choices they make and in the resources available to them. In short, political ecology needs to attend to both of its theoretical roots.

Concepts and Applications: The Case of Maritime Anthropology

Maritime anthropology is a domain within a domain. Anthropologists and kindred social scientists who study fishing communities and intervene in fisheries policy have faced, and sometimes fashioned, many of the issues at the forefront of a larger environmental anthropology. These include the nature of property rights. Fish, like pastures, forests, and the atmosphere, are prone to the tragedy of the commons, and fisheries anthropologists have worked long and hard to find, document, and recommend solutions to the problem of a resource that has no owners. Maritime social scientists have also been concerned with issues of sustainability, as have those throughout the domain of environmental anthropology. On this score, the record for the world's fisheries is not good. Thus, maritime anthropologists and their colleagues have studied fisheries science, often with the conviction, and frequently the conclusion, that such science has failed the world's fisheries. They have studied and advocated traditional ecological knowledge as a complement to big science. They have made significant contributions to the new ecology of chaos and have drawn clear policy implications from this research. Most significantly, perhaps, they have placed notions of co-management—the call for local communities to share in the management of their own resources—firmly on the agendas of state and international resource management. A handful of anthropologists have taken their seats in those agencies. They have, to one extent or another, fostered what John van Willigen distilled as the "new synthesis" for applied anthropology, building on local knowledge, participation, empowerment, critical consciousness, and sustainability (van Willigen 2002, 44). Here I assess some of these forays into an applied maritime anthropology.

Questioning Common Property

Garrett Hardin's elegant argument in "The Tragedy of the Commons" (1968) sparked several decades of rebuttal work by anthropologists, political scientists, geographers, legal scholars, and others. Much of the anthropological response drew upon fisheries cases. In fact, economist H. Scott Gordon had earlier formulated Hardin's tragedy around the fishery. Gordon concluded that there is substantial truth to the notion that everybody's property is nobody's property: "The fish in the sea are valueless to the fisherman, because there is no assurance that they will be there for him tomorrow if they are left behind today" (1954, 124).

Hardin's tragedy also played out on the village commons, where a rational herder would graze more and more head, garnering all the proceeds from the additional animals but bearing only a fraction of the costs of overgrazing. Inevitably the pasture would be destroyed: "the freedom of the commons brings ruin to all" (Hardin 1968, 1244). His two solutions to the common property dilemma would prove unpalatable to many social scientists: privatization or government regulation.

There was a concerted effort to more precisely define the problem and the nature of property rights regimes. Strictly, the regime Hardin was modeling was one of open access, the absence of well-defined property rights where access to resources was unregulated and open to all. A private property regime entailed the right of an owner to exclude access to resources and, typically, transfer or sell these resources to others. State property regimes vested resource rights exclusively in governing bodies, empowering such entities to make decisions on access and levels of exploitation. Distinguished from these regimes is communal property, under which resources are held by identifiable communities of interdependent users. These users regulate use by members of the community and prevent outsiders from exploiting those resources. As David Feeny and his colleagues have defined communal property, rights to resources within the community are often rights of equal access and use, not of exclusive property. These rights may be legally recognized. In other cases they may be de facto, "depending on the benign neglect of the state" (Feeny et al. 1990, 2).

Many researchers were inclined to accept Hardin's model of the human being as a rational, self-interested actor, but they argued that after several years of declining yields or deteriorating environmental conditions, these actors would come together to make and enforce rules for resource use (cf. Ostrom 1990). Anthropologist James Acheson painstakingly documented one such case on the lobster fiefs of Maine, first publishing his results in 1975 (cf. Acheson 1988). Lobster fishers working out of individual harbors formed "lobster gangs" and defined and defended territories, in effect turning an open-access property regime into a communal one. In territories that are strongly guarded—perimeter-defended territories—harbor gangs also agreed to self-regulate their fishing effort. Acheson was able to document the biological and economic benefits of this system. In perimeter-defended territories, there were fewer boats and fewer fishermen per square mile and lower levels of fishing effort. Local conservation measures, such as closed seasons and limits on the number of traps, controlled fishing efforts. As Acheson noted, these measures did not affect the total lobster catch, but they reduced lobster mortality and increased the proportional catch of larger, more valuable lobsters. Finally, "[g]reater stock density in the perimeter-defended areas suggests that reduced effort has halted the process of overexploitation" (Acheson 1987, 57–58).

Folk Management, Co-Management

Acheson's important work, in which both the economy of fishing and the ecology of lobsters were well documented, invigorated the field of maritime anthropology. A number of researchers set out to find similar "folk management" schemes in the world's fisheries, leading however to overzealous and poorly documented claims to ecological sustainability. Prefacing a collection of these studies, Christopher Dyer and James McGoodwin defined this arena as follows:

> Folk management in the fisheries is management by and for fishing people themselves. It naturally arises as an inevitable outcome of resource utilization by fishing peoples. Formally defined, it is any localized behavior originating outside state control that facilitates the sustainable utilization of renewable natural resources. (1994, 1)

The inevitability of folk management systems and their durability would be questioned (cf. King and Durrenberger 2000, 9). Indeed, few of the case studies assembled by Dyer and McGoodwin support their faith in folk management. Caroline Pomeroy's analysis of Mexico's Lake Chapala fisheries disclosed failed efforts to maintain exclusive resource boundaries, little support by government agencies for local organizational initiatives, and a resultant tragedy of the commons (Pomeroy 1994). McGoodwin's own study of Mexico's coastal shrimpers revealed that efforts at local management are "hardly worth the effort, given the pervasive pessimism about ever seeing the more valuable marine resources return to their former abundance" (McGoodwin 1994, 50). William Ward and Priscilla Weeks evaluated offers by the Texas Coastal Fisheries Division (CFD) to suspend state regulation of oyster harvesting. The industry itself rejected the offer, believing it to be a covert attempt to destroy the industry. Ward and Weeks suggested, then, that the industry's view of human nature coincided with that of the CFD biologists: "if humans are given a public resource to use with no restrictions, they will 'keep taking until the last one is gone'" (1994, 108).

Evelyn Pinkerton (1994) concluded the Dyer and McGoodwin collection with a careful specification of the conditions required for effective folk management and a warning that neither the state nor the market will go away. Folk management systems may be expected to arise, she suggests, when a community has experienced a long period of stable population size, affording it an opportunity to experiment, learn, and adapt to local resources. Such adaptations would occur through trial and error where the resource base is forgiving—where mistakes could be made that were not fatal to that resource. Based on the case studies presented, she suggested that such conditions are rare.

As an alternative to folk management, Pinkerton and others call for schemes of co-management. Resource regulatory agencies incorporate legitimate local management practices into regulatory regimes, provide legal backing for local activities, and foster local participation in management decisions. Responsibilities for initiating regulations are shared by local users and their managers. Svein Jentoft situated co-management between the property regimes of communal and state, as "a meeting point between over-all government concerns for efficient resource utilization and protection, and local concerns for equal opportunities, self-determination, and self-control" (1989, 144). Jentoft thus acknowledged that the tragedy of the commons may occur in unregulated fisheries but suggested that the partici-pation of local fisheries organizations in the framing of regulations will enhance the legitimacy of such regulations and increase the possibility that local fishers will comply with those regulations (Jentoft 1985).

Although there was a general consensus in the fisheries social sciences that co-management was a desirable goal, there was a rather categorical rejection in these same circles of what was becoming the dominant tool in state-sponsored fisheries management in the 1980s and 1990s: individual transferable quotas. Quotas are a form of output control, efforts to limit catches to a sustainable level over the long term. They are also a form of private property because individual fishermen or boats are accorded the right to obtain a specific quantity of fish out of the total allowable catch (TAC) as estimated by fisheries scientists for a given season. In early schemes, individual quotas could be transferred, bought, and sold on the free market, and anthropologists quickly raised objections on equity grounds. There were concerns about the fairness of initial allocations, and then concerns about the acquisition and consolidation of quotas in the hands of large operators (National Research Council 1999; Pálsson 1998). A deeper critique of quotas and TAC, and the fisheries science upon which these are based, would surface in the 1990s. This critique drew upon the "new ecology" of chaos and complexity, producing calls for management policies that foster flexibility and resiliency (Berkes and Folke 1998). Before examining the new direction, I turn to a spectacular failure in fish-eries management.

The Collapse of the Cod

The collapse of northern cod stocks, and the indefinite moratorium imposed in 1992, affected 35,000 fishers and fish plant workers in New-foundland and Labrador. This has rightly been labeled "the classic case of the failure of conventional science-based fisheries management" (Finlayson and McCay 1998, 311). It is also, I have argued, a test case for linking the ana-lytical traditions of political economy and cultural ecology (McGuire 1997).

Prior to 1977, the waters off Canada had been fished by voracious factory freezer trawlers from a dozen European nations as well as by Canada's own fleet. In the early 1970s, the International Commission for the Northwest

Atlantic Fisheries (ICNAF) introduced quotas, which were weakly enforced by member states over their own fleets. Quotas were set at "maximum sustainable yield," which proved to be unsustainable. Average catches had plummeted from 800,000 metric tons in the 1960s to 214,000 tons by 1977, when Canada unilaterally declared a 200-mile exclusive fisheries jurisdiction and commenced a rebuilding process. Quotas were set by scientists from the Department of Fisheries and Oceans (DFO) at more modest fishing mortality targets, providing, it was thought, "a buffer against stock assessment errors and enforcement deficiencies" (Lear and Parsons 1993, 66). By the end of the 1980s, it became increasingly clear that even these targets were excessive, and the science underlying them came under intense scrutiny.

DFO scientists based their annual targets on two sources of data: research surveys performed by the department and the catch per unit effort (CPUE) reported by the country's offshore fishing fleet. Through the 1980s, these data sets diverged significantly; the surveys showed that stocks had grown very little since 1978, whereas the CPUE data showed stocks at about three times what they were in the late 1970s. DFO scientists resolved this discrepancy by essentially averaging the two data sets.

Warnings within and outside the scientific community that quotas were too high and that assessments were wrong went largely unheeded until 1989, when quotas for the 1990 offshore fishery were substantially reduced. Even then, the two integrated fishing and processing firms resisted any reductions in total allowable catches. One deep-sea trawler skipper wrote to St. John's newspaper: "I've been fishing northern cod for eight years, and I tell you there are more fish there now than there were eight years ago" (quoted in Finlayson and McCay 1998, 326).

Christopher Finlayson and Bonnie McCay offered a partial hypothesis for the failure of fish science, one that draws on the relations of power—the political economy of the industry and its managers. Scientists know the truth but are not listened to by fisheries policymakers, who have a vested interest in portraying the stocks under their care as healthy. They further suggest that the heavy debts of offshore fishery companies and the high number of jobs at stake in their processing plants "may have played a role in closing eyes and ears until it was too late" (1998, 326).

One set of truths that was emerging, and that went largely unheard until the cod stock collapsed, came from inshore fishermen. Larry Felt and Barbara Neis, sociologists at the Memorial University in St. John's, had been gathering local knowledge from these fishermen, through interviews and archival research, and the material pointed quite clearly to signs of a declining stock, such as the decrease in the numbers of larger, breeding fish (cf. Felt and Neis 1996). Fishermen themselves were (mal)adapting to this stock decline by increasing their fishing effort and adopting more efficient technology. David Hearn from Petty Harbour increased the number of cod traps he operated: "Even though we were increasing our gear the fish were getting smaller. Fish wasn't half the size the last few years as they had been years before that. We had to catch twice as much fish for the same amount of weight" (quoted in Neis 1992, 163).

Other researchers linked humans, technology, and the environment in a cultural ecology of faulty science and resource collapse (e.g., Steele, Andersen, and Green 1992). My own postmortem is an argument against a political ecology that slights ecology. In retrospect, three processes were at work in the collapse. First, in the euphoric though cautious optimism after Canada declared its 200-mile exclusive zone, Canadian deep-water trawlers were upgraded with new technologies for finding and harvesting fish, even though the actual number of vessels was fixed. Second, skippers were encouraged to fish in areas that had theretofore been the province of the foreign distant water fleets, and they quite rapidly learned how to fish those grounds. Third, the ecology of the cod came into play. There was an apparent increase in cod stock concentrations as these stocks declined in the 1980s, increasing their "catchability." Together, these processes worked to distort the interpretation of catch per unit effort. High trawler catch rates coincided with declining stocks because fishers were discovering where to find the last northern cod (McGuire 1997).

Chaos

Faced with such failures in conventional resource management, a number of anthropologists incorporated the metaphor of chaos into their thinking about marine systems and how they should be managed (Acheson and Wilson 1996; Smith 1990; Wilson et al. 1991). The thrust of one such effort, the University of Maine Chaos Project, was to generate a multispecies ecosystem model for the Gulf of Maine fish stocks that more accurately represented ecosystem behavior than the dominant modes of stock assessment utilized by fisheries scientists. Those "numeric" modes were predicated on a stock-recruitment assumption—that the size of the stock available to be exploited in one year is a function of the size of the breeding stock that survived the fishery in the previous year. Models using this assumption form the basis for most management regimes, calculating the total allowable catch and restraining fishing efforts to the appropriate level. However, the evidence of numerous crises in the world's fisheries that are managed this way suggests that it was not working.

The University of Maine's modeling exercise began by setting a few constant parameters, representing spawning potential, growth rates, habitat, and migration, that in the real world remain relatively stable over time. Stable parameters lend a degree of order to chaotic systems; fish populations will vary in unpredictable ways, but they will remain within a normal range of historical limits (Acheson and Wilson 1996, 584; cf. Acheson, Wilson, and Steneck 1998). Acheson and Wilson offered a simple recommendation to fisheries regulators: Manage fisheries by managing the parameters, not the numbers. The goals of management should be to maintain critical life processes such as spawning; to outlaw fishing during certain parts of the life cycle; and to maintain areas such as breeding grounds, migration routes, and nurseries that are essential for the growth of the species. This can be done by rules governing fishing locations, fishing areas, and fishing techniques, an approach to management, they observed, "that is taken in so many tribal and peasant societies" (Acheson and Wilson 1996, 584–85).

Parametric management has not displaced numeric management in the world's fisheries, but its implications are consonant with the growing interest in ecosystem management, refugia, and marine protected areas (cf. Gadgil, Hemam, and Reddy 1998; Pitcher, Hart, and Pauly 1998). Parametric management, however, draws its inspiration from folk management, and both are beset by the problems of evidence. Acheson and Wilson acknowledged this:

> [T]here is very little statistical data that local-level folk management rules are effective in conserving the resource. The evidence is largely anecdotal. . . . [A]uthors have noted that resources have not crashed and have assumed that the sustained yields are due to folk management rules. (1996, 586)

Nevertheless, Acheson and Wilson marshaled the ethnographic materials from dozens of tribal and peasant fishing societies (none of which were managed through quotas) to support the case for parametric management of industrial fisheries. Much of this evidence was collected by American maritime anthropologists working within a tradition of cultural ecology. And, as previously noted, much of this research was undertaken to contest Hardin's model of the tragedy of the commons and the self-interested and shortsighted actor who, if unfettered, would bring about the tragedy.

Canadian anthropologists and sociologists turned to political economy rather than cultural ecology to analyze the industrialized fisheries of the Maritimes and Newfoundland. Observing a landscape of failing fish stocks and socioeconomic crisis in Nova Scotia in the 1980s, Anthony Davis looked to government fisheries policies. Those policies fostered the professionalization of small-boat fishers through training in accounting, small business operations, and taxation and fiscal planning. Davis argued that these policies, aimed at the goal of turning fishing into a small business enterprise rather than a way of making a living, in fact spawned a class of very Hardinesque "rapacious fishers": "government management policies, which were predicated on the premise that fishers were irresponsible self-seekers and, thus, prone to over exploit ocean resources, have created the very conditions necessary to fulfill their prophecy" (1991, 20). Davis and others are doubtful that the localized practices and norms governing fishing for a living can survive the ingestion of competitive, utilitarian rationality peculiar to industrial capitalism.

Maritime Anthropology in the Policy Process

In the final analysis, maritime social scientists have not prevented fisheries disasters. But Bonnie McCay, long a participant in fisheries policy forums, is guardedly optimistic about the contributions anthropologists and others are making to resource management thinking and practice. They have added their voice to the growing numbers of fisheries scientists who question the logic of managing by numbers (Ludwig, Hilborn, and Walters 1993). They have championed the idea that ecosystems, not single species, should be the units of management (Pauly and Maclean 2003; Pitcher, Hart, and Pauly 1998). They have promoted the notion that fishers themselves should have a say in how they are managed, and co-management is now on the agenda for resource managers worldwide (Haroldsdottir 2000). They are less enamored now with some of the unrealistic claims made in the name of folk management, which should add credibility to anthropological interventions in policy. Most recently, McCay is making the case for participatory research, in which scientists and fishers collaborate to define community needs and find workable and acceptable solutions (Finlayson and McCay 1998; McCay 2000; McCay 2001). This mode of intervention is the touchstone of the backyard anthropology promoted by the collaborative effort of the EPA and the SfAA; participatory research also plays a significant role in the endeavors to scale up to study human-environment relations beyond the local community.

Scaling Up: Mapping and Countermapping

The driving forces for scaling up are multiple. Land degradation, soil loss, deforestation, and desertification have been concerns of social and environmental scientists as well as of those whose livelihoods depend on the resources of these landscapes. The loss of biological diversity and the recognition that this diversity can best be maintained by preserving the integrity of terrestrial and marine areas have been acknowledged by local resource users, environmental activists, and land managers. Assaults on indigenous people and their traditional territories have not ceased. These processes take place across wide geographic spaces, and the ethnographic tradition of localized, community-oriented fieldwork holds little promise of analyzing and ameliorating these larger processes. Anthropologists, nonetheless, are increasingly inserting their skills, methods, and values into scaled up exercises. One exercise is pulled and facilitated by advances in technology over the last two decades, such as the availability and refinement of remote sensing and Geographical Information Systems (GIS) hardware and software: Anthropologists have become "ground-truthers" of the snapshots from space. The other exercise is driven by the anthropological, and human, concern for human rights and social justice. Anthropologists and other social scientists are assisting indigenous peoples throughout the world in mapping and defending their lands and resources. The collection, preservation, and use of local knowledge are elements common to both of these projects.

Mapping

Anthropologist Priscilla Reining is credited with the first use of satellite imagery within the discipline, in an effort to identify individual Mali villages from data provided by the Landsat system in the 1970s (Conant 1990, 359). The technology was crude by today's standards, and Reining had to confirm the identifications by fieldwork. In general, though, social scientists were slow to form partnerships with remote sensing scientists; many of the problems of interest were not amenable to measurement from space. As Ronald Rindfuss (a demographer) and Paul Stern (a social psychologist) observed:

> Changing land use, road and building construction, and the like are regarded as manifestations of more important variables, such as government policies, land-use rules, distribution of wealth and power, market mechanisms, and social customs, none of which is directly reflected in the bands of the electromagnetic spectrum. (1998, 2)

There was concern also that the technology, as it developed, would diminish the need for anthropologists in the field, despite the early experiences of Reining. Indeed, the National Aeronautics and Space Administration (NASA), which launched the first Landsat platform in 1972, promoted remote sensing as a means to carry out analysis and interpretation at home, lessening the necessity for field observations (Conant 1994, 407). Nonetheless, a few anthropologists undertook the difficult task of acquiring a working knowledge of remote sensing, sufficient to know its possibilities and limitations. Francis Conant, enthused by Reining's work, apprenticed at the Goddard Institute for Space Studies in New York and developed the Human Ecology and Remote Sensing Laboratory in Hunter College's anthropology department. Emilio Moran, an ecological anthropologist with decades of work in the Amazon, utilized a senior scholar training grant from the National Science Foundation to acquire the skills. At Indiana University, he established the Anthropological Center for Training and Research on Global Environmental Change, an ongoing program to bring the social and remote sensing communities together.

Moran was led to remote sensing because studies of Amazonia in the 1970s and early 1980s presented a picture of "devastating deforestation, desertification in the humid tropics, and wholesale conversion of tropical forest to pasture" (Moran and Brondízio 1998, 94), a portrayal at odds with Moran's own understanding of land-use change in the region and the testimony of local farmers about rapid regrowth of vegetation after forests had been cut and burned. The methodology Moran and his colleagues have developed involves, first, the selection of study areas with contrasting soil characteristics, land-use patterns, and population distributions. Satellite imagery is explored, and preliminary land cover classifications are made. Researchers then go to the field, images in one hand, Global Positioning System (GPS) devices in the other, and conduct observations of actual land cover and interview land users. Detailed household surveys are undertaken, focusing on land-use histories and economic practices. A sample of sites with representative vegetation is then drawn, and teams measure a variety of soil and vegetation characteristics and record these data directly on spreadsheets. Back home, Moran and his teams use these field observations to perform refined classifications of the satellite imagery and to translate, if possible, the spectral data from space into the land-use patterns on the ground. They have been successful in identifying stages of vegetative regrowth in cleared land and in differentiating between unmanaged and actively manipulated floodplain forests.

The research process has been carried out, to date, in five regions across Amazonia. The land-use histories of these disparate sites include cattle ranching, extraction of forest products such as rubber and logs, small-scale shifting cultivation and gardening, and mechanized export agriculture; the effects on the ecosystems are equally varied. One picture to emerge, however, is the viability of agroforestry: management to increase the frequency of trees that produce valuable products such as palm fruits. On the ground, this has been shown to be economically productive; from space, it shows up as widespread. Through time, by comparing satellite imagery from the 1980s and 1990s, Moran and his co-workers have determined that such a system does not increase the rate of deforestation in the region. They conclude that the conceptualization of local forest users should be changed, from "extractivist" sharecroppers on plantations to managers of a sustainable landscape (Brondízio et al. 1994; Brondízio and Siqueira 1997).

Countermapping

Introducing a collection of studies on participatory action research mapping (PARM) for *Human Organization*, geographers Peter Herlihy and Gregory Knapp put forward a bold claim: The methodology may be "one of the more important contributions to the understanding and solution of social and environmental problems" of this century (2003, 310). As an activist's tool, frequently called countermapping, PARM seeks to empower indigenous communities in the delimitation and defense of traditional territories. It is closely linked to the environmentalists' interest in inventorying and preserving biodiversity. Fundamental to both of these purposes is a reliance on local people to convey their knowledge of spatial and environmental features to facilitators, researchers who then transform hand-drawn sketches into the map products used in negotiating and managing landscapes.

Gaining popularity through the 1990s, and typically funded by environmentally oriented nongovernmental organizations (NGOs) such as the World Wildlife Fund and the Nature Conservancy, participatory mapping has been put to a number of uses: to record spatial features of land use and occupancy, to develop management plans for conservation areas and indigenous reserves, to assess biodiversity, to document land claims and titles, and to build consensus and foster conflict resolution over natural resources and lands (Herlihy and Knapp 2003, 308). One of the early exercises in countermapping was directed by anthropologists Mac Chapin and Anthony Stocks of Cultural Survival, an indigenous rights organization, in the Darién region of eastern Panama (Chapin, Herrera, and González 1995).

Covering 17,000 square kilometers, the Darién contains the country's largest remaining piece of intact forest, the only uncompleted segment of the Pan-American Highway, and a population of 45,000, mostly indigenous Kuna, Emberá, and Wounaan. Increasingly, though, the region has become a conflict zone between the native inhabitants and newcomers, such as loggers, cattle ranchers, land speculators, and landless colonizers from Panama's overcrowded interior. To assess these threats, Cultural Survival joined with two Panamanian organizations, the General Congress of the Emberá, Wounaan, and Kuna People and the Centro de Estudios y Acción Social Panameño, to map the Darién. A team of indigenous "surveyors" was recruited from local communities, trained in land-use questionnaire and cartographic techniques, and sent off by bus, by canoe, and on foot through the region. They eschewed the official government base maps. The intent was to do an ethnocartography, in which villagers create their own maps with their own symbols. Surveyors, in collaboration with village elders, made detailed drawings of river systems, hunting, fishing, and gathering areas, and the locations of medicinal and other forest products.

The surveyors then joined with cartographers from the University of Panama and Peter Herlihy, the geographer, to construct composite maps, this time using the official government base maps. It was a countermap, however. Place names, river systems, and significant local landmarks were all recorded in the indigenous language. Surveyors returned to the field with this draft map to consult with community members, correct errors, fill in gaps, and confirm boundary lines. With the corrected master map in hand, the indigenous groups addressed a forum in Panama City on the lands and resources of the Darién. Attended by 500 people, including government officials, leaders of indigenous groups from several Central and South American countries, and representatives of conservation organizations, the forum induced Panama's minister of government and justice to recognize the importance of indigenous rights.

Chapin and his colleagues linked the two underpinnings of the mapping effort: the protection of indigenous lands and the conservation of biodiversity. The maps of the Darién show that the areas of indigenous land use are also zones of relatively intact forest: "The implication of this is that perhaps the best way to preserve what is left is to strengthen indigenous control over the land, and work toward common conservationist goals" (Chapin, Herrera, and González 1995, 36).

Scaling Down: Backyard Anthropology and Environmental Justice

Maritime anthropology has developed, by and large, within the comfortable confines of academic and research institutions. Some of the information- and technology-intensive projects of a scaled up environmental anthropology have their locus there as well. This is the institutional context where theories, methods, and skills are acquired. However, it may not be the ultimate working environment for practicing environmental anthropologists. Barbara Rose Johnston, in preparing the ground rules for the Environmental Anthropology Program (EAP), a cooperative venture between the SfAA and the EPA, surveyed the anthropological workforce engaged in environmental issues in the United States. The largest segment, she found, worked outside academia in local communities, grassroots groups, and NGOs. Their efforts were problem focused and public service oriented. Their roles were varied: program evaluators, advisors, consultants, organizers. Their engagement was often a result of deep personal commitment. Their work was seldom recognized and valued by the academic profession. She ruefully noted, "such work rarely was a means to making a living" (Johnston 2001a, 3). The EAP was designed to foster these efforts, to further what Johnston called a "backyard anthropology," to create opportunities for asserting anthropological methods and engagement in community-based environmental protection efforts (2001a, 2–3).

Backyard Anthropology

Under the program, the EPA provided funding for interns, fellows, and consultants to collaborate with local entities in environmental protection efforts. The projects were framed as technical assistance, addressing a wide range of locally defined needs: watershed planning, protection, and restoration, sustainable development issues, environmental planning and restoration, and exposure to environmental risks. The program provided anthropologists with opportunities to hone technical skills, to understand policy processes and develop a role in policy formation, to expand networks of contacts, and to "demonstrate the unique contributions of disciplinary methods and techniques in environmental planning and problem solving processes" (Johnston 2001a, 5). Many of the participants parlayed these skills and contacts into professional employment.

David Driscoll's efforts under the EAP to instill a participatory decision-making process surrounding brownfields—contaminated properties—in Miami-Dade County, Florida, illustrate the potential, and problems, of technical assistance projects. Brownfields are a conundrum for policymakers and local communities. With passage of the Comprehensive Environmental Response, Compensation, and Liability Act (CERCLA), the EPA was mandated to undertake environmental risk assessments of brownfields and to collect monetary damages from current or former owners and operators of such sites. In response, many owners hastily sold or abandoned contaminated sites, in turn resulting in initiatives by states and the federal government to weaken enforcement of CERCLA. These initiatives, as Driscoll observed, "are founded on the idea that independent (if incomplete) cleanup and redevelopment is better than abandonment and continued contamination" (2001, 8). The EPA's program, the Brownfields Economic Redevelopment Initiative (BERI), provides risk assessment and cleanup funds to local communities and calls for resident input in redevelopment activities.

The Poinciana Industrial Center (PIC) and its surrounding neighborhoods in Miami were targeted as a pilot BERI site in 1997, and Driscoll, with graduate training in both public health and anthropology, was enlisted to develop and implement a participatory model of brownfield redevelopment, largely through involvement in public meetings. PIC is an industrial park that was abandoned after several of its enterprises were burned during riots in 1989. Driscoll's goal was to identify those residents who would be most affected by redevelopment by using participant observation of foot traffic and resident behavior on and around the site, community mapping, and developing a database of community organizations.

Driscoll then proceeded to identify audiences with shared perceptions about the redevelopment of the industrial park and to assess the perceived benefits of and constraints to participation for these community segments. He spent several weeks working with key informants to develop outreach messages and to identify means of communication most likely to reach specific, receptive subpopulations—means of communication that would, it was hoped, convince the segments of the community to participate in public hearings on the remediation and development of the local brownfield (2001, 9).

The participatory process unraveled at this point. The outreach efforts to attract local residents to public hearings were administered by a "local advisory committee" with grants from the EPA. As Driscoll noted, these individuals were hired on the basis of their ethnicity and involvement with issues of environmental justice. The EPA officials had expected that these activists would "reassure skeptical community residents that this was not like other 'top-down' government intrusions into their community, and thus encourage their participation" (Driscoll 2001, 10). The activists, none of whom were residents of the community or the county, accused agency officials of whitewashing the health risks of brownfields, called for the complete cleanup of all brownfields in the area, and prevented the dissemination of outreach materials containing messages other than those of the potential health risks of the proposed redevelopment: "The idea that some residents might be willing to negotiate a partial remediation for local jobs was particularly refuted by the activists" (10). These disagreements led to the curtailment of the outreach process and disappointing attendance at local public hearings. With some optimism, Driscoll noted that the local advisory committee had begun to meet again after the EPA contracts with both Driscoll and the activists had ended.

Environmental Justice

Driscoll's issues are ones of environmental justice, and this is an arena where applied anthropologists will meet environmental activists again. Patterns of environmental injustice—the siting of hazardous activities disproportionately in minority and poor communities—have been documented in the United States (Bullard 1990; United Church of Christ 1987). Environmental justice has been institutionalized in U.S. policy. In 1994, President Bill Clinton issued an executive order, "Federal Actions to Address Environmental Justice in Minority Populations and Low-Income Populations." Ensuing regulations now require all federal agencies to evaluate actions that pose environmental risks on minority and low-income members of communities. Barbara Rose Johnston views this as a significant opening for anthropologists.

We can document and articulate subsistence patterns and lifeways that might contribute to increased vulnerability. We can work with vulnerable communities to understand environmental threats, recognize "high-risk" behavior, and generate culturally appropriate strategies for reducing risk. By using applied ethnographic techniques to conduct baseline surveys we can facilitate educational outreach and informed participatory involvement in environmental planning and decision-making processes. (2001b, 146)

Agencies are still in the process of designing policies and procedures for addressing issues of environmental justice. It is not unreasonable to expect that at least some of the backyard anthropologists will make a living at this. But environmental justice, raised to the level of public policy by Bill Clinton, has its own political economy. Barbara Rose Johnston acknowledged this: "Even in the context of strong legal protection for human rights and environmental quality, human rights are abused when cultural forces and economic greed co-opt and corrupt the implementation of legal structures" (1994, 12).

Those legal structures have remained largely in place under the administration of President George W. Bush. The president signed legislation in 2002 for brownfield revitalization and restoration (albeit with liability relief for small businesses seeking to develop hazardous sites), and the EPA has joined 20 other agencies in the Federal Partnership Action Agenda to assist communities in assessing, cleaning up, and developing brownfields. The Superfund Trust Fund, however, is running out of money. During Clinton's watch, Congress refused to reauthorize the "polluter taxes" on producers of petroleum and chemical products that had underwritten clean-up efforts, and subsequent efforts to revive the tax have fallen on congressional cold shoulders (U.S. Commission on Civil Rights 2003; for a preliminary assessment of Bush's overall environmental record, see Cohen 2004).

The U.S. Supreme Court may have the final word on environmental protection during the Bush presidency. It has an unusually high number of environmental cases on its docket; one of the eight cases has been decided to date. In *Alaska v. EPA* (2004), the Court ruled in favor of the EPA, allowing it to impose more costly antipollution measures on the Red Dog Mine, against the wishes of Alaska. It was a narrow decision, however. Four of the nine justices dissented.

Retrospect and Prospect

In the domain of the environment, the matter-of-fact materialism of Julian Steward, through subsequent debates and permutations, has produced the better knowledge and yielded the better action that Eric Wolf and his fellow students hoped it would. Some of the casualties in those debates, such as ecosystems in balance, for one, have been replaced by another framework: chaotic ecosystems. This has led to coherent policy recommendations, for instance, managing fisheries by managing the parameters of the ecosystem. And the limits of Steward's worldview have been addressed by theorists of world systems, the expansion of capitalism, and the environmental consequences of relations of power. The liberation ecologies promoted by Arturo Escobar, Michael Watts, and others put those in power on notice that there are alternate world views about the environment. Mapping the terrains of those with little power may be an effective route to empowerment.

Anthony Paredes contends that many of the openings for an applied anthropology have come from the top down. He traces his own career of research and application to the spaces created by prevailing public policies and consequent funding opportunities: John Kennedy's Peace Corps in the context of Cold War competition for alliances with developing countries, Lyndon Johnson's War on Poverty, the promulgation of the U.S. Fishery Conservation and Management Act of 1976, and the Native American Graves Protection and Repatriation Act of 1990 (Paredes 1997). To such openings, such opportunities, Barbara Rose Johnston would add the realm of environmental justice that Bill Clinton put on the national agenda in 1994. Climate change is now firmly on the international agenda, as is the concern for the loss of biodiversity. Anthropologists are increasingly called upon to probe and document the roles of communities and cultures in global environmental change.

For Paredes, the opportunities provided by such prevailing public policies are attractive precisely because they call for "close-to-the-ground" fieldwork, as Wolf put it, the prospect of studying a real world of real people. An applied environmental anthropology requires the skills of an anthropologist: the ability to closely observe real people doing real things, to understand the causes and consequences of those actions, and to communicate those observations in an honest and credible way. These skills will continue to be acquired in a variety of settings: academic training in method and theory, practical internships during the course of undergraduate and graduate study, consultancies and careers with governmental and nongovernmental organizations, participatory research with communities and neighborhoods, and institutes for advanced training in the technologies to assess global environmental change.

Concerns over the environment and its human inhabitants are not likely to wane. But anthropologists practicing in the environmental arena need to be vigilant, ready to critique any sign that public policies and programs are working against the premise of the Rio Summit: that a healthy and productive life—in harmony with nature—is indeed a human entitlement.

References

Acheson, James M. 1987. The lobster fiefs revisited: Economic and ecological effects of territoriality in the Maine lobster industry. In *The question of the commons: The culture and ecology of communal resources*, edited by Bonnie J. McCay and James M. Acheson. Tucson: University of Arizona Press.

———. 1988. *The lobster gangs of Maine*. Hanover, N.H.: University Press of New England.

Acheson, James M., and James A. Wilson. 1996. Order out of chaos: The case for parametric fisheries management. *American Anthropologist* 98 (3): 579–94.

Acheson, James M., James A. Wilson, and Robert S. Steneck. 1998. Managing chaotic fisheries. In *Linking social and ecological systems*, edited by Fikret Berkes and Carl Folke. Cambridge: Cambridge University Press.

Bebbington, A. J., and S. P. J. Batterbury. 2001. Transnational livelihoods and landscapes: Political ecologies of globalization. *Ecumene* 8 (4): 369–80.

Bennett, John. 1969. *Northern plainsmen: Adaptive strategy and agrarian life*. Chicago: Aldine.

Berkes, Fikret, and Carl Folke, eds. 1998. *Linking social and economic systems: Management practices and social mechanisms for building resilience*. Cambridge: Cambridge University Press.

Biersack, Aletta. 1999. Introduction: From the "new ecology" to the new ecologies. *American Anthropologist* 101 (1): 5–18.

Blaikie, Piers, and Harold Brookfield. 1987. *Land degradation and society*. London: Methuen.

Botkin, Daniel B. 1990. Discordant harmonies: A new ecology for the 21st century. New York: Oxford University Press.

Bowen, William M., Mark J. Salling, Kingsley E. Haynes, and Ellen J. Cyran. 1995. Toward environmental justice: Spatial equity in Ohio and Cleveland. *Annals of the Association of American Geographers* 85 (4): 641–63.

Brondízio, Eduardo S., and Andréa D. Siqueira. 1997. From extractivists to forest farmers: Changing concepts of Caboclo agroforestry in the Amazon estuary. In *Research in economic anthropology*, edited by Barry L. Isaac, vol. 18. Greenwich, Conn.: JAI Press, Inc.

Brondízio, Eduardo S., Emilio F. Moran, Paul Mausel, and You Wu. 1994. Land use change in the Amazon estuary: Patterns of Caboclo settlement and landscape management. *Human Ecology* 22 (3): 249–78.

Brosius, J. Peter. 1999. Analyses and intervention: Anthropological engagements with environmentalism. *Current Anthropology* 40 (3): 277–309.

Bryant, Raymond L. 1998. Power, knowledge and political ecology in the Third World: A review. *Progress in Physical Geography* 22 (1): 79–94.

Bullard, Robert. 1990. *Dumping on Dixie: Race, class and environmental quality*. Boulder, Colo.: Westview Press.

Chapin, Mac, Francisco Herrera, and Nicanor González. 1995. Ethnocartography in the Darién. *Cultural Survival Quarterly* 18 (4): 34–37.

Cohen, Maurie J. 2004. George W. Bush and the Environmental Protection Agency: A midterm appraisal. *Society and Natural Resources* 17 (1): 69–88.

Conant, Francis Paine. 1990. 1990 and beyond: Satellite remote sensing and ecological anthropology. In *The ecosystem approach in anthropology: From concept to practice*, edited by Emilio F. Moran. Ann Arbor: University of Michigan Press.

————. 1994. Human ecology and space age technology: Some predictions. *Human Ecology* 22 (3): 405–13.

Davis, Anthony. 1991. Insidious rationalities: The institutionalisation of small boat fishing and the rise of the rapacious fisher. *Maritime Anthropological Studies* 4 (1): 13–31.

Descola, Philippe, and Gísli Pálsson, eds. 1996. *Nature and society: Anthropological perspectives*. London and New York: Routledge.

Driscoll, David L. 2001. Urban brownfields in south Florida: Lessons learned from a consultancy project. *Practicing Anthropology* 23 (3): 7–11.

Dyer, Christopher L., and James R. McGoodwin, eds. 1994. Folk management in the world's fisheries: Lessons for modern fisheries management. Niwot: University Press of Colorado.

Escobar, Arturo. 1998. Whose knowledge, whose nature? Biodiversity, conservation, and the political ecology of social movements. *Journal of Political Ecology* 5: 53–82.

————. 1999. After nature: Steps to an antiessentialist political ecology. *Current Anthropology* 40 (1): 1–30.

Feeny, David, Fikret Berkes, Bonnie J. McCay, and James M. Acheson. 1990. The tragedy of the commons: 22 years later. *Human Ecology* 18 (1): 1–19.

Felt, Lawrence F., and Barbara Neis. 1996. A bridge over troubling waters: Social science and interdisciplinarity in sustainable fisheries management. Prepared for the Symposium on Reinventing Fisheries Management, University of British Columbia, February 20–24, 1996.

Finlayson, A. Christopher, and Bonnie J. McCay. 1998. Crossing the threshold of ecosystem resilience: The commercial extinction of the northern cod. In *Linking social and ecological systems: Management practices and social mechanisms for building resilience*, edited by Fikret Berkes and Carl Folke. Cambridge: Cambridge University Press.

Frank, Andre Gunder. 1967. *Capitalism and underdevelopment in Latin America: Historical studies of Chile and Brazil*. New York: Monthly Review Press.

Gadgil, Madhav, Natabar Shyam Hemam, and B. Mohan Reddy. 1998. People, refugia and resilience. In *Linking social and ecological systems: Management practices and social mechanisms for building resilience*, edited by Fikret Berkes and Carl Folke. Cambridge: Cambridge University Press.

Glantz, Michael H. 2001. *Currents of change: Impacts of El Niño and La Niña on climate and society*. 2nd ed. Cambridge: Cambridge University Press.

Gordon, H. Scott. 1954. The economic theory of a common property resource: The fishery. *Journal of Political Economy* 62: 124–42.

Hardin, Garrett. 1968. The tragedy of the commons. *Science* 162: 1243–48.

Haroldsdottir, Gudrun. 2000. Tradition, co-management, diversity, and the FAO in small-scale inland fisheries in Africa. In *State and community in fisheries management: Power, policy, and practice*, edited by E. Paul Durrenberger and Thomas D. King. Westport, Conn.: Bergin and Garvey.

Herlihy, Peter H., and Gregory Knapp. 2003. Maps of, by, and for the peoples of Latin America. *Human Organization* 62 (4): 303–14.

Hvalkof, Søren, and Arturo Escobar. 1998. Nature, political ecology, and social practice: Toward an academic and political agenda. In *Building a new biocultural synthesis: Political-economic perspectives on human biology*, edited by Alan H. Goodman and Thomas L. Leatherman. Ann Arbor: University of Michigan Press.

Jentoft, Svein. 1985. Models of fishery development: The cooperative approach. *Marine Policy* 9 (4): 322–31.

———. 1989. Fisheries co-management: Delegating government responsibility to fishermen's organizations. *Marine Policy* 13 (2): 137–54.

Johnston, Barbara Rose. 1994. Environmental degradation and human rights abuse. In *Who pays the price? The sociocultural context of environmental crisis*, edited by Barbara Rose Johnston. Washington, D.C.: Island Press, for the Society for Applied Anthropology.

———. 2001a. Backyard anthropology and community-based environmental protection: Lessons from the SfAA environment anthropology project. *Practicing Anthropology* 23 (3): 2–6.

———. 2001b. Anthropology and environmental justice: Analysts, advocates, mediators, and troublemakers. In *New directions in anthropology and environment: Intersections*, edited by Carole L. Crumley. Walnut Creek, Calif.: AltaMira Press.

Kempton, Willett, James S. Boster, and Jennifer A. Hartley. 1995. *Environmental values in American culture*. Cambridge: MIT Press.

King, Thomas D., and E. Paul Durrenberger. 2000. Introduction. In *State and community in fisheries management: Power, policy, and practice*, edited by E. Paul Durrenberger and Thomas D. King. Westport, Conn.: Bergin and Garvey.

Kottak, Conrad P. 1999. The new ecological anthropology. *American Anthropologist* 101 (1): 23–35.

Lear, W. H., and L. S. Parsons. 1993. History and management of the fishery for northern cod in NAFO divisions 2J, 3K, and 3L. In *Perspectives on Canadian marine fisheries management*, edited by L. S. Parsons and W. H. Lear. *Canadian Bulletin of Fisheries and Aquatic Sciences* No. 226.

Little, Peter D., and Michael M. Horowitz. 1987. *Lands at risk in the Third World: Local-level perspectives*. Boulder, Colo.: Westview Press.

Ludwig, Donald, Ray Hilborn, and Carl Walters. 1993. Uncertainty, resource exploitation and conservation: Lessons from history. *Science* 260 (5104): 17, 36.

Magistro, John, and Carla Roncoli. 2001. Anthropological perspectives and policy implications of climate change research. *Climate Research* 19 (2): 91–96.

McCay, Bonnie J. 1978. Systems ecology, people ecology, and the anthropology of fishing communities. *Human Ecology* 6 (4): 397–422.

———. 2000. Sea changes in fisheries policy: Contributions from anthropology. In *State and community in fisheries management: Power, policy, and practice*, edited by E. Paul Durrenberger and Thomas D. King. Westport, Conn.: Bergin and Garvey.

———. 2001. Environmental anthropology at sea. In *New directions in anthropology and environment: Intersections*, edited by Carole L. Crumley. Walnut Creek, Calif.: AltaMira Press.

McGoodwin, James R. 1994. "Nowadays, nobody has any respect": The demise of folk management in a rural Mexican fishery. In *Folk management in the world's fisher-*

ies, edited by Christopher L. Dyer and James R. McGoodwin. Niwot: University Press of Colorado.

McGuire, Thomas R. 1997. The last northern cod. *Journal of Political Ecology* 4: 41–54.

Milton, Kay, ed. 1993. *Environmentalism: The view from anthropology*. London and New York: Routledge.

Mohai, Paul, and Bunyan Bryant. 1998. Is there a "race" effect on concern for environmental quality? *Public Opinion Quarterly* 62 (4): 475–505.

Moran, Emilio F. 1990. Ecosystem ecology in biology and anthropology: A critical assessment. In *The ecosystem approach in anthropology: From concept to practice*, edited by Emilio F. Moran. Ann Arbor: University of Michigan Press.

Moran, Emilio F., and Eduardo Brondízio. 1998. Land-use change after deforestation in Amazonia. In *People and pixels: Linking remote sensing and social science*, edited by Diana Liverman, Emilio F. Moran, Ronald R. Rindfuss, and Peter C. Stern. Washington, D.C.: National Academy Press.

Murphy, Robert F. 1970. Basin ethnography and ethnological theory. In *Languages and cultures of western North America*, edited by E. H. Swanson, Jr. Pocatello: Idaho State University Press.

National Research Council. 1999. *Sharing the fish: Toward a national policy on individual fishing quotas*. Washington, D.C.: National Academy Press.

Neis, Barbara. 1992. Fishers' ecological knowledge and stock assessment in Newfoundland. *Newfoundland Studies* 8 (2): 155–78.

Odum, Eugene. 1953. *Fundamentals of ecology*. Philadelphia: Saunders.

Oliver-Smith, Anthony. 1996. Anthropological research on hazards and disasters. *Annual Review of Anthropology* 25: 303–28.

Oliver-Smith, Anthony, and Susanna M. Hoffman, eds. 1999. *The angry earth: Disasters in natural perspective*. London and New York: Routledge.

Orlove, Benjamin S. 1980. Ecological anthropology. *Annual Review of Anthropology* 9: 235–73.

Orlove, Benjamin S., and Stephen B. Brush. 1996. Anthropology and the conservation of biodiversity. *Annual Review of Anthropology* 25: 329–52.

Ortner, Sherry B. 1984. Theory in anthropology since the sixties. *Comparative Studies in Society and History* 26 (1): 126–66.

Ostrom, Elinor. 1990. *Governing the commons: The evolution of institutions for collective action*. Cambridge and New York: Cambridge University Press.

Painter, Michael. 1995. Introduction. In *The social causes of environmental destruction in Latin America*, edited by Michael Painter and William H. Durham. Ann Arbor: University of Michigan Press.

Painter, Michael, and William H. Durham, eds. 1995. *The social causes of environmental destruction in Latin America*. Ann Arbor: University of Michigan Press.

Pálsson, Gisli. 1998. Learning by fishing: Practical engagement and environmental concerns. In *Linking social and ecological systems*, edited by Fikret Berkes and Carl Folke. Cambridge: Cambridge University Press.

Paredes, J. Anthony. 1997. The influences of government policies and academic theories on the practice of applied anthropology in the United States: Some personal observations. *Human Organization* 56 (4): 484–89.

Paulson, Susan, Lisa L. Gezon, and Michael Watts. 2003. Locating the political in political ecology: An introduction. *Human Organization* 62 (3): 205–17.

Pauly, Daniel, and Jay Maclean. 2003. *In a perfect ocean: The state of fisheries and ecosystems in the North Atlantic Ocean.* Washington, D.C.: Island Press.

Peet, Richard, and Michael Watts. 1993. Introduction: Development theory and environment in an age of market triumphalism. *Economic Geography* 69 (3): 227–53.

————, eds. 1996. *Liberation ecologies.* London: Routledge.

Peluso, Nancy Lee. 1992. *Rich forests, poor people: Resource control and resistance in Java.* Berkeley: University of California Press.

Pinkerton, Evelyn W. 1994. Summary and conclusions. In *Folk management of the world's fisheries: Lessons for modern fisheries management,* edited by Christopher L. Dyer and James R. McGoodwin. Niwot: University Press of Colorado.

Pitcher, Tony J., Paul J. B. Hart, and Daniel Pauly, eds. 1998. *Reinventing fisheries management.* Dordrecht, The Netherlands: Kluwer Academic Publishers.

Pomeroy, Caroline. 1994. Obstacles to institutional development in the fishery of Lake Chapala, Mexico. In *Folk management in the world's fisheries: Lessons for modern fisheries management,* edited by Christopher L. Dyer and James R. McGoodwin. Niwot: University Press of Colorado.

Rappaport, Roy A. 1968. *Pigs for the ancestors.* New Haven, Conn.: Yale University Press.

————. 1990. Ecosystems, populations and people. In *The ecosystem approach in anthropology: From concept to practice,* edited by Emilio F. Moran. Ann Arbor: University of Michigan Press.

Rindfuss, Ronald R., and Paul C. Stern. 1998. Linking remote sensing and social science: The need and the challenge. In *People and pixels: Linking remote sensing and social science,* edited by Diana Liverman, Emilio F. Moran, Ronald R. Rindfuss, and Paul C. Stern. Washington, D.C.: National Academy Press.

Roseberry, William. 1988. Political economy. *Annual Review of Anthropology* 17: 161–85.

Schmink, Marianne, and Charles H. Wood. 1987. The "political ecology" of Amazonia. In *Lands at risk in the Third World: Local-level perspectives,* edited by P. D. Little and M. M. Horowitz. Boulder, Colo.: Westview Press.

Schroeder, Richard A. 1993. Shady practice: Gender and the political ecology of resource stabilization in Gambian Garden/Orchards. *Economic Geography* 69 (4): 349–65.

Sillitoe, Paul. 1998. The development of indigenous knowledge: A new applied anthropology. *Current Anthropology* 39 (2): 223–52.

Smith, M. Estellie. 1990. Chaos in fisheries management. *Maritime Anthropological Studies* 3 (2): 1–13.

Steele, D. H., Jr., R. Andersen, and J. M. Green. 1992. The managed commercial annihilation of northern cod. *Newfoundland Studies* 8 (1): 34–68.

Steinberg, Ted. 2000. *Acts of God: The unnatural history of natural disaster in America.* New York: Oxford University Press.

Steward, Julian H. 1938. *Basin-plateau Aboriginal sociopolitical groups.* Washington, D.C.: Smithsonian Institution.

————. 1955. *Theory of culture change: The methodology of multilinear evolution.* Urbana: University of Illinois Press.

Steward, Julian H., Robert A. Manners, Eric R. Wolf, Elena Padilla Seda, Sidney W. Mintz, and Raymond L. Scheele. 1956. *The people of Puerto Rico: A study in social anthropology.* Urbana: University of Illinois Press.

Stonich, Susan C. 1995. Development, rural impoverishment, and environmental destruction in Honduras. In *The social causes of environmental destruction in Latin America*, edited by Michael Painter and William H. Durham. Ann Arbor: University of Michigan Press.

Tsing, Anna. 2001. Nature in the making. In *New directions in anthropology and environment: Intersections*, edited by Carole L. Crumley. Walnut Creek, Calif.: AltaMira Press.

United Church of Christ. 1987. *Toxic wastes and race in the United States.* New York: United Church of Christ.

U.S. Commission on Civil Rights. 2003. Not in my backyard: Executive Order 12,898 and Title VI as tools for achieving environmental justice. Draft report for commissioners' review, September 4, 2003. Washington, D.C.: Office of the General Counsel, U.S. Commission on Civil Rights.

van Willigen, John. 2002. *Applied anthropology: An introduction.* 3rd ed. Westport, Conn.: Bergin and Garvey.

Vayda, Andrew P. 1983. Progressive contextualization: Methods for research in human ecology. *Human Ecology* 11 (3): 265–81.

Vayda, Andrew P., and Bonnie J. McCay. 1975. New directions in ecology and ecological anthropology. *Annual Review of Anthropology* 4: 293–306.

Vayda, Andrew P., and Bradley B. Walters. 1999. Against political ecology. *Human Ecology* 27 (1): 167–79.

Vayda, Andrew P., and Roy A. Rappaport. 1968. Ecology: Cultural and non-cultural. In *Introduction to cultural anthropology: Essays in the scope and methods of the science of man*, edited by J. A. Clifton. Boston: Houghton Mifflin.

Ward, William, and Priscilla Weeks. 1994. Resource managers and resource users: Field biologists and stewardship. In *Folk management of the world's fisheries: Lessons for modern fisheries management*, edited by Christopher L. Dyer and James R. McGoodwin. Niwot: University Press of Colorado.

Watts, Michael. n.d. For political ecology. Unpublished manuscript.

Wilson, James A., John French, Peter Kleban, Susan R. McKay, and Ralph Townsend. 1991. Chaotic dynamics in a multiple species fishery: A model of community predation. *Ecological Modelling* 58: 303–22.

Wolf, Eric R. 1972. Ownership and political ecology. *Anthropological Quarterly* 45 (3): 201–205.

———. 2001. Remarks on *The people of Puerto Rico.* In *Pathways of power: Building an anthropology of the modern world.* Berkeley: University of California Press. Reprinted from 1978.

Young, John A. 2001. Assessing cooperation and change: The SfAA and the EPA. *Practicing Anthropology* 23 (3): 47–49.

Zimmerer, Karl S. 1991. Wetland production and smallholder persistence: Agricultural change in a highland Peruvian region. *Annals of the Association of American Geographers* 81 (3): 443–63.

5 Applied Anthropology and Health and Medicine

Linda M. Whiteford and Linda A. Bennett

Introduction

Would you like to reduce the spread of HIV/AIDS? Help improve communication between practitioners and their patients? Unravel the complexities of alcohol or drug abuse? Assist local communities in fighting a cholera epidemic? These are all things that applied medical anthropologists do. Applied medical anthropologists do many more things as well: they teach in medical schools and in departments of anthropology, consult with international health organizations, and work with local governments and nongovernmental organizations. In this chapter, we will share some of the excitement about applied medical anthropology that we experience and describe its historical roots and contemporary applications.

What is applied medical anthropology, and where does it fit in the field of anthropology as a whole? Medical anthropology is a relatively recent major addition to the field of anthropology, gaining momentum in the United States in the 1960s and 1970s, with critical pioneering studies a decade earlier. Some, however, trace the conceptual roots of applied medical anthropology to British colonial experiences and the use of social observers in India, Africa, and Melanesia. This chapter tells a story of the early development of the field, illustrates some of its current applications, and imagines some future directions its practitioners might take. Case studies from the authors' experiences are used to exemplify major concepts and applications of applied medical anthropology to the domains of health and medicine.

Medical anthropologists are often trained in the four-field approach of anthropology, comprised of knowledge from cultural, biological, linguistic, and archaeological studies. This provides medical anthropology with unusual breadth and depth, allowing medical anthropologists to build on findings from forensic biology, ethnopaleontology, historical reconstructions of disease, and the linguistic and cultural patterns employed in the social construction and understanding of disease.

In general, medical anthropology seeks to understand the interplay between culture and biology, particularly as that interplay is expressed in health and illness and in their associated belief and practice systems. By system we mean the conceptual framework that links variables together following particular and specific rules. As Joralemon notes (1999, 13), medical anthropology is not unique in attempting to understand the interplay between culture/biology and humans/disease. However, it can be differentiated from the other medical social sciences by two factors: first, by its wider geographic range and time spread because it builds on archaeological and paleontological research, and, second, by its explicit focus on the cultural and biological determinants of disease. We can think about the ways in which cultural rules about disease recognition and treatment intersect with germ pathology of disease; that intersection is what medical anthropologists refer to as the biocultural synthesis.

The importance of conceptualizing and analyzing this biocultural synthesis had led some medical anthropologists to acquire special training. While they are being trained in anthropology, often specializing in either sociocultural or biological anthropology, they often acquire additional expertise in allied fields, such as public health, nutrition, counseling, nursing, or medicine. Some graduate programs in anthropology offer specialized courses in medical as well as applied anthropology. Others now even offer students the chance to acquire two degrees simultaneously: one in applied anthropology, the other in public health. This dual training, combined with an in-depth education in anthropology, makes medical anthropology an immensely varied field, with practitioners studying such subjects as prenatal testing, genetic counseling, immigration laws and health policy, aging in a cross-cultural perspective, and even the forensic analyses of ethnic cleansing.

For this chapter, we conceptualize health as a state of being, an equilibrium of sorts in which one's physiological, emotional, and mental functions work in harmony. We also think of medicine as a cultural system of knowledge and practice designed to promote and maintain that harmony. Using these definitions of health and medicine as complex, interrelated, and constructed systems, we can see how necessary it is to employ what is referred to as a biocultural perspective or synthesis in medical anthropology. A biocultural perspective is one that integrates knowledge of biological systems with knowledge of cultural systems. That perspective acknowledges the co-primacy and power of both biology and culture and recognizes that their interplay forms an integral part of biocultural analysis.

Current anthropological interests in health and medicine continue a history of analysis of the complex interactions of physical/ideational and cultural/biological systems, which has become known as medical anthropology. As if that were not complicated enough, most medical anthropologists are also applied anthropologists. Some might argue, as we do, that *all* medical anthropology is applied anthropology. That is, all research in medical anthropology has direct or indirect applications to human health and medicine.

Medical anthropologists now teach and conduct research in medical schools, in schools of nursing and public health, and in more traditional settings such as anthropology departments. They also work in state departments of health and national health agencies such as the Centers for Disease Control and Prevention (CDC), for international health agencies like the World Health Organization (WHO) and the U.S. Agency for International Development (USAID), and for nongovernmental organizations (NGOs) such as the Red Cross, to name a few. It is clear that anthropologists make contributions in numerous arenas in an effort to better our understanding of health and medicine. Knowledge that is generated by medical anthropologists, be they teachers, researchers, consultants, or practitioners, has applied implications and often results in changes in policies, programs, or practices. That is why we think that all medical anthropology is applied, whether in universities, international agencies, or local consulting.

Applied medical anthropologists come from a variety of theoretical, epistemological, and methodological orientations. That is, although they all may be interested in some aspect of the dynamic interplay between cultural beliefs, practices, and physical expressions, they approach the design of their research or analysis from a number of distinct bases. In this chapter we will discuss some of these perspectives. Regardless of approach, whether political/economic, interpretive, ecological, critical, or hermeneutic, applied medical anthropologists tend to share a commitment to the holistic perspective of anthropology, that is, a perspective that takes into account the larger nonbiological context. Such an approach takes into account multiple relevant factors rather than narrowing in on a single aspect. In medical anthropology, we draw heavily upon the biological and cultural facets of the human experience of health and illness. An ability to consider the cultural context in which actions occur and a capacity to bridge what is too often thought of as a conceptual chasm between culture and biology make the applications of a medical anthropology perspective of great utility not only in anthropology but also in allied fields such as medicine, social work, nursing, addictions research, and public health policy and practice.

Historical Overview and Current Theoretical Approaches

In all cultures, humans create systems of thinking and behavior to protect themselves from future possibilities of becoming sick, having bad luck, and suffering ill fortune. All people have beliefs and practices designed either to keep them healthy or to make them healthy if they fall ill. Have you ever taken vitamin C when you thought you were getting sick? Have you ever had a good luck charm, worn a lucky shirt, or saved a four-leaf clover? People in other cultures do similar things. In all societies people develop cultural systems designed to maintain health or restore individuals to healthy states. These cultural systems of beliefs and practices vary widely, and they may include patterns of dietary constraints, behavioral admonitions, recourse to spiritual or specialist guidance, and self-diagnosis and treatment. Going to a doctor, a midwife, a mental health counselor, a spiritualist, or a pastor are examples of relying upon specialists to help maintain or return to health. Neighbors, mothers, sisters, grandmothers, and other friends and family members also form part of the system of information and communication we use.

In the early part of the twentieth century, European colonial expansion into the Pacific islands, India, and Africa brought colonial administrators into contact with cultures radically different from their own. The Dutch, French, and British governments found themselves trying to control people whose cultural beliefs and practices were unintelligible to them. They turned to people they called social observers, whose job it was to observe and understand local rules, regulations, and cultures. In turn, these social observers were to help the colonial administrators understand and rule the colonies. Some of the social observers were members of the foreign office; others were physicians or educators; and many became what today we would call anthropologists. Anthropologists and social observers like E. E. Evans-Pritchard and W. H. R. Rivers were introduced firsthand to non-Western cultures in places like Melanesia, the Nuer, and the Azande through their government's activities in those areas. They became intrigued by how social relations and cosmological beliefs were tightly intertwined. They learned how people defined who was a member of their family and how those kin relations were shaped not by biology but by cosmology (religious beliefs). They noticed and described how systems of religion and social organization reflected and supported those kinship systems of beliefs and practices.

One result of the colonial expansion was the development of a rich body of literature describing beliefs and practices of non-Western peoples. Some of those early social observers, like Evans-Pritchard and Rivers, sought to conceptually link their analyses of non-Western systems of beliefs and practices used in magic and religion to those Western practices used to try to keep people safe and in good health. Magic, religion, and medicine, they saw, were all systems of thought based on assumptions with sometimes limited physical evidence. Rivers, who was a physician as well a social observer, found his experience with Melanesian practices to be directly applicable to the situation of the shell-shocked British soldiers. As a result of his field observations, he challenged the accepted wisdom of the time in Britain about how to "treat" soldiers thought to be suffering from shell shock.

The accepted medical practice during World War I (and in previous wars) was to treat soldiers who suffered from unseen or psychological wounds by forcing them back into the field of war immediately or by labeling them as cowards. Soldiers were not encouraged to speak about what they saw or their fears. Rivers, however, believed that their minds needed healing and that the wounded men were not necessarily cowards trying to escape the front lines. His decision to give soldiers time to recover from what they had seen and experienced and a chance to speak about the experience was almost prescient of what has come to be called post-traumatic stress disorder (PTSD) some 80 years later.

For many, medical anthropology is traced to a much later start—in the 1950s and 1960s—with two seminal books: Benjamin Paul's edited collection, *Health, Culture, and Community: Case Studies of Public Reaction to Health Programs* (1955) and Rene Dubos's *Man Adapting* (1965). Paul's book is a classic in both applied and medical anthropology. He presented a cultural "systems model" that embedded responses to public health medicine within the contrasting set of traditions and expectations of the clients' culture and community. His case studies are exemplars of cultural systems in conflict. The chapters are drawn from Paul's consulting work at Many Farms, Arizona, where the U.S. Public Health Service provided clinical health care to the Navajos. The clinic was new and well staffed, and the Public Heath Service was particularly concerned when few patients attended. Diabetes, tuberculosis, alcoholism, and many other illnesses associated with poverty and isolation were common on the reservations, yet few people attended the clinic. Paul and several other anthropologists were asked to observe the clinic and help the Public Health Service administrators understand why the clinic was so underutilized.

The anthropologists found that a series of barriers existed. Cultural differences in expected behaviors and anticipated outcomes, in combination with contrasting perceptions of modesty, manners, and time, created an almost insurmountable gulf between the practitioners and the clients they were to serve. The cultural expectations of the public health practitioners were based on their training with non-Navajo groups, and this led the physicians and nurses to expect their patients to come to the clinic at the appointed time, to look the public health official in the eye, and to declare a set of physical medical symptoms. The cultural expectations of the Navajos, on the other hand, were based on religious cycles related to weather, crops, and seasons in which time was fluid and based on complex rituals rather than on clocks and months. Fixed time appointments were not part of their lives. In addition, cultural norms of modesty prevented many Navajos from making direct eye contact and prescribed an unspoken set of rules concerning which relatives and nonrelatives could be spoken to. Navajo beliefs about illness causation were often at odds with those held by the public health doctors and nurses. The lack of shared understanding about personal presentation, time, who could be spoken to, and even whose names could be spoken caused serious communication problems. These problems were, in part, resolved when the anthropologists helped the clinic staff see that the problems stemmed from cultural differences rather than a lack of need or a lack of respect. Understanding differences about when and how things should be done, what could make one sick, the range of ways to get better, and even how to talk about these things made it possible to design policies and practices that bridged the two cultural systems.

Paul's book was seminal for the development of the field because it clearly articulated the need to contextualize medical care as a cultural system that may or may not fit with other cultural systems. Until that time, little attention had been paid to the cultural biases of both practitioners and patients or to the fact that those biases were rooted in cultural systems. The Many Farms experience is classic because the models were so distinctive: the public health service practitioners were trained to emphasize efficiency, science, confidence, punctuality, and individuality, whereas the Navajo clients' model of the world emphasized humility, modesty, respect, spirituality, and community. In retrospect, we can see that a clash between these models of the world is avoidable, and now more attention is paid to patient-practitioner interactions, their communication patterns, and their cultural systems of belief and practice.

Whereas Ben Paul's model laid the groundwork for a systems approach to applied medical anthropology in the United States, Rene Dubos's contribution to the evolving specialization was his book *Man Adapting* (1965). Along with Dubos's earlier book *The Mirage of Health* (1959), it provided the basis for articulating the biocultural and ecological perspectives. Dubos suggested that, although there may be negative aspects to human adaptability, it was that very ability to be adaptive that allowed humans to survive in divergent and constantly changing environments. In the 1960s and 1970s, the key terms denoting the biocultural perspective were adaptation and ecological and featured evolutionary themes (Janzen 2001, 32). Adaptation, according to McElroy and Townsend, involved "changes, modifications, and variations enabling a person or group to survive in a given environment" (2004, 14). They went on to note that humans "adapt through a variety of biological mechanisms and behavioral strategies" (14). With an ecological perspective, the focus is on the interrelationships between the various components seen to constitute an ecosystem: populations and their environment (37). This perspective continues to capture the attention of medical anthropologists by providing a useful and practical method to connect humans to their environment through both biology and behavior.

Charles Leslie also shaped the nascent field of medical anthropology in significant ways. Leslie's writings from 1960 to 2000 took the field to new horizons. Although his contributions are many, his book from 1976, *Asian Medical Systems: A Comparative Study*, was seminal because it introduced many medical anthropology students to the tremendous variation in medical systems throughout Asia and the rest of the world.

Contemporary Applied Medical Anthropology

Contemporary applied medical anthropologists look at how people in different societies, as well as in their own, ritualize universal life stages: birth and death, childhood, and old age. Such life stages provide researchers a common biological experience that can be examined using the biocultural perspective. Birth, for instance, occurs biologically the same way among all humans but with immense variation in practice across cultures. The biology of birth does not vary. Babies are born in a limited number of ways: vaginally or by caesarian section (surgery). However, the cultural range of birth practices is exceptional. Some societies, the United States, for instance, encourage women to give birth in sterile, medically controlled rooms with men or women in gloves, masks, and gowns. However, among the Bariba of Benin, women are expected to give birth alone, often away from their homes and the prying eyes of family or friends (Sargent 1982). Still other societies welcome the presence of family members—children, fathers, mothers, and sisters—while the woman labors and gives birth. Why is there such cultural variation on a universal biological process? According to those who have studied the social context of the biocultural synthesis of birth, birthing rituals reflect the norms and needs of the society of which they are a part.

Brigitte Jordan's (1978, 1997) studies of women in four different cultures showed how the rules about who attends the birth and even the physical position of the laboring woman—whether she sits in a birthing chair, squats back on her heels on the floor, or lies on her back with her legs strapped onto a horizontal table—all depend on the cultural beliefs about life and death, gender relations, power and authority, and religion. Jordan's work opened up a whole area of research in applied medical anthropology and, equally importantly, provided women, their families, and their medical assistants with knowledge of alternative ways to situate the birth: with a midwife, at home, in a birthing room at a medical facility, with family or without them. For many women, this research transformed the birth experience into a more positive and emotionally significant moment in their lives.

Gender—another universal cultural category—also has provided an important focus for medical anthropology. Just as Jordan and others researched how birth is culturally situated, questions of how biocultural categories like gender shape medical experiences have stimulated anthropologists to ask why women are treated differently than men in, for instance, clinical settings in the United States. In the 1980s and 1990s, medical anthropologists sought to understand how the cultural biases toward a group become replicated in their medical treatments (Sargent and Brettell 1996; Rapp 1989, 2001; Ginsberg 1989). Others explored the consequences of cultural biases on the medical treatment of various ethnic and socioeconomic groups. Do African Americans receive the same quality of care in the United States as non-African Americans? Do the poor in Britain receive the same type of medical attention as the rich? Do immigrants in France receive the same quality of care as the native-born French? These are all examples of the kinds of issues that capture the attention of medical anthropologists as they apply their anthropological training in cultural analysis to medical systems.

Investigating the cultural underpinnings of beliefs and practices associated with various universal life stages provides important information that helps us understand both cultural variation and the reasons for the continuation of such cultural practices. The application of the results of medical anthropological studies such as those of Jordan or Sargent may be part of the original research design, or it may follow once the research has found a public audience.

The emergence and reemergence of communicable diseases is another area of contemporary research among applied medical anthropologists. The reemergence of dengue fever, the geographic spread of malaria, and the emergence of new diseases such as HIV/AIDS and SARS require the stereoscopic and biocultural approach that has become the hallmark of applied medical anthropology. Anthropologists have made significant contributions to understanding the sociocultural basis of risky behaviors implicated in the spread of communicable diseases (Page and Trotter 1999). For instance, in an effort to reduce the spread of HIV/AIDS, researchers at the Hispanic Health Council in Hartford, Connecticut, studied the cultural rules that shaped patterns of HIV/AIDS transmission. They interviewed men and women who used sex for income or as barter. They interviewed homeless women and men, sex workers, and others to learn if there were alternatives to sex exchange or if the use of condoms was an option in reducing transmission (Romero-Daza, Weeks, and Singer 2003). Although gender and ethnicity were certainly categories considered in the research, the political variables that controlled access to resources, jobs options, and education were considered primary in their analysis.

Theoretical Approaches

The example from the Hispanic Health Council demonstrates what is known in medical anthropology as a critical medical perspective. This approach focuses on class structure and access to resources and modes of production (Singer 1992; Baer 1989). It brings together many of the concerns held by those studying health and medicine by looking at economic patterns and their distribution as related to socially constructed categories such as gender, class, and ethnicity. That is, the economic underpinnings of cultural systems and how they affect health and health care became an explicit focus of research (Singer et al. 1998; Morsy 1996; Whiteford 1995). The political economy of health (Morsy 1996), or critical medical anthropology of health (Singer and Baer 1995), brings a more Marxist and political orientation to framing the research question. This framework pays explicit attention to differences in socioeconomic levels as they affect peoples' access to health care and economic resources. It focuses on the unequal distribution of wealth and power as they affect health outcomes.

This is one of the several perspectives currently employed in the analysis of health and medicine. In addition to the critical medical perspective, the three other most frequently encountered are the ecological/evolutionary approach, the interpretive approach to health, and the clinically applied approach. In addition, consensus and cultural modeling is sometimes considered a fifth approach. Each is associated with a central set of concepts that shape the research design, data analysis, and interpretation of findings.

The ecological/evolutionary approach emphasizes the biocultural synthesis between biological and environmental conditions (McElroy 1990; McElroy and Townsend 1989, 1996; Leatherman, Goodman, and Thomas 1993), employing the concept of adaptation as a key tool for analyzing the interactions. In many ways, this approach is a direct descendent of the writings of Dubos and others in the early history of the subdiscipline. In contemporary medical anthropology, some biocultural research focuses on microevolutionary processes within the context of particular and changing environments. Studies of malaria and sickle cell anemia are good examples of the gains from such an approach (Frisancho 1981).

The interpretive approach, sometimes referred to as the constructivist approach, takes as key ideas that experiences of health and illness are culturally constructed and their interpretation may include the experiences of the sufferers themselves. Those experiences can only be understood by recourse to the cultural assumptions from which they emerge (Scheper-Hughes and Lock 1987; Kleinman, Das, and Lock 1997).

Any one of these approaches may be utilized in applied and clinical settings. Some anthropologists place clinical medical anthropology in a category separate from applied anthropology, just as others conceptualize epidemiology as a separate theoretical perspective, distinct from applied anthropology. We see each as a cluster of techniques used in the application of medical anthropological theories and practice. Epidemiology (the study of the determinants and distribution of disease) comprises concepts and methods that can usefully be employed in conjunction with anthropological theories and applied to medicine and health. Although medical anthropology is strengthened by attending to epidemiological data, epidemiology without the encompassing cultural context is quite limited and often results in misleading conclusions. In order to truly understand disease within its behavioral, cultural, social, political, economic, and environmental milieus, it is essential to look beyond epidemiological data.

Cultural models and consensus theory is also used in medical anthropology to investigate the relationship between peoples' cognitive models and health statuses (Weller and Romney 1988). Cultural models are frameworks designed to represent how people think about something in particular, for instance high blood pressure, diabetes, or other health problems (Dressler 1996a, 1996b). Consensus theory is based on the assumption that if a certain level of agreement is achieved about the model of disease causation (a consensus), then the constructed model is an accurate reflection of the cultural beliefs of the group. In the cultural model approach, data are collected as responses to questions posed to cultural representatives, rather than exclusively based upon observations of behavior.

In all these approaches, a concern with ethics and ethical conduct is central, and thus, ethical issues have come into mainstream applied medical anthropology discussions. Federally mandated Institutional Review Boards (IRBs) began in the 1970s to review research proposals in an attempt to protect research subjects. Initially, IRBs were established to protect research subjects from possible untoward effects of clinical medical research; however, most universities now mandate that research proposals involving humans be approved by their institutional review board. Applied medical anthropologists using patient medical records, for instance, must demonstrate they have secured permission from both the medical institution and the patient. In addition, researchers must devise measures to ensure that patient confidentiality is protected. Research among people who are disabled, very young, elderly, or in some way considered to be members of vulnerable groups must be conducted in such a way that the subjects are protected.

Likewise, many activities of interest to applied medical anthropologists could put either the researcher or the subject in legal danger. Interviews, for instance, on barriers to medical care for immigrants are fraught with difficulties because of potential recriminations if the person being interviewed does not have the necessary legal status or could lose his or her rights to medical care. Researchers who observe illegal activities while studying homelessness must take steps to protect subjects involved as well as themselves.

Anthropologists in academia, as well as those practicing anthropology outside of its confines, are faced with difficult questions: Do universal ethical standards exist? Are all values situationally and culturally relative, or are there some absolute values? They question the ethics of selling human organs, of selling human knowledge, and even of selling, trading, or borrowing cultural traditions (Marshall and Daar 2000). Professional organizations such as the Society for Applied Anthropology (SfAA) and the American Anthropological Association (AAA) developed codes or guidelines for the ethical practice of anthropology, but infringement of these codes carries few professional consequences. Although these codes are designed to cover the practices of all anthropologists, some would argue that the research conducted by medical anthropologists might be more intrusive than other anthropological research because it often deals with biological materials or practices.

Anthropologists specializing in ethics, such as Patricia Marshall (Marshall and Daar 2000), ask whether, for instance, the international proliferation of human tissue "gifts" will change the way we conceptualize both gift and exchange if human organs are the commodity of use. Other themes in the field question the ethics of using people for research to enhance the knowledge of the discipline, and some seek ways to protect people from being used by anthropologists for career development. Codes of ethics, IRBs, and federal policy concerning the Protection of Human Subjects are all designed to reduce the endangerment of people being studied. Justice, equity, respect for diversity, autonomy of decisions, and a commitment to the leveling of the playing field for all participants are key ethical issues (Whiteford 2000).

How Is All This Applied?

This quick review of some of the history and trends in medical anthropology begs the question: How is this research applied? We know applied medical anthropologists are policymakers and advisors. We know them as administrators and practitioners. We know they work as consultants and advocates. In each of those roles, they apply principles and theories from anthropology to data generated using medical anthropological methods. And they are all engaged in the resolution of human social problems, such as improving access to medical care for the disenfranchised, alerting the public through careful research to the hidden inequities brought about by racial, ethnic, and gender prejudices, and reflecting critically on the unobserved status quo.

As we suggested at the beginning of this chapter, we see all medical anthropological research as having applied components; however, sometimes they need to be made more explicit. We began by identifying three seminal works, each embodying a concept that has become central to applied medical anthropology: Ben Paul's use of a systems model, Rene Dubos's development of the concept of the biocultural synthesis, and Charles Leslie's use of a comparative framework. Each of these concepts (although not necessarily simultaneously) provides a bridge between research and application. They allow research in medical anthropology to be applied in the development of health care policy, practice, and programs. Jordan's work (1978, 1997) helped transform birthing practices in the United States; it gave a rationale for birthing rooms in hospitals, increased the use of midwives, gave people permission to employ a variety of physical positions during labor and birth, and changed hospital policies to allow family members to be present during the birth.

Likewise, Paul Farmer's eloquent indictment of the use of blame and stereotyping to associate HIV/AIDS with a particular group of people contributed to a reevaluation of hospital admission policies (Farmer 1988, 1992, 1999). Medical anthropology was also applied to uncover policies that doubly disenfranchised drug-using pregnant women, by both putting them in jail immediately following the birth and separating them from their newborns. Medical anthropology research brought to light the unequal application of the maternal drug-screening policy and the harm being done to poor women and their babies (Whiteford and Vitucci 1997). Public concern later resulted in the policy being challenged and changed. Both Myra Bluebond-

Langer's (1978) and Jill Korbin's (1981) work with dying and chronically ill children, which demonstrated the need for the children to be included in medical decision making, changed hospital policies about children's rights and their roles in being able to make decisions about their care. Whether the topic is HIV/AIDS, children's mental health, spouse abuse, or community participation in medical care, the work of applied medical anthropologists is often used to make a difference. It does so by documenting patient and practitioner experiences; assessing systems of care; contextualizing medicine in its personal, political, and economic frameworks; and finding patterns where none were found before.

Policymakers (and their legislative aides) are not the only group that benefits from the application of medical anthropological research. Practitioners such as social workers, addiction counselors, nurses, and physicians use anthropologists to help them reach and treat their clientele more effectively. Anthropologists like Michael Agar (1973, 1980, 1996; Agar, Underwood, and Woolard 1981), Merrill Singer (1992, 1996, 1999, 2000), and Robert Trotter (Trotter, Bowen, and Potter 1995) and others have all found that their research on alcohol, heroin, and other addictions has been used by policymakers and practitioners alike. Some populations are particularly difficult for social service providers to reach and are often invisible to the public. For example, homeless people or domestic violence victims have been made visible through the work of medical anthropologists like Kim Hopper (1988, 1990, 1991) or Jay Sokolovsky (1993, 1997a, 1997b). By making these invisible groups visible, anthropologists help make programs and policies take them into account.

Applied medical anthropology shares a natural affinity with public health. The work of medical anthropologists is used in both public health classrooms and agencies. For instance, the work of Jeannine Coreil used cognitive or decision-making models and helped to design therapeutic interventions like self-help groups for filariasis sufferers in Haiti (2004). Holly Mathews conducted a decision analysis of social support mechanisms for women with breast cancer in the United States (1987, 1990, 1998). Some medical anthropology research is designed specifically to be used by policymakers. Carol Bryant's research on the U.S. federal Women, Infants, and Children (WIC) program (1993, 2001), for instance, used focus groups to gather women's perceptions of its uses and limitations. The research resulted in a revitalization of that program nationwide. Her work combined careful analysis of the policies, services, and practices in the WIC programs she studied, illuminated by the women's words and descriptions that were gathered during focus groups. Their voices captured and amplified the research findings generated by the analysis of programs and policies, resulting in real and measurable policy changes.

Areas of Current Interest

As we have emphasized, contemporary applied medical anthropologists continue the legacy of Ben Paul, Rene Dubos, and Charles Leslie by focusing on cultural systems, using a biocultural perspective, or employing comparative analysis in their research. Often medical anthropologists focus on the interplay of culture and biology on life stages; the effects of sociocultural categories like gender, race, and ethnicity on the distribution and treatment of disease; and factors accounting for the emergence and reemergence of infectious and contagious diseases such as malaria, dengue fever, cholera, tuberculosis, and HIV/AIDS.

The HIV/AIDS epidemic provides both an impetus and urgency for applied medical anthropologists to work toward prevention by understanding behavior within its political, economic, and medical contexts. The epidemic has made it clear that no magic vaccine is going to control its spread. Even if such a vaccine were available, the costs of providing it to all the people at risk would be prohibitive; therefore, other ways have to be found to control the disease. The key is to understand the beliefs that underlie the behaviors implicated in the spread of the disease (Feldman 1985, 1986, 1990a; Singer 1992, 1996; Trotter et al. 2000).

What Evans-Pritchard and Rivers noticed in the early 1900s is still true a century later. Behaviors are embedded in larger and more encompassing belief systems, and to understand the behaviors, we must study the larger cultural system. AIDS researchers found that behaviors associated with high risks of negative outcomes (i.e., unprotected sex or sharing needles increases the chance of spreading HIV/AIDS) are extremely difficult to change without understanding how those behaviors fit and—in some sense—provide positive outcomes within a larger set of options, alternatives, and risks (Feldman 1985, 1990b; Singer 1992, 1998; Trotter et al. 2000). Intervention policies that fail to recognize the larger cognitive rules of the intended population fail to reach the intended population.

Medical anthropology is also applied through program assessments and evaluations, program and policy monitoring, and policy development and advocacy. Partners in Health (PIH), an NGO organized by Paul Farmer and others, epitomizes how applied medical anthropology can be effectively used in advocacy research. Farmer, an anthropologist and physician, both practices medicine and applies anthropology by being on the ground with local people in clinics in Haiti, Peru, Russia, and Cuba. Simultaneously, PIH works to understand the larger global political and economic picture that shapes those local realities (Farmer 1999, 1992, 2004). The work by PIH and Farmer clearly and eloquently situates disease in the context of disparities and inequalities. Co-morbid diseases, such as HIV/AIDS and tuberculosis (TB), exist in conjunction with prejudice and poverty. Advocates like Farmer and PIH give life and leadership to the fight for justice and equity by applying medical anthropology on a global scale.

Infectious and contagious diseases like HIV/AIDS and TB attract the attention of applied medical anthropologists, as do diseases once thought to be controlled and almost eradicated. The spread of malaria and dengue fever continues to increase, both in the number of cases and also in its geographic range (Brown 1997, 1998; Whiteford 1997; Coreil 1997). Like HIV/AIDS, both malaria and dengue fever have no vaccine, and such prevention is unlikely to be developed. Unlike HIV/AIDS, malaria and dengue fever rarely result in death but, rather, they result in prolonged poor health and increased susceptibility to other diseases. The primary hope in controlling HIV/AIDS, malaria, dengue, and other infectious diseases lies in our ability to understand peoples' beliefs and practices that are implicated in the spread of these diseases.

Just as life stages, biocultural categories, and infectious and contagious diseases have drawn applied medical anthropologists' interest, chronic diseases like heart disease, hypertension (Dressler 1996a, 1996b; Dressler, Baliero, and Dos Santos 1997), and diabetes (Weller et al. 1993; Weller and Baer 2001) are all areas in which anthropologists and clinical researchers are currently working together. Dressler has been working for almost two decades with his Brazilian counterparts—a team that includes physicians and social scientists—to understand relationships among cultural models, lifestyles, hypertension, and heart disease. His work has furthered our understanding of the theory and methods behind consensus modeling and chronic disease research.

Alcohol and drug addiction continues to be a major area of applied medical research with many anthropologists actively engaged in understanding the cultural construction of addiction (Bennett and Ames 1985; Douglas 1990; Eber 1995; Heath 2000; MacAndrew and Edgerton 1969; Marshall 1979).

Case Study: The Disease Concept of Alcoholism

Medical anthropologists, in particular, have contributed to the debate on the disease concept of alcoholism. What exactly is meant by the disease concept of alcoholism or addiction more generally? When people attribute the etiology, development, or expression of alcoholism to biological factors, they are articulating this concept. Arthur Kleinman's work helps put this somewhat specific idea into a broader theoretical framework. When Kleinman published *Patients and Healers in the Context of Culture* in 1980, he articulated a theoretical dichotomy in medical anthropology between illness and disease within the overall phenomenon of sickness: "*Disease* refers to a malfunctioning of biological and/or psychological processes, while the term *illness* refers to the psychosocial experience and meaning of perceived disease" (1980, 72). Kleinman submitted this distinction as an ideal dichotomy, not necessarily as reality. He noted that professional practitioners, such as physicians, are more oriented toward viewing sickness as a disease, whereas nonprofessional practitioners tend to be more inclined toward the illness perspective. He observed that for chronic disorders, such as alcoholism, it can be particularly difficult to distinguish between illness and disease. As this case study demonstrates, one's orientation can be critical for constructing an understanding of the source, course, and treatment of alcoholism.

Noel Chrisman (1985) focused precisely on the question of whether alcoholism is an illness or a disease. He referred to the earlier writing of Horatio Fabrega Jr., who defined disease as "altered body states or processes that deviate from norms as established by Western biomedical science" (1972, 213). Similarly, Leon Eisenberg took the position that "patients suffer 'illnesses'; physicians diagnose and treat 'diseases'" (1977, 11). In considering alcoholism, Chrisman observed that "neither alcoholism as an illness nor as a disease is well defined" within the biomedical health culture (1985, 14). A long-standing debate revolves around issues such as the role of psychosocial versus genetic factors in the susceptibility of certain individuals to alcoholism. Chrisman noted that the psychosocial and biological complexity of alcoholism has made it very difficult to arrive at any consensus about the specific factors that "cause" alcoholism. He also observed that because there is no consensus about the disease/illness dichotomy of alcoholism, health practitioners diagnose and treat alcoholism in a variety of ways. In other words, they take particular approaches that are congruent with their worldview of alcoholism. These approaches include the moral, social, spiritual, and biological (1985, 15).

The moral-medical model of alcoholism has provoked lively and relevant discussion to which anthropologists and sociologists, in particular, have contributed. In addressing American beliefs about alcoholism, Genevieve Ames reviews the history of the moral-medical model (1985) that is particularly relevant to our understanding of the etiology, course, and treatment of alcoholism. Ames noted that in the disease concept, alcoholism is viewed as a progressive disease that can be divided into symptomatic phases. The primary distinction between being an alcoholic and a nonalcoholic is the stage when the drinker loses control of alcoholic beverage consumption. In contrast to the moral model prominent during the temperance and prohibition eras in the early twentieth century, in which drinkers were deemed responsible for their drinking and its consequences, the medical model evolved after World War II as medical professionals and alcohologists depicted alcoholism as a series of stepping stone experiences with alcoholic beverage consumption (Jellenik 1952, 1960). This shift in thinking about alcoholism still does not have full support across the United States, but alcoholism has become viewed less and less as a sign of moral weakness. This shift could be heralded as a positive development in the public mindset toward dealing effectively with alcoholism. Working clinically with alcoholics from a medical (or disease) perspective, for example, can relieve them from at least some of the blame of their addiction.

Or does it really work that way? From the perspective of American families living with an alcoholic parent, accountability for the alcoholism is complicated (Bennett 1995). This study asked how family members incorporated the concepts of illness versus disease and the moral versus medical model into their comprehension and explanation of alcoholism. Drawing on a subset of ten alcoholic families interviewed in a study of family cultural influences on the well-being of school age children, Bennett examined the interview transcripts for statements about accountability for alcoholism. These statements, as glimpses of worldviews, were organized into three domains: causes, forms, and consequences of alcoholism. Three other concepts are important to consider: shame, guilt, and blame. These are common emotional responses to "irresponsibility" around drinking and drinking-related behavior. Such emotional responses are more likely to emerge in families when the alcoholic and family members subscribe to a moral model of alcoholism rather than a medical model. At the other end of the spectrum, if the family endorses the medical model, the alcoholic and the family are much less likely to feel or express shame, guilt, or blame. However, if the alcoholic does not find a way to resolve the problem, such emotional reactions are more likely to emerge. All ten families studied evidenced all three of these emotions in their attempts to resolve the question of who or what was responsible for the alcoholism.

Beyond this generalization, though, there was wide variation among the families and family members about these emotions. With regard to the cause, or etiology, of alcoholism, no one interviewed suggested that its etiology was biological or genetic. Instead, these were the five most often noted precipitating influences: (1) family pressure to drink or not drink; (2) traumatic life events; (3) occupational situation; (4) emotional problems in the family; and (5) loving alcohol. This final influence is the one that is most likely to connect with the disease/biological/genetic causation. Among all families interviewed, however, "I loved the stuff from the start" was a rare response. One particular impetus to drink came from the wider political-social context: the Vietnam War. Wartime experiences repeatedly came to the fore in discussions with one couple, who identified this as the time when the husband began drinking with a vengeance: "Vietnam changes the life of everyone who goes through it. I don't suppose I am the same person I was before I went over. It made indelible changes in my psyche. A lot of drunks came back from Vietnam" (author's fieldnotes, n.d.)

Contrary to the opinion that alcoholics and their families spend much of their lives in denial about alcoholism, it is more accurate to see them as using various cognitive and behavioral strategies to grapple with the problem and resolve it. Understanding this is important for designing effective intervention strategies for families with alcoholism. Relating the emic perspectives of these husbands and wives in trying to account for the cause of alcoholism, Bennett concluded that they clearly draw upon an illness rather than a disease model. They tend to view alcoholism neither as a moral nor as a medical phenomenon in terms of its etiology. However, in attempting to find a *solution* to the problem, they do expect the alcoholic, with the help of others, to resolve the problem. At this point, the "sickness" of alcoholism is still regarded in Kleinman's terms as an illness, but if no solution is reached, the family begins to regard alcoholism and the alcoholic in moral terms.

The following quote shows the complexity of one wife's understanding of her husband's lifelong extremely heavy drinking and how she tries to encompass the disease concept within her understanding:

> With drinking, you get to the point of saturation where you can't do anything about it, and it's affecting your life so much you try to push it away. There is only so much you can take, and then you don't want any more part of it. I've known for a few years that alcoholism is a disease, but the thing is how long can you live with a disease and go along as if it's all right. There is a point you get to and then, the hell with it, I've had enough and want no part of it because *the disease is getting to you then*. (Bennett 1995, 17)

This woman's struggle to comprehend alcoholism demonstrates the importance of taking a biocultural perspective in research on addictions.

In addition to studying topics like birth and reproduction, chronic and contagious diseases, and alcohol and drug abuse, two others areas stand out as examples of applied medical research: ethnomedicine and health systems analysis. Finerman and Sackett (2003) demonstrated, for example, how ethnomedicine and traditional curing remain embedded in contemporary family health in the Ecuadorian Andes. Their most recent study revealed that most plants grown in Saraguro home gardens are intended for medicinal application and that the selection of healing herbs cultivated in gardens is tailored to suit the unique health needs of the household. Kedia and van Willigen (2001) provided an example of the place of the health system within the broader sociopolitical system of India. Specifically, they examined the impact of forced population displacement (due to building hydroelectric dams) on the mental health of older people living in Northern India.

Methods Used by Applied Medical Anthropologists in Studying Health and Medicine

Applied medical anthropologists have found a number of ways to study health and medicine, relying on the traditional anthropological toolkit of techniques employed in ethnographic studies, such as participant observation, surveys, and oral histories (Angrosino 1987, 1989, 2002; LeCompte and Schensul 1999a, 1999b; LeCompte et al. 1999). But they have also developed new methodologies like rapid appraisal (RAP) (Scrimshaw and Hurtado 1987), community elicitation, and network models (Trotter et al. 2000). RAPs were designed to be used in community health appraisals, and they require shorter periods of fieldwork. RAPs often involve both community members and people from outside of the community to design questions that elicit responses about illness categories and locally specific names. This is a critical step in being able to discuss health and illness beliefs and practices using locally appropriate words. The use of local terminology allows people to speak comfortably and allows researchers to learn names of illnesses, diagnoses, and treatment modes. Rapid research techniques have been found to be effective ways to collect basic information for many applications to medical anthropology, including designing health care programs, especially in primary health areas (Pelto and Pelto 1996). Scrimshaw and Hurtado (1987) developed the *Rapid Assessment Procedures* manual to be used in evaluating health care programs and nutrition programs. By using the RAP approach, they found that "[a] great deal of practical, diagnostic, and applied work can be accomplished in a shorter time by using a simple approach" (1987, 1).

Applied medical anthropologists train in the theories and methods of traditional anthropology but then superimpose or integrate methods derived from other disciplines to expand their toolkits. Epidemiology, which we defined earlier as the study of the determinants and distribution of disease, provides population-based data on who is getting sick, what groups of people are sick, and locations where people got sick, and who is getting well. Although there are valuable discussions about the application of epidemiological techniques to anthropology research (McCombie 1990), some applied medical anthropologists (Janes, Stall, and Gifford 1986; Trostle 1986; Trostle and Sommerfeld 1996; Yacoob and Whiteford 1995) appear to have found them useful. They used epidemiology to provide a measurable set of indicators from data gathered on a large scale, with specific ranges of time and space, within which to contextualize ethnographic analysis.

Focus group research also has become a popular and useful technique for gathering information about identified themes, and at least one university provides a biannual conference on focus group research and application. Earlier we mentioned Carol Bryant's work using focus groups to gather colloquial terms and ideas about particular topics, which enabled her to use that initial set of interactions to shape further research. Sometimes focus groups are used to teach the researcher what the target population thinks about a product or a program. Once the focus groups are completed, that data can be used to shape questionnaires or other research instruments to gather larger numbers of responses.

Oral history techniques, although not unique to applied medical anthropology, have been used effectively to understand the experience of being disabled (Frank 1980, 2000), the kinds of personal interactions people have with health care professionals (M. H. Becker 1974) and living with stigmatized conditions such as infertility (G. Becker 1990; Sandelowski 1993). An oral history might entail soliciting information about a person's personal experience and perspectives on a specific health issue. By collecting oral histories from different people with varying viewpoints about a common health problem, we reach a better understanding of complex health problems.

The Integration of Theory, Concepts, and Methods

Applied medical anthropologists have contributed to our understanding of health and medicine in a variety of ways: by contributing to interdisciplinary, collaborative investigations of health problems, by applying theoretical models from anthropology to medical systems, and by incorporating ethnographic and other anthropological methods to global problems. The biocultural perspective, in particular, offers significant advances over less inclusive analyses of health. The following case study is an example of how applied medical anthropological research uses the concepts, research methods, and theories to work with a community to design an appropriate and long-lasting intervention.

Case Study: Cholera Epidemic in Ecuador

This case study exemplifies how interdisciplinary and collaborative research using traditional anthropological field methods, along with focus groups and epidemiological record reviews, provided critical and practical insights into understanding the transmission of cholera in two rural Andean states during the 1990s cholera epidemic in South America.

In March 1991, the El Tor cholera pandemic hit Ecuador. By the time it began to subside 24 months later, more that 85,000 cases of cholera had been identified, almost 1,000 people had died, and many more cases had gone undiagnosed. Cholera is caused by water-borne bacteria, making communities with unreliable or insecure water supplies the most vulnerable to and at risk for the disease. Indeed, epidemiological data showed that fully 80 percent of the cases in Ecuador came from a corner of the country with the poorest and most marginalized citizens. Within months of the onset of the epidemic, the Ecuadorian Ministry of Health (MOH), along with the Pan American Health Organization (PAHO), WHO, and other international governmental and nongovernmental aid organizations, had successfully reduced the transmission, particularly in urban areas, through health education campaigns and improved access to water and sanitary facilities.

In the rural areas mostly populated by indigenous groups, the epidemic continued unabated. In an attempt to break the chain of transmission in the rural areas, the MOH requested aid from a variety of international aid donors; one was USAID, which contracted with the Environmental Health Project (EHP) to undertake an in-depth investigation of cholera-related behaviors in the communities at greatest risk of contracting and continuing the spread of the disease. An international, interdisciplinary team, which included an applied medical anthropologist, a physician/epidemiologist, and a community educator, was brought to the project. The aim of the project was the development and implementation of what came to be named the Community Participatory Intervention (CPI) model, based on the following assumptions: (1) Members of the community needed to lead the community in its fight against the disease—the fight had to be a grassroots movement; (2) simultaneously, local concepts of risk, disease and health, as well as local beliefs and behaviors had to be elicited; (3) biological information about the disease vectors and environment needed to be shared; and finally, (4) a culturally appropriate, locally designed, and regionally sustainable intervention had to be agreed upon.

The research and implementation took place over an 18-month period in four rural communities in the two Andean states with the highest cholera rates. Using an ecological framework, the project gathered information about water resources, land tenure patterns, community organization, health statistics, and the regional public health system. Ethnographic techniques were used to train local participants to elicit community terms and categories related to health beliefs and behaviors implicated in oral and fecal transmissions. Participatory teams were recruited from local communities; regional multidisciplinary teams were brought together from regional health and educational agencies. The MOH coordinated the activities.

Within a year of the implementation of the CPI model, the number of new cholera cases in the research sites dropped drastically (from 32,430 cases in 1992 to only 6,883 cases in 1993). And the reductions were sustained. Equally important, the rates of other water-borne diseases dropped significantly and the reduction was sustained. Two years (and even ten years) later, some of the participants trained in the CPI model were still local health advocates, and the model implementation sites demonstrated lower water-borne infection rates than did neighboring communities and states where the CPI model was not implemented. Not only did water-borne infectious disease rates drop, but local leadership was also developed as part of the CPI model.

Why did the CPI model work? It worked because the participating communities were anxious for relief from the visible and often deadly threat of cholera. When the project began, almost every household in the study communities had lost someone, and everyone knew someone who had died from cholera; people were very motivated. But the model also actively validated local knowledge and local understandings of the threats—from cholera as well as from other sources—that people perceived in their surroundings. This validation of local beliefs, in conjunction with the incorporation of new information about disease vectors, provided local inhabitants with means to combat cholera.

The model worked because, although the focus was on cholera, it was not an exclusive focus. Other foci were brought to light by ethnographic interviews and team members' experiences. It worked because it followed community-based research with community-determined actions and interventions. Creative health education and leadership training were not the only means used to combat cholera. The locally designed intervention combined community leadership, new information about disease transmission, and a commitment from the community to participate. New, closed water containers kept hands from dipping into them. The containers also had a spigot that could be easily cleaned. Locally available chlorine was used to disinfect water. Each of these factors shaped the outcome, and, with this combination, the project succeeded. Communities beyond the original research site became so excited about the water containers and the participatory training that they also asked for the CPI process to be conducted in their community. Participants from the original intervention communities created a small group to train other communities, thereby spreading the intervention.

The CPI model succeeded on many levels. It was grounded in the local community but had support from regional, state, and national offices of the government. It trained local people in things they were interested in and concerned about. And the results were transferable to other communities, were locally sustainable, and resulted in national policy changes. As one Ecuadorian CPI team member noted, "People have been changed by participating in the project; before they were quiet, compliant, and unquestioning. Now they express their opinions, question others and feel they are right."

Future Directions

The worldwide HIV/AIDS pandemic has brought into sharp focus the need for social science researchers to work closely with medical researchers and forces us all to look at new ways to prevent the spread of disease and to understand the underlying causes, not only the biological basis for disease but also the cultural conditions that enhance and accelerate it. HIV/AIDS is emblematic of but one of the consequences of unequal distribution of wealth and access to resources throughout the world.

Applied medical anthropologists have significant contributions to make in our understanding of disease prevention and to the reform of health care systems. Following the trajectory begun by Ben Paul and others, the systems approach directs medical anthropologists to identify the various pieces of a system and how they fit together and to consider how change in one element affects the entire system. In health care reform, this view is particularly critical because of the various and often competing perspectives, such as those of the clients, practitioners, and insurers—whether they are private or public. Governments throughout the world are struggling to provide health care in a privatizing world where not all voices are heard equally. Anthropologists have a role to play in providing data and analysis of these different system changes and their consequences.

The ability to conceptually bridge culture and biology (the biocultural synthesis) and its evolutionary basis are critical components of applied medical anthropology. Just as Dubos perhaps hoped, the vigorous subdiscipline continues in new and innovative directions largely because of its appreciation for how culture and biology are inexorably intertwined. Addictions research, for instance, demonstrates this meshing of boundaries between the cultural construction of disease and the physiological understanding of its expression.

Charles Leslie recently wrote that medical anthropology has cultivated a "humanistic interdisciplinary natural science tradition" (2001, 437). One would hope (and imagine) that the future of the discipline will continue that tradition. The future is harder to realize than to imagine, but we agree with Leslie that "most anthropologists have considered the discipline, and our recent subdisciplinary part of it, to be more than science. It has been a worldview, an occupation, a way of life, an entertainment, and . . . an existential search for meaning" (2001, 437). Let us hope that students and others will continue to recognize the importance of the humanistic and scientific tradition of applied medical anthropology.

References

Agar, Michael H. 1996. Recasting the "ethno" in "epidemiology." *Medical Anthropology* 16 (4): 391–403.

———. 1980. *The professional stranger: An informal introduction to ethnography.* San Diego: Academic Press.

———. 1973. *Ripping and running: A formal ethnography of urban heroin addicts.* New York: Seminar Press.

Agar, Michael H., Charles Underwood, and Kathryn Woolard. 1981. The commonalities quest: Toward a theory of "problem behavior." *Journal of Psychoactive Drugs* 13 (4): 333–43.

Ames, Genevieve M. 1985. American beliefs about alcoholism: Historical perspectives on the medical-moral controversy. In *The American experience with alcohol: Contrasting cultural perspectives,* edited by Linda A. Bennett and Genevieve M. Ames. New York: Plenum Press.

Angrosino, Michael V. 2002. *Doing cultural anthropology: Projects for ethnographic data collection.* Prospect Heights, Ill.: Waveland Press.

———. 1989. *Documents of interaction: Biography, autobiography, and life history in social science perspective.* University of Florida Monographs. Social sciences, no. 74. Gainesville: University of Florida Press.

———. 1987. *A health practitioner's guide to the social and behavioral sciences.* Dover, Mass.: Auburn House.

Baer, Hans A. 1989. American dominative medical system as a reflection of social relations in the larger society. *Social Science and Medicine* 28 (1): 1103–12.

Becker, Gay. 1990. *Healing the infertile family.* New York: Bantam Press.

Becker, M. H., ed. 1974. *The Health Belief Model and personal health behavior.* Health Education Monographs 2: 323–508.

Bennett, Linda A. 1995. Accountability for alcoholism in American families. *Social Science and Medicine* 40 (1): 15–25.

Bennett, Linda A., and Genevieve M. Ames. 1985. *The American experience with alcohol: Contrasting cultural perspectives.* New York: Plenum Press.

Bluebond-Langer, Myra. 1978. *The private worlds of dying children.* Princeton, N.J.: Princeton University Press.

Brown, Peter J. 1997. Malaria, *miseria,* and underpopulation in Sardinia: The "malaria blocks development" cultural model. *Medical Anthropology* 17 (3): 239–54.

———. 1998. *Understanding and applying medical anthropology.* Mountain View, Calif.: Mayfield Publishing.

Bryant, Carol A. 2001. Social marketing approach to increasing enrollment in a public health program: A case study of the Texas WIC program. *Human Organization* 60 (3): 234–46.1993.

———. 1993. A supportive environment in health care for breastfeeding. *Genesis: Promoting excellence in childbirth education* 3 (July): 1, 5.

Chrisman, Noel J. 1985. Alcoholism: Illness or disease? In *The American experience with alcoholism: Contrasting cultural perspectives,* edited by Linda A. Bennett and Genevieve M. Ames. New York: Plenum Press.

Coreil, Jeannine. 2004. Cultural models of illness and recovery in breast cancer support groups. *Qualitative Health Research* 14 (7): 905–23.

———. 1997. More thoughts on negotiating relevance. Commentary on special issue, Negotiating relevance of anthropological theory and methods. *Medical Anthropology Quarterly* 11 (2): 252–5.

Douglas, Mary, ed. 1990. *Constructive drinking: Perspectives in drinking from anthropology.* Cambridge: Cambridge University Press.

Dressler, William W. 1996a. Culture and blood pressure: Using consensus analysis to create a measurement. *Cultural Anthropology Methods Journal* 8 (3): 6–8.

———. 1996b. Culture, stress, and disease. In *Medical anthropology: Contemporary theory and method,* edited by Carolyn F. Sargent and Thomas M. Johnson. Rev. ed. Westport, Conn.: Praeger.

Dressler, William W., Mauro Campos Baliero, and Jose Ernesto Dos Santos. 1997. Cultural construction of social support in Brazil: Associations with health outcomes. *Culture, Medicine, and Psychiatry* 21 (3): 303–35.

Dubos, Rene. 1965. *Man adapting.* New Haven, Conn.: Yale University Press.

———. 1959. *The mirage of health: Utopias, progress, and biological change.* New York: Harper and Row.

Eber, Christine. 1995. *Women and alcohol in a highland Maya town: Water of hope, water of sorrow.* Austin: University of Texas Press.

Eisenberg, L. 1977. Disease and illness: Distinctions between professional and popular ideas of sickness. *Culture, Medicine, and Psychiatry* 1: 9–23.

Fabrega, Horacio, Jr. 1972. Medical anthropology. In *Biennial review of anthropology 1971,* edited by B. J. Siegel. Stanford, Calif.: Stanford University Press.

Farmer, Paul. 2004. *Pathologies of power: Health, human rights, and the new war on the poor.* Berkeley: University of California Press.

———. 1999. *Infections and inequalities: The modern plagues.* Berkeley: University of California Press.

———. 1992. *AIDS and accusation: Haiti and the geography of blame.* Comparative Studies of Health Systems and Medical Care, no. 33. Berkeley: University of California Press.

———. 1988. Bad blood, spoiled milk: Bodily fluids as moral barometers in rural Haiti. *American Ethnologist* 15 (1): 62–83.

Feldman, Douglas A. 1990a. Assessing viral, parasitic, and sociocultural cofactors affecting HIV-1 transmission in Rwanda. In *Culture and AIDS,* edited by Douglas A. Feldman. Berkeley, Calif., and New York: Praeger.

———. 1990b. *Culture and AIDS.* New York: Praeger.

———. 1986. Anthropology, AIDS, and Africa. *Medical Anthropology Quarterly* 17 (2): 38–40.

————. 1985. AIDS and social change. *Human Organization* 44 (4): 343–48.

Finerman, Ruthbeth, and Ross Sackett. 2003. Using home gardens to decipher health and healing in the Andes. *Medical Anthropology Quarterly* 17 (4): 459–82.

Frank, Gelya. 2000. *Venus on wheels: Two decades of dialogue on disability, biography, and being female in America.* Berkeley: University of California Press.

————. 1980. Life histories in gerontology: The subjective side to aging. In *New methods for old-age research,* edited by Christine L. Fry and Jennie Keith. Chicago: Center for Urban Policy, Loyola University of Chicago.

Frisancho, A. Roberto. 1981. *Human adaptation: A functional interpretation.* Ann Arbor: University of Michigan Press.

Ginsburg, Faye D. 1989. *Contested lives: The abortion debate in an American community.* Berkeley: University of California Press.

Heath, Dwight B. 2000. *Drinking occasions: Comparative perspectives on alcohol and culture.* Philadelphia: Brunner/Mazel.

Hopper, Kim. 1991. Some old questions for the new cross-cultural psychiatry. *Medical Anthropology Quarterly* 5(4): 299–330.

————. 1990. Research findings as testimony: A note on the ethnographer as expert witness. *Human Organization* 49 (2): 110–13.

————. 1988. More than passing strange: Homelessness and mental illness in New York City. *American Ethnologist* 15 (1): 155–67.

Janes, Craig, Ron Stall, and Sandra Gifford. 1986. *Anthropology and epidemiology.* Dordrecht, The Netherlands: D. Reidel.

Janzen, John M. 2001. *The social fabric of health: An introduction to medical anthropology.* Boston: McGraw-Hill.

Jellenik, E. M. 1960. *The disease concept of alcoholism.* New Haven, Conn.: College and University Press.

————. 1952. Phases of alcohol addiction. *Quarterly Journal of Studies on Alcohol* 13: 673–84.

Joralemon, Donald. 1999. *Exploring medical anthropology.* Needham Heights, Mass.: Allyn and Bacon.

Jordan, Brigitte. 1997. Authoritative knowledge and its construction. In *Childbirth and authoritative knowledge: Cross-cultural perspectives.* Berkeley: University of California Press.

————. 1978. *Birth in four cultures: A crosscultural investigation of childbirth in Yucatan, Holland, Sweden, and the United States.* Monographs in Women's Studies. Montreal and St. Albans, Vt.: Eden Press Women's Publications.

Kedia, Satish, and John van Willigen. 2001. Effects of forced displacement on the mental health of older people in North India. *Hallym International Journal of Aging* 3 (1): 81–93.

Kleinman, Arthur. 1980. *Patients and healers in the context of culture: An exploration of the borderland between anthropology, medicine, and psychiatry.* Berkeley: University of California Press.

Kleinman, Arthur, Veena Das, and Margaret Lock. 1997. Displacing suffering: The reconstruction of death in North America and Japan. In *Social suffering,* edited by Arthur Kleinman, Veena Das, and Margaret Lock. Berkeley: University of California Press.

Korbin, Jill. 1981. *Child abuse and neglect: A cross-cultural perspective.* Berkeley: University of California Press.

Leatherman, Thomas J., Alan Goodman, and R. Brooke Thomas. 1993. On seeking common ground between medical ecology and critical medical anthropology. *Medical Anthropology Quarterly* 7 (2): 202–207.

LeCompte, Margaret D., Jean J. Schensul, Margaret R. Weeks, and Merrill Singer. 1999. *Researcher roles and research partnerships.* Ethnographer's toolkit, no. 6. Walnut Creek, Calif.: AltaMira Press.

LeCompte, Margaret D., and Jean J. Schensul. 1999a. *Analyzing and interpreting ethnographic data.* Ethnographer's toolkit, no. 5. Walnut Creek, Calif.: AltaMira Press.

————. 1999b. *Designing and conducting ethnographic research.* Ethnographer's toolkit, no. 1. Walnut Creek, Calif.: AltaMira Press.

Leslie, Charles M. 2001. Backing into the future. *Medical Anthropology Quarterly* 15 (4): 428–39.

————. 1976. *Asian medical systems: A comparative study.* Berkeley: University of California Press.

MacAndrew, Craig, and Robert B. Edgerton. 1969. *Drunken comportment: A social explanation.* Chicago: Aldine Publishing.

Marshall, Mac. 1979. *Weekend warriors: Alcohol in a Micronesian culture.* Mountain View, Calif.: Mayfield Publishing.

Marshall, Patricia, and Abdullah Daar. 2000. Ethical issues in human organ replacement: A case study from India. In *Global health policy, local realities: The fallacy of the level playing field*, edited by Linda M. Whiteford and Lenore Manderson. Boulder, Colo.: Lynne Rienner Publishers.

Mathews, Holly F. 1998. Methodological approaches to the study of reasoning. *Medical Anthropology Quarterly* 12 (3): 358–62.

————. 1990. Applying cognitive decision theory to the study of regional patterns of illness treatment choice. *American Anthropologist* 92 (1): 155–70.

————. 1987. Predicting decision outcomes: Have we put the cart before the horse in anthropological studies of decision making? *Human Organization* 46 (1): 54–61.

McCombie, Susan. 1990. AIDS in a cultural, historic, and epidemiological context. In *Culture and AIDS*, edited by Douglas A. Feldman. New York: Praeger.

McElroy, Ann. 1990. Biocultural models in studies of human health and adaptation. *Medical Anthropology Quarterly* 4 (3): 243–65.

McElroy, Ann, and Patricia K. Townsend. 2004. *Medical anthropology in ecological perspective.* 4th ed. Boulder, Colo.: Westview Press.

————. 1996. *Medical anthropology in ecological perspective.* 3rd ed. Boulder, Colo.: Westview Press.

————. 1989. *Medical anthropology in ecological perspective.* 2nd ed. Boulder, Colo.: Westview Press.

Morsy, Soheir A. 1996. Political economy in medical anthropology. In *Medical anthropology: Contemporary theory and method*, edited by Carolyn Sargent and Thomas M. Johnson. Rev. ed. Westport, Conn.: Praeger Publishers.

Page, J. Bryan, and Robert T. Trotter II. 1999. To theorize or not to theorize: Anthropological research in drugs and AIDS. In *Integrating cultural, observational, and epidemiological approaches in the prevention of drug abuse and HIV/AIDS*, edited by

Patricia L. Marshall and Michael C. Clatts. *USD/AIDS*. U.S. Department of Health and Human Services and the National Institute on Drug Abuse. NIH Pub. No. 994565.

Paul, Benjamin, ed. 1955. *Health, culture, and community*. New York: Russell Sage Foundation.

Pelto, Pertti J., and Gretel H. Pelto. 1996. Research designs in medical anthropology. In *Medical anthropology: Contemporary theory and method*, edited by Carolyn F. Sargent and Thomas M. Johnson. Rev. ed. Westport, Conn.: Praeger Publishers.

Rapp, Rayna. 2001. Thinking about women and the origin of the state. In *Gender in cross-cultural perspective*, edited by Caroline B. Brettell and Carolyn F. Sargent. Upper Saddle River, N.J.: Prentice Hall.

———. 1989. Chromosomes and communication: The discourse of genetic counseling. *Medical Anthropology Quarterly* 2 (2): 143–57.

Romero-Daza, N. M. Weeks, and M. Singer. "Nobody gives a damn if I live or die": Experiences of violence among drug-using sex workers in Hartford, CT. *Medical Anthropology* 11 (3): 233–59.

Sandelowski, Margarete. 1993. *With child in mind: Studies of the personal encounter with infertility*. Philadelphia: University of Pennsylvania Press.

Sargent, Carolyn. 1982. *The cultural context of therapeutic choice: Obstetrical decisions among the Bariba of Benin*. Dordrecht, The Netherlands: D. Reidel.

Scheper-Hughes, Nancy, and Margaret M. Lock. 1987. Mindful body: A prolegomenon to future work in medical anthropology. *Medical Anthropology Quarterly* 1 (1): 6–41.

Scrimshaw, Susan C. M., and Elena Hurtado. 1997. *Rapid assessment procedures for nutrition and primary health care: Anthropological approaches to improving programme effectiveness*. Tokyo: United Nations University, UNICEF, and UCLA Latin American Center.

Singer, Merrill. 2000. Drug-use patterns: An ever-whirling wheel of change. *Medical Anthropology* 18 (4): 299–303.

———. 1999. Why do Puerto Rican injection drug users inject so often? *Anthropology and Medicine* 6 (1): 31–58.

———. 1998. Articulating personal experience and political economy in the AIDS epidemic: The case of Carlos Torres. In *The political economy of AIDS*, edited by Merrill Singer. Amityville, N.Y.: Baywood.

———. 1996. Evolution of AIDS work in a Puerto Rican community organization. *Human Organization* 55 (1): 67–75.

———. 1992. Biomedicine and the political economy of science. *Medical Anthropology Quarterly* 6 (4): 400–404.

Singer, Merrill, and Hans A. Baer. 1995. *Critical medical anthropology*. Critical Approaches in the Health Social Sciences series. Amityville, N.Y.: Baywood.

Singer, Merrill, Freddie Valentin, Hans Baer, and Zhongke Jia. 1998. Why does Juan Garcia have a drinking problem? The perspective of critical medical anthropology. In *Understanding and applying medical anthropology*, edited by Peter J. Brown. Mountain View, Calif.: Mayfield Publishing.

Sokolovsky, Jay. 1997a. Aging, family, and community development in a Mexican peasant village. In *The cultural context of aging: Worldwide perspectives*, edited by Jay Sokolovsky. Westport, Conn.: Bergin and Garvey.

―――. 1997b. One thousand points of blight: Old, female and homeless in New York City. In *The cultural context of aging: Worldwide perspectives,* edited by Jay Sokolovsky. Westport, Conn.: Bergin and Garvey.

―――. 1993. Culture, society, and aging. In *Growing old in different societies: Cross-cultural perspectives,* edited by Jay Sokolovsky. Ann Arbor, Mich.: Copley Publishing Group.

Trostle, James A. 1986. Anthropology and epidemiology in the twentieth century: A selective history of collaborative project and theoretical affinities, 1920 to 1970. In *Anthropology and epidemiology,* edited by Craig Janes, Ron Stall, and Sondra Gifford. Dordrecht, The Netherlands: D. Reidel.

Trostle, James A., and Johannes Sommerfeld. 1996. Medical anthropology and epidemiology. *Annual Review of Anthropology* 25: 253–74.

Trotter, Robert, Richard Needle, Eric Goosby, Christopher Bates, and Merrill Singer. 2000. A methodological model for rapid assessment, response, and evaluation: The RARE Program in public health. *Field Methods* 13 (2): 137–59.

Trotter, R. T. II, A. M. Bowen, and J. M. Potter. 1995. Network models for HIV outreach and prevention programs for drug users. In *Social network analysis: HIV prevention and drug abuse.* NIDA Monograph 151: 144–80. Bethesda, Md.: National Institute on Drug Abuse.

Weller, Susan C., and Roberta D. Baer. 2001. Intra- and intercultural variation in the definition of five illnesses: AIDS, diabetes, the common cold, empacho, and mal de ojo. *Cross-Cultural Research* 35 (2): 201–26.

Weller, Susan C., Lee M. Pachter, Robert T. Trotter II, Roberta D. Baer, Robert E. Klein, Javier E. Garcia de Alba Garcia, and Mark Glazer. 1993. Empacho in four Latino groups: A study of intra- and inter-cultural variation in beliefs. *Medical Anthropology* 15 (2): 109–36.

Weller, Susan C., and A. Kimball Romney. 1988. *Systematic data collection.* Qualitative research methods, vol. 10. Newbury Park, Calif.: Sage Publications.

Whiteford, Linda M. 2000. Local identity, globalization, and health in Cuba and the Dominican Republic. In *Global health policy, local realities: The fallacy of the level playing field,* edited by Linda Whiteford and Lenore Manderson. Boulder, Colo.: Lynne Rienner Publishers.

―――. 1997. The ethnoecology of dengue fever. *Medical Anthropology Quarterly* 11 (2): 202–23.

―――. 1995. Political economy, gender, and the social production of health and illness. In *Gender and health: An international perspective,* edited by Carolyn Sargent and Caroline Brettell. Upper Saddle River, N.J.: Prentice Hall.

Whiteford, Linda M., and Judi Vitucci. 1997. Pregnancy and addiction: Translating research into practice. *Social Science and Medicine* 44 (9): 1371–80.

Yacoob, May, and Linda M. Whiteford. 1995. An untapped resource: Community-based epidemiologists for environmental health. *Environment and Urbanization* 7 (1): 219–30.

6 Nutritional Anthropology and Its Application to Nutritional Issues and Problems

David A. Himmelgreen and Deborah L. Crooks

Introduction

The whole of nature, it has been said, is a conjugation
of the verb to eat, in the active and passive.
William Ralph Inge (1922)

As a domain of application within anthropology, nutrition encompasses an array of topics, from food ideology to food production, availability, access, and consumption. Anthropology is particularly well suited for the study of nutrition because of its theoretical underpinnings and its applied focus. Theoretically, the application of the holism concept along with the biocultural perspective and evolutionary theory provide a lens through which we can view the interactions between biological and cultural processes in the evolution of human food use and its nutritional consequences. On the one hand, anthropologists study the significance of the food quest in terms of survival, health, and reproductive fitness. On the other hand, they also know that people eat food for a variety of reasons that have little, if anything, to do with nutrition, health, or survival. Within anthropology, it is well known that the availability of food is dependent upon ecological and economic resources, but food choice and the strategies human groups employ to gain access to and distribute food are deeply embedded in specific cultural patterns related to social organization, social relations, symbolic systems, and political and economic systems. In the end, biological factors cannot be separated from cultural ones, and the study of nutrition can benefit from a perspective that combines both the sociocultural determinants of food intake and the biological effects of food choice on nutritional status and health.

According to van Willigen, "applied anthropology is a complex of related, research based, instrumental methods which produce change or stability in specific cultural systems through the provision of data, initiation of direct action, and/or the formulation of policy" (2002, 10). In applied nutritional anthropology, data are provided from a variety of sources. Primary data, such as anthropometric and dietary indicators of an individual's or group's nutritional status, are provided through field or clinical research, and secondary data may come from the analysis of national data sets on food consumption and nutritional status, such as the National Health and Nutrition Examination Surveys (NHANES). These data inform policy both directly, through anthropologists who have a hand in developing food and nutrition policy, or, more frequently, indirectly, through policy makers who translate the findings of nutritional anthropological research into policy statements and programs. Action often follows in the form of interventions to improve nutritional status, such as the formulation of culturally tailored nutrition education programs or the development and evaluation of food assistance programs (examples of these are provided at the end of the chapter).

Our aim in this chapter is to provide an overview of applied nutritional anthropology, especially as it relates to public health nutrition. As part of this overview, we will briefly discuss the history and development of the broader field of nutritional anthropology, but this will not be a comprehensive treatment. To this end, the chapter has six goals. First, we will discuss what nutritional anthropology is and describe its emphasis on holism and the biocultural approach. Second, we will briefly examine the history of nutritional anthropology, focusing on its application to programs of change. Third, we will discuss some of the theoretical models. Fourth, we will examine some of the methods and forms of analysis currently used by nutritional anthropologists. Fifth, we will provide a number of topical areas, current trends, and case studies of the application of nutritional anthropology research to the development of policy, interventions, and direct services. And sixth, we will discuss future trends in nutritional anthropology, providing recommendations to anthropology students who are interested in public health nutrition.

What Is Nutritional Anthropology?

Kandel and colleagues wrote that "food by virtue of its pivotal place in the human experience is, at once, a bundle of energy and nutrients within the biological sphere, a commodity within the economic sphere, and a symbol within the social and religious spheres" (Kandel, Pelto, and Jerome 1980, 1). Although some nutrition and dietetic approaches examine the relationship among these spheres, nutritional anthropology is uniquely explicit in its goal of understanding the linkages between the biological significance of nutrients and the sociocultural and economic meaning of food. Nutritional anthropology has been defined as being "fundamentally concerned with understanding the interrelationships of biological and social forces in shaping human food use and the nutritional status of individuals and populations" (Pelto, Goodman, and Dufour 2000, 1). Nutritional anthropology deals with nutrition as a process of the ways "in which humans utilize food to meet the requirements of biological and behavioral functioning" (Johnston 1987, ix). At the same time, nutritional anthropology is a science in that it focuses on the chemical processing and biological use of food (Kreutler 1980). This holistic approach means that there is a wide array of topical areas and expertise covered in nutritional anthropology, as we shall demonstrate throughout this chapter.

Some nutritional anthropologists focus on the process side of nutrition, looking, for example, at the political economy of food production, availability, and consumption patterns. Others may focus on the science of the biology of nutrition and may, for instance, examine the relationship between energy intake and expenditure in a particular ecological setting. Still other nutritional anthropologists bring together the process and science sides of nutrition, analyzing, for example, the relationship among changing food consumption patterns, nutritional status, and nutrition-related conditions, such as obesity and diabetes, in the context of globalization. In each of these scenarios, the opportunity exists for the nutritional anthropologist to generate information, inform policy, provide theory and data for policy development, and develop interventions addressing a particular nutrition problem.

Professional Recognition of Nutritional Anthropology

Nutritional anthropology, as a distinct, organized topic of interest within anthropology, has a fairly recent history. In the early 1970s, anthropologists utilizing biocultural approaches to the study of food and nutrition came together at the annual meetings of the American Anthropological Association (AAA) to discuss common interests and to present research in a series of three symposia (Quandt and Ritenbaugh 1986). These discussions and the symposia papers led to the publication of *Nutritional Anthropology: Contemporary Approaches to Diet and Culture* by Jerome and colleagues, which organized the field of nutritional anthropology around the combination of four traditional, and previously separate, lines of research: dietary survey studies, food habits and foodways, the cognitive aspects (or meaning) of food, and ecological theory (Jerome, Kandel, and Pelto 1980). This was followed some years later by the *Training Manual in Nutritional Anthropology* (Quandt and Ritenbaugh 1986), which detailed methodological approaches in nutritional anthropology. Taken together, these symposia, along with their associated publications, set out a course by which the newly emerging field of nutritional anthropology could address local and global nutritional problems through the integration of the biocultural approach, evolutionary theory, and methods from cultural and physical anthropology and the nutritional sciences.

By the mid-1980s, the Committee on Nutritional Anthropology had merged with the AAA as an interest group within the Society for Medical Anthropology (SMA), a section of the AAA; later on, the renamed Council on Nutritional Anthropology (CNA) was established as a separate section of the AAA. In 2004, the CNA was renamed as the Society for Anthropology of Food and Nutrition (SAFN). Today, the SAFN is a small but viable section that has the following objectives: (1) to encourage research and exchange of ideas, theories, and methods; (2) to provide a forum for communication and interaction; and (3) to promote practical collaboration among social and nutritional scientists (Council on Nutritional Anthropology 1998). The SAFN promotes the understanding of sociocultural, behavioral, and political-economic factors related to food production, availability, access, preparation, and biological utilization.

Like its parent organization (the AAA), the SAFN covers a wide range of interests; nutritional anthropologists work from a variety of theoretical perspectives within all subdisciplines of anthropology. Thus, research and job-related interests span a range of food and nutrition topics, for example, infant feeding, child growth and development, gender issues in food consumption and nutritional status, food security and malnutrition, diet and chronic illness, local and global development policies and programs, and public and community health. Nutritional anthropologists do not always work alone to solve problems in these diverse fields of interest; many of them partner with colleagues from nutrition and dietetics, public health, medicine, and development in an effort to gain a greater understanding of how nutritional statuses of individuals and populations are produced and how policies and interventions might more effectively improve nutritional status among populations in communities around the world.

A Brief History of Nutritional Anthropology

Contributions from the First Half of the Twentieth Century

Whereas the professional recognition of nutritional anthropology as a distinct field of interest is relatively recent, anthropology has a rich history of food and nutrition research. Early in the twentieth century, studies in nonindustrial societies examined the links among food production, distribution patterns, and social organization (Messer 1984). Prior to World War II, British social anthropologists were interested in how food supply, social organization, and nutrition were interrelated among different cultural groups in colonial Africa. Although the anthropological goal was to define and analyze the basic units of social organization, the research documented changing social relations as well and provided details on cultural change resulting from the social disruption caused by British rule; these changes have affected nutritional status (Messer 1984).

In her classic study of the Bemba, Richards (1939) found that Bemba males under British colonization were drawn away from their traditional agricultural roles to work in the mining industry and other British controlled enterprises. As a result of male migration, local food production declined and malnutrition set in. Similarly, in their work among the Tallensi of West Africa, Fortes and Fortes (1936) documented seasonal drops in food production during the planting season, a time when nutritional needs were the greatest. These reductions in food availability were related to food scarcity prior to the new harvest. In addition, Firth (1929) documented the symbolic and emotional values of foods and their use in rituals and as indicators of social status among the Maori of New Zealand. These and other studies contributed to theory building in anthropology, enhancing understanding of the structure and evolution of social organization and cultural change, but they also had practical implications for human productivity, nutrition, and health.

At the same time, U.S. anthropologists were using social psychological approaches to understand how attitudes toward food developed across cultures, and how they affected later social relationships and behaviors (Messer 1984). Some studies focused on small nonindustrial societies, such as Alorese and the Trobriand Islanders (DuBois and Kardiner 1944; Malinowski 1948); others aimed at characterizing ethnic and national personality types (Kardiner 1945). Although these studies are often criticized for inattention to cultural heterogeneity within and across societies, they were thought to be prudent at the time, when war was imminent.

Margaret Mead in particular was interested in the development of food habits (i.e., foodways) and the ease with which they could be changed in light of anticipated wartime food rationing. She is often credited with being the first anthropologist to apply an anthropological approach directly to the solution of nutrition-related problems; her work with the Committee on Food Habits of the National Academy of Sciences resulted in the publication of *Manual for the Study of Food Habits* (National Research Council 1945) and *Food Habits Research: Problems of the 1960s* (Mead 1964), which updated many of the issues in the earlier volume. The intent of the committee's work was to foster improvement in the nutritional habits of people in the United States and around the world by applying "scientific knowledge" gained through nutritional, social, and behavioral research. These and other efforts would eventually lead to applied research on food preference, which is defined as the degree to which an individual likes or dislikes a food. Research of this type has been used by food marketers to predict sales of particular food items to improve marketing schemes and by cancer researchers, who have looked at changes in food preferences in relation to treatment modalities (e.g., chemotherapy) and the progression of disease (Carson and Gormican 1977).

Contributions since World War II

Symbolic, or semiotic, research on food prohibitions, prescriptions, and the meaning of foods in the context of social identity and social relations became fairly common following the World War II (Himmelgreen 2002). Levi-Strauss (1963, 1966) looked at the relationship between food symbolism and totems and found that food rules cement group identity and define social rank, status, and power. Ferro-Luzzi (1977) examined Hindu food classifications and food exchange rules within the caste system, and Harper (1964) showed that foods, like castes, are classified according to their relative degree of purity and pollution. Douglas (1975) analyzed eating patterns and argued that they reveal much about social structure, later bridging her ideas about the "meaningfulness of food" (1985, 5) into the policy arena by demonstrating that hunger in the West is a consequence of social attitude, not availability of food.

Whereas most, if not all, of these and other similar studies were done to advance cultural theory, more recent studies have practical implications for dealing with nutrition-related problems. For instance, the high consumption of Coca-Cola in the Yucátan Peninsula—a drink virtually unknown to Mayan Indians 25 years ago—has been associated with the belief that this soft drink is healthy and with the high status it holds as a Western item

(Goodman, Dufour, and Pelto 2000). Likewise, anthropological studies on the marketing of fast-food chains like McDonalds (Kottak 1978) are especially relevant today in light of the global obesity epidemic.

During the 1950s, cultural materialism came into vogue and was applied to the study of food and nutrition. Although many of the materialist explanations were criticized for their lack of empirical data (Ross 1978; Chagnon and Hames 1979), they did provide insight into the nature of subsistence strategies and food habits in different ecological settings. Examples of this research include Harris's materialist explanations for both the Hindu prohibition against beef consumption (1978) and the prohibition against pork consumption among Jews and Muslims (1974), Aztec cannibalism (Harner 1977), and various animal taboos in South America (Ross 1978). Later research examined the relationship between ecosystem energy flow (e.g., food availability, access, and consumption) and the way cultural systems could produce, harness, and use that energy. For example, in his classic study of the Maring of New Guinea, Rappaport (1968) showed how ritualized pig festivals regulated the distribution of highly prized protein. Other studies showed how specific food-processing techniques are used to detoxify some foods (e.g., cyanide in bitter manioc root) or to enhance the nutritional quality of others (e.g., niacin in maize) (Dufour 1995; Katz, Hediger, and Valleroy 1974). Although cultural materialism and human ecology studies have generally not been used in applied food and nutrition research, they have meshed well with the ecological and adaptation models used in nutritional anthropology.

With the rise of the social consciousness movement beginning in the 1960s, there was an increased interest in the relationship between nutrition and economic development. In particular, there was an emphasis on the impact of economic development on diet in the developing world. For example, research focused on topics such as how the changing economic roles of women affected food production, preparation, and distribution (Cowan 1978) and the impact of cash-cropping on local food self-sufficiency among rural producers (Dewey 1980). More recently, this research domain expanded to include studies on poverty, economic development, and nutrition in industrialized countries. Sellen and Tedstone (2000) looked at the nutritional needs of refugee populations in the United Kingdom, and Crooks (1996, 2000) conducted research on dietary quality and nutritional status among children in eastern Kentucky. An increasing number of studies looked at the obesity epidemic, both in countries undergoing economic transition as well as in industrialized nations where there is a strong link between food insecurity and obesity (Martorell et al. 1998; Popkin 2001; Himmelgreen et al. 2001).

Since the 1980s, nutritional research has become the focus of many biological anthropologists because of the increased prominence of nutrition in public health and the "centrality of diet as an issue in human adaptation and evolution" (Huss-Ashmore 1992, 155). In many cases, biological anthropologists develop research models in which growth, body composition, and the functional outcomes of nutritional status are considered the dependent variables, whereas factors associated with the physical, sociocultural, and political-economic environments are independent or determining variables. Some studies focus on social epidemiology, in which the roles of social factors on the etiology of a nutrition-related condition are identified (e.g., breast-feeding duration and infant health) (Pelto, Goodman, and Dufour 2000). Other studies examine biological adaptations (long-term genetic and short-term developmental and physiological adaptations to particular physical environments). Research on the thrifty-genotype (Neel 1962), the short-but-healthy hypothesis (Martorell et al. 1981; Messer 1986), and the association between seasonal ecology and nutritional status (Huss-Ashmore 1988; Simondon et al. 1993; Himmelgreen and Romero-Daza 1994) are but a few examples. Lastly, biological anthropologists have examined the nutritional bases for various behavioral disorders, such as arctic hysteria and calcium deficiency, and the geographical distribution of population differences in the digestion of lactose (Kretchmer 2000).

Nutritional interests in anthropology have grown and expanded considerably over the years. Nevertheless, they are connected, explicitly or implicitly, through holistic perspectives that consider cultural ideologies that underlie social aspects of food organization and distribution, which shape food consumption behaviors and, ultimately, have repercussions for nutritional status among populations and diverse groups. This has certainly been the case with research done during the past decade. Dettwyler's work in Mali (1991, 1994) indicates that cultural notions of who deserves "good food" (i.e., those who work hardest or who may die soonest) results in the channeling of the best foods to adult men and elders in the household and away from infants and growing children, thereby thwarting good, or even adequate, growth and development. Daltabuit and Leatherman's work in the Yucatán (1998) makes clear that the impact of Western culture disseminated through globalization policies has changed consumption patterns among Mayan households in Yalcoba. At the same time, local engagement of the development process alters traditional economic production patterns, as well as patterns of social interaction. The consequences for women and children are particularly egregious, as indicated by poor nutritional status and high illness rates. Economic development policies can have negative, unintended consequences for the health and nutritional status of select groups in local communities; in other words, the costs of development may far outweigh the benefits for some. The lesson for policymakers is that programs intended to improve nutritional status must take into account, among other things, cultural ideologies in the economic system that affect both what is consumed and the distribution of food within households.

Although globalization is associated with recent and rapid changes in diet and health status, it should be noted that there is a long history of research on how sociocultural, economic, and political systems have had an influence on food consumption patterns. For example, Mintz (1979) documented the diffusion of sugar from the Old World to the New World in the seventeenth century and the concomitant increase in consumption rates. Brenton (1998) provided a historical overview of the political and economic factors associated with maize production, low-protein diets, and the development of pellagra dating back to the Irish Famine. Research by biological and nutritional anthropologists along with archeologists has also provided evidence of nutritional evolution and changes in health status dating back to the Paleolithic period, with significant changes taking place with the advent of horticulture and animal husbandry occurring during the post-Pleistocene epoch (Eaton and Konner 1985; Gordon 1987; Katz 1987; Cavalli-Sforza 1981; Stini 1981; Cassidy 1980).

As in these examples, and many others (e.g., Alderman and Garcia 1993; Baer 1998; DeWalt and DeWalt 1991; Howard and Millard 1997; Huss-Ashmore and Curry 1994), the work of nutritional anthropologists is organized around an attempt to sort out the complex threads that make up the fabric of people's lives and the way these threads connect directly or indirectly to nutritional status. This research provided, and continues to provide, important information for agents of change who directly target nutritional improvement or whose programs have indirect consequences for nutritional status of diverse groups of people in the United States and around the world.

Theoretical Models Used in Nutritional Anthropology

The field of nutritional anthropology includes individuals from the four subdisciplines of anthropology (cultural, biological/physical, archeological, and linguistic), as well as from other disciplines such as nutrition, public health, sociology, food studies, and so on. Hence, it incorporates theory from all of these areas, but it maintains most notably a biocultural perspective, which extensively uses theory from the biological and social sciences. Moreover, the humanities provide data through the examination of the cultural and historical aspects of food (Pelto, Goodman, and Dufour 2000).

Depending on the topic of research, nutritional anthropologists use different heuristic models to examine the relationship between biology and culture in relation to food and nutrition. What follows is a brief description of three of the better-known models used in nutritional anthropology.

The Ecological Model

Over the years, several ecological models have been proposed, yet all of them have a common focus: the intersection of the social and physical environments and their effects on food and nutrition (Steward 1972; White 1949). In 1980, Jerome and colleagues developed an ecological model in response to food scarcity in many developing countries, the overabundance of food in industrialized ones, and the failure of many policies and interventions aimed at the alleviation of malnutrition. This model, which was recently reexamined by Pelto and colleagues (Pelto, Goodman, and Dufour 2000), integrates biological, social, cultural, psychological, and economic factors in the analysis of human food systems.

The model begins with the individual's biological needs for nutrients and psychological needs for nurturance. These needs are based not only on the general requirements for the species but also on individual and population genetic characteristics, developmental stage, reproductive demands, and activity and stress levels (Jerome, Kandel, and Pelto 1980). In other words, the model incorporates a life-cycle approach and takes into account individual and population variations in nutritional needs for biological and psychobiological functioning. Interacting with individual needs is a series of environmental features that determine the food system. The physical environment includes climate, water resources, soil characteristics, and the flora and fauna. The social environment refers to many features that have an influence on food availability, access, and consumption; they include political and economic institutions, division of labor, and even household-level decisionmaking regarding food acquisition and redistribution. Technology is another environmental feature, and it includes the innovations and tools associated with food production, distribution, storage, processing, and preparation. The cultural environment refers to the ideas and beliefs about food and the way in which they shape food consumption patterns. As Jerome, Kandel, and Pelto state, "the ecological approach is valuable for delineating elements of the dynamic system, determining how the various elements work together, identifying hazards or potential stress areas, predicting the types and direction of change, and assessing adaptive and deleterious responses to both planned and unplanned changes" (1980, 15).

Whatever the iteration of the ecological model, it is one that is useful in applied food and nutrition research because of its focus on the dynamics of change at micro- and macro-levels. Recently, aspects of the ecological model have been applied to the promotion of healthy eating and physical activity in an effort to better understand the environmental influences on obesity in the United States (see Nutritional Reviews 2001).

The Adaptation Model

Under the adaptation model, the physical and social environments may limit availability and access to nutrients, causing nutritional stress and, in doing so, presenting a set of challenges to which individuals and populations must respond. Responses may be biological, cultural, and behavioral, and they are often termed "adaptive" or "maladaptive" (Jerome, Kandel, and Pelto 1980). Biological adaptive responses include body weight fluctuations in response to seasonal food scarcity (Himmelgreen and Romero-Daza 1994), the plasticity of human body size in relationship to environmental resources (Bogin 1988), and the genetic variability of lactose sufficiency to maintain lactose tolerance and the ability to drink fresh milk products (Kretchmer 2000). Cultural and behavioral responses include food preservation technologies (e.g., salting and curing, smoking) and practices (e.g., ritual feasting, use of high-yield grains) and food processing techniques (e.g., detoxification of cyanide-containing cassava and niacin liberation of maize).

This model also allows for responses that are maladaptive. Maladaptive biological responses include the development of nutritional deficiencies such as anemia in the presence of an iron deficient diet or the development of obesity as the result of an excess intake of calories. Cultural and behavioral maladaptations could include the high consumption of fast foods in the United States.

As can be seen from this brief discussion, the adaptation model systematically examines the social and physical environments in terms of the nutritional stress they present and how humans respond to that stress, either through the adaptive process or through maladaptation. This model can be useful in the development of interventions and food and nutrition programming, especially in areas where the risk of nutritional stress is high.

The Political Economy of Health Model

The political economy of health model focuses on the relationship between class and health, and it can be traced back to the work of Engels and Virchow (Singer 1998). With the rise in industrialism during the mid-nineteenth century, there was growing interest in how the social and physical environments of the working class were associated with illness and early mortality (Himmelgreen 2002). The political economy of health model is especially relevant in applied nutritional anthropology and can be used to study the impact of social structural factors on food availability, access, and consumption. For example, even though the United States is a food-rich nation, there are segments of the population that experience food insecurity and for whom the availability of nutritionally adequate and safe foods is limited or uncertain (Anderson 1990). If this problem is chronic, it can result in hunger and undernutrition, including illnesses and conditions related to micronutrient deficiencies (e.g., iron deficiency anemia). Food insecurity can also result in an unbalanced diet that is high in fat or refined sugar, resulting in obesity, which is a major epidemic in the United States and a growing public health problem worldwide. In applied nutritional anthropology, the political economy of health model can be used to factor in social structural conditions in the design, implementation, and evaluation of food assistance programs, nutrition education services, and social marketing programs, especially those targeting economically marginalized populations (Himmelgreen 2002).

Methodologies Used by Nutritional Anthropologists

Because of the complexity of issues in which nutritional anthropologists are interested, they must be trained in a variety of both quantitative and qualitative data gathering and analysis techniques. The information base from which solutions to nutritional problems can be derived is created through the integration of methodologies borrowed from biological anthropology, cultural anthropology, and nutrition and dietetics. Approaches are focused at various levels of inquiry—individual, household, community, and population (e.g., Quandt and Ritenbaugh 1986; Johnston 1987). Nutritional anthropologists do not utilize all methods for each project; however, the best training in nutritional anthropology should include all methodological procedures.

Because the production of nutritional status takes place in sociocultural settings, nutritional anthropologists must often be trained in, or at least be familiar with, methods and techniques from other diverse fields of interest such as agriculture, economics, epidemiology, public health, development, and, more recently, geography (e.g., Geographic Information Systems). Today, local food consumption cannot be divorced from national or global economic policies, so nutritional anthropologists seeking to improve local dietary behaviors may need, for example, to understand how the economic behaviors of smallholder producers in a global environment shape dietary behaviors at the household level. Moreover, because diet interacts with disease in producing nutritional status, nutritional anthropologists interested in understanding malnutrition among children would do well to be trained in both health and public health assessment methods, if their intent is to foster change.

The next section discusses methods that should be considered the most basic for adequate training in nutritional anthropology. Again, these methods are adopted from biological anthropology, cultural anthropology, and nutrition and dietetics.

Methods of Analysis for Growth, Body Composition, and Nutritional Status

Jelliffe has defined nutritional anthropometry as "measurements of the variations of the physical dimensions and the gross composition of the human body at different age levels and degree of nutrition" (cited by Gibson 1993, 41). Anthropometric measures are often used to evaluate the nutritional status of individuals and populations. The advantages of anthropometry are that it is relatively easy to do, it is safe and noninvasive, and it provides information on past long-term and current nutritional history. Anthropometry is widely used and especially useful in cross-sectional and longitudinal studies that evaluate growth and body composition over time (Weiner and Lourie 1981; Frisancho 1990; Gibson 1993). Nutritional anthropologists should be able to take accurate and reliable measures of growth and body composition. Some of the more frequently used measures are stature, body weight, arm circumference, and skin folds. Indices derived from these measurements include weight-for-height, height-for-age, weight-for-age, body mass index (i.e., kg/m^2), and mid-upper arm muscle and fat areas. Procedures for collecting these data and creating these indices are well detailed by Gibson (1993) and Lohman and colleagues (1988), with alternatives and additions provided by Frisancho (1990).

Anthropometric and other body composition assessment methods rely on indirect techniques to estimate body fat and fat-free or muscle mass. Although methods such as hydrostatic weighing and Magnetic Resonance Imaging (MRI) are considered gold standards, they are usually prohibitively expensive and not feasible in field-based studies. Anthropometric skin-fold measurements are inexpensive and suitable for field studies, but they are not accurate for estimating small changes in body fat. One method for the assessment of body composition that provides more accurate results, is less expensive than the gold standard methods, and is better suited for field studies is Bioelectrical Impedance Analysis (BIA) (Heyward 1996).

Once anthropometric or other data have been collected, assessment of nutritional status from those data must follow. Assessment of the adequacy of growth and nutritional status is often made by comparing anthropometric measures and indices to percentiles of a reference population or converting them to z-scores based on a nationally representative reference population. National Center for Health Statistics (NCHS) references, provided by the Centers for Disease Control (CDC), are commonly used by nutritional anthropologists, and the CDC provides a computer-based program (EPI-Info) to facilitate assessment of growth and nutritional status. However, there is often debate as to what is representative for populations from countries other than those from which references are constructed (in this case, other than U.S. populations). Because of this, some nutritional anthropologists will use both international and local reference data when available. Nevertheless, while there is an effort underway to develop new international growth references (Semba and Bloem 2001), the World Health Organization (WHO) has accepted the NCHS references for most international work (1995).

Food Consumption Methods and Dietary Analysis

Food consumption methods differ by level of assessment (i.e., individual, household, community, or national). Assessment of national food consumption is seldom the responsibility of nutritional anthropologists and will not be discussed here (see Gibson 1993 for a discussion of methods used). Individual and household assessment of food consumption is the primary focus of dietary data collection for nutritional anthropologists. These data are then aggregated to provide group information (e.g., age, gender, socioeconomic status). Data collection methods include 24-hour dietary recalls, estimated food records, weighed food records, dietary histories, and food frequency questionnaires (FFQs). The kinds and quality of data collected, along with respondent and interviewer burden, vary by method. The 24-hour food recall has been frequently used in nutritional anthropology research, and, more recently, there has been increased use of the FFQ. What follows is a brief discussion of these two methods. (For more information on these and other methods, see Gibson 1993 and Quandt and Ritenbaugh 1986.)

The 24-hour food recall is a method for estimating food intake during a 24-hour period or the day prior to the interview. This method provides information on the mean intake of a population (Gibson 1993). In general, the 24-hour food recall has the following advantages: low respondent burden, high compliance, low cost, use of standardized interview, and ease of administration. Thus, this method is ideal in community-based studies of population food intake; however, researchers must take care to administer repeated 24-hour recalls on different days of the week to capture weekday, weekend, and seasonal variability.

Several limitations of the 24-hour recall must be acknowledged, including reliance on memory (a potential problem when studying older adults and young children), the flat-slope syndrome (the overestimation of low intake and underestimation of high intakes), and inaccurate estimates of portion sizes (Gibson 1993; Gersovitz, Madden, and Smiciklas-Wright 1978). The flat-slope syndrome can be accommodated by observing actual food consumption on sample days. Issues with memory and accurate recall of portion sizes can be accommodated as well. For example, in her work with 8- to 12-year-old schoolchildren in eastern Kentucky, Crooks (2000) reminded children the day before a 24-hour recall interview that she would be seeing them the next day so that they could pay attention to what they were eating on the "data" day. When interviewing the children, she verbally walked them through their day, which helped them recall eating events. In addition, because snack foods are often overlooked when recalling food consumption, she provided posters with pictures of the snack foods children were most likely to consume. And to overcome the difficulties in recalling portion sizes, she used plastic food models and presented children with various plates, cups, and glasses to aid in their recall. For example, children might recall they had mashed potatoes for lunch but were not able to define portion size in ounces or cups. However, they could determine that they had more or less mashed potatoes than represented by the model, or that the potatoes covered a certain portion of a plate, using their hands to show where as well as how high the potatoes were piled. Or they might recall that they had a glass of milk, but while they could not determine portion size in ounces, they could say that the glass was the same size as one of the models, and when asked, they might offer that they drank only half.

The food frequency questionnaire (FFQ) provides qualitative and semi-quantitative dietary assessment through retrospective information on food consumption patterns over longer and less precisely defined time periods than those used for quantitative assessment methods, such as the 24-hour food recall (Gibson 1993). The FFQ contains a list of categorized foods (e.g., dairy, fruits and vegetables, and meat and poultry) and associated categories indicating the frequency-of-consumption (e.g., daily, weekly, monthly, or yearly). The food list may be extensive, providing estimates of total dietary intake (i.e., dietary diversity), or it may be shorter, focusing on specific food items or groups of foods (Gibson 1993) associated with a particular health problem (e.g., nutrition-related cancers). Data from the FFQ may be collapsed into food groups and compared to the number of servings per day as recommended by the United States Department of Agriculture (USDA) Food Pyramids or other country recommendations. FFQ data may also be collapsed into composite food groups that more accurately reflect the food consumption patterns of different cultural or ethnic groups. For example, a starchy vegetables food group (*viandas* in Spanish) may be created in order to capture the relatively high intake of complex carbohydrates such as yucca, breadfruit, taro root, and yams among Hispanic/Latino groups such as Puerto Ricans (Himmelgreen et al. 1998; Pérez-Escamilla, Himmelgreen, and Ferris 1997). Sometimes the FFQ is modified to estimate usual portion sizes with the aid of food models, photographs, or actual foods. The validity of the FFQ for estimating food and nutrient intakes (with the exception of some nutrients such as vitamin A) has been demonstrated (Willett 1998a, 1998b).

Once food intake data have been collected, assessment of macronutrients and energy (i.e., carbohydrates, lipids, and proteins) and micronutrients (i.e., vitamins and minerals) can be made with the use of food composition tables such as *Bowes & Church's Food Values of Portions Commonly Used* (Pennington 1997) or computer-based nutrient databases.

Computerized databases, such as the U.S. Nutrient Data Bank (Nutrient Data Research Group, USDA Consumer Nutrition Center) and Nutritionist Pro (First DataBank), facilitate calculation of nutrient intake from individual data collected with 24-hour recalls, food histories, and food frequency questionnaires. These can be used to compare individual nutrient and food intake against recommendations (e.g., recommended daily allowances or daily recommended intakes).

Other kinds of dietary evaluations may be of interest to nutritional anthropologists (see Gibson 1993). For example, overall dietary quality can be assessed by aggregating individual nutrient adequacy ratios (of the actual daily intake of a nutrient to the recommended intake) to provide a mean adequacy ratio (MAR), or by computing the index of nutritional quality (INQ). And food frequency data can be used to rank individuals (e.g., as low, medium, or high), with respect to intake of certain foods or categories of foods, or to calculate food scores based on the frequency of consumption of foods compared to various recommendations.

Qualitative Methods in Nutritional Anthropology

A hallmark of nutritional anthropology, as mentioned previously, is a biocultural approach, which necessitates training in qualitative methods in addition to quantitative ones. The *Training Manual in Nutritional Anthropology* (Quandt and Ritenbaugh 1986) provides information on qualitative data collection methods that are commonly used by nutritional anthropologists, but other texts are also helpful (Bernard 1998; LeCompte and Schensul 1999; Emerson, Fretz, and Shaw 1995).

In general, the ethnographic process, which involves close observation and the recording of the daily lives of people (Marcus and Fischer 1986), can provide keen insights into food consumption patterns, for example, seasonal events and unusual happenings in which food and diet were involved, that are not usually captured through other methods, such as the 24-hour food recall or the FFQ. Nutritional anthropologists may use participant observation, surveys, and focus group interviews to ascertain the variety of foods available to and within communities and what may be selected for consumption (or what may be avoided) by individuals and groups. They may use these same techniques, along with other forms of interviewing (structured, semistructured, or unstructured), to gain insight into how households make decisions about food acquisition, preparation, and allocation. Focus group interviews and sorting techniques may help in the identification of various food categories (e.g., everyday vs. special-occasion foods, age-grade [including weaning] foods, gendered foods, and foods that have special health or medicinal significance).

Because applied anthropologists must often do their work more quickly than other anthropologists, rapid assessment procedures (RAPs) are often helpful. Scrimshaw and Hurtado (1987) cover techniques to assist the nutritional anthropologist in the rapid collection of relevant data from various records and from survey, interview, observation, and focus group procedures.

Preparation and analysis procedures for qualitative data are far different from those used with quantitative data. Open coding is followed by more focused coding as questions are asked of the data and themes are identified (Emerson, Fretz, and Shaw 1995). Coding techniques are described in various texts, including Emerson and colleagues (1995), Strauss and Corbin (1990), and LeCompte and Schensul (1999). Additionally, there is now powerful software that can perform qualitative analysis on unstructured and text-based data. These programs include Ethnograph 5, one of the first programs developed to analyze qualitative data; NUD*IST 6, a program that can search plain text documents (e.g., transcripts of interviews and focus groups) and external documents (e.g., media such as tape recordings and videos); and ATLAS.ti, a graphics-based program that can be used to build models.

Combining Methodologies and Analysis

It should be clear from the preceding discussion that training in nutritional anthropology is multifaceted, combining methods of data collection and analysis from a variety of subdisciplines in anthropology. In addition, the application of nutritional anthropology to solving real-world problems may require training in techniques from other disciplines, for example, policy formulation. In this area, applied nutritional anthropologists may benefit from training in program evaluation, needs assessment, and social impact assessment (see van Willigen 2002).

Probably the biggest methodological challenge in applied nutritional anthropology is bringing quantitative and qualitative data together to allow them to speak to each other in a meaningful way. Biocultural research designs are theoretically powerful, but they are difficult to carry out. One reason is the lack of training and experience in combining qualitative and quantitative methods and analytical techniques. Although many cultural anthropologists have a sound background in ethnographic interviewing and text-based qualitative data analysis, they may not have a firm understanding of quantitative methods for assessing diet, growth, and body composition, and they may have inadequate training in statistics. Conversely, whereas biological anthropologists are using cutting-edge methods in genetics, energetics, and dietary assessment to study human biology, their utilization of qualitative methods is often limited or absent; this affects the soundness of their theoretical models and sometimes the validity of their interpretation of biocultural interactions. Although there are graduate programs that provide training in combining qualitative and quantitative methods, more needs to be done so that students get adequate exposure to and experience with both. Finally, even though an increasing number of funding agencies (e.g., National Institutes of Health) are requesting proposals that combine methods, more needs to be done to increase the number of grant reviewers who give equal weight to both methodologies. In the end, qualitative data can provide insight and meaning into the patterns and trends described by numbers.

Topical Areas and Current Trends

Because nutritional anthropology is interdisciplinary and includes anthropologists from the four subfields, there are myriad topical areas of interest within the domain.

Some of these topical areas include evolutionary perspectives on human diet; food processing techniques and nutrient liberation among contemporary and historic populations; food production and nutrient deficiencies (e.g., pellagra); the adaptive significance of body size; the nutrition-infection cycle and child survival; the development of growth reference curves; sociocultural and economic factors associated with infant feeding; malnutrition and developmental delays; the impact of malnutrition on physical activity, work capacity, and reproductive fitness; prenatal nutrition and birth outcomes; nutrition and health disparities across classes and ethnic groups; genetic and environmental factors associated with obesity; biocultural factors associated with food preferences and choices; development of culturally tailored nutrition education services; access and utilization of food assistance; diet, nutrition, and agricultural development; socioeconomic factors in adult body composition; and migration and changes in family food habits.

What follows is a brief overview of some of the topical areas that are currently being explored in nutritional anthropology.

Malnutrition and Child Survival

More than 800 million people throughout the world are not meeting their basic energy and protein needs, 230 million children are malnourished (as indicated by growth stunting), and 6.6 million of the 12.2 million child (birth to five years old) deaths every year are associated with malnutrition (World Health Organization 1996, 1997). For many years now researchers, policy experts, donor agencies, governmental agencies, and nongovernmental organizations (NGOs) have been addressing malnutrition, but the complexity of the problem has made it difficult to find workable solutions. There is a myriad of intertwined causes of malnutrition, including poor diet, illness, inadequate access to food, feeding practices, inadequate health care, economic constraints, and cultural practices related to food.

During the last decade, anthropologists have made important contributions toward better understanding the role that malnutrition plays in child mortality in developing countries. For example, Pelletier (2000, 1999) and colleagues (1994, 1993) have developed a methodology to better estimate the contribution of malnutrition to child mortality. Through meta-analysis of a series of epidemiological studies, they have found that the relationship between malnutrition and mortality is consistent across populations throughout the world, that there is a significant effect of mild-to-moderate and severe malnutrition on child mortality, and that malnutrition is the most important underlying cause of child mortality in most developing countries—even after controlling for socioeconomic factors. These findings have important implications for developing models of child health and survival, which can be used to develop policy and to design and implement food and nutrition programs.

Aside from its contribution to child mortality, malnutrition in children and adults is of grave concern because of its relationship to health in general, to cognitive development and cognitive functioning, and to work capacity and productivity, in other words, to what Per Pinstrup-Andersen has called a "diminished capacity to earn and learn" (2001, v). Anthropologists are working side by side with colleagues in both the governmental and nongovernmental sectors to solve the persistent problems of malnutrition among the world's poor people and nations. We cannot provide a full list of text citations here because they are numerous, but readers may access the Web sites of organizations such as the International Food Policy Research Institute (IFPRI) (http://www.ifpri.org); the various Development Banks, for example, the Asian Development Bank (http://www.adb.org); CARE International (http://www.care.org); Save the Children (http://www.savethechildren.org); U.S. Agency for International Development (USAID) (http://www.usaid.gov); Food First (http://www.foodfirst.org); the World Bank (http://www.worldbank.org); the World Health Organization (http://www.who.int); United Nations Children's Fund (UNICEF) (http://www.unicef.org); and the Food and Agriculture Organization (http://www.fao.org) for information, policy statements, and program and other reports. An especially valuable site is Tufts University's Hunger-Web, which provides links to organizations working to solve the ongoing problems of hunger and malnutrition (http://nutrition.tufts.edu/academic/hungerweb).

Food Insecurity and Overnutrition

During the past decade, the concept of food security has been developed to describe the adequacy and reliability of food supplies at the individual and household levels. Food insecurity can result in undernutrition and overnutrition and, in some cases, both in the same population. Whereas chronic food insecurity can result in undernutrition and even micronutrient deficiencies, less severe food insecurity may affect dietary quality rather than quantity, resulting in the overconsumption of high fat or refined sugared foods and leading to overweight and obesity.

Today, an estimated 300 million people in industrialized (185 million) and developing countries (115 million) are obese (World Health Organization 2002). In addition to food insecurity, other individual, familial, and environmental factors are related to the obesity epidemic. Recently, the term globesity was coined to describe the magnitude of the problem and to emphasize the need to combat this largely preventable disease through alterations in behavior, most notably diet and physical activity (2002).

Biocultural and evolutionary perspectives are especially useful when looking at rising rates of global obesity. Brown (1991) and Brown and Konner (2000), among others, have discussed the discordance between human biological evolution and cultural evolution as precipitating factors in the evolution of obesity. Biologically, humans evolved to maximize weight gain in past environments, where food was scarce and famine was an ever-present threat. Culturally, over the last several hundred years, the human species has developed technologies that maximize food production and the availability of food, reducing the threat of food scarcity and precipitating overweight among people in many places throughout the world.

In addition to a better understanding of the biological consequences associated with modernization, there has been research on the sociocultural meanings of obesity and ideal body types, which can be useful for the development of culturally tailored obesity prevention programs (Chanman 1968; Ritenbaugh 1982). These studies and others provide insights into the perceived association of obesity with health and social status in some societies, the social stigmatization of obesity in other societies, and the ways in which health messages on obesity prevention may or may not promote positive behavior change.

Finally, there has been research on the impact of globalization on dietary changes in developing and industrialized countries. Whiteford (1992) documented a shift away from traditional foods such as *gallo pinto* (rice and beans) toward processed foods such as chips and other snack foods in rural Costa Rica. In a study among the Blackfoot in Montana, Johnston (2001) showed generational changes in sources and choices of food, including an increased reliance on off-reservation food sources (e.g., convenience stores), a decline in the use of homegrown foods, more episodic use of wild food, and a reduction of wild food sources through time.

Numerous anthropologists report worldwide changes in nutritional status (not always for the better), resulting from the effects of globalization and economic development processes on dietary strategies and food consumption patterns, including agricultural commercialization and cash cropping, higher food prices, dietary delocalization, and the penetration of junk foods and other generally low-quality foods into local markets (Daltabuit and Leatherman 1998; DeWalt and DeWalt 1991; Fleuret and Fleuret 1980; Huss-Ashmore and Curry 1994; Whiteford 1992).

Nutritional Anthropology in Action: Selected Case Studies

What follows are three case studies documenting the ways in which research in applied nutritional anthropology can be used to develop nutrition education services and a social marketing program targeting low-income Hispanic/Latino families in Hartford, Connecticut, and Tampa, Florida.

Case Study 1: The Family Nutrition Program for Infants, Toddlers, and Children

In the mid-1990s, just as welfare reform was becoming a reality, the Department of Nutritional Sciences at the University of Connecticut and the Hispanic Health Council (a community-based organization) co-founded the Family Nutrition Program for Infants, Toddlers, and Children (FNP-IT). Funded by the USDA Food Stamp Program through the Connecticut Department of Social Services, FNP-IT has the mission to provide nutrition education to households enrolled in the Food Stamp Program in and around the city of Hartford, Connecticut (Pérez-Escamilla and Himmelgreen 1999). Hartford is one of the ten poorest moderate-size cities in the United States; it has a large Hispanic/Latino population, predominantly Puerto Rican, and more than half of its Hispanic/Latino children live in poverty.

The first step in implementing FNP-IT was to conduct formative research to examine food security and nutritional needs among Puerto Rican preschoolers and their families. The main findings from this study showed a high degree of food insecurity, including episodic child hunger (one in five children studied), suboptimal infant feeding practices, poor dietary quality among children, child obesity (one in five children), and more than 20 hours per week of TV watching among preschool children (Pérez-Escamilla, Himmelgreen, and Ferris 1997). Additional research has confirmed that Puerto Rican children and their caretakers living in inner-city Hartford have serious food insecurity and suffer from nutrition- and physical-inactivity–related health problems. As a group, they experience growth stunting, a high rate of obesity, high rates of iron deficiency anemia and lead poisoning, very low intake of fresh fruits and vegetables, and frequent intake of high fat foods (Himmelgreen et al. 2000; Himmelgreen et al. 2004; Pérez-Escamilla and Himmelgreen 1997; Pérez-Escamilla et al. 2001; Pérez-Escamilla et al. 1998; and Tanasescu et al. 2000). Additionally, other studies were done on various segments on this population (e.g., Latino drug-users and their families) to examine determinants of nutritional status and household coping strategies with food insecurity (Himmelgreen et al.1998; Romero-Daza et al. 1999). The results from these studies and others (Boulanger et al. 2002; Pérez-Escamilla et al. 2001) were used to develop a culturally tailored nutrition education program, Pana (*pana* means breadfruit, which is part of the traditional Puerto Rican diet, and is also a word used to describe a close friend in Puerto Rico and other Latin American countries); food and nutrition social marketing campaigns (such as SALUD) to reach the larger community; and a peer counseling program, the Hispanic Health Council's "Breastfeeding: Heritage and Pride."

A community participatory and empowerment model was applied in all FNP-IT activities (Himmelgreen et al. 1999). For example, most FNP-IT staff resided in the community, and many of them went on for additional academic training. In addition, input and feedback were sought from at-large community members through focus groups, key informant/ethnographic interviews, and the evaluations of FNP-IT service programs. The Pana program was a bilingual, culturally tailored nutrition education program targeting parents and children from low-income families. Pana used sound public health nutrition recommendations, including the USDA's 2000 edition of *Dietary Guidelines for Americans.* The program was divided into three areas: Pana for children (age-appropriate interactive educational activities such as puppet shows and nutrition "Jeopardy"); Pana for adults (presentations and workshops on the food guide pyramid, food safety, and food labels and shopping tips for parents, educators, and other community members); and development and education tools (a Puerto Rican Food Guide Pyramid and color-coded bilingual food labels) (Haldeman et al. 2000). Pana primarily reached the community through health fairs, schools, community-based agencies, day-care centers, and radio shows.

Based on the findings from the needs assessments, FNP-IT developed the SALUD social marketing campaign around several themes—increasing the consumption of fresh fruits and vegetables; increasing knowledge both of links among diet, physical activity, and chronic diseases and of the link between folic acid deficiency and neural-tube defects. Various media (e.g., radio, TV, and print) were used to reach the target population through public service announcements, street billboards, advertisements in the mass transit system, and newspaper and magazine advertisements. Overall, approximately 200,000 Hispanic/Latinos in Connecticut and southwestern Massachusetts (almost eight out of ten target individuals) were exposed to the campaign, and most of them liked it, understood the nutrition messages, and found them to be useful (Boulanger et al. 2002; Motkar et al. 2002; Pérez-Escamilla et al. 2001; Pérez-Escamilla et al. 2000; Pérez-Escamilla et al. 1999; Stopka et al. 2002).

Case Study 2: The Acculturation and Nutritional Needs Assessment of Tampa and Projects PAN and New Life, Good Health

In 1998, the model used in FNP-IT was utilized by the Department of Anthropology at the University of South Florida in a study among low-income Hispanic/Latino families in Tampa. Although not as far along as its Hartford counterpart, the Tampa program has led to several studies and to the development of smaller-scale food and nutrition services. As in the case of Hartford, the first step in Tampa was to conduct a community-based food security and nutritional needs assessment among low-income Hispanic/Latino families. Tampa's Hispanic/Latino population is much more heterogeneous than Hartford's, and it includes a larger percentage of recent immigrants. There were many challenges in reaching the target population and in developing research instruments that could capture the variability in Tampa's Hispanic/Latino community. For example, because there are many undocumented families in the area, it took time to establish rapport and trust and to find the most appropriate venues for the delivery of nutrition education services. Moreover, during the research phase, a food frequency questionnaire had to be developed that would capture the dietary differences found among this heterogeneous population as well as the linguistic differences in the names given for the same or similar foods.

After careful pretesting of the instruments, the Acculturation and Nutritional Needs Assessment of Tampa (ANNA-T) was completed. Although the sociodemographic makeup of the Tampa sample was much different than that found in Hartford, the nutritional needs and problems were similar. There was a high degree of food insecurity, very low intake of fresh fruits and vegetables, high intakes of fat and refined sugar foods, and high rates of pediatric and adult obesity (Himmelgreen 2001, 2002). To further investigate these issues, a series of focus groups were conducted following ANNA-T in which questions on nutritional knowledge, food habits, food access, and food and nutrition needs were addressed. The findings were then used to solicit funding for nutrition education services targeting this population.

Project PAN (Promoting Adequate Nutrition) included a series of community-based and culturally tailored nutrition education seminars that promoted healthy eating and disease prevention among low-income Hispanic/ Latino families in Hillsborough County, Florida. Topics covered in the PAN curriculum included (1) enhancing nutrition knowledge; (2) improving food access (e.g., teaching how to stretch food dollars and developing a pamphlet on local food assistance and social service programs); (3) eating healthy for disease prevention (e.g., diet and diabetes); (4) showing the link between physical activity and health; and (5) discussing ways to build community empowerment. Over the course of one year, eight nutrition education seminars were conducted, reaching a total of 106 adults. The evaluation of the nutrition education seminars was highly positive, with 80 percent of the participants rating the seminars as excellent, 100 percent finding them useful, 93 percent saying the seminars helped/motivated them a lot, and 95 percent agreeing to attend another seminar (Himmelgreen and Martinez 2001).

Focus group data collected during Project PAN revealed the desire on the part of the community to improve their access to fresh fruits and vegetables through the development of a community-based farmers' market. Additionally, a small pilot study was done to examine the relationship between acculturation and food consumption patterns among recent Hispanic/Latino immigrants. In talking about their food consumption patterns since coming to the United States, 50 percent of the participants reported that they consumed fewer of their native foods from their respective countries, 42 percent consumed less fresh fruits and vegetables, 75 percent reported an increase in the consumption of processed foods, and 60 percent reported an increase in the consumption of soft drinks and artificially flavored juices and punches. Often these dietary changes were due to limited income available for food purchases and reduced access to fresh foods (i.e., many participants had small gardens or farms in their native countries). All of this information was used to write another grant proposal for Project New Life, Good Health, a community-participatory nutrition and health education program for the larger Hispanic/Latino community but especially targeting recent immigrants.

Working with several community-based agencies and local churches, the project provided free nutrition education services, health screenings, social services referrals, and a farmers' market with fresh produce at a reduced cost. Specific nutrition education services included cooking demonstrations with low-fat alternatives, presentations on diet and diabetes (a significant problem in the community), a nutrition "Jeopardy" game, and various games for adults and children that emphasized a healthy diet and being physically active. The project also offered interactive nutrition education seminars on other topics such as diet and health among older adults, child nutrition, and nutrition during the teen years. In addition to services, there was a process and evaluation component for Project New Life, Good Health.

In both of the preceding case studies, it was imperative that the community, including key individuals and agencies, play a central role in developing the proposal and in carrying out the research and service provision. For example, in Hartford, the Hispanic Health Council (which conducted research and provided services and advocacy) was an ideal setting because of its location in the heart of the Hispanic/Latino community and because of its reputation as an agency deeply committed to the community. In Tampa, several agencies, including the Hispanic Services Council (which provided referral services), the Center for Family Health (primary health care), the Multi-Cultural Resource Center (English-Spanish classes), and the San Francisco Episcopal Church (resources for promotion and space for the farmers' market) were key for gaining access to the target population. Finally and especially in the case of Tampa, it was important to start out by seeking local funding instead of federal funding. For example, the Children's Board of Hillsborough County provided resources for linking community partners and for developing proposals that were in line with the needs of the county as outlined by legislators and community representatives. Moreover, these kinds of agencies linked community groups with state and federal funding sources for longer-term projects.

Case Study 3: The Positive Deviance Approach to Household Food Insecurity

In "Addressing the Immediate Causes of Malnutrition: The Positive Deviance Approach to Household Food Security," anthropologist Thoric Cederstrom described a program for improving child nutrition that is "economical, sustainable, and promotes community empowerment" (2000, 10). The Hearth Nutrition Program is based on the statistical notion of positive deviance, that is, in any normally distributed trait, such as growth z-scores, some scores will be to the right of zero. Those individuals on the right exhibit good nutritional status, and, when the population from which the sample is drawn is generally poorly nourished, the positive deviant children and families can be used as models for improving the nutritional status of others in the community.

The positive deviance (PD) model is based on the work of Zeitlin and colleagues (1990) in Nicaragua and is participatory, with community members working together with program staff to identify how some families in a generally poor community are providing adequately for the nutrition of their children. In other words, the program asks, "what are these families doing well?" and then staff and villagers formulate home-based interventions from the identified best practices of these families to assist other families who are not doing as well.

Sternin and colleagues (1999) provide additional insight into the program as it was developed and used in four communes in Thanh Hoa province, Vietnam, in the early 1990s. First, using the existing social structure, program staff members identified and trained local health volunteers in each commune. These volunteers were trained in health, nutrition, and management practices, and they became primarily responsible for analyzing, and later monitoring, malnutrition in their own communes and for identifying PD children and the strategies employed by their parents, particularly those related to feeding and child-care practices. In this case, the PD inquiry led to the recognition of different feeding strategies among the families of poorly growing when compared to those of adequately growing children, specifically the inclusion of seasonal but readily available, free or inexpensive foods in the diets of PD children. This, then, became the basis of the intervention program, which was designed not only to rehabilitate poorly nourished children in the short-term through provision of additional food but also to provide families with the tools needed to sustain these successes in their own homes over the long-term, for example, through nutrition and child-care education sessions, including cooking demonstrations that took place in homes throughout the commune. The various aspects of the program—the Growth Monitoring Program, the Nutritional Education/Rehabilitation Program (already described), the Nutrition Revolving Loan Program, and the Healthy Pregnancy/New Mother Program (described in Sternin, Sternin, and Marsh 1999)—involved the entire community and placed nutrition at "center stage in the community's consciousness" (1999, 102). At the end of two years, second- and third-degree malnutrition was reduced from 36 percent to 4 percent in children under three years of age (the targets of the intervention), and over 93 percent of the 1,000 participating children were rehabilitated, achievements which were sustained even after children graduated from the program (Cederstrom 2000, 13).

Conclusion and Future Directions

Because of its theoretical underpinnings, the use of qualitative and quantitative methods, and the emphasis on applied research, nutritional anthropology is particularly well suited for addressing nutrition-related problems. The combination of the holistic approach, the biocultural perspective, and evolutionary theory in anthropology offers an ideal framework for the examination of the interaction between biological and cultural processes in the evolution of human food use and its nutritional consequences. Moreover, other theoretical orientations (e.g., political economy of health and human adaptation models) provide heuristic devices for studying the influences of the physical, economic, and political environments on food production, availability, access, and consumption.

Methodologically, although nutritional anthropologists have borrowed specific methods and techniques from dietetics and nutritional science (e.g., food recalls and food frequency questionnaires), there have been significant anthropological contributions to methodology in nutrition. For example, nutritional anthropometry is derived from nineteenth-century physical anthropology, and modern-day biological anthropologists have made important contributions to our understanding of the relationship between anthropometric measurements of growth and body composition and health status of individuals and populations. Methods from cultural anthropology, such as participant observation and ethnography, have been used to provide an in-depth understanding of how the pulse of everyday life impacts food habits, information that is not usually captured by dietary intake surveys. Life histories and open-ended interviews can provide recollections of the lifetime experience of individuals, which can be especially important for understanding the etiology of chronic diseases (Himmelgreen 2002). Bioarcheology has provided techniques for analyzing the nutritional content of skeletal and other human remains, which yields important nutritional information on past populations. There have also been innovations within nutritional anthropology, in which well-established methods and techniques have been modified to fit the needs of anthropological research. For instance, Christine Wilson, one of the original founders of the CNA, was one of the first to use the child-following method for studying child food consumption patterns.

Within each of the subfields of anthropology is an applied component in which practical problems are addressed. Applied anthropologists use research to bring about change in different cultural systems through the provision of data, policy formulation, or action (van Willigen 2002). Applied nutritional anthropologists often provide primary, secondary, and meta-analysis of data to policy planners for use in the formulation of local, national, and international food and nutrition policies. They also conduct ethnographic analyses of governmental, nongovernmental, and donor organizations in order to examine the ways in which sociopolitical and economic factors influence the institutional priorities and the consequential development and implementation of food and nutrition programming.

One area in which applied nutritional anthropologists are likely to make great contributions is that of nutrition education. Because of the increasing attention to the obesity epidemic in the United States and the world, clinicians and patients are finding themselves increasingly drawn into a negotiation of health and health management strategies that involve dietary change. And just as medical professionals are becoming increasingly aware of the need to understand patients' concepts of and ideas about health and health care, they will need to do the same with food and diet. As an example, we present an experience from our own fieldwork during the late 1980s.

Our field site was a hospital clinic for women with gestational diabetes mellitus (GDM). As biocultural anthropologists, we weighed, measured, and talked with women who attended the clinic, and we observed provider-patient interactions and discussions about the relationship between glucose level and food consumption. During one of these provider-patient encounters, one of us (Crooks) was privy to a discussion between a nurse and a woman with GDM, in which the nurse was trying to determine why the patient's glucose level was highly deviant during one period of the previous day. The nurse assumed the patient had not eaten properly (i.e., not from the approved list of foods), but the patient insisted she had done so—she had chicken, dumplings, and vegetables, as approved on the list. Crooks asked the patient to tell her about the chicken and dumplings; in other words, the anthropologist asked for the patient's story. She confirmed that her understanding of chicken and dumplings was a rich stew of meat, vegetables, and gravy to which dumplings were added at the end of the cooking process. The nurse's understanding of chicken and dumplings, at least for consumption by a woman with GDM, was a rather dry version of broiled chicken with a separately steamed dumpling. Once these different understandings were made known, the nurse and patient could negotiate a healthier diet that either included these foods prepared "healthfully" or one that eliminated them entirely until the patient delivered her baby, and, hopefully, her glucose returned to a more normal state.

In this way, anthropology can make a valuable contribution to nutrition education programs that hope to foster dietary changes to improve health. Anthropologists can work with clinicians, dietitians, public health workers, and others to foster the realization that their clients/patients may hold different understandings of the same phenomenon. Understandings are not always shared, but they can be known, as indeed they must be if programs to change behavior are to be successful in the short term and sustainable in the long run. We saw an example in the Health Nutrition Program case study in which change agents grounded their nutrition intervention program in locally available foods and knowledge about them (Cederstrom 2000).

In a similar way, nutritional anthropologists can contribute to the cultural competence movement that currently holds such force within the medical and allied health professions. For some time now, the medical profession has aggressively pursued the attainment of "cultural competence" vis-à-vis its patients. As anthropologists have pointed out (e.g., Taylor 2003), the concept as most often used is flawed because it assumes that culture is a thing "out there" that one inherits, puts on, and wears in order to fit into society. Culture is not a thing out there, nor a template for behavior that providers can come to know in order to "minimize cultural barriers to health care" (Hunt 2003). Culture is enacted through a process of negotiations that attempt to make meaning of one's world and one's place in it. That is why the patient with GDM could have one understanding of chicken and dumplings and the nurse could have another; they do not share the exact same cultural space, or, as Hunt and Arrar (2001) put it, the same "life-worlds." We can think about these differences in experience and meaning with respect to current nutrition edicts to "increase consumption of fresh fruits and vegetables." For many, fresh fruits and vegetables are not available or accessible; thus this message cannot be made operational, although it may be heard and understood by the target population. But anthropologists and local communities can work together to create nutrition programs that make sense, that is, programs that are meaningful in the context of community needs and resources. Project New Life, Good Health described in the case study is an excellent example.

Nutritional anthropologists are also having a larger role in the development of policies, interventions, and programs, providing especially important insights into how sociocultural factors might limit or facilitate the effectiveness of a particular policy or program. For example, Sellen (2002) recently published an article on how anthropological approaches can be used to understand breast-feeding variations and promotion of "baby friendly" communities. Sellen used evolutionary and political-economic theory, along with the biocultural perspective and examples from the ethnographic and human biology literature, to examine the discordance between breast-feeding practices and infant feeding practices. He discussed the implication of this literature for research and intervention. This article provides a clear example of how nutritional anthropology research can be used for policy and program development.

Finally, nutritional anthropologists can play an important role in addressing the problem of food insecurity and the global HIV/AIDS epidemic. Because AIDS often strikes the most economically productive segment of society, adolescents and adults between 15 and 49, the toll it is taking on economic development and on society as a whole is monumental. For example, sub-Saharan Africa experienced 3.5 million new HIV infections and 2.4 million deaths in 2001. This becomes a humanitarian crisis when one takes into account the projection that 63 percent of all hungry people will reside in sub-Saharan Africa by 2010 (Shapouri and Rosen 2001). Research indicates that African households affected by HIV/AIDS have difficulty in maintaining their livelihoods (whether in agricultural or nonagricultural activities), increasing the risk for hunger and malnutrition (du Guerny 1999; Egal and Valstar 1999). Through time, as more households are affected, functioning and economic productivity within communities is reduced. In time, as increased numbers of those individuals responsible for economic production become sick and die, traditional social and cultural institutions break down and the safety net in place to protect the most vulnerable members (children and the elderly) becomes overwhelmed.

Recently, Mtika explored the relationship between HIV/AIDS and social immunity and the threat to household food security in 65 rural households in rural Malawi. Social immunity is defined as "the collective resistance against problems" (2001, 178). Mtika stated that "social immunity is rooted in networks of interpersonal ties. Its bedrock is social capital, defined as the abundance of information, trust, and help that diffuses across networks of interaction among people, and through which individuals are obligated to exchange their resources, goods, and services to deal with problems or respond to opportunities" (179). When HIV/AIDS first strikes a community, it activates social immunity through increased sharing of labor, food, and income among the network of households. However, as the epidemic worsens, affecting more individuals and households, the people become overwhelmed and social immunity weakens. In the end, networks become fractured, social capital endowments become unfavorable, and redistribution and reciprocity mechanisms fall apart, resulting in food insecurity and malnutrition.

Applied nutritional anthropology has the potential to make significant contributions in addressing the nutritional problems of the twenty-first century. These problems include the global obesity epidemic, the intersection of diet and physical activity in the development of obesity related diseases (e.g., type 2 diabetes), the continuing problems with undernutrition and micronutrient deficiencies, the ongoing problem of food insecurity in a food-rich world and its contributions to under- and overnutrition, the impact of globalization on food consumption patterns, infant feeding recommendations in the face of HIV/AIDS, the utilization of genetically modified foods, and the need to develop culturally tailored nutrition education programs that meet the needs of increasingly diverse populations.

Throughout this chapter the main focus has been on nutritional anthropology as a means for addressing contemporary issues in public health nutrition. There are other topical areas that are covered by nutritional anthropology, which may or may not be applied. Some of these include the history of food; the relationship among food, body, and culture; the symbolic meaning of food in ritual; and the cross-cultural medicinal use of food, to name just a few (Counihan and Van Esterick 1997). Students who are interested in nutritional anthropology with the intent of specializing in public health nutrition or nutritional epidemiology should have a well-rounded background in anthropology, nutritional anthropology, human biology, nutrition and dietetics, community nutrition, and public health. Courses in qualitative and quantitative research methods, along with specific classes on nutritional assessment and analysis, are also highly desirable. The aim should be to combine the strengths of anthropology and nutrition-related disciplines to be able to truly conduct biocultural research that will add to our understanding of human food systems, provide data for policy formation, and inform the development and implementation of effective food and nutrition programs.

References

Alderman, Harold, and Marito Garcia. 1993. *Poverty, household food security, and nutrition in rural Pakistan.* Research Report 96. Washington, D.C.: International Food Policy Research Institute.

Anderson, Sue Ann. 1990. Core indicators of nutritional state for difficult-to-sample populations. *Journal of Nutrition* 120 (115): 1555–1600.

Baer, Roberta D. 1998. *Cooking—and coping—among the cacti: Diet, nutrition and available income in Northwestern Mexico.* Amsterdam: Gordon and Breach Publishers.

Bernard, H. Russell, ed. 1998. *Handbook of methods in cultural anthropology.* Walnut Creek, Calif.: AltaMira Press.

Bogin, Barry. 1988. *Patterns of human growth.* Cambridge: Cambridge University Press.

Boulanger, Paula M., Rafael Pérez-Escamilla, David A. Himmelgreen, Sofia Segura-Millan, and Lauren Haldeman. 2002. Determinants of nutrition knowledge among low-income Latino caretakers in Hartford, Conn. *Journal of the American Dietetic Association* 102 (7): 978–81.

Brenton, Barrett P. 1998. Pellagra and nutrition policy: Lessons from the Great Irish Famine to the New South Africa. *Nutritional Anthropology* 22 (1): 1–11.

Brenton, Barrett P., and Robert R. Paine. 2000. Pellagra and paleonutrition: Assessing the diet and health of maize horticulturists through skeletal biology. *Nutritional Anthropology* 23 (1): 2–9.

Brown, Peter J. 1991. Culture and evolution of obesity. *Human Nature* 2 (1): 31–57.

Brown, Peter J., and Melvin Konner. 2000. An anthropological perspective on obesity. In *Nutritional anthropology: Biocultural perspectives on food and nutrition*, edited by Alan H. Goodman, Darna L. Dufour, and Gretel H. Pelto. Mountain View, Calif.: Mayfield Publishing.

Carson, Jo Ann S., and A. Gormican. 1977. Taste acuity and food attitudes of selected patients with cancer. *Journal of the American Dietetics Association* 70: 361.

Cassidy, Claire M. 1980. Nutrition and health in agriculturalists and hunter-gatherers: A case study of two prehistoric populations. In *Nutritional anthropology: Contemporary approaches to diet and culture*, edited by Norge W. Jerome and Gretel H. Pelto. New York: Redgrave.

Cavalli-Sforza, Luigi L. 1981. Human evolution and nutrition. In *Food, nutrition, and evolution: Food as an environmental factor in the genesis of human variability*, edited by Dwain N. Walcher and Norman Kretchmer. New York: Masson.

Cederstrom, Thoric. 2000. Addressing the immediate causes of malnutrition: The positive deviance approach to household food security. *Nutritional Anthropology* 23 (1): 10–14.

Chagnon, Napoleon, and Ray Hames. 1979. Protein deficiency and tribal warfare in Amazonia: New data. *Science* 203: 910–13.

Chanman, Werner J. 1968. The stigma of obesity. *Sociology Quarterly* 9: 294–97.

Council on Nutritional Anthropology. 1998. Promotional brochure. Arlington, Va.: American Anthropological Association.

Counihan, Carole, and Penny Van Esterick, eds. 1997. *Food and culture: A reader*. New York and London: Routledge.

Cowan, Ann B., ed. 1978. A conference on the role of women in meeting basic food and water needs in developing countries: Focusing on the United Nations World Food Conference resolution on women and food. *The International Conference on Women and Food*. 3 vols. Consortium for International Development, USAID.

Crooks, Deborah L. 2003. Trading nutrition for education: Nutritional status and the sale of snack foods in an eastern Kentucky school. *Medical Anthropology Quarterly* 17: 182–99.

———. 2000. Food consumption, activity and overweight among elementary school children in an Appalachian Kentucky community. *American Journal of Physical Anthropology* 112: 159–70.

———. 1999. Understanding children's nutritional status: Combining anthropological approaches in poverty research. *Nutritional Anthropology* 22 (2): 1–12.

———. 1996. Dietary quality among poor Appalachian school children: A question of food security. *Communicator* 19 (2): 5–13.

———. 1995. American children at risk: Poverty and its consequences for children's health, growth, and school achievement. *Yearbook of Physical Anthropology*. New York: Wiley-Liss, Inc.

Daltabuit, Magali, and Thomas L. Leatherman. 1998. The biocultural impact of tourism on Mayan communities. In *Building a new biocultural synthesis: Political-*

economic perspectives on human biology, edited by Alan H. Goodman and Thomas L. Leatherman. Ann Arbor: University of Michigan Press.

Dettwyler, Katherine A. 1994. *Dancing skeletons: Life and death in West Africa.* Prospect Heights, Ill.: Waveland Press.

———. 1991. Growth status of children in rural Mali: Implications for nutrition education programs. *American Journal of Human Biology* 3 (5): 447–62.

DeWalt, Billie R., and Kathleen M. DeWalt. 1991. The results of Mexican agriculture and food policy: Debt, drugs, and illegal aliens. In *Harvest of want: Hunger and food security in Central America and Mexico*, edited by Scott Whiteford and Ann E. Ferguson. Boulder, Colo.: Westview Press.

Dewey, Kathryn G. 1980. The impact of agriculture development on child nutrition in Tabasco, Mexico. *Medical Anthropology* 4 (1): 21–54.

Douglas, Mary. 1984. Standard social uses of food. In *Food in the social order: Studies of food and festivities in three American communities*, edited by Mary Douglas. New York: Russell Sage Foundation.

———. 1975. Deciphering a meal. In *Implicit Meanings: Essays in anthropology.* London: Routledge and Kegan Paul.

DuBois, Cora, and Abram Kardiner. 1944. *The people of Alor: A social-psychological study of an East Indian island.* Minneapolis: University of Minnesota Press.

Dufour, Darna L. 1995. A closer look at the nutritional implications of bitter cassava use. In *Indigenous peoples and the future of Amazonia: An ecological anthropology of an endangered world*, edited by Leslie E. Sponsel. Tucson: University of Arizona Press.

du Guerny, Jacques. 1999. AIDS and agriculture in Africa, can agricultural policy make a difference. *Food Nutrition and Agriculture* 25: 12–18.

Eaton, S. Boyd, and Melvin Konner. 1985. Paleolithic nutrition: A consideration of its nature and current implications. *New England Journal of Medicine* 312 (5): 283–89.

Eaton, S. Boyd, Stanley B. Eaton III, and Melvin Konner. 1999. Paleolithic nutrition revisited. In *Evolutionary Medicine*, edited by Wenda R. Trevathan, Euclid O. Smith, and James J. McKenna. New York: Oxford University Press.

Egal, Florence, and Arine Valstar. 1999. HIV/AIDS and nutrition: Helping families and communities to cope. *Food Nutrition and Agriculture* 25: 20–26.

Emerson, Robert M., Rachel I. Fretz, and Linda L. Shaw. 1995. *Writing ethnographic fieldnotes.* Chicago: University of Chicago Press.

Ferro-Luzzi, Gabriella F. 1977. Ritual as language: The case of south Indian food offerings. *Current Anthropology* 18 (3): 507–14.

Firth, Raymond. 1929. *Primitive economics of the New Zealand Maori.* London: George Routledge.

Fleuret, Patrick, and Anne Fleuret. 1980. Nutrition, consumption and agricultural change. *Human Organization* 39 (3): 250–60.

Fortes, Meyer, and Sonia L. Fortes. 1936. Food in the domestic economy of the Tallensi. *Africa* 9: 237–76.

Frisancho, A. Roberto. 1990. *Anthropometric standards for the assessment of growth and nutritional status.* Ann Arbor: University of Michigan Press.

Gersovitz, Mitchell, J. Patrick Madden, and Helen Smiciklas-Wright. 1978. Validity of the twenty-four-hour dietary recall and seven-day record for group comparisons. *Journal of the American Dietetic Association* 73: 48–55.

Gibson, Rosalind S. 1993. *Nutritional assessment: A laboratory manual.* New York: Oxford University Press.

———.1990. *Principles of nutritional assessment.* New York: Oxford University Press.

Goodman, Alan H., Darna L. Dufour, and Gretel H. Pelto, eds. 2000. *Nutritional anthropology: Biocultural perspectives on food and nutrition.* Mountain View, Calif.: Mayfield Publishing.

Goodman, Alan H., and Thomas L. Leatherman, eds. 1998. *Building a new biocultural synthesis: Political-economic perspectives on human biology.* Ann Arbor: University of Michigan Press.

Gordon, Kathleen D. 1987. Evolutionary perspectives on human diet. In *Nutritional anthropology,* edited by Francis E. Johnston. New York: Alan R. Liss.

Haldeman, Lauren, Rafael Pérez-Escamilla, Ann Ferris, Linda Drake, and David A. Himmelgreen. 2000. Development of a color-coded bilingual food label for low-literacy Latino caretakers. *Journal of Nutrition Education* 32 (3): 152–60.

Harner, Michael. 1977. The ecological basis for Aztec sacrifice. *American Ethnology* 4 (1): 117–35.

Harper, Edward B. 1964. Ritual pollution as an integrator of caste and religion. In *Religion in South Asia,* edited by Edward B. Harper. Seattle: University of Washington Press.

Harris, Marvin. 1978. India's sacred cow. *Human Nature Magazine* (February): 28–36.

———. 1974. *Cows, pigs, wars, and witches: The riddles of culture.* New York: Random House.

Heyward, Vivian H. 1996. Evaluation of body composition. *Sports Medicine.* 3rd ser. 22 (3): 146–56.

Himmelgreen, David A. 2002. You are what you eat and you eat what you are: The role of nutritional anthropology in public health nutrition and nutrition education. *Nutritional Anthropology* 25 (1): 2–12.

———. 2001. Acculturation and lifestyle changes as factors in obesity among Latino adults. Presented at the Society for Applied Anthropology Annual Meeting, Merida, Yucatán, Mexico, March 28–April 1.

Himmelgreen, David A., and Dinorah Martinez. 2001. Programmatic report project PAN (Promoting Adequate Nutrition). Submitted to Children's Board of Hillsborough County, Tampa, Fla.

Himmelgreen, David A., and Nancy Romero-Daza. 1994. Changes in body weight among women from highland Lesotho. A study of seasonal coping in households with different socioeconomic conditions. *American Journal of Human Biology* 6 (5): 599–612.

Himmelgreen, David A., Rafael Pérez-Escamilla, Anir González, Yukuei Peng, Harby Bonello, Ivette Mendez, and Sofia Segura-Millan. 1999. Cultural competence and nutrition education: The example of PANA. *Social Marketing Quarterly* 4: 83.

Himmelgreen, David A., Rafael Pérez-Escamilla, Sofia Segura-Millan, Nancy Romero-Daza, Mihaela Tanasescu, and Merrill Singer. 1998. A comparison of the nutritional status and food security of inner-city drug using and non-drug using Latino women. *American Journal of Physical Anthropology* 107 (3): 251–61.

Himmelgreen, David A., Rafael Pérez-Escamilla, Sofia Segura-Millan, Yukuei Peng, Anir Gonzalez, Merrill Singer, and Ann Ferris. 2000. Food insecurity among low-income Hispanics in Hartford, Connecticut: Implications for public health policy. *Human Organization* 59 (3): 334–42.

Himmelgreen, David A., Rafael Pérez-Escamilla, Dinorah Martinez, Ann Bretnall, Brian Eells, Yukuei Peng, and Angela Bermudez. 2004. The longer you stay, the bigger you get: Length of time and language in the U.S. are associated with obesity in Puerto Rican women. *American Journal of Physical Anthropology* 125 (1): 90–96.

Himmelgreen, David A., Rafael Pérez-Escamilla, Yukuei Peng, Dinorah Martinez, Ann Bretnall, and Brian Elles. 2001. Length of time in the U.S., acculturation status, and overweight and obesity among Latinos in two urban settings. Presented at the 70th Annual Meeting of the American Association of Physical Anthropologists, March 28–31, Kansas City, Mo.

Howard, Mary, and Ann V. Millard. 1997. *Hunger and shame: Poverty and child malnutrition on Mount Kilimanjaro.* New York: Routledge.

Hunt, Linda M. 2003. The notion of "culture" in the clinical context: Meanings, interpretations and implications. Paper delivered at the Cultural Competence Conference, University of Kentucky Chandler Medical Center, Kentucky Health Education Training Center, September 19–20, Lexington, Ky.

Hunt, Linda M., and Nedal H. Arar. 2001. An analytical framework for contrasting patient and provider views of the process of chronic disease management. *Medical Anthropology Quarterly* 15: 347–67.

Huss-Ashmore, Rebecca. 1992. Introduction: Nutrition and diet as issues in human biology. *American Journal of Human Biology* 4 (2): 155–57.

Huss-Ashmore, Rebecca, ed. 1988. Introduction: Why we study seasonal constraints. MASCA Research Papers in Science and Archaeology, vol. 5. Philadelphia: University Museum.

Huss-Ashmore, Rebecca, and John J. Curry. 1994. Diet, nutrition, and agricultural development in Swaziland. 3. Household economics and demography. *Ecology of Food and Nutrition* 33 (1–2): 107–21.

Inge, William Ralph. 1922. Confessio Fidei. *Outspoken essays: Second series.* London: Longmans.

Jerome, Norge W., Randy F. Kandel, and Gretel H. Pelto, eds. 1980. An ecological approach to nutritional anthropology. In *Nutritional anthropology: Contemporary approaches to diet and culture,* edited by Norge W. Jerome, Randy F. Kandel, and Gretel H. Pelto. Pleasantville, N.Y.: Redgrave Publishing.

Johnston, Francis E. 1986. Reference data for physical growth in nutritional anthropology. In *Training manual in nutritional anthropology,* edited by Sara A. Quandt and Cheryl Ritenbaugh. Washington, D.C.: American Anthropological Association.

———, ed. 1987. *Nutritional anthropology.* New York: Alan R. Liss.

Johnston, Susan L. 2001. Food choice is shaped by accessibility: How sources of food have changed over time for the Blackfeet. *Nutritional Anthropology* 24 (2): 3–9.

Kandel, Randy F., Gretel H. Pelto, and Norge W. Jerome. 1980. Introduction. In *Nutritional anthropology: contemporary approaches to diet and culture,* edited by Norge W. Jerome, Randy F. Kandel, and Gretel H. Pelto. Pleasantville, N.Y.: Redgrave Publishing.

Kardiner, Abram. 1945. The concept of basic personality structure as an operational tool in the social sciences. In *The science of man in the world of crisis,* edited by Ralph Linton. New York: Columbia University Press.

Katz, Solomon H. 1987. Food and biocultural evolution: A model for the investigation of modern nutritional problems. In *Nutritional Anthropology*, edited by Francis E. Johnston. New York: Alan R. Liss.

Katz, Solomon H., M. L. Hediger, and L. A. Valleroy. 1974. Traditional maize processing techniques in the New World. *Science* 184: 549–61.

Kottak, Conrad P. 1978. Rituals at McDonald's. In *Natural History*. New York: American Museum of Natural History.

Kretchmer, Norman. 2000. Genetic variability and lactose tolerance. In *Nutritional anthropology: Biocultural perspectives on food and nutrition*, edited by Alan H. Goodman, Darna L. Dufour, and Gretel H. Pelto. Mountain View, Calif.: Mayfield Publishing.

Kreutler, Patricia A. 1980. *Nutrition in perspective*. Englewood Cliffs, N.J.: Prentice Hall.

LeCompte, Margaret D., and Jean J. Schensul. 1999. *Analyzing and interpreting ethnographic data*. Ethnographer's Toolkit 5. Walnut Creek, Calif.: AltaMira Press.

Levi-Strauss, Claude. 1966. *The savage mind*. Chicago: University of Chicago Press.

————.1963. *Totemism*, translated by Rodney Needham. Boston: Beacon Press.

Lieberman, Leslie S. 1986. Nutritional anthropology at the household level. In *Training manual in nutritional anthropology*, edited by Sara A. Quandt and Cheryl Ritenbaugh. Washington, D.C.: American Anthropological Association.

Lohman, Timothy G., Alex F. Roche, and Reynaldo K. Martorell, eds. 1988. *Anthropometric standardization reference manual*. Champaign, Ill.: Human Kinetics.

Malinowski, Bronislaw. 1948. Introduction. In Audrey Richards, *Hunger and work in a savage tribe*. Glencoe, Ill.: Free Press.

Marcus, George E., and Michael M. J. Fischer. 1986. *Anthropology as cultural critique: An experimental moment in the human sciences*. Chicago: University of Chicago Press.

Martorell, Reynaldo, H. L. Delgado, V. Valverde, and E. Klein. 1981. Maternal stature, fertility, and infant mortality. *Human Biology* 53 (3): 303–12.

Martorell, Reynaldo, Laura K. Khan, Morgen L. Hughes, and Laurence M. Grammer-Strawn. 1998. Obesity in Latin American women and children. *Journal of Nutrition* 128 (9): 1464–73.

Mead, Margaret. 1964. *Food habits research: Problems of the 1960s*. National Academy of Sciences, National Research Council, Publication 1225. Washington, D.C.: National Academy of Sciences.

————. 1962. The social psychology of food habits. In *Malnutrition and food habits*, edited by Anne Burgess and R. F. A. Dean. New York: Macmillan.

Messer, Ellen. 1986. The "small but healthy" hypothesis: Historical, political, and ecological influences on nutrition standards. *Human Ecology* 14: 57–75.

————. 1984. Sociocultural aspects of nutrient intake and behavioral responses to nutrition. In *Nutrition and Behavior*, edited by Janina R. Galler, vol. 5. New York: Plenum Press.

Mintz, Sidney. 1979. Time, sugar, and sweetness. *Marxist Perspectives* 2: 56–73.

Motkar, Chandrasekhar R., Sofia Segura-Pérez, Yukuei Peng, David A. Himmelgreen, Grace Damio, and Rafael Pérez-Escamilla. 2002. The SALUD Campaign: Coverage, consumer satisfaction, and nutrition knowledge influence. Experimental Biology Meetings, New Orleans, Louisiana, April 20–24 (Abstract no. 1991).

Mtika, Mike M. 2001. The AIDS epidemic in Malawi and its threat to household food security. *Human Organization* 60 (2): 178–88.

National Research Council. 1945. *Manual for the study of food habits: Report of the committee on food habits.* Bulletin of the National Research Council, no. 111. Washington, D.C.: National Research Council, National Academy of Sciences.

Neel, James V. 1962. Diabetes mellitus: A thrifty genotype rendered detrimental by "progress." *American Journal of Human Genetics* 14 (4): 354–62.

Nutritional Reviews. 2001. Summit on promoting healthy eating and active living: Developing a framework for progress. Lawrence, Kans.: International Life Sciences Institute.

Pelletier, David L. 2000. The potential effects of malnutrition on child mortality: Epidemic evidence and policy implications. In *Nutritional anthropology: Biocultural perspectives on food and nutrition,* edited by Alan H Goodman, Darna L. Dufour, and Gretel H. Pelto. Mountain View, Calif.: Mayfield Publishing.

———. 1999. Ecological, social and institutional influences on nutritional policy. *Nutritional Anthropology* 22 (2): 4–12.

Pelletier, David L., Edward A. Frongillo, and Jean Pierre Habicht. 1993. Epidemiologic evidence for a potentiating effect of malnutrition on child mortality. *American Journal of Public Health* 83 (8): 1130–33.

Pelletier, David L., Edward A. Frongillo, D. G. Schroeder, and Jean Pierre Habicht. 1994. A methodology for estimating the contribution of malnutrition to child mortality in developing countries. *Journal of Nutrition* 124 (105): 2106S–2122S.

Pellett, Peter L. 1991. Commentary: Nutrition, sustainable development and the environment. *Ecology of Food and Nutrition* 26 (3): 187–201.

Pelto, Gretel H., Alan H. Goodman, and Darna L. Dufour. 2000. The biocultural perspective in nutritional anthropology. In *Nutritional anthropology: Biocultural perspectives on food and nutrition,* edited by Alan H. Goodman, Darna L. Dufour, and Gretel H. Pelto. Mountain View, Calif.: Mayfield Publishing.

Pennington, Jean A. T. 1997. *Bowes & Church's food values of portions commonly used,* 17th ed. Philadelphia and Toronto: Lippincott Williams & Williams.

Pérez-Escamilla, Rafael, and David A. Himmelgreen. 1999. Promoting better dietary habits through nutrition education in an impoverished USA community: The PANA Program and the Salud Campaign. *United Nations Newsletter* 17: 31.

———.1997. *Connecticut family nutrition program: Infants, toddlers, and children 1996–1997 Annual Report.* Department of Nutritional Sciences, College of Agriculture and Natural Resources, University of Connecticut, Storrs.

Pérez-Escamilla, Rafael, David A. Himmelgreen, and Ann Ferris. 1997. Community nutritional problems among Latino children in Hartford, Connecticut. Family Nutrition Program Technical Report no. 1, Storrs and Hartford, Connecticut.

Pérez-Escamilla, Rafael, David A. Himmelgreen, Harby Bonello, Anir González, Lauren Haldeman, Ivette Mendez, and Sofia Segura-Millan. 2001. Nutrition knowledge, attitudes, and behaviors among Latinos in the USA: Influence of language. *Ecology of Food and Nutrition* 40 (4): 321–45.

Pérez-Escamilla, Rafael, David A. Himmelgreen, Harby Bonello, Yukuei Peng, Gloria Mengual, Anir Gonzalez, Ivette Mendez, Jocelyn Cruz, and Lisa M. Phillips. 2000. Marketing nutrition among urban Latinos: The SALUD Campaign. *Journal of the American Dietetic Association* 100 (6): 698–701.

Pérez-Escamilla, Rafael, David A. Himmelgreen, Sofia Segura-Millan, Anir Gonzalez, Ann Ferris, Grace Damio, and Angela Bermudez-Vega. 1998. Prenatal and perinatal factors associated with breast-feeding initiation among inner-city Puerto Rican women. *Journal of the American Dietetic Association* 98 (6): 657–63.

Pérez-Escamilla, Rafael, David A. Himmelgreen, Sofia Segura-Millan, Anir Gonzalez, Ivette Mendez, and Jocelyn Cruz. 1999. Knowledge of folic acid and neural tube defects among inner-city residents: Have they heard about it? *Journal of the American Dietetic Association* 99 (1): 80–83.

Pinstrup-Andersen, Per. 2001. Foreward. In *Attacking the double burden of malnutrition in Asia and the Pacific,* edited by Stuart Gillespie and Lawrence Haddad. Manila, Philippines: Asian Development Bank, and Washington, D.C.: International Food Policy Research Institute.

Popkin, Barry M. 2001. The nutrition transition and obesity in the developing world. *Journal of Nutrition* 131 (3): 871S–873S.

———. 1994. The nutrition transition in low-income countries: An emerging crisis. *Nutrition Reviews* 52 (9): 285–98.

Quandt, Sara A. 1986. Nutritional anthropology: The individual focus. In *Training manual in nutritional anthropology,* edited by Sara A. Quandt and Cheryl Ritenbaugh. Washington, D.C.: American Anthropological Association.

Quandt, Sara A., and Cheryl Ritenbaugh. 1986. Introduction. In *Training manual in nutritional anthropology,* edited by Sara A. Quandt and Cheryl Ritenbaugh. Washington, D.C.: American Anthropological Association.

Rappaport, Roy A. 1968. *Pigs for the ancestors.* New Haven, Conn.: Yale University Press.

Richards, Audrey L. 1939. *Land, labour and diet in northern Rhodesia: An economic study of the Bemba tribe.* London: International Institute of African Languages and Cultures by the Oxford University Press.

Ritenbaugh, Cheryl. 1982. Obesity as a culture-bound syndrome. *Culture, Medicine and Psychiatry* 6: 347–61.

Romero-Daza, Nancy, David A. Himmelgreen, Rafael Pérez-Escamilla, Sofia Segura-Millan, Mihaela Tanasescu, and Merrill Singer. 1999. Taking care of yourself when you are an addict: Food habits of addicted Hispanic women in Hartford, Connecticut. *Medical Anthropology* 18 (3): 281–98.

Ross, Eric B. 1978. Food taboos, diet, and hunting strategy: The adaptation to animals in Amazon cultural ecology. *Current Anthropology* 19 (1): 1–36.

Scrimshaw, Susan C. M., and Elena Hurtado. 1987. *Rapid assessment procedures for nutrition and primary health care: Anthropological approaches to improving programme effectiveness.* Tokyo: United Nations University; Los Angeles: UCLA Latin American Center Publications, University of California.

Sellen, Daniel W. 2002. Anthropological approaches to understanding the causes and variation in breast-feeding and promotion of "baby friendly" communities. *Nutritional Anthropology* 25 (1): 19–29.

Sellen, Daniel W., and Alison Tedstone. 2000. Nutritional needs of refugee children in the UK. *Journal of the Royal Society of Medicine* 93 (7): 360–64.

Semba, Richard D., and Martin W. Bloem, eds. 2001. *Nutrition and health in developing countries.* Totowa, N.J.: Humana Press.

Shapouri, Shahla, and Stacey Rosen. 2001. Food security assessment: Regional overview. *USDA, Agriculture Information Bulletin* 765 (1).

Simondon, Kirsten B., Eric Bénéfice, François Simondon, Valerie Delaunay, and Anouch Chahnazarian. 1993. Seasonal variation in nutritional status of adults and children in rural Senegal. In *Seasonality and human ecology*, edited by S. J. Ulijaszek and S. S. Strickland. Great Britain: Cambridge University Press.

Singer, Merrill. 1998. Forging a political economy of AIDS. In *The political economy of AIDS*, edited by Merrill Singer. Amityville, N.Y.: Baywood Publishing.

Sternin, Monique, Jerry Sternin, and David Marsh. 1999. Scaling up a poverty alleviation and nutrition program in Vietnam. In *Scaling up, scaling down: Overcoming malnutrition in developed countries*, edited by Thomas J. Marchione. The Netherlands: Overseas Publishers Association.

Steward, Julian. 1972. *Evolution and ecology: Essays in social transformation.* Urbana: University of Illinois Press.

Stini, William A. 1981. Body composition and nutrient reserves in evolutionary perspective. *World Review of Nutrition and Dietetics* 37: 55–83.

Stopka, Thomas, Sofia Segura-Pérez, Donna Chapman, Grace Damio, and Rafael Pérez-Escamilla. 2002. An innovative community-based approach to encourage breastfeeding among Hispanic/Latino women. *Journal of the American Dietetic Association* 102: 766–67.

Strauss, Anselm L., and Juliet Corbin. 1990. *Basics of qualitative research: Grounded theory procedures and techniques.* Newbury Park, Calif.: Sage.

Tanasescu, Mihaela, Ann Ferris, David A. Himmelgreen, Nancy Rodriguez, and Rafael Pérez-Escamilla. 2000. Biobehavorial factors are associated with obesity in Puerto Rican children. *Journal of Nutrition* 30 (7): 1734–42.

Taylor, Janelle S. 2003. The story catches you and you fall down: Tragedy, ethnography, and "cultural competence." *Medical Anthropology Quarterly* 17: 159–81.

van Willigen, John. 2002. *Applied anthropology: An introduction.* 3rd ed. Westport, Conn.: Bergin and Garvey.

Weiner, J. S., and J. A. Lourie. 1981. *Practical human biology.* London: Academic Press.

White, Leslie A. 1949. *The science of culture. A study of man and civilization.* New York: Farrar, Straus.

Whiteford, Michael B. 1992. From gallo pinto to Jack's Snacks: Observations on dietary change in a rural Costa Rican village. *Ecology of Food and Nutrition* 27 (3–4): 207–18.

Willett, Walter C. 1998a. Invited commentary: Comparison of food frequency questionnaires. *American Journal of Epidemiology* 148 (12): 1137–47.

———. 1998b. *Nutritional Epidemiology.* 2nd ed. New York: Oxford University Press.

World Health Organization. 2002. *Controlling the global obesity epidemic.* From http://www.who.int/nut/obs.htm

———. 1997. *Fact sheet: Reducing mortality from major childhood killer diseases.* From http://www.who.int/child-adolescent-health/New_Publications/IMCI/fs_180.htm

———. 1996. *Fact sheet: Child malnutrition.* From http://www.who.int/inf-fs/en/fact119.html

————. 1995. An evaluation of infant growth: The use and interpretation of anthropometry in infants. WHO Working Group on Infant Growth. *Bulletin of the World Health Organization* 73 (2): 165–74.

Zeitlan, Marian F., Hossein Ghassemi, Mohamed Mansour, Robert A. Levine, Maria Dillanneva, Manuel Carballo, and Suganya Sockalingham. 1990. *Positive deviance in child nutrition: With emphasis on psychosocial and behavioral aspects and implications for development.* Tokyo: United Nations University.

7 Applied Anthropology and Development-Induced Displacement and Resettlement

Anthony Oliver-Smith

Introduction

There are few more bitterly contested issues in the field of development today than the displacement and resettlement of people and communities by large-scale infrastructural projects. The World Bank has calculated that publicly and privately funded development projects displace approximately 10 million people a year (Cernea and McDowell 2000). Characteristically, people and communities are displaced by capital-intensive, high technology, large-scale development projects that convert farmlands, fishing grounds, forests, and homes into dam-created reservoirs, irrigation schemes, mining operations, plantations, colonization projects, highways, urban renewal, industrial complexes, and tourist resorts favoring regional, national, or global interests. Putatively designed to spur economic growth and spread general welfare, many of these projects leave local people permanently displaced, disempowered, and destitute (Koenig 2000). Anthropologists in the mid-twentieth century were among the first to recognize, report on, and work toward mitigating the serious impoverishment and gross violations of human rights that occurred among populations resettled by development projects (Butcher 1971; Brokensha and Scudder 1968; Colson 1971; Hansen and Oliver-Smith 1982).

Despite the participation of other fields, anthropology can reasonably claim to be the foundational discipline of the field of development-induced displacement and resettlement research (DIDR). Because DIDR impacts virtually every domain of community life, anthropology's holistic approach equips it well to address the inherent complexity of the resettlement process. It is also in DIDR that anthropology has arguably made the single strongest, tangible, and internationally documented and recognized contribution to development policy and practice over the last quarter century. Since the 1950s, anthropologists have spanned the entire field of DIDR in basic and applied research, policy formulation, theory building, evaluation, planning, implementation, and community- and NGO-based resistance movements. Anthropologists have helped to frame and contribute to current debates concerning DIDR on human and environmental rights, policy frameworks and guidelines, implementation, evaluation, the limits of state sovereignty, and the agendas of international capital. In the context of current intensified development agendas, because of its central role in the field, anthropology has a responsibility to expand the array of approaches and methods that address the challenges presented by DIDR at the local community and project level, in national and international political discourse, and in the policy frameworks of multilateral institutions.

Despite the fact that in the phrase development-induced displacement and resettlement three basic ideas—development, displacement, and resettlement—are linked, there has not always been, nor is there now, any necessary relationship among them. Development obviously can take place without displacement or resettlement. Many people who are displaced by development projects are never resettled, and they either succumb to the impacts of dislocation or find themselves consigned to the margins of society and economy. Further, the vast majority of those displaced by development who are in fact resettled suffer the outcomes of inadequately financed, poorly designed, and incompetently implemented resettlement projects that bear no resemblance to any honestly rendered interpretation of the concept of development. Hence, there is no necessary or inevitable linkage between development, displacement, and adequate, humane resettlement.

The trauma and hardships experienced by the displaced pose critical moral questions about the nature, scale, and ethics of such development models and practices. Generally, development as a goal of public policy is aimed at improving levels of well-being through enhancing productive capacity, based on the premise that increased production and income will filter through the system to enhance general patterns of consumption. Enhanced productive capacity is posited on a principle of efficient use of resources to render maximum market value (Penz 1992, 107). National governments and private developers assess that local users do not efficiently exploit resources, and they argue that large-scale projects produce greater value, thereby enhancing levels of overall economic development. Projects that displace communities justify themselves ethically with the belief that greater value production increases consumption and welfare at all levels of society. When projects force people to resettle, the process may be defined in economic terms, but resettlement is fundamentally a political phenomenon, involving the use of power by one party to relocate another. Current trends suggest that development strategies will continue to stress large-scale projects that will result in the resettlement of large numbers of people. The extent to which this process can be carried out ethically, democratically, and effectively is an issue of considerable dispute.

For local people, often members of indigenous or minority groups and their allies in the global networks of social movements and NGOs, the rights to land and other resources, self-determination, cultural identity, environmental protection, and more sustainable forms of development are central to the survival of their communities. Their claims emphasize the rights of the less powerful, the significance of cultural diversity, and the sustainability of environments over what they consider ecologically risky, economically questionable, and socially destructive projects (Oliver-Smith 2001). They point to the consistent failures of governments and private developers to adequately fund, plan, and train personnel for the complex tasks of DIDR, resulting in the impoverishment of the displaced. Deploying international covenants, they have actively broadened the agenda to include questions of human and environmental rights and justice in development, frequently converting their discourses of resistance into alternative models and strategies for socially responsible development. The central issue in DIDR is the democratic character of the development process.

Development-Induced Displacement in the Twentieth Century

In terms of sheer numbers, the twentieth century saw more people displaced and set in motion against their will than any other in recorded history. The wars and environmental havoc that have uprooted millions have been compounded by the global drive to develop. Despite sharing many similarities, displacement caused by development projects is different in important ways from the dislocation experienced by participants in voluntary relocation schemes, victims of natural or technological disasters, or refugees from civil or international conflicts. In DIDR people are "pushed" to move rather than "pulled" or attracted by better possibilities elsewhere. DIDR is entirely involuntary, despite the inducements devised to attract people to voluntarily resettle. Furthermore, although wars that turn people into refugees are the outcome of intentional decisions taken by political authorities, the general consensus is that they should be avoided whenever possible. However, large development projects, also the result of intentional decisions by authorities, are seen to fit well within national ideologies of development. In effect, empowered by international standards that grant the state the right to take property for national goals, such projects are justified by a cost-benefit analysis that assigns losses and gains on a political basis. Finally, unlike the victims of disasters or wars, there is no returning home once the situation has stabilized. DIDR is permanent. There can be no return to land that is submerged under a dam-created lake or a neighborhood that is under a stadium or a highway. Thus, the solutions that are devised to meet the needs of development-induced displacees must be durable rather than contingency-based emergency strategies to meet immediate needs until people can return home (Guggenheim and Cernea 1993, 3–4).

The problem of development-induced displacement and resettlement expresses the frequent tensions in development between local and national needs. In DIDR the needs of societies to develop their infrastructure to produce more energy, better water supplies, more efficient transportation systems, or more productive agriculture are balanced against the welfare of the local communities that face displacement and possible resettlement to make room for such projects. The costs of DIDR that are born by local people are balanced against the benefits that the entire society will purportedly enjoy from the implementation of the project.

Applied Anthropological Research in Displacement and Resettlement

Despite the long history of involuntary displacement by development projects, systematic research on its effects and outcomes, whether people were formally resettled or not, did not begin until the 1950s. Research on displacement emerged from the postwar concern for the welfare and fate of the enormous numbers of refugees in World War II. The pioneer document was Alexander Leighton's *The Governing of Men: General Principles and Recommendations based on Experiences at a Japanese Refugee Camp* (1945). Although based on a case of politically forced relocation, Leighton introduced in his research many of the issues that would become central to the concerns of anthropologists who undertook research with development-induced displacement in the 1950s, particularly in the realms of stress, social organization, and forms of resistance. In 1952 Elizabeth Colson and Thayer Scudder began long-term research on the social and ecological consequences of resettlement among the Gwembe Tonga, who were relocated by the construction of the Kariba Dam in what was to become Zambia and Zimbabwe (Colson 1971; Scudder 1973; Scudder and Colson 1982). The 1950s saw the topic attract increasing interest elsewhere in Africa (Chambers 1970; Fahim 1983), as well as in Asia (Dobby 1952) and Latin America (Villa Rojas 1955), as postwar and, subsequently, postcolonial development efforts accelerated.

In roughly the same period, sociologists in the United States began to consider the impacts of displacement on neighborhoods affected by urban renewal and large-scale construction projects, developing important perspectives on grief and mourning for lost homes among resettled people (Fried 1963; Gans 1962). In the 1960s, efforts at developing conceptual models of the displacement and resettlement process began to appear. Robert Chambers proposed a three-stage model based on voluntary land settlement projects in Africa (1969). Nelson, working on new land settlements in Latin America, developed a similar approach (1973). The problems associated with DIDR provoked a response in the form of an organizational manual for resettlement from the United Nations Food and Agriculture Organization (FAO) (Butcher 1971).

In the 1970s the problems experienced by people affected by the growing number of development projects were linked to those of people displaced by the expansion of conflicts as well as major natural disasters (Hansen and Oliver-Smith 1982). At that time, Scudder and Colson, addressing the responses of dislocated peoples regardless of cause, proposed a stress-based four-stage process of recruitment, transition, potential development, and incorporation (1982; see below for more discussion). The field of displacement and resettlement studies expanded considerably in the 1980s, especially because concern about the environmental and social impacts of large infrastructure projects, particularly dams, began to be expressed. Indeed, two World Bank research and policy specialists speculated that the 1980s might go down in history as "the decade of displacement" (Guggenheim and Cernea 1993, 1). A key element in the growth of this concern about DIDR was the expansion of well-organized and widely publicized resistance movements in regions where projects were displacing and resettling many thousands of people, such as Brazil, India, Thailand, Mexico, and many other nations. As the resistance movements publicized the many inadequacies of displacement and resettlement policies and practices, the problem of DIDR moved to center stage in the debates regarding the development process, and it gained the attention of the general public and the research community alike.

Many of the studies stimulated by the massive increase in the number of people displaced by development projects in the 1980s followed the lead of Colson and Scudder in documenting the social impacts and injustices of the displacement process, focusing on the characteristics of the stresses of dislocation and resettlement, patterns of individual and group reactions, the similarities and differences among the various forms of displacement and resettlement, and assessment of the negative outcomes imposed on people in the resettlement process. The researchers as well as the locations of research were international. Particularly in those nations in which large-scale infrastructural development processes were being funded from national, international, and multilateral sources, a considerable body of DIDR research began to emerge. Those governmental and multilateral institutions, as well as international private consulting organizations, began to produce increasing amounts of material on DIDR in the form of a substantial "gray literature" composed of feasibility studies, project evaluations, and in-house reviews of policies and outcomes, many of them researched and authored by anthropological staff or consultants (e.g., Rew and Driver 1986).

In similar fashion, NGOs that allied themselves with the displaced also called on anthropologists to produce lengthy documentation substantiating the deficiencies of DIDR policy and negative project impacts (e.g., Aspelin and Coelho dos Santos 1981; Barabas and Bartolome 1973; Feit and Penn 1974). In India, for example, researchers documented the displacement of thousands by development projects, the lack of any resettlement efforts for many of the displaced, and the failures and inadequacies of those resettlement projects that were provided for the affected peoples (Fernandes and Thukral 1989). By the same token, in Mexico, where researchers had begun documenting the social impact of dam construction in the early 1950s, analysis of the displacement and relocation process for the Cerro de Oro Dam assessed the impacts as a process of "ethnocide" (Barabas and Bartolome 1973). Other dam projects that resettled people were also documented (Ballesteros, Edel, and Nelson 1970). Researchers in Brazil, where the government had proposed a nationwide 80-dam hydropower development initiative, also began to explore the implications of large-scale relocation and resettlement projects, particularly for indigenous and peasant populations in the Amazon region (Santos and de Andrade 1990; Sigaud 1986).

The case of the Tucurui Dam in Northeast Brazil is emblematic of the problems caused by poorly planned and implemented resettlement projects. The Tucurui Dam, the largest in the tropics and fourth largest in the world, is part of an overall plan of the Brazilian government to build 80 dams to reduce national dependence on petroleum-generated power. Before the gates closed in 1984, flooding 2,850 square kilometers of forest, including part of the Parakana Indian reservation, between 20,000 and 30,000 people had to be relocated. The Brazilian government and the administrating agency, Eletronorte, had a woefully inadequate resettlement policy that affected only a minority of those relocated upstream from the dam and obligated many to fend for themselves in settlements upriver and along the trans-Amazon highway (Biery-Hamilton 1987). Even those who were included in the resettlement scheme were inadequately compensated for their losses. Environmental impacts both upstream and downstream of the dam became the motors for significant protest and resistance that eventually empowered local people for future negotiations with the state (Scudder 1996).

Upstream from the dam, an area known as the Parakana Glebe, located close to the bank of the reservoir, suffered severe environmental impacts. Many people displaced by the reservoir were relocated to the Parakana Glebe. In effect, the filling of the dam had transformed the Glebe from a forest fluvial environment to a lacustrine ecosystem. The reservoir area closest to the Glebe had not been deforested prior to submersion, and when the reservoir was filled in early 1986, the decaying and floating vegetation provided an ideal spawning habitat for mosquitoes. The insects proliferated uncontrollably and soon became a virtual plague. They soon spread from the lakeside to secondary breeding grounds on roads and to certain trees in the forest whose foliage collects considerable water. Initially, the resettled communities attempted to endure the conditions, going about their normal activities, but the infestation became "unbearable. Nobody could work anymore, or even sleep. . . . Then desperation came, we became really desperate. People abandoned their lots and went to look for some solution. The government should have helped people in that calamity" (interview with a Union leader/STR-NR, February 1996, quoted in Acselrad and da Silva 2000, 5).

A series of epidemics, including malaria and leishmaniasis, a disfiguring and potentially fatal skin infection, swept over the area, and many of the roughly 8,000 people living close to the reservoir had to abandon their farms and homes (McCully 2001, 93). Indeed, as people experienced these new conditions of misery and disease, their interpretations linking the lack of deforestation in the submerged area closest to them with the creation of ideal breeding conditions for mosquitoes generally coincided with scientific assessments. However, scientific caution, based on a lack of field studies, resulted in no assignment of direct causality and enabled Eletronorte to challenge these conclusions and assign blame to the population itself. Eletronorte claimed that waste runoff from the communities themselves created conditions that allowed mosquitoes to proliferate, thereby setting up an environmental debate between the resettlement authority and the people. However, in 1991 evidence confirmed that mosquito larvae were present in the vegetation that emerged after the filling of the reservoir. The lack of an effective policy to combat the plague, the problematic nature of the empirical information, and the severe impact on health and living conditions led the people to begin negotiations with land-tenure agencies, ministries, local governments and politicians, and subsequently to Brasilia to the ministries, the national congress, and the president. From these negotiations a new settlement project was established, albeit with new sets of problems, primarily competing landlords and their hired thugs (unless otherwise noted, this section is based on Acselrad and da Silva 2000).

In addition, approximately 40,000 *caboclos* (peasants) who lived downstream on the hundreds of islands between the dam and the mouth of the river began to suffer serious ecological and economic impacts. In the course of research undertaken by Magee four years after the close of the dam gates, it was found that traditional subsistence strategies of riverine peasants were totally disrupted. As Magee noted, "if peasants above the dam suffered the loss of their land, peasants below the dam suffered the loss of their water" (1989, 6–7). The water below the dam became seriously polluted from decomposing trees in the flooded areas that were not cleared before the floodgates closed. In the four years after the dam began operation, the pollution of the water caused a series of outbreaks of waterborne diseases of various sorts, ranging from serious vaginal infections to gastrointestinal ailments, particularly among children, and skin rashes in the general population. Island crops suffered also from the polluted water. Cacao and *acai* palm production was crippled. However, the most serious consequence of the dam was the destruction of the river's shrimp and fish populations, the very base of the local subsistence economy and an important source of exchange value as well (Magee 1989).

Faced with the continuing destruction of their resource base by the dam, the riverine caboclos were left with two options: migration and resettlement or resistance designed to obligate the government to both recognize and compensate their losses and also to diminish the damaging impacts of the dam. In this effort, the Tucurui River peasants began to engage in new forms of political mobilization to defend their way of life. They acquired two extremely important allies: the Catholic Church and the Rural Workers Union. At the top of the agenda of the new union leadership was the commencement of negotiations with Eletronorte and its consulting companies to establish responsibilities for the effects of the dam (Magee 1989). In the process, the peasants began to acquire the political skills that enabled them to represent their own interests. However, as Magee (1989, 10) noted, it remained to be seen whether the Tocantins Islanders could muster the international support they needed to survive on the islands or whether they would join the ranks of the other disenfranchised groups competing for scarce land on the mainland.

Among the problems investigated by other researchers in many other nations were the failures of governments and government agencies to adequately fund resettlement projects or to adequately plan for them along with the infrastructural project and to train personnel to handle such a complex task. To some degree, the failure to take seriously the human rights of the affected people and the failure to understand the complexity and gravity of the impacts of the DIDR process characterized the arrogance and ignorance of authorities in many countries in both the developed and the developing worlds. Other researchers focused on failures in planning and implementation, such as land replacement, social stress, differential gender-based effects, ideological impacts, legal issues, compensation problems, lack of participation in project planning and implementation by local people, problems experienced by host populations, failure to provide economic support, ecological impacts, and urban planning and housing.

Although much of this research still focused on the negative outcomes of poorly planned and implemented resettlement projects and the lessons to be learned from these failures, a number of investigators turned their attention to the question of successful resettlement in those relatively few cases where it could be claimed. Recognizing the difficulty inherent in establishing a set of criteria against which such a multidimensional social process that usually transpired over many years, and sometimes decades, might be assessed for success, several researchers highlighted those projects that enjoyed partial success at one stage or another of development as beacons of light in the otherwise dismal record of DIDR.

Partridge, for example, considered that the Arenal Hydroelectric Project in Costa Rica succeeded in improving the standards of living and returning control over their own lives to the resettled people within five years of implementation of the project (all information on Arenal is drawn from Partridge 1993). The Arenal Hydroelectric Project involved the construction of a dam 70 meters high to produce a reservoir of 1,750 cubic meters, and it necessitated the displacement and resettlement of about 2,500 people (roughly 500 families). The final cost of the project was $179 million, almost twice the originally estimated cost of $91 million.

The area in which the project was located was a humid tropics cattle-ranching complex, a system that went through three developmental phases. The first phase involved the colonization of tropical forest by migrants who use slash-and-burn agriculture to begin small farms. The second phase involved the absorption of these small holdings by large cattle-ranches, which continued clearing the forest for pasture. The third phase resulted in the depopulation of the region as land was taken over for pasture and both farming and employment opportunities decreased. The region to be affected by the dam was fully in the third phase, having already lost roughly a fourth of its population. The principal economic activity was cattle ranching, with little or no commercial agriculture. Subsistence agriculture was declining as well. In other words, the potential for the region for supporting the existing population was in rapid decline.

When the dam project was approved, resettlement planning began two years before actual construction began. The preparatory period consisted of 11 steps or phases. These 11 phases were:

Phase I: Ethnographic Sample Survey of Communities
Phase II: Information Campaign and Meetings with Families
Phase III: Census of People and Property to be Affected
Phase IV: Making Public the Planning Data
Phase V: New Settlement Site Selection
Phase VI: Action Plan for Resettlement Prepared
Phase VII: Land Acquisition
Phase VIII: Participation of the Affected Population
Phase IX: Financial Mechanism for Restitution of Property
Phase X: Construction of New Settlements
Phase XI: Community and Agricultural Development

The first several years (1976–79) of the new communities were difficult. The resettled people cleared land and planted traditional crops such as maize, manioc, plantains, and bananas. Seeds and cuttings were made available to the farmers as soon as their new plots had been allocated. The agricultural system in the new settlements initially used the traditional slash-and-burn technology. Subsequently, new vegetable, tree, and pasture crops, which had been field-tested during the construction phase, began to be cultivated, particularly a new variety of coffee. Individual farmers obtained loans from the National Bank of Costa Rica to intensify production, and the farmers as a group organized a marketing cooperative. Income from coffee increased by roughly 100 percent over preresettlement levels. New grasses for cattle fodder also enabled farmers to increase the number of cattle pastured per hectare from one animal to three. A new road constructed by the Instituto Costarricense de Electrificación (ICE) linked the new communities to market centers and fostered the development of several small dairy farms.

Income from these initiatives stimulated purchases of additional farmlands, construction of outbuildings on farms, purchase of vehicles, and construction of a rural school building with no assistance from the government.

The success of the families in the farming sector nourished success in the commercial sector. Shopkeepers and their families benefited by the increased levels of cash income in the communities. Levels of fixed capital and inventory values in the new communities ranged between 50 and 200 percent greater than those in the old settlements. Furthermore, social organizational features developed in the new communities in the form of a school committee, a sports committee, and the continuation of the Catholic Church committee. Finally, the population of the new communities remained stable, halting the flight of people from an area they perceived as unable to sustain them.

Partridge attributed the successes achieved in the project to three basic steps in the preparation process. Good data collection and community studies carried out by social scientists resulted in a resettlement plan than was both realistic and practical. He also emphasized the importance of consultation with the people to be relocated and their meaningful participation in the preparation process. Also significant in the success of Arenal was the strategy of establishing the new farms on the basis of traditional crops and technology, allowing the farmers to continue with known practices for the initial period of adjustment. After three years, innovations were introduced when people were more able to assume risks, and the results significantly enhanced income generation, leading to long-term acceptance of the new settlements (Partridge 1993, 367).

Two recent publications of the World Bank, while acknowledging that major problems remain for people uprooted by development projects, maintain that improvements are being made in resettlement in DIDR planning and implementation. The Impoverishment Risks and Reconstruction (IRR) model developed by Cernea provides a significant tool for the prediction, diagnosis, and resolution of problems associated with DIDR (Cernea and McDowell 2000). A study by the World Bank's Operations Evaluation Department (OED) of five major bank-funded dam projects concluded that although better planning has occurred, it has not generally led to better involuntary resettlement. Furthermore, the public agencies charged with resettlement have not responded adequately to the challenge of resettlement. They also find that income restoration strategies, whether based on land-for-land or other options, have not in general been successful. The key to success, in their opinion, is genuine commitment to the resettlement process as a development opportunity by the borrower country (Picciotto, van Wicklin, and Rice 2001).

Generally, nondam-related of DIDR have been less fully documented and analyzed. Other forms of development-induced displacement, such as conservation, urban renewal, mining, public-use complexes, transportation, and pipelines, have received generally less attention as causes of resettlement. One example of a well-documented nondam case is the Singrauli region of central India (Clark 2003). Although the initial transformation of the region and significant population displacement began in 1960 with the Rihand Dam, subsequent environmental destruction and the displacement of ultimately between 200,000 and 300,000 people, some of them displaced as many as three to five times, have been due to the massive exploitation of large deposits of coal that are found beneath the surface in the region. With World Bank loans, the National Thermal Power Corporation (NTPC) established nine open-pit coal mines, which operate 24 hours a day, and it constructed the Singrauli Super Thermal Power Plant, the Vindhyachal Super Thermal Power Plant and the Rihand Power Plant, all on the banks of the reservoir created by the original Rihand Dam. Three other power plants, although not run by the NTPC, have been added close by. The power plants subsequently attracted hundreds of factories and plants for chemical, aluminum, cement, and other forms of industrial production.

Local people were relocated into resettlement colonies as their agricultural land was appropriated for the dam and reservoir and later for the coal mines, power plants, roads, and markets, homes, and recreational grounds for NTPC workers. Ninety percent of the local people were relocated at least once, and 34 percent were uprooted several times as development in the region expanded. A study commissioned by the World Bank and the NTPC found that resettlement projects were unsuccessful in almost all the cases, failing to provide adequate facilities and equipment for water supply, sewage treatment, schools, education, or medical care. Moreover, industry-driven air, water, and soil pollution seriously contaminated the food chain and compromised the health of the population consigned to the resettlement colonies. Displacement forced formerly self-sufficient agriculturalists to become beggars seeking occasional labor in the industrial complex. The livelihoods and way of life of the resettled communities were utterly destroyed, and neither the NTPC nor the local government was willing to assume responsibility for their losses. Now known as the energy capital of India, Singrauli has also been compared to "the lower reaches of Dante's Inferno" (Clark 2003, 167–272).

As mentioned earlier, urban renewal and, more recently, gentrification in the developed world have been closely examined since the 1950s (e.g., Gans 1962; Fried 1963; Squires et al. 1987). With rapid urban growth in both the developed and developing worlds, projects ranging from public-use facilities (such as stadia, conference centers, government complexes) to slum clearance to major transportation redevelopment have displaced hundreds of thousands of people. Local authorities are increasingly employing eminent domain to transfer property to private developers to spur economic growth (Cauchon 2004).

Conservation-driven resettlement is also receiving increasing attention (Brechin et al. 2003). In 1980 the International Union for the Conservation of Nature published the *World Conservation Strategy*, challenging the national park model and advocating the incorporation of local people into the conservation process. The World Bank followed this initiative with a program called Integrated Conservation and Development Projects (ICDP), intended to integrate local people into projects to enable them to benefit economically.

However, more recently, dissatisfaction with the outcomes of such projects has generated a more exclusionary strain within the conservation movement, dubbed the "protectionist paradigm" (Brechin et al. 2003). It calls for a radical transformation of nature, namely the removal of all human inhabitants from environments deemed endangered (Terborgh 1999). This strategy entails the forced removal of people from their homelands, producing another variety of environmental refugee (Geisler and Da Sousa 2001). Barring outright displacement, the new protectionist paradigm advocates radically restricting resource-use practices employed by people resident in reserves and parks. Such restrictions constitute a form of structural displacement in that, although people have not been geographically moved, the norms and practices with which they have engaged the environment in the process of social reproduction have become so altered as to effectively change their environment from one that is known to one that must be newly encountered with new norms and new practices if social reproduction is to continue.

There is still considerable need for research on other forms of development-induced displacement. Much greater attention should be paid to privately funded development projects that induce displacement. The significance of this form of research will only increase in the coming decade as privatization of previously publicly provided services increases. Some private sector projects have developed their own resettlement plans and policies (Rio Tinto 2001). However, most privately funded development, such as the outcome of market factor speculation, presents significantly different problems for people affected by DIDR, in the disguised involuntary quality of market exchanges between parties of unequal power. Although private projects must agree to DIDR guidelines to get World Bank guarantees for lower interest rates, other private sector infrastructural initiatives that do not want or need the guarantees are free to subordinate the human and environmental rights of affected communities to corporate agendas and market logic.

Applied Anthropological Practice in Development-Induced Displacement and Resettlement

Anthropologists have been involved in an extremely wide array of activities and domains in their work on DIDR, spanning the entire field in activities as diverse, yet related, as applied research, policy formation, theory building, evaluation, planning, implementation, and resistance. They have also played major roles in the development of more appropriate policies within multilateral institutions such as the World Bank, the Inter-American Development Bank (IADB), and the Asian Development Bank regarding the planning and implementation of resettlement projects that accompany infrastructural development. They have authored the guidelines for best practices and procedures that such institutions require that borrower nations must comply with. World Bank Operational Directive 4.30: Involuntary Resettlement (OD 4.30), written by anthropologist Michael Cernea, called for minimal resettlement; improvement or restoration of living standards, earning capacity, and production levels; resettler participation in project activities; a resettlement plan; and valuation and compensation for assets lost (World Bank 1990, 1–2). Although these guidelines were hailed as an important step toward the reduction of damages, costs, and losses incurred by resettled peoples, their implementation in borrower nations has been consistently problematic. Although some have contended that, without the guidelines, the outcomes of many projects would have been incalculably worse, others assert that the guidelines have actually made things worse because they allow restoration of previous levels of development, which research has shown are rarely reached, leaving people in greater poverty. The Bank's response to this problem was to advocate the formulation and implementation of resettlement legislation in borrower nations, producing policy changes in several developing nations, such as Brazil, Colombia, and Mexico, as well as other development agencies, like the Organization for Economic Cooperation and Development (OECD) and the IADB (Cernea 1993, 32; Shihata 1993).

A number of nations see the OD 4.30 guidelines as an infringement of national sovereignty. Furthermore, adoption of formal policies, either by the World Bank or borrower nations, is no assurance of adequate implementation. In addition, the degree to which projects financed by private capital must adhere to the Bank's now modified guidelines and procedures is far from clear. The World Bank commissioned an independent report on the Narmada Sardar Sarovar Project in India (Morse and Berger 1992). The report recommended cessation of the project pending major improvements in environmental and social monitoring and implementation, resulting in the rejection of further World Bank funding of the project by the government of India. Most recently, however, World Bank policy and guidelines have been weakened. The Board of Executive Directors approved revisions of the policy on involuntary resettlement that undermine protection for indigenous peoples and other peoples lacking formal title to lands, thus making it easier to carry out resettlement and, in some circumstances, reducing the World Bank's responsibility for certain kinds of displacement and resettlement impacts (Clark 2002, 10–11).

Often as consultants to these and other institutions, anthropologists have carried out the applied research necessary for informed planning and implementation of humane and development-oriented resettlement projects. Through the lifetime of projects, anthropologists have also evaluated the performance of projects in restoring incomes and enhancing social rearticulation among the resettled for individual and community recovery. For example, Partridge's study of the successful Arenal Hydroelectric Project was based on an evaluation that he did for IADB (1993).

By the same token, anthropologists have been actively engaged in advocacy work on behalf of affected communities. Working closely with groups and communities, anthropologists have joined in, legally contesting the decisions and actions of international financial institutions (IFIs) on behalf of communities facing DIDR. Anthropologists currently are in leadership roles in many NGOs that work at various levels to assist communities facing resettlement to gain better conditions or in resisting resettlement. They are part of the larger community of activists and scholars who keep close watch on policy formulation in lending institutions to guard against the dilution or weakening of any policy relating to DIDR (Fox and Brown 1998; Colchester 1993; Waldram 1980).

Grassroots organizations, NGOs, and social movements involved in resistance to DIDR have also acquired or developed legal personnel, expertise, and general knowledge that enable them to sue projects for violation of national civil and human rights law as well as international accords. The aforementioned growth of international human rights norms supplies a series of conventions and covenants that, although difficult to enforce in local circumstances, can be used to portray projects as being in violation of internationally accepted standards. The European Convention on Human Rights (1950), the International Covenant on Civil and Political Rights (1966), the Universal Declaration of Human Rights (1948), the United Nations Declaration on the Rights to Development (1986), the Declaration on the Rights of Persons Belonging to National or Ethnic, Religious or Linguistic Minorities (1992), the Articles of the International Labour Organization

(1944), and the United Nations Draft Declaration on the Rights of Indigenous Peoples (1994) all provide articles and protocols that can be used to portray projects in violation of human rights on the international stage. There are now much more active efforts to use these and other documents as means to achieve reparations for past injustices as well (Johnston 2000).

Theoretical Perspectives on Development-Induced Displacement and Resettlement

Initial attempts at theorizing DIDR focused less on rights to resources than on the most immediate and visible outcomes for the people involved. Although a number of models of the nature of voluntary planned settlement processes were developed in the late 1960s (Chambers 1970; Nelson 1973), there was little theoretical work on DIDR until Thayer Scudder and Elizabeth Colson developed a model based on the concept of stress to describe and analyze the process of involuntary dislocation and resettlement (1982). They posited that three forms of stress resulted from involuntary relocation and resettlement: physiological stress, psychological stress, and sociocultural stress. Physiological stress is seen in increased morbidity and mortality rates. Psychological stress has four manifestations: trauma, guilt, grief, and anxiety. Sociocultural stress is manifested as a result of the economic, political, and cultural effects of relocation. These three forms of stress, referred to as multidimensional stress, are experienced as affected people pass through the displacement and resettlement process. Scudder and Colson represented the process itself as occurring in four stages, which they label recruitment, transition, potential development, and handing-over/incorporation. Recruitment refers to the decisions taken by authorities regarding the population to be relocated, particularly those that influence the length and severity of the stressful transition stage. The transition stage begins when the population to be relocated is first affected. Generally speaking, the transition stage is the longest, and it is the stage in which the most severe multidimensional stress is experienced. The general attitude of people during the transition stage is conservative, in order to avoid the possibility of further risk and stress. The stage of potential development begins when people begin to abandon their conservative risk-avoidance strategies and express greater initiative and risk-taking behavior. Scudder and Colson emphasized that this stage is often never realized because many DIDR projects remain trapped in the transition stage by inept and inappropriate policy and implementation. Equally difficult to attain is the final stage of handing-over, or incorporation.

Achieving the incorporation stage signifies that the DIDR project has been successful. They define success as the achievement of local management of economic and political affairs and the phasing out of external agencies and personnel from day-to-day management of the community. The community has become able to assume its place within the larger regional context, which includes host communities and other regional systems.

At roughly the same time that Scudder and Colson were developing their model, an approach began in the political ecology literature focused on the linked ideas of vulnerability and risk. The concept of vulnerability was initially employed in disaster research to characterize the vast differences among societies in disaster losses from similar agents. An alternative perspective on human-environment relations, one that emphasizes the role of human interventions in generating disaster risk and impact, found that these sets of relations coalesced in the concept of vulnerability (Hewitt 1983). Vulnerability and risk, therefore, refer to the relationships among people, the environment, and the sociopolitical structures that frame the conditions in which people live. The concept of vulnerability thus integrates not only political and economic conditions but also environmental forces in terms of both biophysical and socially constructed risk. This understanding of vulnerability enabled researchers to conceptualize how social systems generate the conditions that place different kinds of people, often differentiated along axes of class, race, ethnic, gender, or age, at different levels of risk.

As these concepts gained currency, Cernea began to write about the risks of poverty resulting from displacement by water projects (1990). He subsequently developed his well-known Impoverishment Risks and Reconstruction (IRR) approach to understanding (and mitigating) the major adverse effects of displacement, in which he outlined eight basic risks to which people are subjected by displacement (1995; Cernea and McDowell 2000). The model is based on the three basic concepts of risk, impoverishment, and reconstruction. Deriving his understanding of risk from Giddens's (1990) notion of the possibility that a certain course of action may produce negative effects, Cernea modeled displacement risks by deconstructing the "syncretic, multifaceted process of displacement into its identifiable, principle and most widespread components": landlessness, joblessness, homelessness, marginalization, food insecurity, increased morbidity, loss of access to common property resources, and social disarticulation (Cernea 2000, 19). He further asserted that the probability of these risks producing serious consequences is extremely high in badly planned resettlement.

Cernea noted that "While some degree of population territorial rearrangement is unavoidable, such inequitable distribution of benefits and losses is neither mandatory nor inevitable . . . socially responsible resettlement

... can prevent impoverishment and can generate benefits for the regional economy and host populations" (Cernea 1996). Basically he argued that development should avoid displacement where at all possible, but where projects are determined to be necessary, the risks of negative effects can be reduced by political commitment, appropriate legal protection, and adequate resource allocations. His IRR model is designed to predict, diagnose, and resolve the problems associated with DIDR. He also maintained that the hardship of resettlement may be less responsible for resistance than the fact that policy and legal vacuums leave people little alternative (1996, 258).

Dwivedi's research on the Narmada Dam complex in western India has significantly contributed several refinements to the risk approach by elaborating on the social and political construction of risk. Drawing on Beck (1992), he approached risk as "a subjective calculation of different groups of people embedded differentially in political-economic and environmental conditions" (Dwivedi 1999, 47). People in different structural positions define risk differently, but their risk calculations are also affected by cultural norms as well as legal and policy frameworks for compensation (Beck 1995, 43). Risk is calculated on the basis of information that allows people to make judgments about relative degrees of certainty or uncertainty of outcomes. People facing DIDR very often spend a considerable amount of time under conditions of uncertainty, in which a lack of information about what is going to happen seriously hampers their ability to assess conditions and act, compounding their disorientation and trauma. Uncertainty and the lack of predictability heighten the perception of risk because, without adequate information, no calculations of losses and benefits are possible (Dwivedi 1999, 47). Most mandated resettlement projects deprive people of control over fundamental features of their lives and have generally been derelict in providing affected populations with the kinds of information necessary to reassert satisfactory control and understanding over the resettlement process or the changed circumstances of their lives. Understanding of and control over circumstances are fundamental for human beings to deal productively and positively with the forces of change. Therefore, if people find that their understanding and control are diminished, change will be characterized by conflict, tension, and, perhaps, active resistance. The often extremely negative concrete impacts of resettlement projects on affected peoples compound the disorientation generated by the loss of control and understanding as motivations for resistance. Resistance is a reassertion of both a logic and a sense of control (Oliver-Smith 1996; Turner 1991). The resistance to the Sardar Sarovar Dam of the Narmada River in western India offers a case in point.

The Sardar Sarovar Project (SSP) is but one part of the Narmada Valley Project (NVP) which includes the construction of ten major dams on the Narmada and 20 others on its tributaries (Baviskar 1992, 233). The Sardar Sarovar dam is projected to provide irrigation water for 1.8 million hectares of land. The dam is also intended to provide drinking water for 4,720 villages and 131 towns, while generating 1,450 MW of electricity. The damming of the Narmada will submerge roughly 37,000 hectares of land and displace an estimated 163,500 people (Parasuraman 1999, 179; Fisher 1995, 13). The estimates of benefits to be generated and costs to be incurred by construction of the dam are hotly contested by a variety of people representing many interests. Economic costs are criticized for being grossly underestimated. The human and environmental costs are said to be based on low estimates of the number of people to be affected and a lack of understanding of the cultural disruption that the tribal people in particular will suffer in dislocation. The alleged benefits in the form of irrigation and drinking water are also said to be vastly unrealistic (Fisher 1995, 17). Critics also argue that there were no provisions for appropriately informing the people to be affected, much less any remotely adequate plans for their humane and constructive resettlement.

Like many of India's tribal groups, the people of the Narmada Valley have a tradition of resistance to any attempts by outsiders to compromise their autonomy and their resource base (Parasuraman 1999, 232). Although protest against the dam began appearing earlier, active resistance began to evolve in 1980, when two voluntary organizations started working with the people to improve resettlement conditions and to help in legal actions related to land. A second stage of resistance developed in 1987 after the Indian government displaced roughly 2,000 families. The government neither informed nor consulted the affected people because it believed that the tribal peoples would not understand the issues even if they had the information (1999, 237). In 1985 Medha Patkar, a social scientist and activist, began organizing in the project-affected villages of Maharashtra. She and other activists framed the issues in development terms based on the absolute lack of basic services that the villages suffered. They organized village committees, instituted adult education programs, and established health care programs. They provided information about the dam to the villages, including submergence levels, the numbers of people who would face dislocation, the resettlement and rehabilitation programs, and other issues (1999, 238). The villages themselves began to collect comprehensive household data on potential losses to inform the government so that adequate compensation levels could be set. Furthermore, they demanded that the government provide the right to information on all aspects of the dam, more comprehensive land surveys for adequate compensation, a comprehensive resettlement plan, the right to resettle within their own state, and the extension of resettlement and rehabilitation benefits to all those affected by the subsidiary projects of the dam such as the colony, canal, sanctuary, and compensatory afforestation programs (1999, 239).

By the late 1980s it was clear that the government of India and the state governments were not willing to establish a coherent policy for compensation for a variety of losses to be incurred by the people, leading to the evolution of a position of total opposition to the SSP (Parasuraman 1999, 240–41). The local organizations united and formed the Narmada Bachao Andolan (NBA), or "Save the Narmada Movement," under the leadership of Mehda Patkar. Their opposition was voiced in the slogan *Koi nahin hatega! Baandh nahin banega!*—"No one will move! The dam will not be built!" (Baviskar 1992, 238). The NBA initiated a campaign of resistance on a broad front. In addition to efforts to mobilize the villages in the valley, the NBA established linkages with NGOs and social movements in both rural and urban areas in India as well as with international NGOs that pressured the international financial community to withdraw economic support from the project. In 1989 the Environmental Defense Fund, the Environmental Policy Institute, and the National Wildlife Federation urged the U.S. Congress to pressure the World Bank to undertake an independent review of the project, which turned out to be highly critical (Morse and Berger 1992). The NBA also brought suit in state courts against the SSP, charging improper land acquisition and forcible eviction, state repression, and denial of the constitutionally guaranteed right to life (Baviskar 1992, 239–40). The NBA also sued the project in the Supreme Court in 1994, which, although it was defeated, led the NBA to renew efforts at resistance, including groups of people willing to drown themselves in the waters rising behind the partially completed dam in villages below the expected submergence lines.

The NBA has gained the support of celebrities, including rock stars, prize-winning authors, and supreme court justices, and it has also won a number of international environmental awards. With its increasing international fame, tensions between the local priorities of people in the valley and the broader agenda of the NBA have appeared. Some NGOs have criticized the NBA for making decisions without consulting the people in the valley (Patel and Mehta 1995, 404). Some local people have felt that the NBA has exploited them, urging them to resist rather than accept resettlement in order for the NBA to gain political capital in their struggle against the dam (Dwivedi 1998, 167). Nonetheless, the NBA appears to have the support of most of the people in the valley, and it has continued its opposition in the form of meetings, marches, demonstrations, petitions, strikes, public confrontations with authorities, roadblocks, hunger strikes, refusals to move, and "save or drown squads." The NBA has adopted Gandhian resistance strategies, including the *satyagraha*, a nonviolent mass social action event. They have also acquired a voluntary support group, Friends of River Narmada, which provides a sophisticated Web site chronicling the history of the movement and up-to-date information on the struggle, as well as information on opportunities to contribute resources and participate. There is also a Narmada Solidarity Network, composed of six organizations from various cities in the United States.

Mediating institutions, such as NGOs and independent commissions, also frame and may politicize uncertainties and risks, and they may be pivotal in the way people construct risk as well. The World Commission on Dams (WCD) links risk with the concept of rights by advocating that an "approach based on 'recognition of rights' and 'assessment of risks' (particularly rights at risk)" be elaborated to guide future planning and decisionmaking on dams (2000, 206). The global review of the WCD stressed the need to address the five values of equity, efficiency, participatory decisionmaking, sustainability, and accountability as justification for the elaboration of a rights-and-risks approach to dam construction. Rights that were seen to be relevant in large dam projects included constitutional rights, customary rights, legislated rights, and property rights (of both landholders and developers and investors). These rights can be grouped by their legal status, their spatial or temporal reach, or their purpose. In the case of spatial or temporal dimensions, rights of local, regional, or national entities or the rights of present or future generations can be perceived. In terms of purpose, rights are cited that pertain to material resources such as land, water, forests, and pasture or to spiritual, moral, or cultural resources such as religion, dignity, and identity (2000, 206).

Most recently, Chris de Wet has sought to incorporate Cernea's important insights into a more comprehensive approach (de Wet, forthcoming). Asking why resettlement so often goes wrong, de Wet sees two broad approaches to responding to the question. The first approach is what he calls the inadequate inputs approach, which argues that resettlement projects fail because of a lack of appropriate inputs: national legal frameworks and policies, political will, funding, predisplacement research, careful implementation, and monitoring. Optimistic in tenor, the inadequate inputs approach posits that the risks and injuries of resettlement can be controlled and mitigated by appropriate policies and practices. De Wet, on the other hand, finds himself moving toward what he calls the inherent complexity approach. He argues that there is a complexity in resettlement that is inherent in "the interrelatedness of a range of factors of different orders: cultural, social, environmental, economic, institutional and political—all of which are taking place in the context of imposed space change and of local level responses and initiatives" (de Wet, forthcoming). Moreover, these changes are taking place simultaneously in an interlinked and mutually influencing process of transformation. And further, these internal changes from the displacement process are also influenced by and respond to the imposition of external sources of power as well as the initiatives of local actors. Therefore, the resettlement process emerges out of the complex interaction of all these factors in ways that are not predictable and that do not seem amenable to a rational planning approach.

De Wet suggests that a more comprehensive and open-ended approach than the predominantly economic and operational inadequate inputs approach is necessary to understand, adapt to, and take advantage of the opportunities presented by the inherent complexity of the displacement and resettlement process. Although some might see this perspective as unduly pessimistic, the fact that authorities are limited in the degree of control they can exercise over a project creates a space for resettlers to take greater control over the process. The challenge thus becomes the development of policy that supports a genuine participatory and open-ended approach to resettlement planning and decisionmaking (de Wet, forthcoming).

Applied Anthropological Frameworks for Analysis and Action

The three perspectives proposed for applied anthropological frameworks for analysis and action are advocacy anthropology, stakeholder analysis, and political ecology ethnography, and an approach adapted from Little's analysis of environmental conflicts in Amazonia (1999). The advocacy anthropology approach is characterized by an activist stance that privileges a particular group's perspective over competing or contesting positions. This approach has been shown to be particularly valuable in situations where groups, such as the Native Americans of Amazonia, may be facing acute sociopolitical forces that may amount to ethnocide, to which DIDR has been likened (Barabas and Bartolome 1973), or even genocide. Little suggests that one limitation of an advocacy approach is that only one point of view, of the many that may be relevant in resettlement issues, is presented, eclipsing the possibility of presenting the view that each contesting social actor may have its own sources of legitimacy. Thus, advocacy anthropology may forfeit the analysis of positions taken, for example, by anthropologists within the World Bank on behalf of peoples affected by DIDR. Conversely, it can equally be argued that advocacy anthropology often articulates a view that otherwise might not be heard, thus promoting dialogue and negotiation.

Stakeholder analysis is an approach to environmental conflict that has emerged recently to resolve conflicts and thereby reduce levels of environmentally destructive activities and processes. Stakeholder analysis employs methods of conciliation, negotiation, and mediation for reducing levels of conflict and managing disputes. Such efforts at establishing truly effective methods for cross-cultural negotiation in DIDR can play meaningful roles in enhancing the capacity of local peoples to effectively represent their interests. On the other hand, one criticism of stakeholder analysis is that it frequently assumes that all actors have equal or symmetrical stakes in the conflict, something that is rarely the case. For example, although monetary values of the loss of home, land, and community may allegedly be compensated at levels established by the project, it is not often that they adequately reflect the true nature of the project in terms of the social, spiritual, and emotional losses that are at stake for people facing DIDR. Moreover, stakeholder approaches also assume that all participants in the disputes hold citizenship and have the abilities to employ their rights within the larger political space of the nation. Again, assumptions of this sort are far from warranted, especially in cases involving ethnic minorities or indigenous peoples, whose positions in national social and cultural hierarchies generally eliminate the exercise of such basic rights (Little 1999). In the view of Laura Nader, the "neutral" position of stakeholder approaches is largely fictional in that it is ideologically based on a kind of functionalist harmonics that is less about the representation and interplay of diverse interests than it is about pacification and hegemonic control (Nader 1996, as quoted in Little 1999).

Political ecology ethnography is characterized by methods that aim to generate a social scientific approach that incorporates multiple perspectives. This goal is achieved by methods and tools—aimed at inclusion of multiple groups at multiple levels—to explore not only the political dimensions of these conflicts but also to bring new participants into the political frame of action and to initiate new approaches to viewing power relationships across multiple social and natural scales (Little 1999, 4). Importantly, this approach has the potential of creating concepts that may be adopted by the new participants to question established public policy and generate new alternatives for action. The methods that are employed in this approach focus on identification of all the different participants in the conflicts, a task that can be challenging in light of their numbers and the diverse historical and cultural traditions that have helped to situate them in the dispute. Most essentially, the task must reveal the basic claims to resources and territory that are made by participant social actors, and it must analyze the forms by which such claims are promoted and defended within broader political spheres of action in ways that display the competing discourses of cultural and political legitimacy (1999, 5). In this fashion the disputes over eligibility for DIDR compensation may hinge on the legitimacy of various kinds of claims to land.

All three of these perspectives have significant advantages and disadvantages in approaching DIDR. In point of fact, unlike Little, I tend to see them as nested, interacting, and complementary rather than as exclusive. Each approach roughly corresponds to a level of action in resettlement politics. As in all research conceptual frameworks and methodologies, there are moments and places of inconsistency or less-than-perfect fit, even contradiction. In that sense, the methodological approaches reflect the tensions and inconsistencies of relations within and among the various levels of resettlement politics. Advocacy research, stakeholder analysis, and political ecology ethnography, focusing on the rights and risks in DIDR, correspond to the levels or scales of interaction. Advocacy anthropology is appropriate for work at the level of the community to be resettled. In some instances, applied social scientists have found themselves carrying out research in the midst of the crisis of resettlement while people are facing a virtually life-threatening process (Colson 1971; Oliver-Smith 1986). In these contexts, researchers adopting an advocacy stance fulfill a necessary function in assisting communities in their efforts to deal with the crisis and in articulating their views in nonlocal contexts. Similarly, when DIDR projects are underway and communities are involved in bargaining or negotiating the terms and conditions of resettlement with planners and other authorities, stakeholder analysis can prove useful both in assisting people in the negotiation process and in demarcating the issues and limits that are "in play" in the process. Enlightened stakeholder analysis can reveal the differentials in value positions that are being negotiated among very disparate participants. Stakeholder analysis that is culturally sensitive can frame the issues in ways that help to balance those situations where, as one historian put it, one party has "a continent to exchange and the other, glass beads."

Finally, a political ecology ethnography helps to place DIDR in the context of global conversations about development. The political ecological perspective reveals the commonalities that specific communities, which are engaged with specific projects in diverse regions, contribute to the emergence of new forms of discourse in the shaping of alternative approaches to development that are less destructive to environments and human rights. By revealing the interplay of multiple interests across scales and levels, political ecology ethnography informs both the policy and practice to the communities and the affected peoples of the dimensions, scale, and implications of their roles, not only in specific projects but also in larger conversations, calling for more sustainable forms of development around the world.

Conclusion

The total environment of development planning and funding is rapidly changing, particularly issues at the core of DIDR that impact social and environmental justice advocacy. The role of applied anthropology as both participant and observer in the evolving nature of the local-global politics of social and environmental advocacy needs to be critically assessed, building on the substantial work already done, to develop new understandings and approaches to the challenges of DIDR. For example, DIDR-affected peoples are developing novel strategies in defense of their rights in their relations with the state and the global capital market by invoking international human rights covenants. Political power is emerging in supranational organizations, NGOs, and private institutions to expand the claims for disempowered subjects under the law (Clark, Fox, and Treakle 2003). Project-affected communities provide a point of convergence for the human rights and environmental movements to create an arena for an expanded international civil society across borders (Fisher 1995). This convergence entails a critique of development models that accept the necessity of relocating people, but also a questioning of the scale of development interventions that create major disruption for people, their ways of life, and their environments. Further, this discourse also reassesses the extent of state sovereignty and invokes changes in global political culture.

There is currently an active debate among powerful interests on the role of dams and other large infrastructure projects. Renewed efforts by national governments and private interests to promote development projects with DIDR components but without significant legal and economic protection are threatening increasing numbers of people and communities. Despite widespread criticism, the actual practice of development continues to favor large infrastructural expansion and economic growth over ecological and cultural concerns (Flyvbjerg, Bruzelius, and Rothengatter 2003; Josephson 2002). For example, the recent reframing of dams by the World Bank, nation-states, and industry associations as environmentally benign, socially productive, and efficient technologies reflects an energized perspective favoring "high risk, high reward" projects. India's enormous river-linking scheme, for example, defies every major recommendation of the World Commission on Dams. The recent weakening of World Bank guidelines regarding both involuntary resettlement and the protection of indigenous people affected by development projects has also alarmed the activist community (Downing and Moles 2001). Further, the lack of clarity about the responsibilities of privately funded development projects to affected peoples is cause for concern.

However, these trends have been met by such initiatives as the World Commission on Dams (2000), the Extractive Industries Review (2003), and the Equator Principles (2003), which are aimed at creating what Jonathan Fox has called "accountability politics" to ensure socially and environmentally responsible development (Fox 2003, xii). The World Bank Inspection Panel, which allows people affected by bank-funded projects to file complaints and request independent investigations regarding a bank's compliance with its own social and environmental guidelines, is another element in the quest for accountability, although its results since its creation in 1993 have been uneven (Clark, Fox, and Treakle 2003). Furthermore, gaining prior informed consent from people to be affected by projects (Goodland 2004) and strengthening the legal basis and procedures for payment of reparations for injuries and costs imposed on individuals and communities by projects have recently emerged as strategic priorities (Johnston 2000). It is fair to say that an opportunity now exists for applied anthropology to make further contributions to the development of socially and environmentally responsible DIDR policy and practice in the future.

As the debates on development evolve in the twenty-first century, the concerns for continued infrastructural and economic growth will continue to be countered by concerns for more environmentally sustainable and more democratic forms of development, particularly at the local level. Development projects have increasingly become the sites in which these interests and issues are contested and played out through different models of development by individuals and groups from a variety of communities, both local and nonlocal. To some extent, both sides of the discussion share similar rhetorics of social justice and material well being, but they differ markedly on the deeper philosophical meaning of development as a social goal and the means by which that goal should be achieved. The meanings, means, and implications of development in the discussion reflect the internal heterogeneity of both the development industry and those who propose alternative visions (Fisher 1995, 8).

Reigning development models, promoting large-scale infrastructural projects, transform social and physical environments and espouse the concept of "the greatest good for the greatest number" while attempting to safeguard local rights and well-being. Although generally the record has yet to reflect it, such a position assumes that the less powerful will eventually benefit from the project through well-designed and implemented resettlement programs. For some, within the framework of current economic structures and conditions, realism dictates acceptance of this development ideology. The opposing view tends to emphasize the rights of the less powerful and the significance of cultural and environmental diversity over projects it considers to be ecologically risky and economically questionable. The fact that applied anthropologists of good faith have employed their knowledge, analytical skills, and energies on both sides of the debate testifies to the complexity and the urgency of the issues.

References

Acselrad, Henri, and Maria das Gracas da Silva. 2000. Social conflict and environmental change at the Amazon Tucurui Dam Region. Paper presented at the meetings of the International Rural Sociology Association Meetings in Rio de Janeiro, Brazil, August 4, 2000.

Aspelin, Paul, and Claudio Coelho dos Santos. 1981. *Indian areas threatened by hydroelectric projects in Brazil.* Copenhagen: IWGIA.

Ballesteros, J., M. Edel, and M. Nelson. 1970. *La colonización del Papaloapan.* Serie de estudios sobre tenencia y uso de la tierra, no. 1. Mexico: Centro de Investigaciones Agrarias.

Barabas, Alicia, and Miguel Bartolome. 1973. *Hydraulic development and ethnocide: The Mazatec and Chinantec people of Oaxaca, Mexico.* Copenhagen: IWGIA.

Baviskar, Amrita. 1992. Development, nature and resistance: The case of the Bhilala Tribals in the Narmada Valley. PhD dissertation, Cornell University, Ithaca, New York.

Beck, Ulrich. 1995. *Ecological politics in an age of risk.* London: Frank Cass.

———. 1992. *Risk society: Towards a new modernity.* Thousand Oaks, Calif.: Sage Publications.

Biery-Hamilton, Gaye. 1987. Coping with change: The impact of the Tucurui Dam on an Amazonian community. PhD dissertation, Department of Anthropology, University of Florida.

Brechin, S. R., P. R. Wilshusen, C. L. Fortwangler, and P. C. West. 2003. *Contested nature: Promoting international biodiversity with social justice in the twenty-first century.* Albany: SUNY Press.

Brokensha, David, and Thayer Scudder. 1968. Resettlement. In *Dams in Africa,* edited by N. Rubin and W. M. Warren. London: Frank Cass.

Butcher, David. 1971. *An organizational manual for resettlement: A systematic approach to the resettlement problem created by man-made lakes, with special reference for West Africa.* Rome: Food and Agriculture Organization.

Cauchon, Dennis. 2004. Pushing the limits of public use. *USA Today* April 1: 3A.

Cernea, Michael M. 2000. Risk, safeguards, and reconstruction: A model for population displacement and resettlement. In *Risk and reconstruction: Experiences of settlers and refugees,* edited by Michael Cernea and Christopher McDowell. Washington, D.C.: World Bank.

———. 1999. *The economics of involuntary resettlement: Questions and challenges.* Washington, D.C.: World Bank.

————. 1997. The risks and reconstruction model for resettling displaced populations. *World Development* 25 (10): 1569–88.

————. 1995. Eight main risks: Impoverishment and social justice in resettlement. Washington, D.C.: Environment Department, World Bank; ESSD processed.

————. 1993. Anthropological and sociological research for policy development on population resettlement. In *Anthropological approaches to resettlement: Policy, practice, and theory,* edited by Michael M. Cernea and Scott E. Guggenheim. Boulder: Westview Press.

————. 1990. Poverty risks from population displacement in water resources development. HIID Development Discussion Paper no. 355. Cambridge, Mass.: Harvard University Press.

Cernea, Michael M., and Christopher McDowell. 2000. *Risk and reconstruction: experiences of settlers and refugees.* Washington, D.C.: World Bank.

Chambers, Robert, ed. 1969. *Settlement schemes in Africa.* London: Routledge and Kegan Paul.

————. 1970. *The Volta resettlement experience.* New York: Praeger; Volta River Authority, Accra; and University of Science and Technology, Kumasi, Ghana.

Clark, Dana. 2003. Singrauli: An unfulfilled struggle for justice. In *Demanding accountability: Civil society claims and the World Bank Inspection Panel,* edited by Dana Clark, Jonathan Fox, and Kay Treakle. Lanham, Md.: Rowman and Littlefield.

————. 2002. World Bank resettlement policy compromised. *World Rivers Review* 17 (1): 10.

Clark, Dana, Jonathan Fox, and Kay Treakle, eds. 2003. *Demanding accountability: Civil society claims and the World Bank Inspection Panel.* Lanham, Md.: Rowman and Littlefield.

Colchester, Marcus. 1993. Salvaging nature: Indigenous peoples, protected areas, and biodiversity conservation. Discussion Paper no. 55. UNRISD; World Rainforest Movement; and WWF.

Colson, Elizabeth. 1971. *The social consequences of resettlement.* Manchester: Manchester University Press.

De Wet, Chris. Forthcoming. Risk, complexity, and local initiative in involuntary resettlement outcomes. In *Towards improving outcomes in development induced involuntary resettlement projects,* edited by Chris de Wet. Oxford and New York: Berghahn Books.

Dobby, E. H. 1952. Resettlement transforms Malaysia: A case history of relocating the population of an Asian plural society. *Economic Development and Cultural Change* 50: 163–89.

Downing, Ted, and Jerry Moles. 2001. The World Bank denies indigenous peoples their right to prior informed consent. *Cultural Survival Quarterly* (Winter).

Dwivedi, Ranjit. 1999. Displacement, risks and resistance: Local perceptions and actions in the Sardar Sarovar. *Development and Change* 30: 43–78.

————. 1998. Resisting dams and "development": Contemporary significance of the campaign against the Narmada Projects in India. *European Journal of Development Research* 10 (2): 135–79.

The Equator principles: A framework for banks to manage environmental and social issues in project financing. 2003. Retrieved from http://www.equator-principles.com

Extractive Industries Review. 2004. Striking a better balance: Consultation on the future of the World Bank Group in the extractive industries. Retrieved from http://siteresources.worldbank.org/INTOGMC/Resources/finaleirmanagementrespon-seexecsum.pdf

Fahim, Hussein. 1983. *Egyptian Nubians: Resettlement and years of coping.* Salt Lake City: University of Utah Press.

Feit, Harvey, and Alan F. Penn. 1974. *The northward diversion of the Eastmain and Opinaca Rivers as proposed: An assessment of impacts on the native community at Eastmain Village.* Montreal: Grand Council of the Crees (Quebec).

Fernandes, Walter, and E. G. Thukral. 1989. *Development, displacement and rehabilitation.* New Delhi: Indian Social Institute.

Fisher, William F., ed. 1995. *Toward sustainable development: Struggles over India's Narmada River.* Armonk, N.Y., and London: M. E. Sharpe.

Flyvbjerg, Bent, Nils Bruzelius, and Werner Rothengatter. 2003. *Megaprojects and risk: An anatomy of ambition.* Cambridge: Cambridge University Press.

Fox, Jonathan. 2003. Introduction: Framing the inspection panel. In *Demanding accountability: Civil society claims and the World Bank Inspection Panel,* edited by Dana Clark, Jonathan Fox, and Kay Treakle. Lanham, Md.: Rowman and Littlefield.

Fox, Jonathan A., and L. David Brown, eds. 1998. *The struggle for accountability: The World Bank, NGOs, and grassroots movements.* Cambridge, Mass.: MIT Press.

Fried, Marc. 1963. Grieving for a lost home. In *The urban condition: People and policy in the metropolis,* edited by Leonard Duhl. New York: Basic Books.

Gans, Herbert J. 1962. *The urban villagers: Group and class in the life of Italian Americans.* Glencoe, Ill.: The Free Press.

Geisler, C., and R. da Sousa. 2001. From refuge to refugee: The African case. *Journal of Public Administration and Development* 21: 159–70.

Giddens, Anthony. 1990. *The consequences of modernity.* Cambridge: Polity Press.

Goodland, Robert. 2004. Prior informed consent and the World Bank Group. American University Center for International Environmental Law, Washington College of Law: Conference: Prior Informed Consent.

Guggenheim, Scott, and Michael Cernea. 1993. Anthropological approaches to involuntary resettlement: Policy, practice and theory. In *Anthropological approaches to resettlement: Policy, practice and theory,* edited by Michael Cernea and Scott Guggenheim. Boulder: Westview Press.

Hansen, Art, and Anthony Oliver-Smith, eds. 1982. *Involuntary migration and resettlement.* Boulder: Westview Press.

Hewitt, Kenneth, ed. 1983. *Interpretations of calamity.* Boston: Allen and Unwin.

Johnston, Barbara Rose. 2000. Reparations and the right to remedy. Briefing paper prepared for the World Commission on Dams, July 2000. Retrieved from the WCD Web site, http://www.dams.org/thematic/contrib._papers.php

Josephson, Paul R. 2002. *Industrialized nature: Brute force technology and the transformation of the natural world.* Washington, D.C.: Island Press.

Koenig, Dolores. 2000. Toward local development and mitigating impoverishment in development-induced displacement and resettlement. Final Report prepared for ESCOR R7644 and the Research Program on Development-Induced Displacement and Resettlement, organized by the Refugee Studies Centre, University of Oxford.

Leighton, Alexander. 1945. *The governing of men: General principles and recommendations based on experiences at a Japanese relocation camp.* Princeton, N.J.: Princeton University Press.

Little, Paul E. 1999. Political ecology as ethnography: The case of Ecuador's Aguarico River Basin. *Serie Antropologia,* no. 258. Brasilia: Departamento de Antropologia, Universidade de Brasilia.

Magee, Pennie L. 1989. Peasant political identity and the Tucurui Dam: A case study of the island dwellers of Para, Brazil. *The Latinamericanist* 24 (1): 6–10.

McCully, Patrick. 2001. *Silenced rivers: The ecology and politics of large dams.* 2nd ed. London: Zed Books.

Morse, Bradford, and Thomas Berger. 1992. *Sardar Sarovar: Report of the independent review.* Ottawa: Resource Futures International, Inc.

Nader, Laura. 1996. A civilizacao e seus negociadores: A harmonia como tecnica de pacificao. In *XIX Reuniao Brasileira de Antropologia,* translated by M. L. L. B. de Menezes. Niteroi, Brazil: UFF, ABA.

Nelson, M. 1973. *Development of tropical lands: Policy issues in Latin America.* Baltimore: Johns Hopkins University Press.

Oliver-Smith, Anthony. 2001. Displacement, resistance and the critique of development: From the grassroots to the global. Final Report prepared for ESCOR R7644 and the Research Programme on Development Induced Displacement and Resettlement, Refugee Studies Centre, University of Oxford.

———. 1996. Fighting for a place: The policy implications of resistance to resettlement. In *Understanding Impoverishment: The Consequences of Development Induced Displacement,* edited by Christopher McDowell. Providence and London: Berghahn Books.

———. 1994. Resistance to resettlement: The formation and evolution of movements. *Research in Social Movements, Conflict and Change* 17: 197–219.

———. 1986. *The martyred city: Death and rebirth in the Andes.* Albuquerque: University of New Mexico Press.

Parasuraman, S. 1999. *The development dilemma: Displacement in India.* New York: St. Martin's Press.

Partridge, William. 1993. Successful involuntary resettlement: Lessons from the Costa Rican Arenal Hydroelectric Project. In *Anthropology and involuntary resettlement: Policy, practice and theory,* edited by Scott Guggenheim and Michael Cernea. Boulder: Westview Press.

Patel, Anil, and Ambrish Mehta. 1995. The independent review: Was it a search for truth? In *Toward sustainable development: Struggles over India's Narmada River,* edited by William F. Fisher. Armonk, N.Y., and London: M. E. Sharpe.

Penz, G. Peter. 1992. Development refugees and distributive justice: Indigenous peoples, land and the developmentalist state. *Public Affairs Quarterly* 6 (1): 105–31.

Picciotto, Robert, Warren van Wicklin, and Edward Rice. 2001. *Involuntary resettlement: Comparative perspectives.* World Bank Series on Evaluation and Development, vol. 2. Washington, D.C.: World Bank.

Rew, A. W., and P. A. Driver. 1986. Evaluation of the social and environmental impact of the Victoria Dam Project. Overseas Development Administration Evaluation Report EV 392, London: Evaluation Department, ODA.

Rio Tinto. 2001. *Murowa Project Newsletter.* Harare, Zimbabwe: Rio Tinto.

Santos, Leinad Ayer de O, and Lucia M. M. de Andrade. 1990. *Hydroelectric dams on Brazil's Xingu River and indigenous peoples.* Cambridge, Mass.: Cultural Survival.

Scudder, Thayer. 1996. Development-induced impoverishment, resistance and river-basin development. In *Understanding Impoverishment: The Consequences of Development Induced Displacement,* edited by Christopher McDowell. Providence and London: Berghahn Books.

———. 1973. The human ecology of big projects: River basin development and resettlement. *Annual Review of Anthropology* 2: 45–61.

Scudder, Thayer, and Elizabeth Colson. 1982. From welfare to development: A conceptual framework for the analysis of dislocated people. In *Involuntary migration and resettlement,* edited by Art Hansen and Anthony Oliver-Smith. Boulder: Westview Press.

Shihata, Ibrahim F. I. 1993. Legal aspects of involuntary population resettlement. In *Anthropological approaches to resettlement: Policy, practice, and theory,* edited by Scott Guggenheim and Michael Cernea. Boulder: Westview Press.

Sigaud, Ligia. 1986. Efeitos Sociais de Grades Projetos Hidroeletricos: as Barragens de Sobradinho y Machadinho. *Comunicacao* 9. Rio de Janeiro: Programa de Pos-Graduacao en Antropologia Social/Museo Nacional.

Squires, Gregory D., Larry Bennett, Kathleen McCourt, and Philip Nyden. 1987. *Chicago: Race, class and the response to urban decline.* Philadelphia: Temple University Press.

Terborgh, J. 1999. *Requiem for nature.* Washington, D.C.: Island Press.

Turner, Terry. 1991. Representing, resisting, rethinking: Historical transformations of Kayapo culture and anthropological consciousness. In *Colonial situations: Essays on the contextualization of ethnographic knowledge,* edited by George W. Stocking, Jr. History of Anthropology, vol. 7. Madison: University of Wisconsin Press.

Villa Rojas, Alfonso. 1955. *Los Mazatecos y el Problema Indigena de la Cuenca del Papaloapan.* Mexico: Instituto Nacional Indigenista.

Waldram, James. 1980. Relocation and political change in a Manitoba native community. *Canadian Journal of Anthropology* 1 (2): 173–78.

World Bank. 1990. Operational Directive 4.30: Involuntary resettlement. In *The World Bank operational manual.* Washington, D.C.: World Bank.

World Commission on Dams. 2000. *Dams and development: A new framework for decision making.* London: Earthscan Publications.

8 Anthropological Practice in Business and Industry

Marietta L. Baba

Scope of the Domain

Three core knowledge domains enable anthropologists to bring new knowledge and skills to private sector organizations: general knowledge of culture and culture theory, competency in the practice of ethnography, and specialized knowledge of particular cultures and languages. These anthropological assets intersect with the two major subdomains of business and industry: (1) the marketplace and its consumers and (2) corporate work organizations. In each of these subdomains, there are several areas of need where anthropologists can add value. For example, in the market and consumer area, anthropologists are playing a central role in consumer behavior research, which in turn contributes to improvements in product design and innovation. In the area of corporate organizations, anthropologists are helping companies adapt to rapid changes in their competitive environments. In each of the subdomains, anthropological knowledge of culture (general and specific) and skill in ethnography adds value by providing richly detailed, empirically grounded, and comprehensively developed understanding of human social practices and systems of meaning that can help businesses do a better job of recognizing and responding to human and societal needs. The cross-cultural approach contributes to both of the business subdomains by providing businesses with the new understandings needed to operate effectively in diverse cultural contexts around the globe.

Historical Development of the Field

The notion of anthropologists working in business and industry may seem novel, but actually it has its roots in the 1930s. More than seven decades ago, anthropologists working in industry contributed to one of the most important discoveries ever made in social science research, and that contribution established the foundation for our practice in the private sector today.

The Invention of Industrial Anthropology: 1927–32

The invention of industrial anthropology took place inside the Western Electric Company (now part of Lucent Technologies), at its Chicago-based Hawthorne Works, through a series of controlled experiments aimed at increasing the productivity of the workforce (i.e., increasing outputs relative to inputs). Beginning in the early 1920s and continuing for several years, Western Electric tried to find out how to improve working conditions so that worker fatigue and dissatisfaction would be reduced, and the experimenters believed that a single variable (such as factory illumination) could be manipulated to make this happen (Roethlisberger and Dickson 1946). In these particular experiments, however, the results did not appear to make sense. The experimenters found that worker productivity increased when the lights were made brighter (as expected), but productivity also increased or stayed the same when lighting was decreased, even to the dim level of moonlight. This result definitely was not expected and could not be explained by any prevailing theory of the time.

To examine this anomaly, the company set up another series of tests, the most famous being the Relay Assembly Test Room (RATR) experiment. In this experiment, initiated in 1927, five women were isolated in a special room where their rate of production was carefully measured. The women's working conditions were improved through a series of rewards (rest breaks, free lunches, incentive pay), and these rewards were gradually withdrawn over a period of more than one year. Again, productivity seemed to improve, independent of the changes in working conditions. Even when rewards were withdrawn, improved results were sustained or increased. This phenomenon is now known as the Hawthorne Effect, meaning that experimental results are affected by nonexperimental variables, for example, working more diligently to impress the observers (Finlay 1991). At the time, however, the findings were inexplicable.

The company called in a Harvard psychologist, Elton Mayo, to help interpret the mysterious results. With the help of Mayo's colleague Frederick Roethlisberger, the RATR researchers came to realize that they had inadvertently introduced changes into the social situation of the women beyond simply changing their working conditions. For example, the researchers took over the role of the women's supervisor and established a congenial relationship with the women to secure their cooperation (more congenial than would normally be the case in an ordinary industrial setting). The researchers further noticed that the women themselves developed a kind of team spirit, helping each other if anyone fell behind. These observations suggested that a social system was in operation, meaning that a change in one variable (e.g., replacing the supervisor) affected many others (e.g., the work group's attitudes and interactions). Now, rather than continuing to study the impact of single variables (e.g., illumination, rewards) on output, the researchers became interested in understanding the social system of the work group as a whole (Roethlisberger and Dickson 1946).

Enter anthropology. Elton Mayo was familiar with anthropology through his friendship with two prominent anthropologists, Bronislaw Malinowski and A. R. Radcliffe-Brown. He knew that anthropologists study natural social systems in the field, and it was this approach that Mayo wanted to adopt for the final phase of the Hawthorne study. Mayo was introduced to one of Radcliffe-Brown's students, W. Lloyd Warner, who had just returned from fieldwork in Australia. Warner consulted with the Hawthorne researchers in designing and conducting the next phase of the experiment and, with this act, gave birth to industrial anthropology.

The final phase of the Hawthorne project was the famous Bank Wiring Observation Room (BWOR), designed to explore what workers actually *do* on the job in contrast to what they *say* during interviews (a central goal of ethnography). The BWOR was a replica of the shop floor at Western Electric. A typical work group (14 male bank wirers and their supervisors) was transferred to the experimental facility. The workers performed their tasks as usual while a trained observer watched them and recorded their interactions for several months in 1931 and 1932, during the Great Depression. A second researcher, not present in the observation room, conducted periodic interviews with the workers to gain a better understanding of their point of view. Warner encouraged the researchers to read anthropological theory and to analyze their observational data much as an anthropologist would in studying a small society such as a band or tribe. As a result, the BWOR study became the first systematic observational investigation of a work group's social system, or, as we would call it today, the work group's organizational culture (Chapple 1953).

The BWOR study revealed a complex interplay between managerial intent, on the one hand, and work group interpretation and response, on the other, and it showed how this interaction shaped work group productivity on the shop floor. In keeping with the concept of the economic man (i.e., workers are rational actors who respond to economic incentives), the Hawthorne management had devised a complex piece rate system for rewarding output by the BWOR workers. In this payment system, workers received a guaranteed hourly wage in exchange for a minimum daily standard of production (the *bogey*), plus an additional sum that was determined by the amount of output produced by the entire group in excess of that which guaranteed the minimum hourly wage. Managers believed that this policy created an economic incentive that would spur individuals within the group to increase their rate of production up to the point at which fatigue and discomfort stymied additional effort.

In reality, the effect of the piece rate system on the workers was exactly the opposite of what managers predicted. The workers had the concept of a "fair day's work" that was considerably below that which management envisioned as desirable under the piece rate incentive system. The workers' informal standard was translated into a certain number of units to be produced by each man during the day (basically, the amount required to produce the bogey). Anything in excess of this minimum was frowned upon and negatively sanctioned by the group. A worker who set a fast pace and produced more than the minimum standard was subjected to verbal abuse (e.g., called a slave), "binging" (using the thumb to snap the third finger against the violator's arm), and, eventually, ostracism. Often, the workers would produce their quota early in the day and then subtly scale back effort in the afternoon while enjoying one another's company (all the while keeping an eye out for management). This work culture arose from the workers' belief that a higher daily rate of production would prompt management to raise the bogey (the minimum daily standard of production), cut the hourly rate, or lay off some of them. Because this study took place during the depths of the Great Depression, it is not surprising that workers feared the worst from management.

These findings produced the first solid empirical evidence of informal organization, defined as the actual patterns of social interaction and relationships among the members of an organization that arise spontaneously and are not determined by management (Roethlisberger and Dickson 1946). Researchers mapped this informal organization by quantifying interactions among workers and graphically depicting networks of relationships between different work groups or cliques, much as network analysis today reveals informal patterns of communication and exchange among individuals. The informal organization that was depicted very much contrasted with the formal organization (interactions defined by the rules and policies of the corporation) that management had put in place to enable pursuit of the company's goals. The corporation thus was comprised of two kinds of organization that were not aligned with each other: a rational organization designed for instrumental purposes and a spontaneous, natural form of human social interaction that arose in response to inherent human interests and needs. These findings made clear that workers were not simply "factors" in production, much like machines, but were sentient beings who assigned their own meaning to phenomena and who protected their interests through mechanisms of their own design.

Perhaps the most significant finding that emerged from the Hawthorne project was that workers exerted considerable influence over industrial productivity. As long as machines did not control the work process, workers could manipulate the pace of production in many subtle ways that would be difficult to detect without an army of supervisors. From a theoretical perspective, management was no longer fully in control of the corporation but had to deal with a powerful natural force that, from management's perspective, did not respond to the logic of economic incentives. Of course, from the workers' point of view, the people in the BWOR were being quite logical because any behavioral pattern other than that which they exhibited could end up costing them in the long run.

As a consequence of the Hawthorne findings, a new school of thought emerged in organizational theory—the human relations school. This school of thought rested upon functional equilibrium theory, widespread in the social sciences at that time, which viewed human organizations as integrated social systems with specific structures that interacted to maintain a smoothly operating whole (Holzberg and Giovannini 1981). Within the context of this theory, conflict between management and workers was seen as pathological, reflecting the disruption of an equilibrium state, and the conflict was to be ameliorated by making adjustments in the pattern of interaction among individuals and organizational structures. A disruption of the equilibrium state could affect worker morale in a negative way, and this, in turn, would interfere with efficient production. The human relations school aimed at creating harmonious worker-manager relationships that would ensure optimal productivity in a company. For the next 20 years, through the 1950s, this school of thought was prominent in American industry, and it was highly influential in shaping the practices of the first generation of industrial anthropologists.

Industrial Anthropology in the Human Relations Movement: 1940–60

W. Lloyd Warner, the founder of industrial anthropology, had a larger theoretical agenda that he hoped to advance through the study of modern institutions such as industrial organizations:

When I went to Australia . . . my fundamental purpose in studying primitive man was to know modern man better . . . some day I proposed to
investigate (just how I did not know) the social life of modern man
with the hope of ultimately placing the researches in a larger framework of comparison which would include the other societies of the
world. (Cited in Partridge and Eddy 1978, 16)

The anthropologists at Harvard during the time of the Hawthorne project
were influenced by Warner's interest in modern institutions, and they found
many opportunities to conduct observational studies in large corporations
and to apply their insights toward the goal of industrial harmony from the
1940s through the 1950s. This first generation of industrial anthropologists,
including Conrad Arensberg, Eliot Chapple, Burleigh Gardner, Robert
Guest, Solon Kimball, Frederick Richardson, Leonard Sayles, and William
Foote Whyte (who was trained as a qualitative sociologist), undertook a series
of important studies of both workers and managers, with the goal of discovering factors and forces that could be manipulated to achieve an equilibrium
state in the organizational system (i.e., the elimination of conflict). The
anthropologists did not question the asymmetrical relations of power in a
company as a key source of conflict; these were taken as given.

During the 1940s and 1950s, anthropologists were hired by management
to work on problems in specific plants, such as high turnover, remoteness,
strikes, and poor worker-management cooperation. They studied various
aspects of social structure and relationships within the industrial enterprise,
such as informal relationships among workers, actual work processes, status
hierarchies, relations between workers and managers, union-management
interaction, and voluntary associations in the workplace. Companies that hired
anthropologists during this period included Sears, Roebuck & Company, the
Container Corporation of America, International Business Machines (IBM),
Inland Steel Container Company, Libby McNeil & Libby, Bundy Tubing
Company, and the Eastern Corporation. Some of the anthropological studies
of these firms produced industrial ethnographies (case studies) of the entire
company, with a focus on the factors and forces that influenced human relations within an integrated social system.

After the Hawthorne project, W. Lloyd Warner shifted his focus to the
contemporary community in his Yankee City studies (Newburyport, Massachusetts). Especially important to our understanding of industrial anthropology in this period was Warner and Low's (1946) study of a major strike
affecting several Yankee City shoemaking factories. The intensity and duration of the strike, which took place during the depths of the Depression,
were a surprise to many observers because the workers in the plant had
never before mounted a job action in the many decades of the factory's his-

tory. Warner and Low were able to trace the roots of the strike to changes in the technology, work process, and social relations within the factory; they also linked these microlevel changes to larger technological and economic transformations unfolding within the surrounding community and the nation. During the decades before the strike, shoemaking production technology had gradually evolved, reducing once highly skilled craftsmen to less skilled (known as deskilling, or degradation of skills [Braverman 1974]) and more interchangeable workers in a more heavily mechanized production process. The deskilling of the workforce had destroyed the traditional social system within the factory, which was based on a hierarchy of increasing levels of skill in the craft of shoemaking. Workers' identity and self-esteem were tied to their capacity to move up the skill hierarchy as they gained experience and expertise. But technological changes destroyed the skill hierarchy, reducing once proud craftsmen to a more or less undifferentiated mass of unskilled workers. Such changes generated a sense of loss of control and autonomy among the workers, drawing them into a group with shared interests. At the same time, the ownership of the factories had changed hands, shifting from local ownership to distant owners in New York City. The remoteness of the factory owners removed social constraints against strikes that had been in place when the owners were integral members of the local community. As a result, members of the community supported the strike in a way that would have been unlikely before, and this support made a lengthy strike possible. As a result of the strike and its community support, the workers organized an industrial union and were successful in their demands against management, reflecting similar changes that were taking place across the country. Through this study, Warner and Low showed that behavior inside a plant cannot be understood fully without also knowing the connections between the plant and its historical, social, economic, political, and technological contexts.

By the early 1950s, with many significant discoveries about organizations to its credit, the future looked bright for industrial anthropology. Unfortunately, the first generation of anthropologists in industry failed to produce a second generation, and as a result, the study of corporations declined and virtually vanished from the anthropological landscape (at least for the time being). Reasons for the decline of industrial anthropology are numerous and complex.

Theoretical Shift
The theoretical foundation for the human relations school assumed that labor-management collaboration and organizational harmony were desirable objectives in an industrial organization. This assumption was not

compatible with the emerging reality of labor relations in American industry, which was increasingly characterized by severe labor-management conflict and strife. As the organized labor movement grew in strength, the collective bargaining agreement gradually came to be the answer to labor-management relations on a daily basis, and the human relations school slowly faded into obsolescence (Burawoy 1979). The anthropologists themselves appeared to not realize what was happening until it was too late. Historians of social science have criticized this generation of industrial anthropologists for being too close to management (management-centric) and not sufficiently connected to the working class to foresee the rising tide of unionization and its theoretical consequences (Baba 1998). In the meantime, other disciplines such as industrial sociology were developing new theories to explain organizational behavior. The most prominent of these (and still dominant) is contingency theory, which explains what is happening in an organization by using correlations among formal variables that rely upon quantitative data drawn from surveys of large numbers of organizations and rigorous statistical analysis of survey results. Anthropological methods were sidelined as appropriate mainly for case studies, which, in those days, were suspect as unreliable and nongeneralizable to a large population of organizations.

Changes in Academia

In the 1960s, American higher education was entering a period of enormous growth; many more professors were needed to teach a flood of college-age baby boomers (Partridge and Eddy 1978). At the same time, the U.S. government was eager to continue the technological advances that had helped the Allies to win World War II, and toward that objective the National Science Foundation was established to fund academic research. These developments meant that the field of academic anthropology, and federal funds for fieldwork in foreign countries, grew both in size and stature. Anthropologists now had the means to travel abroad to conduct research, and the academic discipline of anthropology emphasized the significance of foreign fieldwork as necessary to the creation of a "real anthropologist." Those conducting research in the United States (such as the industrial anthropologists) were relegated to a second-class citizen status, which ultimately pushed many of them out of anthropology and into the business world. Some became professors in business schools (e.g., Frederick Richardson, William Foote Whyte, and Leonard Sayles), whereas others started businesses or became business consultants (e.g., Burleigh Gardner and Eliot Chapple; see Schwartzman 1993). This meant that they were not able to produce a second generation of industrial anthropologists (i.e., they were not training future anthropologists to study business in departments of anthropology).

Political and Ethical Issues

Beginning in the 1960s and continuing through the 1970s, academic anthropologists in the United States developed serious concerns regarding the ethical propriety of conducting research under the auspices of powerful sponsors such as government agencies and corporations (Partridge and Eddy 1978). A wariness and suspicion of applied anthropology erupted in the 1960s, when it became known that certain government agencies had attempted to engage anthropologists in research that would become part of a counterinsurgency program in the developing world (e.g., Project Camelot). Such revelations, together with a growing antiwar movement in the United States, turned anthropologists away from government service and fostered a suspicion of any powerful sponsor who could use anthropological research in ways that might injure those studied, injuring anthropology in the process. In addition to the government, multinational corporations also were identified as potentially dangerous sponsors. Given the devastation of Europe as a result of World War II, the United States became the dominant global economic power in the 1960s. American industry was making inroads into foreign markets and was setting up factories in developing countries to reduce the cost of production. Academic anthropologists who were conducting fieldwork in the very places that American businesses were investing often saw the negative consequences of industrialization, including increasing poverty, new disease threats, and the disintegration of traditional communities and social support systems.

One notorious example of such tragedy was the malnutrition and infant death that followed Nestlé's introduction of infant formula in the developing world. Often, Third World women could not afford to continue to buy formula in the amounts recommended, nor could they ensure that bottles were sterile or that water to mix the formula was pure. Formula was often heavily diluted with contaminated water, leading to infant diarrhea, malnutrition, and outright starvation. Women who relied on formula instead of breast-feeding could not switch back to the breast because their milk supply dried up when not used. Nestlé was aware of these problems, yet it would not withdraw the formula from countries where these problems were manifest, triggering a massive global boycott of Nestlé products. Such instances of unethical corporate behavior further alienated anthropologists from industry and caused some to label any work for industry as unethical. This label stuck, as the American Anthropological Association promulgated principles of professional responsibility in 1971 that prohibited any research that could not be freely disseminated to the public. Because industrial research some-times is proprietary (i.e., owned by the company and not publishable with-out its permission), this code of ethics virtually banned anthropological practice in industry for the next two decades.

The Fragmentation of Industrial Anthropology in Academia: 1960–80

There was little anthropological practice in business and industry during the two decades between 1960 and 1980. This was a time of high productivity in the development of anthropological theory, however, and most of the the-oretical frameworks that are employed by practitioners today were devel-oped in this era (but they were not applied in business until later). Anthropological interest in industry fragmented into several different streams during this period. In one stream, anthropologists working abroad became critics of the hypothesis that industrialization in developing coun-tries requires cultural changes that parallel those experienced in the West. These anthropologists showed that industrial development is compatible with many different cultural traditions and does not require other societies to copy our practices at work or at home (Holzberg and Giovannini 1981). In another stream of research, Marxist anthropologists documented the strategies that working people use to cope with management practices aimed at increasing profit margins (i.e., surplus revenue over expenditure). For example, managers often employ improvements in technology and automation to wrest control over the work process from workers, and they use technology to reduce both the overall number of workers needed to do a job as well as the skills required (deskilling associated with the rise of tedious, repetitive industrial jobs that are demeaning, boring, and alienat-ing). Anthropologists and qualitative sociologists were among the first to empirically document the informal working knowledge that people use on the job, both to get the work done and to protect their jobs, skills, and earn-ings (Kusterer 1978; Burawoy 1979; Lamphere 1979). It was not until much later that management scholars similarly discovered that workforce knowl-edge is a valuable economic asset (Nonaka and Takeuchi 1995).

During this same period there was a third stream of anthropological research in industry that had a more direct connection with the develop-ment of management and organizational theory: the anthropology of work among occupational and professional groups (e.g., construction trades, rail-way workers, accountants, and musicians). Members of occupational or professional groups often have characteristics that parallel those found in small-scale societies, such as a unique system of meanings, practices, and a language that distinguishes them from other work groups (Applebaum

1984). The common life of occupational members gives rise to an occupational community, which may be defined as a social group that establishes its own boundaries; derives its identity from work-related roles; looks to other members as a primary reference for values, beliefs, and norms; and adopts activity patterns that blur the boundary between work and leisure activity (Van Maanen and Barley 1984). The features of a given type of work promote certain patterns of behavior while suppressing others; these patterns are reinforced through selective hiring, formal training, and the informal enculturation of new recruits.

A work culture lends itself well to application of the concept of culture and the ethnographic method, and anthropologists have used ethnography to record the distinctive cultures of many different occupations and professions. For example, Herbert Applebaum's (1981) ethnographic account of life as a construction worker depicts a world in which highly skilled craftspeople (carpenters, masons, electricians, cement finishers, ironworkers, sheet metal workers, plumbers, and others) often own their tools, accessories, and trucks and, in many cases, have been in business for themselves at one time or another. They know their business better than anyone else, and they control the work process, with an emphasis on quality. If a general manager places too much emphasis on speed, the worker is likely to walk off the job. Workers gain the respect of others through the quality of their finished work, and highly respected journeymen consider themselves to be the peers of the engineers and other overseers. It is the craftspeople and their supervisors who make most of the decisions at a work site, and because the latter have come from the ranks, they are usually on friendly terms with the workers. Hiring and firing happen on the job site, not in the home office. The personal networks of the supervisors and foremen are the sources from which workers are selected, based on experience. Workers also determine whether or not conditions are safe enough to commence or continue working. These conditions create a work culture that is highly satisfying to its members, who take pride in work that they control.

According to Applebaum (1981), a number of factors have intersected to create the special conditions found in the construction industry. Unlike many other areas of commerce, the construction industry has not been affected by the increasing mechanization of work processes and specialization of tasks that have led to deskilling in other industries. Rather, construction workers have maintained a high level of skill, so workers control much of the work process, and trade unions have great strength. These features, in turn, are related to the technological requirements of the industry, including the uniqueness of each building and site, the temporary duration of a given project, the variation in work processes due to changes in weather, and the inability to stockpile a product. All of these requirements have prevented the advance of mechanization and have enabled construction workers to maintain their independence and autonomy.

Over the years, anthropologists, sociologists, folklorists, and others working in the qualitative research tradition have contributed to our knowledge of many different occupational and professional work cultures. This includes studies of accountants (Montagna 1974), locomotive engineers (Gamst 1980), longshoremen (Pilcher 1972), medical school students (Becker et al. 1961), nightclub strippers (Boles and Garbin 1977), police (Van Maanen 1973), professional dance musicians (Becker 1951), rodeo workers (Lawrence 1982), social workers (Cohen and Wagner 1982), timber loggers (Bergren 1966), underground miners (Fitzpatrick 1980), waiters (Mars and Nicod 1984), and many others too numerous to mention (Applebaum 1984; Van Maanen and Barley 1984; Trice 1993). Descriptive studies of occupational and professional cultures in so many different industries created a foundation of knowledge that contributed greatly to our understanding of cultural phenomena in organizations in general, and they set the stage for further development of the concept of organizational culture during the 1980s.

The Expansion of Private Sector Practice: 1980–Present

In the decades following World War II (1945–80), American business interests were dominant in much of the world. This was because the nations of Europe had been devastated by World War II and were engaged in a prolonged rebuilding effort, while much of the rest of the world was caught up in the transition from colonial status (with regimes whose economies were dominated by agriculture and the extraction of raw materials) to political independence and the rise of industrialization. American business and industry really had no major world economic competitor (at least not in the private sector), and, as a result, U.S. private enterprise held international monopolies in many industries. Markets of the industrial world were not yet saturated with goods but were hungry for products manufactured in the United States. Many of today's emerging markets did not yet exist. Millions of potential consumers in Asia, Latin America, and Africa still were too impoverished to purchase manufactured goods, meaning that manufacturing industries based in these countries were stunted. It was a U.S. producer's world. American manufacturing corporations were kings with vast territories to rule.

In the 1980s, we began to notice some changes, and the change process became a tidal wave that altered the state of the world as we knew it. The economies of Western Europe and East Asia, especially Japan, South Korea, Taiwan, and Singapore, had recovered sufficiently from the wreckage of

World War II to begin aggressive trade and foreign investment activity that threatened U.S. business interests at home and abroad. Businesses based in Western Europe and East Asia successfully challenged American manufacturers in several industries (e.g., automobiles, steel, and consumer electronics), leading to the reduction of manufacturing jobs in many American locales and the diminution of American industrial preeminence. At the same time, the consumer markets of these competitor nations also were growing. In some parts of Asia, such as Japan and Taiwan, these markets attained, for the first time ever, a level of affluence sufficient to attract the interest of major corporations. U.S. markets by now were saturated with products, and American producers needed new places offshore to sell their goods and services. These new markets looked like prime real estate. Unexpectedly, about a decade into this period, the Soviet Union collapsed, and its many republics broke free to create their own nations, many with economies struggling to transform on the basis of capitalist market principles. Even China, an avowed Communist nation, surprisingly followed suit with its own brand of market economics, bringing billions of new consumers into the global marketplace. Middle classes began to emerge and grow in various nations of Asia and Latin America (e.g., India, Thailand, Mexico, and Brazil), bringing new and different types of consumers into the mix. American corporations knew relatively little about these new consumers, but they did know that these markets were their future.

During this period, the markets of Western Europe and Japan were becoming saturated with goods, just as the U.S. market had, but this didn't mean that consumers in these now wealthy countries would forgo purchases. Instead, the industrial (or postindustrial, as some would say) markets of the West and Japan fragmented into specialty submarkets and niches, some local and some global, with each displaying its own unique patterns of consumer preference and consumption. With the businesses of many other countries now challenging U.S.-based firms around the world, and with saturated and fragmented markets in the developed nations, it was no longer a producer's world in which American manufacturers were dominant. Instead, we witnessed the dawn of a consumer age in which no nation dominated the marketplaces of the world, and all producers had to work very hard to understand and serve the consumers in their own countries and elsewhere.

The implications of these developments for anthropology are profound. Although we cannot forget the factors within our discipline that played a role (e.g., overproduction of PhDs relative to the shrinkage of tenure-track positions in academia, a problem which ultimately forced changes in our professional code of ethics so that anthropologists could take jobs in the private sector), it is demand from industry that has had the most powerful impact on our private sector practice. In the new consumer age, American corporations find that they need new kinds of knowledge in order to compete effectively around the globe. Most importantly, they need the knowledge and skill to understand new kinds of consumers and to understand them in new ways. It is no longer sufficient to use only quantitative tools to understand consumer demographics and purchases (e.g., surveys, censuses) because these approaches may describe the *what* (is being purchased, where, and by whom), but they don't explain the *why*. A company needs to know why consumers are or are not reacting favorably to its products or services if that company is to make future decisions that lead to business success. Even more significantly, traditional means of studying consumers (e.g., focus groups, interviews, product clinics) do not yield sufficient insights into consumers' daily lives, which are needed to generate creative ideas for new and improved products and services. Consumers can provide some of the information (e.g., why they don't like a particular product) needed to generate new product ideas when they participate in focus groups, but there are many things they cannot tell. For example, consumers may not be consciously aware of the way they use products in their daily routines. Or they may not have the time or the inclination to conceptualize totally new kinds of products or services that could help to meet their unspoken needs and interests. Yet this is exactly the sort of knowledge companies need in order to survive in today's highly competitive global markets.

Another dimension of the economic transformations that have taken place since 1980 derives from the need of American corporations to change their own internal practices. When the producer is no longer king, there are many things that must be done differently, from the way new products and services are designed and manufactured to the way these products are sold and serviced. Everyone, from the CEO to the entry-level production worker, has become more consumer-oriented in virtually everything they do, so that the business can offer its consumers attractive, high quality products and services at competitive prices, delivered and serviced in a way that is effective and efficient. If a corporation does not do these things, its competitors will, and the company that is found lacking will face decline, taking hundreds or thousands of jobs down with it.

The need for American firms to change was driven home by the management consultants who wrote several books in the 1980s explaining differences between successful and unsuccessful corporate practices (Deal and Kennedy 1982; Peters and Waterman 1982). The role of corporate culture (distinctive systems of practice and meaning in particular companies) was highlighted in some of these volumes, and the whole idea of culture was elevated by the fact that Japanese firms—which obviously grew out of an entirely different cultural context than American ones—were experiencing such great success in global markets at the time.

The concept of culture thus entered the lexicon of American business, apparently for good. As a result, many corporations came to realize that they needed to change their culture in order to be successful. Even though corporations knew that they needed to change, it did not prove easy to alter traditional corporate practices. Many companies developed new strategies (means to achieve ends) to transform their business operations for success in the consumer age, but they were not always able to modify traditional *practices* within the firm to implement the strategies effectively. Business consultants often blamed this inability to change on resistance from "the culture," and as a result, anyone who could help a company understand and shift its culture was suddenly welcome (including anthropologists).

The preceding scenarios open two major vistas for anthropological practice in business and industry. One vista, the newer and perhaps more expansive of the two, is consumer behavior, product design, and marketing. Anthropologists are making significant contributions to the understanding of consumer behavior, to product design innovation to meet consumer needs, and to the marketing of new products and services in markets within the United States and abroad. The second vista, which is more closely aligned with anthropology's long history of practice in industry, addresses modern corporate needs through anthropological practice that enables the firm to better understand the company's internal cultures and their dynamics. Such understanding is a critical prerequisite to the development of fresh approaches that can help the company implement new strategic directions in culturally sensitive ways.

What Business Needs from Anthropology

Changes in global markets and related shifts in corporate strategy and practice, as described in the previous section, are often considered to be aspects of globalization, which is a process of economic and social transformation that is steadily increasing interdependence among the nations and peoples of the world. Anthropological practice in the private sector has expanded as globalization has gathered strength over the past two decades. Yet, because our practice in business is still relatively new, most companies will not post an advertisement that reads "anthropologist wanted" in marketing or management (although some might). Still, it is the case that anthropological training provides a unique combination of skills that can bring important new assets to the business world, assets that may not be developed in this particular combination through training in any other discipline. In the next sections of this chapter, we first review major areas of business needs and then explore ways in which an anthropological approach can address these needs.

Consumers and the Marketplace

Consumption, defined broadly as the acquisition, utilization, and disposition of goods and services, is the engine of a modern capitalist economy (Arnould, Price, and Zinkhan 2002). Virtually everyone who lives in such an economic system is actively involved in consumption decisions, from the small children who beg their parents for toys they have seen in television commercials to the wage-earning adult whose entire life is structured by and dependent upon the purchase of goods and services from corporations (e.g., home, vehicle, appliances, furniture, wardrobe, food, entertainment, and vacations). It is these consumption activities that keep the capitalist production system operating. If people around the world stopped buying new goods and services for an extended period of time, our economic system probably would collapse.

The consumption of goods and services is far more significant in cultural terms than may appear at first glance (McCracken 1988; Sherry 1995). Indeed, we in the United States tend to take consumption for granted, primarily because it is so pervasive in every aspect of our lives that it has become habitual and almost automatic. We don't often ponder the underlying cultural significance of purchases such as food, clothing, or household items, yet research has shown that such actions are integral to our individual definitions of self and reflect cultural patterns at both the societal and subgroup levels. In a consumer society, people tend to categorize each other based on consumption choices: where do we choose to buy or rent a home, what kind of car do we drive, what type of restaurants do we frequent? All of these choices signal to others what kind of person we are likely to be (or would like to be). Sometimes, we make these choices deliberately because we want to send a signal to others about our identity; sometimes we make these choices unconsciously, and it is the others who read meaning into our selections. This implies that goods and services act as media of interpersonal communication, with the coding and decoding of signals dependent upon deeper meanings that have their roots within a particular cultural context.

The capacity of consumption choices to reflect and signal individual identity and social affiliation suggests that goods and services have symbolic value (Arnould, Price, and Zinkhan 2002). A symbol is anything that stands for, or represents, something else. For example, to the average U.S. consumer, a Ferrari sports car symbolizes wealth, racy glamour, and sophisticated European tastes. The vehicle thus carries a meaning separate from its inherent functional properties, where meaning is defined as the interpretation of a good or service's value-in-use to the consumer. Traditionally, it was believed that the value-in-use of most goods and services was defined by their utilitarian nature—what functional properties the good or service provided (e.g., performance, reliability, durability, number and type of features, and price). It is now recognized, however, that the things we consume have other kinds of meanings as well, including those related to the construction of personal identity or the appropriation of someone else's identity (Belk, Wallendorf, and Sherry 1989), the conveyance of public messages about our social status or membership in a subgroup (i.e., class, ethnicity, religion, gender, or age), differentiation between the sacred and secular realms, and the evocation of specific kinds of feelings such as pleasure, arousal, or misery (known as hedonic meaning [see Arnould, Price, and Zinkhan 2002]). For example, the clothes we choose to wear may have any or all of these kinds of value. They perform the utilitarian function of covering some or all of our bodies. But they also signal who we are (hipster or preppie), where we belong (upper middle class or blue collar), whether we are relating to the sacred or secular (a biker outfit suggests the latter to most, but not necessarily all), or whether we choose to stimulate specific types of feelings (a skimpy bikini or an amusing Halloween costume) (Jordan 2003).

The linkage between a specific good or service and its meaning is quite often arbitrary; that is, there is no inherent reason why some type of clothing (a Halloween costume) may be interpreted as humorous whereas other clothing (choir robe) elicits a feeling of the sacred. The linkage is created within the context of a particular culture, through conventions that are established historically, handed down across the generations, and changeable over time. If we cross from one culture to another (or from one time period to another), the linkages between a particular good and its meaning may shift, causing confusion or misunderstanding. Thus, in modern Japan, we find that a large, multitiered, white wedding cake is present at a marriage ceremony, but the "cake" is inedible and is not served to the guests (Edwards 1982). Its meaning is revealed in a ritual in which the bride and groom cut the cake with a sword, representing the physical union between the man and the woman. To accurately interpret the meaning, or value-in-use, of the wedding cake, or of any other good, it is necessary to have knowledge of the culture in which the good is embedded.

Marketing managers try to supply consumers with the value they seek by making connections between goods and services and authentic meanings that exist within the culture. Thus, a certain brand may be linked in an advertisement with another object that is known to carry specific meaning within the culture. For example, in America, a single red rose symbolizes romance, and this object may be linked with the name of a jewelry store to suggest that purchases from that store will enhance a romantic relationship. It is not necessary for the advertisement to spell out the connection. Potential consumers already have the cultural knowledge requisite for drawing the connection between the rose, its meaning, and the store. Of course, the meaning of cultural objects can change over time and can also vary across consumer groups. A single red rose may have other meanings. People can draw their own idiosyncratic or creative meanings from a symbol, and these are not under anyone else's control, which means that the marketing of meanings is a task fraught with uncertainty. Ultimately, it is the consumer who creates or derives meaning from a product, not the marketer.

Because human behavior is ultimately open-ended, not predetermined, consumers can also create new kinds of meaning through the use of products and services, and these acts of creation suggest innovative uses or designs for products, just as they also may play a role in cultural shifts. For example, Americans spend many long hours inside their automobiles each week, commuting to work and driving children to various activities. Some people actually use their vehicle as mobile offices. As a result, many new features and accessories for automobiles allow the vehicle to function better as a multipurpose space and not just a means of transportation (e.g., sliding doors on both sides of the vehicle for improved access, improved interior lighting, increased capacity to hold objects in the driver's area, and geopositioning systems). These modifications not only represent changes in function but also symbolize a cultural shift toward increasing mobility and a broader geographic scope of operations for a household's activity (Squires and Byrne 2002).

Anthropologists trained in cultural concepts and ethnographic methods are well positioned to gain a deeper understanding of cultural and other behavioral patterns that may affect product concepts, functions, and design, and the subtle cultural meanings that may be attached to various objects and experiences in consumers' lives. This knowledge can be invaluable to corporations in planning for new products and improving product design and functionality and in the overall marketing mix, which includes promotion (advertising), packaging, placement in the market, and pricing. For example, an approach that emphasizes consumers' lifestyles and emerging product needs is the ethnographic investigation of consumer behavior in the home, workplace, or community. In this type of study, the anthropologist spends several weeks or days with specially selected groups of consumers, examining how they live and work, with the objective of recommending new types of products or services that can improve consumers' lives. Often, the study is targeted at a particular class of products (e.g., workplace technology, breakfast foods) and is likely to be sponsored by a firm that makes such products. Usually, anthropologists conduct such studies as members of a team with colleagues from other disciplines, such as artists, product designers, psychologists, and engineers. Insights drawn from ethnographic field studies often have greater validity than those derived from surveys, focus groups, or product clinics, where verbal behavior may be separated from actual practices. Customers may not even be aware of their actual behaviors and may respond to survey questionnaires based on an idealized representation of the subject matter. Direct observation of behavior (including videotaping) and comparison with verbal reports can identify such important distinctions, and these can be highly valuable in and of themselves because they capture two different dimensions of a customer's reality: thought and behavior. Ethnography also places human behavior in its larger social and historical contexts, which helps to explain *why* we do what we do, and often it is the answers to the "why" questions that hold the key to understanding what new product concepts will bring most value to consumers' lives. Several of these points are illustrated in the following case study.

Case Study: Creating New Product Concepts through Ethnography

Sue Squires

The ethnographic approach to conceptualizing new products not only relies upon direct observation of consumers' behavior in natural settings but also gains power by comparing and contrasting what consumers say and what they do. Sue Squires (2002) found that some consumers may not be aware of the conflict between saying and doing when she investigated breakfasting behavior in the home of a consumer who had participated earlier in a focus group.

Squires and her research partner arrived at the consumer's home around 6:30 AM on a weekday to observe a working Mom fixing breakfast for her two sons, Jack, age four, and Kevin, age six. The two boys had only 30 minutes to eat their breakfast, after which Mom would drive them to first grade and a day-care center before going on to work herself. Dad had already left, saying that he would grab something to eat on his way to the office. As Squires set up her videotape equipment, Mom explained that there would be nothing much to see because she had already explained her breakfast-making preferences at a focus group meeting a few days earlier. Mom said she believed that breakfast is the most important meal of the day and that she wanted her boys to have a healthy, wholesome breakfast each morning. She proceeded to heat up packaged, whole grain waffles for the two boys.

Jack and Kevin, however, had other ideas. Four-year-old Jack was watching television and would not come into the kitchen to eat his breakfast. Kevin came to the kitchen, but instead of eating the waffle, he fixed himself a bowl of red, white, and blue Sugar Pebble Crisp cereal and milk. Squires asked Kevin how he liked the cereal and he replied that it turns the milk blue, stirring the bowl to demonstrate. She then asked if Kevin's Mom bought the cereal and Kevin replied, no, his Dad bought it because he likes it too. Kevin left the waffle on his plate, untouched. Mom didn't seem to notice any of this. She kept talking about nutritious food while she prepared lunch for the boys. She then cleared the table, eating Kevin's waffle herself and throwing Jack's into the garbage disposal.

Just before leaving the house with the boys, Mom got a phone call from her mother-in-law, who questioned her about the boys' breakfast. Mom reported again that she had prepared the boys a healthy breakfast of whole grain waffles, juice, and milk. After hanging up, Mom told Squires that her mother-in-law called nearly every morning to see whether she had prepared a good breakfast for the boys. Apparently, the mother-in-law believed that Mom should stay home with the boys. "What does she know?" Mom asked. "In her day, she fed her kids (my husband being one of them) bacon and eggs in the morning—cholesterol. Just goes to show you. I'm watching out for my kids. I'm a good Mom." The three family members left, with Jack having eaten nothing. Later on, Squires visited Jack's day-care center and found him, at around 10:00 AM, sitting by himself on the playground, eating his lunch. He was hungry, he said, so his teacher told him he could have lunch early.

Squires observed several other working families in their homes, following family members to work and other activities and studying other market research data such as focus group results, which she says provide a good picture of what are considered the "right" or "acceptable" responses to a series of questions. Focus group responses consistently emphasized the need for a wholesome, healthy breakfast. After conducting many hours of observation and interviewing and analyzing videotapes, Squires and her partner gradually built up a picture of breakfast behavior in working American households, based in part on discoveries that center upon contrasts between different standards for "good" breakfasting. Breakfast, Squires believes, is under stress in dual-income families. There is very little time for breakfast, and it takes place very early in the morning when children (and adults) may not be hungry. Yet there is a cultural ideal that requires moms to prepare a good breakfast if they want their kids to do well at school. At the same time, there is little agreement on what a good breakfast is. Moms and dads tend to have different standards for this meal, and grandparents are concerned about the generational shift that has taken moms out of the home and into the workplace, even though the older generation's concept of a good breakfast doesn't pass muster by today's standards. As for the kids, they are not cooperating, and their resistance to mom's ideal breakfast creates more stress in the household. As it turns out, most of the family members are not actually eating breakfast at home. Moms, dads, and kids often eat breakfast on the way to work or school, or snack once they arrive (only the "snack" is really breakfast, says Squires). Squires believes the difficulties she observed are the result of a structural conflict in the American middle class—breakfast being forced at a time when people are not really prepared or able to eat it.

Based on Squires's work, the corporate client who sponsored the study developed a new product called Go-Gurt, a yogurt-based snack that tastes good to kids, is fun and nutritious, and can be eaten on the go (e.g., in the car on the way to school). Go-Gurt brought in $37 million in sales its first year, even with a very limited distribution. This product may help to resolve some of the contradictions moms face as they try to raise a healthy family while working full-time.

Several dimensions of Squires's work exemplify the anthropological approach to new product development. Squires went beyond the focus group data (which are the usual means of obtaining consumer input) by exploring breakfasting behavior in its natural context: the home. She carefully recorded detailed descriptions of natural behavior, using videotape to capture and analyze what happened. Anthropologists are trained to obtain detailed descriptive, qualitative data as a basis of their findings. Squires did not restrict her inquiry to the adult's point of view but included conversations with children to gain a better understanding of what was going on. She also ventured beyond the home to visit one of the children at school, where she learned more about breakfasting patterns. All of these choices made by Squires were part of an effort to go beyond the superficial or the obvious to gain a holistic and naturalistic perspective on breakfasting, both key features of anthropological analysis. Squires also utilized her understanding of cultural systems to identify points of conflict between what was said in a focus group (ideal culture) and what actually happened on the ground (real culture). Her analysis of this cultural conflict became the heart of her findings. She was able to link the conflict to larger tensions between social pressure to conform to the image of a "good mom" and economic pressure for women to work outside the home. The tension between these countervailing pressures means that women need new products that will help them provide nutritious food for their children while taking into account work schedules and the constraints of human biology. This insight became the basis for the new product concept.

Corporate Cultures and Organizational Change

Since the Hawthorne studies of the 1930s, it has become apparent that corporations contain social and behavioral patterns that resemble the various forms of culture studied by anthropologists and sociologists in the larger society (e.g., cultures of small-scale and complex societies, subcultures of ethnic groups). The Hawthorne studies proved that human beings in corporate organizations are not strictly bound by the formal, rational organizational designs constructed by management. Indeed, not even the managers themselves are bound by these designs. Rather, groups of people who work together for prolonged periods tend to develop shared and open systems of meaning and practice that persist over time and are taught to newcomers as the correct ways to think and act. These shared systems are not planned but emerge spontaneously in response to human efforts to cope with challenges inside and outside a group's scope of operations. This is, basically, the definition of culture. Cultural patterns in the private sector can form within various contexts (e.g., a work group, divisional or business unit, corporation, or industry) and may be conceptualized as subcultures (i.e., distinctive local patterns of practice and meaning that hold certain elements in common with larger cultural systems, such as those of the nation-state in which they are based or of occupational communities or ethnic or religious groups). Thomas Rohlen's classic work *For Harmony and Strength: Japanese White Collar Organization in Anthropological Perspective* (1974) provides an opportunity to observe the interaction of cultural and subcultural forms operating at the national, organizational, and occupational levels. In this ethnography, Rohlen describes daily life in a Japanese bank, Uedagin, with a special emphasis on the training that young people receive to prepare them for a lifelong career of service with the bank. From this vantage point, we can see how the national culture of Japan shapes the subculture of the banking occupation in a Japanese setting, and of the Uedagin bank in particular. In one training exercise, for example, new employees are sent into a small village dressed in plain white uniforms and are required to go door-to-door asking residents for simple household chores that they may do without pay. The trainees must do this alone and may not return to the training facility until they succeed in finding work. The exercise is not as simple as it may appear because doing a favor for someone in Japan creates an obligation, meaning that strangers are not eager to accept gratuities. After being refused several times, the young trainees usually find that they are happy to do whatever work they are offered, no matter how menial or onerous. This experience is meant to teach them that it is not the nature of the work that determines one's attitude toward work, but rather one's attitude that determines the way in which the nature of work is perceived. We see from this example that occupational training in the bank reflects the larger cultural pattern of aligning individual values and attitudes with group norms and practices.

Some cultural forms within corporations also may reflect countercultures that form in opposition to managerial interests. Martin and Siehl (1983) describe a colorful counterculture at General Motors (GM), founded around the personality of maverick executive John DeLorean, who stood out from other top managers at GM, in both his charismatic personal style and his managerial practices. DeLorean was opposed to the mainstream GM cultural values of team play and fitting in, and he instead emphasized dissent and independence, backing up his views with managerial practices such as measuring performance on the basis of objective criteria, rather than personal loyalty or other subjective bases. DeLorean also signaled dissent in the way he decorated his divisional offices (bright carpets and modern furniture) and in his personal dress (more fashionable than the norm). Corporations may permit such countercultures to co-exist with their mainstream culture because they can be a source of new ideas (e.g., DeLorean's division also designed innovative vehicles that were successful in the marketplace), while remaining sufficiently marginal in size and scope to permit them to be sold off, shut down, or reined in should they become a threat to the corporation.

Anthropologists and other qualitative researchers have written extensively about corporate cultures and subcultures, and they have found complex patterns of interaction among them. Subcultures or countercultures within a corporation may compete with one another for resources, collaborate to achieve mutual interests, or engage in conflictual interactions (Trice 1993; Baba 1995). For example, Baba (1999) describes interactions that reflect distrust between work groups in the automotive and aerospace industries, based on past experiences of negative reciprocity (i.e., exchange relations in which one party attempts to gain something at the expense of the other party). When members of work groups distrust one another, they may attempt to shield themselves from harmful exchanges by building elaborate boundaries to prevent interaction. These boundaries can become barriers to closer cooperation between the work groups. Protective boundaries founded on past experiences of distrust also can retard a company's progress in establishing automated communication links between work groups (e.g., computer-aided design and manufacturing, e-commerce) because workers may fear that new technology will pierce the protective veil they have established by connecting them electronically with distrusted others. Under such conditions, work groups may resist the implementation of new information technology as a threat to their security.

Individuals within a given subculture also may shift their orientation from one subculture to another, depending upon their background and experience. For example, a single employee may be able to participate during the course of a single day in a work group culture (factory), an ethnic culture (Asian-American), and a counterculture (radical union local). Hamada (1995) describes the interesting case of an American female factory employee working in a Japanese-owned company who shifted her cultural orientation away from that of her American co-workers and toward that of the Japanese plant managers. This shift took place as part of a process through which she was being groomed for a position as a junior manager within the plant. The employee's behavioral patterns changed to model those practiced by Japanese managers, until a (somewhat ambiguous) point was reached at which she no longer was able to continue along this path. Then, after a charge of sexual harassment against her Japanese manager, she reoriented herself toward a more American behavioral pattern and eventually left the company altogether. Individual shifts across cultural contexts are an important means by which various forms of culture are integrated within a company, but they also may be a source of tension and conflict, as in the situation described by Hamada.

What is especially fascinating about corporate cultures, subcultures, and countercultures is that their patterns of practice and meaning reflect the intersection of *rational* and *natural* systems in modern organizations (Scott 1998). Rational systems are those deliberately planned and constructed for instrumental purposes, whereas natural systems are those that arise, unplanned and spontaneous, from the fulfillment of basic human social and psychological needs (e.g., the need to identify with, belong to, and have value within a social group; the need to make sense of events; resistance to power). The interaction of these different kinds of organizational systems is responsible for many issues and challenges in corporations, especially in cases where natural systems contradict managerial intent. The implementation of new technology provides an illustration of this point because it is usually considered to be a rational system, one with components that are planned and controlled. Yet the way that technology is used, and its meaning for work groups, may also be part of the natural system because humans appropriate technology for their own purposes. For example, Baba (1995) describes a case in which a large corporation developed a strategy that called for all work groups involved in new product development to adopt a common brand of computing technology to ensure that product design and engineering data could be shared easily, toward the goal of improving time to market (i.e., the time between creation of a product concept and delivery of the new product to the market). In some cases, work groups were willing to adopt the new brand of computing technology (rational), but they were not willing to give up the other brands they were already using (for their own "natural" purposes), with the end result that the corporation's technology strategy actually increased the number of computer brands in use, rather than decreasing it. Clearly, this outcome would not have the intended result of streamlining product development and reducing time to market. From a managerial perspective, this behavior was a serious problem because it thwarted the corporate agenda of improving time to market. This is perhaps one key reason why cultural patterns often are thought to represent resistance to change. Anthropological inquiry, however, revealed that for some work groups, multiple brands of computing were required to ensure compatibility with external suppliers who provided valuable technical services, whereas a shift to a single strategic brand threatened to lock the work groups into relationships with a small set of less desirable suppliers. Thus, natural system responses also were quite rational from the work groups' point of view.

Anthropologists are well equipped to understand the natural systems of the corporation and to investigate how these natural systems interact with management's rational designs. Anthropologists can help the company to better understand its own natural systems and creatively co-design ways for these two types of systems to work together constructively to serve human purposes. In the following case study, we explore one example of the way in which the knowledge of natural systems—gained as a result of anthropological intervention—paid off in terms that the corporation acknowledged as significant.

Case Study: Discovery of Local Knowledge in an Occupational Community

Julian Orr

Xerox Corporation employs a large cadre of repair technicians who perform client services in the field to keep the company's photocopying products in good working order. The context for this service is that of a large corporation in heavy competition with both foreign and domestic rivals, a situation that requires continuous technological innovation. The technology embedded inside the machines is constantly evolving at a rapid pace, meaning that photocopiers sometimes reach the market before anyone understands all of the ways in which the equipment can fail once it comes into contact with customers.

Although the repair technicians receive formal technical training to do their jobs, it is generally acknowledged that their training is not sufficient to allow them any substantial knowledge of how the science inside a photocopier—based on sophisticated physics and engineering principles—actually works. Instead, the repair technicians receive training focused on the mechanical aspects of the equipment, and they also learn diagnostic procedures that allow them to troubleshoot and repair machines without in-depth knowledge of science or engineering.

One might expect that the rapid pace of technological change in the industry, coupled with limitations in the depth of the repair technicians' training, would lead to a situation in which the technicians often could not fix machines in the field. This is not the case, however. The vast majority of repair calls (95 percent) are handled competently by the technicians, without any need to replace the machinery. Nonetheless, Xerox worried about the potential fallibility of the technician's knowledge and created a system of "directive documentation" that supposedly would enable faster resolution of problems in the field. The documentation includes set-up and repair procedures, simplified schematic diagrams, and diagnostic procedures. The diagnostic procedures provide a decision tree that contains a series of instructions described in considerable detail, followed by a yes/no choice, followed by further branching to other actions. Significantly, no rationale for the actions described in the decision tree is provided; the purpose of the tests and interpretation of the results are not explicit and are known only to the engineers who designed the documentation. Although technicians may refer to the documentation during the course of a repair call, they often put the documentation aside and proceed with a diagnosis on their own.

Wondering how the technicians managed to be so successful despite the fact that the documentation often was ignored, Xerox deployed anthropologist Julian Orr (who was once himself a technician) to travel with some of the company's technicians and watch them work. Within a relatively short time, Orr (1990) had discovered the technicians' secret. When they ran into machine failures that could not be resolved with standard diagnostic procedures, technicians had other tools that the company knew nothing about. The most potent was a form of storytelling, in which a technician recounts war stories about past machine failures and heroic saves. The war stories embed diagnostic clues and test procedures that suggest ways to manipulate real machines on the ground, through reference both to a network of abstract representations of the machinery and to contextual details that permit pattern recognition from the story to the immediate situation. By considering clues and trying the tests contained within the stories, technicians were usually able to work themselves out of a jam through trial-and-error problem-solving maneuvers. The story framework is a good way to package and transmit information about machines because the story's structure and the interest it holds for technicians enables easy recall.

The most interesting thing about the war stories was that they originated not only from the past experience of the technician actually facing an immediate problem, but through the experience of *other* technicians as well. War stories were swapped by technicians whenever they had an opportunity, for example, at lunch, on coffee breaks, in training sessions, or during off-duty socializing. The more unusual the story, the more likely it was to be remembered by others and recalled when the need arose. Technicians liked to tell stories about their problem-solving heroics because they gained status on the basis of technical prowess. The more difficult the machine-failure problem, the more status gained by solving the problem and telling a story about it.

Once Xerox found out how technicians solved difficult machine problems, it decided to facilitate and enhance this grassroots approach by equipping technicians with mobile radio phones that would enable them to call each other in the field or to contact a roving "tiger team" comprised of highly skilled troubleshooters. Technicians willingly adopted the radio phones, not only because this technology was compatible with their own preferred practices but also because it would provide technicians with ready access to two-way radio connectivity that could be used for a variety of other purposes (such as staying in contact with family members).

Orr's discovery of the economic value of storytelling within an occupational community provides an unforgettable illustration of the power of culture in an organization. The repair technicians—a community of practice (Lave 1991; Brown and Duguid 1991) whose members create and share a unique system of knowledge and work practices that enhance the overall capabilities of the entire distributed group—add value to Xerox's service operation, not necessarily because they want Xerox to profit but because individual technicians gain a sense of self-worth from their own technical prowess and competency, and they enjoy the experience of winning kudos (and status) from peers when they solve a particularly intractable problem. This example reveals the close intertwining of the rational and natural systems discussed earlier in the chapter. Clearly, these two kinds of organizational systems are informed by different principles, but they are mutually causal and entirely interdependent.

Orr's study was uniquely anthropological in several respects. Orr engaged in a prolonged period of fieldwork, during which he observed technicians doing their normal work; in other words, he observed natural behavior in the field and did not rely on survey data or verbal self-reports. By carefully recording exactly what the technicians *said* while working, as well as what they *did*, Orr was able to connect these two kinds of data to understand their interrelationship and identify a pattern of storytelling by technicians on the job. He noted that these stories were also told off the job, when technicians were in training or relaxing. Orr was able to make this observation because he followed the technicians beyond their normal workday and on to educational and leisure activities. Using his understanding of sociocultural systems, and his own insider knowledge of technicians' occupational culture, Orr was able to connect storytelling to the achievement of status within the technician community, and he was also able to connect the detailed content of the stories to technicians' behavior while they worked. By connecting what technicians said with what they did, Orr discovered that the war stories were a template for solving machine problems, one that is well suited to the nature of human memory. This discovery could only be made by fine-grained analysis of carefully recorded qualitative data, informed by knowledge of human biological and cultural systems, skills and knowledge uniquely provided by anthropological training.

Natural systems, such as those described by Orr, become especially important when a company faces environmental change and has no choice but to adapt. In these times of turbulence in global economic and political arenas, corporations need to be flexible and adaptive to changing demands from their customers and shifts in strategy from their competitors at home and abroad. Yet strategies for change will not be very effective if they do not take into account the local knowledge embedded in natural systems of meaning and practice that people create spontaneously as a means to help them get the work done while satisfying their basic human needs. Many rational strategic plans have come to naught and many resources have been wasted because the planners of change did not bother to consult the people who have to implement the plan on the ground and take their knowledge into account (see Howard and Schneider 1988; Baba 1990, 1999; Sachs 1995). Again, anthropologists can help by learning about and accessing local knowledge that is relevant to an intended course of change and by recommending ways to modify the plan so that local knowledge is incorporated. Such adjustments can help to ameliorate the root causes of human problems that result from corporate policies and plans that are uninformed by such knowledge, especially those that are enacted in a context that is foreign to the corporation. The anthropologist, acting as a kind of knowledge broker between the natural and rational systems within a corporation, may also recommend ways to enable natural systems to adapt to changing circumstances without suffering harm.

The negotiation of a new alignment between rational and natural systems that enables a corporation to pursue its goals while continuing to foster conditions in which people can co-create vibrant work communities is an alternative to older approaches in which managers attempted to manipulate or control the organizational culture, often with unintended negative consequences for hapless employees, as in the case described by Gideon Kunda (1992; for discussion, see also Baba 2001). Kunda described the engineering division of a high technology corporation, in which engineering managers deliberately construct a culture that attempts to enmesh the individual interests of the engineers with those of the corporation through the mechanism of normative control—a subtle means of influencing individuals to internalize the norms and values of the group and voluntarily contribute more effort than they would otherwise. Although this "engineering culture" (a double entendre) is effective in persuading engineers to devote considerable time and energy to the corporation, it may also lead to cases of burnout and diminished lives outside the company. Whether the creation of such high commitment work environments is a positive development for people is debatable. In this example, the engineering managers may have been successful in their efforts because they started their careers as engineers and had insights into engineering culture. Ultimately, no one can truly control the subculture of another group—culture is created by group members, and overt efforts toward control are likely to be met by equal forces of resistance—and it is possible that certain conditions inside a corporation, such as severe downsizing, a hostile takeover, or massive internal transfers, can so profoundly alter or damage a subculture that the knowledge and creative potential it contained are lost forever.

Global Business: Markets and Organizations

Cutting across the marketplace and workplace contexts just described is the international dimension. With the growth of many foreign markets (Asia, Latin America) and opening of new markets (Eastern Europe), corporations often have no choice but to expand internationally or risk being constrained to an increasingly saturated home market. Anthropologists have many opportunities in the international business arena (see Jordan 2003). Knowledge of culture equips the anthropologist to gain a detailed understanding of the lives of consumers from different cultures. Identifying cultural differences that affect product design is critical because companies must determine which products and services may be sold in a generic version that requires few if any modifications and which must be altered significantly for acceptance abroad. Anthropologists also can be helpful in the marketing arena because of their in-depth knowledge of customer lifeways, preferences, and symbolic systems that should be reflected in marketing decisions and materials (e.g., packaging and advertising). The cross-cultural interpretation of symbols is an especially important aspect of the anthropologist's role. Because the meaning of symbols is arbitrary and culturally defined, almost any symbol—from a word, to a picture, to a material artifact—may change meanings when it crosses a cultural boundary. Symbols that are positive in one culture may be negative in another (e.g., Chevrolet's Nova becomes "doesn't go" in Spanish; the American gesture for OK—making a circle with the thumb and first finger—is an obscene expression in Brazil). Anthropologists can help companies to detect and avoid such cultural landmines.

Anthropologists also can add value by explaining culturally grounded systems of practice and meaning that affect people's work behavior, thus requiring modification of corporate policy and practice. For example, we can contribute to diagnosing difficulties and recommending solutions that arise when employees from different cultures work together. Gluesing et al. (2003) described a globally distributed team comprised primarily of French and American employees, based in Paris but with a corporate headquarters located in the U.S. Midwest. The team experienced a near meltdown during a "videoconference from hell" (emic term), reflecting a protracted factional struggle over how to go about improving corporate relationships with a major global French retail customer. French members of the global team preferred the traditional "French way" of doing business, based on long-term personal relationships and hierarchical access to stable functions at the retail company, whereas the Americans wanted to introduce a radically new method of interaction with the retailer that would require reinventing the interface between their company and that of their customer. The factions struggled against each other, largely in silence and behind the scenes, until the team nearly self-destructed. Finally, as a result of the videoconference from hell, during which a key team member threatened to leave the company, everyone realized what was happening and began to correct themselves just in time to negotiate a third way that was both "French" and innovative. The anthropologists who had been studying this global team provided several recommendations for practitioners that would enable virtual work groups to avoid such conflictual situations in the future. One key recommendation involves taking time up front to identify and explore cultural differences in work-related assumptions and interpretations. Even if these differences cannot be resolved immediately, they should be acknowledged, lest they become the unrecognized basis for destructive intrateam conflict (for further discussion, see Baba et al. 2004).

People from different cultures often have divergent interpretations of a situation that can affect their ability to agree on what they are supposed to be doing and how they should do it. Not only can anthropologists explain why different groups of employees may not agree, but we can also support negotiations and compromises that enable people to form effective cross-cultural groups. Finally, anthropological opportunities for employee training and organizational development that may be found in international business are virtually limitless. We can provide knowledge of foreign cultures for training programs aimed at increasing awareness and effectiveness in working with foreign customers or employees (e.g., Hall and Hall 1990). We also can conduct participant observation in international business units to help diagnose and resolve behavior problems involving employees from multiple countries.

What Anthropology Brings to Business

Three core aspects of anthropological expertise bring significant value to private enterprise: (1) general knowledge about culture, (2) skill in ethnographic practice, and (3) specialized knowledge about particular cultures, including language capabilities. Anthropologists are trained in each of these areas of expertise. Although it is possible that individuals trained in other disciplines may possess some of this expertise (e.g., organizational development professionals may be trained in ethnography; persons born and raised in other cultures may possess specialized cultural knowledge), it is the discipline of anthropology that provides the unique combination of these characteristics, and it is this combination that best addresses the needs of global corporations. We will discuss what is important about each of these areas of expertise in a business context, using brief illustrations from cases described in this chapter.

General Knowledge about Culture

To effectively respond to their markets and engage employees, businesses need to know about culture in general. By culture, we mean distinctive, shared patterns of behavior, thought, and feeling that emerge from a group's historical experience in a particular environment and that are taught to new members as the correct way to live. Cultures and subcultures are important aspects of business markets, both at home and abroad, because they influence consumption patterns. Cultures also exist inside the corporation in the form of organizational cultures that influence employees' thinking and behavior.

Some basic questions about culture that are relevant to business interests include the following: What are the key dimensions and domains of culture in our markets and organizations, and how do these affect consumer buying patterns and employee work practices; how does culture come into being and change over time, and can it be consciously managed or influenced; what happens when different cultures meet, and how may their interaction be enhanced? Notice that each question has an applied component—business wants to know *what decisions it should make* and *what actions it should take* in light of its interests and goals, on the one hand, and cultural realities on the other.

To respond effectively to questions posed above, it is first necessary to have mastery of culture theory in general. In practice, these applied questions typically are posed in relation to particular cultures (i.e., the ones the company is interested in), but it is important to have a general approach to framing and answering these questions because, in many cases, the specific answers will not exist in the literature, so it will be necessary for the anthropologist to gather and analyze original data to support an answer. This means conducting research, and sound research practice requires a general theoretical understanding of the phenomenon under investigation, so that we can frame our research questions effectively. It is important to have competence in several different culture theories because each one will have unique strengths for responding to some of these questions but not others. Anthropologists have used many different theories to describe and explain business situations and problems, including functionalism and structural-functionalism (Warner and Low 1946), cultural materialism (Briody and Baba 1991), cultural ecology (Baba 1995), symbolic/interpretativism (McCracken 1988), cognitive theory (Gregory 1983), and postmodernism (Hamada 1995).

The discipline of anthropology is still in its early days, in many respects, so there are many competing schools of thought that seek to explain our central phenomenon of interest: culture. Even though different approaches abound and provide a rich array of concepts with which to understand the human world, our theories of culture share certain characteristics that distinguish the anthropological approach from that of other disciplines. It is important to understand these shared features and the value they bring to business. Many business consultants and practitioners from other disciplines now readily use the culture concept, and we compete with them for employment positions and contracts, so an understanding of our strengths is especially crucial. Here are some aspects of the anthropological value proposition (what we bring to the table and the benefit it provides) that are especially salient in business, illustrated with examples from cases in this chapter.

Our view of culture as a complex, loosely coupled, open system of inter-relationships guides the anthropologist to a *holistic* approach that integrates a wide range of social and behavioral phenomena in describing and explaining culture. We cast a wide net in data gathering, and as a result, we are able to explain more and achieve a significant impact with our recommendations. In business, this means exploring beyond the obvious; for example, we may follow employees to their homes or other venues to find out how they live as a means to better understand what is going on, versus relying on surveys or focus groups. Our approach enables us to discover patterns and variables that may not be uncovered by others. For example, Squires (2002) visited a family at home during breakfast and followed one of the children to school, thereby discovering behavior patterns that contradicted findings from focus group interviews.

Anthropologists often incorporate *history* into their analyses as a means to understanding the origins of cultural patterns and factors shaping them over time. The historical approach identifies the roots of the cultural system and its current manifestations, which means that we are better able to recommend effective ways to change behavior when needed. History can be an invaluable source of information that explains many seemingly inexplicable or irrational behaviors, thus pinpointing strategies for change. In Squires's study (2002), for example, the generational shift in patterns of family activity and values over the past 50 years became an important factor in explaining tension between ideal and real cultures of breakfasting.

We value multiple *emic* (insider) perspectives, and we attempt to understand these by listening directly to the voices of different groups of insiders. This approach allows us to access unique cultural patterns. By staying close to these insider points of view, we avoid the mistakes that come from over-generalization or oversimplification (e.g., from the use of surveys or canned typologies). In a business, the anthropologist should be interested in hearing from multiple groups of managers and employees, including first line workers. Often, there are major discrepancies between the viewpoints of different groups that directly interact with one another, or up and down the chain of command. An example can be found in differences between interpretations of piecework given by managers and workers in the Hawthorne study. Other disciplines' approaches may focus exclusively on management's point of view, or limit the investigation to a small number of elite employee groups, with the result that key data may be missing from the analysis.

Cross-cultural *comparison* is a powerful tool for understanding cultural differences and similarities and how cultures relate to each other. Comparison highlights distinctive cultural features and enables us to project points of both synergy and potential conflict between groups. This approach is particularly effective when the anthropologist is able to compare and contrast two different work groups in the same company, or the same demographic group in two different countries. There are often significant cultural differences in such cases, despite the many control factors, and these differences are likely to be salient in identifying unique cultural patterns. For example, Applebaum (1981) compared construction workers with other occupational groups as a means to understand and explain their unique culture.

Each of these characteristics, especially when combined, helps the anthropologist to obtain a well-grounded, multidimensional, and detailed understanding of culture that is robust in explaining many aspects of cultural phenomena that are relevant to business.

Competency in Ethnographic Practice

Since the late 1990s, business has become aware of the power of ethnography in understanding consumer behavior and employee work practices. By ethnography, we mean a field-based, empirical research strategy that uses multiple methodologies (especially, but not exclusively, direct observation) to depict in fairly minute detail a people's way of life (or some aspect of that life), incorporating insider understandings of the meanings attached to shared behavioral patterns, as well as descriptions of those patterns. Although anthropologists often take this research strategy for granted as "the anthropological way of knowing," we no longer have a monopoly on ethnography, nor can we assume that business will trust the anthropologists to deliver a quality product. Ethnography has escaped the grasp of anthropology, and it has been appropriated by consultants and practitioners from many other fields who claim to do it just as well as we do. Thus, we compete with others to do ethnography in the business market, and others may be asked to evaluate the ethnography we conduct (or vice versa). So we must be clear about how ethnography should be practiced for best results and ensure that we can deliver that to our business clients. Although it is true that ethnography may be (and should be) practiced differently in different situations, there are some general characteristics of good ethnography, both as practice and as product, that we can use as guides in business. Anthropologists Paul Bate (1998) and David Gellner and Eric Hirsch (2001) describe some ethnographic best practices for use in businesses and other organizations. I provide these below, together with my own suggestions and illustrations from the cases. Competent ethnography, either as a process or a product, does the following.

- Requires that we conduct significant *fieldwork*—Ethnography does not rely only on others' reports or on surveys alone. Like naturalists who study species in the wild, we spend time in the field gaining a firsthand understanding of the people we are interested in (as seen in the case studies by Squires and Orr). Often, financial constraints and time pressures limit how much time an ethnographer can spend in a business. Businesses have several concerns that can create pressures for limiting our time in the field.

These include a desire to reduce distractions to employees and a fear that confidential information will be disclosed and released (which can benefit a company's competitors or tarnish the company's public image). Anthropologists can cope with these concerns in two ways. First, rapid assessment approaches can be utilized to enable efficient data collection with minimal distractions to employees (see Beebe 1995). Even as little as three weeks in the field can yield significant ethnographic insights if the study is done properly; this is the amount of time Julian Orr (1990) spent following Xerox repair technicians (although his earlier job experience as a technician facilitated his discoveries). Second, an anthropologist can sign a nondisclosure agreement that protects the corporation's proprietary information from release. This conforms with our professional code of conduct, which requires that we do no harm to those we study.

- Utilizes *multiple* methods and techniques—Ethnography in business relies upon many well-known social science methodologies, including interviewing (structured, semistructured, and unstructured); direct observation and videotape recording of behavior, events, and situations; censuses and surveys; archival analysis; focus groups; network analysis; and computer-aided analysis of qualitative data. Squires, for example, used several of these methods in her study of American breakfasting behavior. Ethnographers who are anthropologists also gain insights through participant observation, in which the ethnographer takes on actual tasks within the business (with knowledge and approval of the company) in order to gain a deeper understanding of the members' experiences. For example, both Orr (1990) and Applebaum (1981) worked as actual members of the occupational groups they studied.

- Conveys a sense of *being there*—Ethnography captures detailed and nuanced portrayals of a particular field site, convincing the client of the ethnographic report's validity and yielding some sense of the site's character and uniqueness. This effect may be achieved by richly detailed descriptions that record and interpret the minutiae of daily situations and events, interspersing quotes throughout the text, or utilizing video clips to highlight key findings. Squires, for example, used videotape to capture contradictory breakfasting patterns, and Orr spliced key sections of technicians' dialogue into his reports. These embellishments are particularly important in business, where decisionmakers often do not have time to read thick descriptions but will read quotes and look at pictures.

- Searches for and provides details and conclusions that are unexpected or *counterintuitive*—Ethnography is exciting, fresh, and "hot" in the business world because it is capable of discovering that which has previously been hidden or unknown and may even contradict a decisionmaker's intuitive understanding. For example, Squires (2002) uncovered what had theretofore been invisible and obscured by inaccurate self-reports in focus groups, and Orr demonstrated that the telling of war stories—which the company previously viewed as a non–value-added activity—actually had significant economic value. Ethnographers are called upon because the business is exploring new ground, and the ethnographer's findings may be highly influential in shaping the early stages of a project. The ethnographer usually does not set out to confirm what has already been discovered by someone else because ethnography may not be the best approach for confirmation. Rather, we work as cultural sleuths, tracking down seemingly obscure pieces of information that depict human experience in new ways.

• Offers a *model* or *theory*—Ethnography, unlike travel writing or journalism, is not just for entertainment. It goes beyond interesting description and also provides explanation, helping the reader to understand *why* a particular site is the way it is. Orr (1990), for instance, explained war stories both as a means for technicians to achieve higher occupational status and as a form of community memory (i.e., he included a cognitive theory). This aspect of good ethnography relates to the requirement for understanding multiple theories of culture because any given model or theory of culture will be better suited to certain situations than others.

• *Contextualizes* its findings—Ethnography relates human thought and behavior to the multiple contexts in which people are situated, including contexts of history, geography, environment, society, politics, and economics. For a business organization and its markets, key contexts may include the nation-state, ethnic or religious groups, the industry in which a company is based, the larger corporation or business unit, and possibly the profession or occupation that relates to the focus of study. Warner and Low's (1946) study of the shoemaking factory strikes provides a prime example. This capability to link data to contextual factors is related to the holism requirement of anthropology—we cast a wide net that captures the background and overall situation of any subject of interest, countering reductionist tendencies that can oversimplify reality.

• Emphasizes both what people *say* and what they *do* and the disconnect between them—Ethnography is not restricted to front-stage performances (what people want us to see) but spends time investigating what goes on behind the scenes. Some of the most valuable insights we achieve in business will be related to discrepancies between verbal behavior and actual practices (e.g., focus group discussion versus actual behavior, as in Squires's study). Often, because of tall chains of command or elite social status, decisionmakers have little or no idea of what is really going on in the trenches, and they are often surprised or shocked when they find out.

• Looks closely at how *language* is used—Ethnography captures emic terms, phrases, and expressions, which are condensed forms of cultural meaning. There is perhaps no better way to obtain the insider's point of view. A single term can reveal much about history and culture (e.g., the "good mother" in Squires, or a "fair day's work" in Hawthorne). In business, there also is a considerable amount of site-specific and occupational jargon, some of which must be mastered just to communicate. For example, Orr's former job experience helped him to decode the repair technician's discourse.

- *Protects* the people we study—Ethnography is firmly committed to the principle of "first, do no harm." This applies both to the immediate project and its long-term effects. We must ensure informed consent (i.e., participation must be voluntary and based on full disclosure regarding the nature of the study and use of the data), respect the confidentiality and privacy of the people we study, and not engage in projects that endanger a people's livelihood or degrade their way of life. If these conditions cannot be met, it is inadvisable to proceed with a project. We also need to make certain that the people we rely on for knowledge receive something of value from the project in exchange for their help. As an illustration, Orr's (1990) work resulted in repair technicians receiving radio phones to extend their communications. Our particular sense of ethics in a business project may be one of the most important features characterizing anthropology in the private sector.

Specialized Knowledge about Particular Cultures and Languages

When a business is planning a significant expansion in a foreign country, it may seek help in understanding the markets or employees of that nation. Generally, the best help comes from either a foreign national (someone born and raised in the country) or someone else with extensive in-country experience and linguistic fluency. An anthropologist who has spent significant time in the country of interest could provide the needed expertise, but it is not out of the question that an anthropologist who does not have expertise in that particular nation but who knows how to learn about other cultures could meet the need. The best time to gain experience abroad and fluency in foreign languages is when one is training to be an anthropologist and has the required time available. Usually, several months or a year are required to achieve language competency, and at least that long is needed to gain a rudimentary understanding of a foreign culture. Later in life, during one's professional career, time or other pressures may prevent extensive stays abroad for the purposes of culture and language training.

Conclusion

The need to understand diverse cultures that comprise the marketplace and the corporate work environment is only expected to grow in the future as business globalization proceeds apace and the demographics of consumer and labor markets change over time. Anthropologists today have unlimited opportunities to work with corporations in enabling adaptation to these environmental changes while also striving to infuse our unique point of view into business practice. Because our contributions relate to innovation and change that is crucial in the global marketplace, we may be more likely to retain our positions within the corporation in turbulent economic times. The anthropological contribution can extend beyond the mere solution of technical problems by bringing a sense of purpose that is dedicated to encouraging more humane approaches to all of a corporation's opportunities and challenges. Our capacity and power to make this happen depends only upon our vision and the will to do so.

References

Applebaum, H. A. 1984. *Work in market and industrial societies.* Albany: SUNY Press.

———. 1981. *Royal blue: The culture of construction workers.* New York: Holt.

Arnould, E., L. Price, and G. Zinkhan. 2002. *Consumers.* Boston: McGraw-Hill.

Baba, M. L. 2001. Beyond Dilbert: The cultural construction of work organizations in America. In *Ethnographic essays in cultural anthropology: A problem-based approach,* edited by R. B. Morrison and C. R. Wilson. Itasca, Ill.: F. E. Peacock.

———. 1999. Dangerous liaisons: Trust, distrust and information technology in American work organizations. *Human Organization* 58 (3): 331–46.

———. 1998. The anthropology of work in the Fortune 1000: A critical retrospective. *Anthropology of Work Review* 18 (4): 17–28.

———. 1995. The cultural ecology of the corporation: Explaining diversity in work group responses to strategic transformation. *Journal of Applied Behavioral Science* 31 (2): 202–33.

———. 1990. Local knowledge systems in advanced technology organizations. In *Organizational issues in high technology management,* edited by L. R. Gomez-Mejia and M. W. Lawless. Greenwich, Conn.: JAI Press.

Baba, M. L., J. Gluesing, H. Ratner, and K. H. Wagner. 2004. The contexts of knowing: Natural history of a globally distributed team. *Journal of Organizational Behavior* 25: 1–41.

Bate, P. 1998. *Strategies for cultural change.* Oxford: Butterworth-Heineman.

Becker, H. S. 1951. The professional dance musician and his audience. *American Journal of Sociology* 57: 136–44.

Becker, H. S., B. Geer, E. C. Hughes, and A. M. Strauss. 1961. *Boys in white: Student cultures in medical school.* Chicago: University of Chicago Press.

Beebe, J. 1995. Basic concepts and techniques of rapid appraisal. *Human Organization* 54 (1): 42–51.

Belk, R., M. Wallendorf, and J. Sherry. 1989. The sacred and the profane in consumer behavior: Theodicy on the Odyssey. *Journal of Consumer Behavior* 16 (1): 1–38.

Bergren, M. 1966. *Tough timber: The loggers of B.C.—their story.* Toronto: Progress Books.

Boles, J., and A. P. Garbin. 1977. Stripping for a living: An occupational study of the night club strippers. In *The social world of occupations*, edited by B. J. Gallagher and C. S. Palazzolo. Chicago: Kendall/Hunt.

Braverman, H. 1974. *Labor and monopoly capital: The degradation of work in the 20th century.* New York: Monthly Review Press.

Briody, E. K., and M. L. Baba. 1991. Explaining differences in repatriation experiences: The discovery of coupled and decoupled systems. *American Anthropologist* 93 (2): 322–44.

Brown, J. S., and P. Duguid. 1991. Organizational learning and communities of practice: Toward a unified view of working, learning, and innovation. *Organization Science* 2 (1): 40–57.

Burawoy, M. 1979. The anthropology of industrial work. *Annual Review of Anthropology* 8: 231–66.

Chapple, E. D. 1953. Applied anthropology in industry. In *Anthropology today: An encyclopedic inventory*, edited by A. L. Kroeber. Chicago: University of Chicago Press.

Cohen, M. B., and D. Wagner. 1982. Social work professionalism: Reality and illusion. In *Professionals as workers: Mental labor in advanced capitalism*, edited by C. Derber. Boston: G. K. Hall.

Deal, T. E., and A. A. Kennedy. 1982. *Corporate cultures.* Reading, Mass.: Addison-Wesley.

Edwards, W. 1982. Something borrowed: Wedding cakes as symbols in modern Japan. *American Ethnologist* 9: 699–711.

Finlay, W. 1991. Review of *Manufacturing knowledge*, by Richard Gillespie. *Science* 254: 1820–21.

Fitzpatrick, J. S. 1980. Adapting to danger: A participant observation study of an underground mine. *Sociology of Work and Occupations* 7 (2): 131–58.

Gamst, F. C. 1980. *The hoghead: An industrial ethnology of the locomotive engineer.* New York: Holt, Rinehart, and Winston.

Gellner, D. N., and E. Hirsch. 2001. *Inside organizations: Anthropologists at work.* Oxford: Berg.

Gluesing, J., T. Alcordo, M. Baba, D. Britt, K. H. Wagner, W. McKether, L. Monplaisir, H. Ratner, and K. Riopelle. 2003. The development of global virtual teams. In *Virtual teams that work: Creating conditions for virtual team effectiveness*, edited by C. B. Gibson and S. G. Cohen. San Francisco: Jossey-Bass.

Gregory, K. 1983. Native-view paradigms: Multiple cultures and culture conflicts in organizations. *Administrative Science Quarterly* 28 (3): 359–76.

Hall, E. T., and M. R. Hall. 1990. *Understanding cultural differences: Germans, French and Americans.* Yarmouth, Maine: Intercultural Press.

Hamada, T. 1995. Inventing cultural others in organizations: A case of anthropological reflexivity in a multinational firm. *Journal of Applied Behavioral Science* 31 (2): 162–85.

Holzberg, C. S., and M. J. Giovannini. 1981. Anthropology and industry: Reappraisal and new directions. *Annual Review of Anthropology* 10 (10): 317–60.

Howard, R., and L. Schneider. 1988. Technological change as a social process: A case study of office automation in a manufacturing plant. *Central Issues in Anthropology* 7 (2): 79–84.

Jordan, A. T. 2003. *Business anthropology.* Prospect Heights, Ill.: Waveland.

Kunda, G. 1992. *Engineering culture: Control and commitment in a high tech corporation.* Philadelphia: Temple University Press.

Kusterer, K. C. 1978. *Know-how on the job: The important working knowledge of unskilled workers.* Boulder, Colo.: Westview Press.

Lamphere, L. 1979. Fighting the piece rate system: New dimensions of an old struggle in the apparel industry. In *Case studies on the labor process,* edited by A. Zimbalist. New York: Monthly Review Press.

Lave, J. 1991. Situated learning in communities of practice. In *Perspectives on socially shared cognition,* edited by L. B. Resnick, J. M. Levine, and S. D. Teasley. Washington, D.C.: American Psychological Association.

Lawrence, E. A. 1982. *Rodeo: An anthropologist looks at the wild and the tame.* Knoxville: University of Tennessee Press.

Mars, G., and M. Nicod. 1984. *The world of waiters.* London: Allen and Unwin.

Martin, J., and C. Siehl. 1983. Organizational culture and counterculture: An uneasy symbiosis. *Organizational Dynamics* (Autumn): 52–63.

McCracken, G. 1988. *Culture and consumption: A new approach to the symbolic character of consumer goods and activities.* Bloomington: Indiana University Press.

Montagna, P. D. 1974. *Certified public accounting: A sociological view of a profession in change.* Houston: Scholars Book Co.

Nonaka, I., and H. Takeuchi. 1995. *The knowledge creating company.* New York: Oxford University Press.

Orr, J. 1990. Sharing knowledge, celebrating identity: War stories and community memory among service technicians. In *Collective remembering: Memory in Society,* edited by D. S. Middleton and D. Edward. London: Sage Publications.

Partridge, W. L., and E. M. Eddy. 1978. The development of applied anthropology in America. In *Applied anthropology in America,* edited by E. M. Eddy and W. L. Partridge. New York: Columbia University Press.

Peters, T. J., and R. H. Waterman. 1982. *In search of excellence.* New York: Warner Books.

Pilcher, W. W. 1972. *The Portland longshoremen: A dispersed urban community.* New York: Holt, Rinehart, and Winston.

Roethlisberger, F. J., and W. J. Dickson. 1946. *Management and the worker.* Cambridge, Mass.: Harvard University Press.

Rohlen, T. 1974. *For harmony and strength: Japanese white collar organization in anthropological perspective.* Berkeley: University of California Press.

Sachs, P. 1995. Transforming work: Collaboration, learning and design. *Communications of the ACM* 38 (10): 36–44.

Schwartzman, H. B. 1993. *Ethnography in organizations.* Newbury Park, Calif.: Sage Publications.

Scott, W. R. 1998. *Organizations: Rational, natural and open systems.* 4th ed. Upper Saddle River, N.J.: Prentice Hall.

Sherry, J. 1995. *Contemporary marketing and consumer behavior: An anthropological sourcebook.* Thousand Oaks, Calif.: Sage Publications.

Squires, S. 2002. Doing the work: Customer research in the product development and design industry. In *Creating breakthrough ideas: The collaboration of anthropologists and designers in the product development industry,* edited by S. Squires and B. Byrne. Westport, Conn.: Bergin and Garvey.

Squires, S., and B. Byrne, eds. 2002. *Creating breakthrough ideas: The collaboration of anthropologists and designers in the product development industry.* Westport, Conn.: Bergin and Garvey.

Trice, H. 1993. *Occupational subcultures in the workplace.* Ithaca, N.Y.: ILR Press.

Van Maanen, J. 1973. Observations on the making of policemen. *Human Organization* 32 (4): 407–18.

Van Maanen, J., and S. Barley. 1984. Occupational communities: Culture and control in organizations. *Research in Organizational Behavior* 6: 287–365.

Warner, W. L., and J. L. Low. 1946. The factory in the community. In *Industry and Society,* edited by W. F. Whyte. New York: McGraw-Hill.

9 Anthropology Applied to Education

Nancy P. Greenman

Introduction

Anthropology applied to education constitutes a very broad and rich domain, especially when one remembers that schooling is just one of the places where education takes place. Anthropologists always have included at least some education in their ethnographic cultural studies. Enculturation, or the acquisition of culture, is a fundamental anthropological construct. How children learn to become successful adults participating in their culture is a question that concerns most ethnographers, and it is a question that leads to many approaches in the anthropological study of education (e.g., Pitman, Eisikovits, and Dobbert 1989). Classic studies about the relationship between mothers and their children explore how children are taught what is expected of them within their culture. This relationship can be seen, for example, in Elsie Clews Parsons's essays about Pueblo mothers and their children (collected in Babcock 1991), Margaret Mead's films, *Bathing Babies in Three Cultures* (1954) and *Four Families* (1960), and Martha Ward's *Them Children: A Study in Language Learning* (1986).

Educational anthropologists seek to understand education within its embedded cultural contexts. In this quest for understanding, epistemological questions, such as "What is considered important knowledge in this culture?," may become questions of curriculum and its importance in enculturation. Other questions, from the pedagogical to the political, illuminate various anthropological dimensions: How do children learn? How are they taught? Where do they learn? Who are their teachers? How does change occur in education? What happens when children receive mixed messages from multiple cultures? Arenas, or domains of concern and interest, emerge from these larger questions.

Literacy, considered essential in educational circles, is a good example of an issue given depth through anthropology. Literacy is defined and redefined by anthropologists. Anthropologists, such as Bloomfield (1964), Bull (1964), Hymes (1964), and Lee (1976), have addressed the essence of literacy, what one must know of the implicit and explicit verbal and nonverbal dimensions of a language to be considered literate in a particular culture and of the use of vernacular language in education. Dell Hymes (1964) investigated the relationship between child-rearing philosophy and language learning and queried what linguistic ability must be acquired to become a competent member of society. Concha Delgado-Gaitan (1990) explored the relationship between literacy and empowerment. Marietta Saravia-Shore and Steven Arvizu (1992) questioned and rejected E. D. Hirsch's limited notion of "cultural literacy,"[1] and Dorothy Lee (1976) questioned the impact of literacy on a culture and its members.

My aim in this chapter is to provide an overview of anthropology and education and a feel for its complexity. I discuss what it is and briefly survey its history. I discuss the embeddedness of application in anthropology and education and the ambivalent attitudes toward advocacy and direct application. I then look at some areas of concern to educational anthropologists, drawing heavily from narratives of professionals who are currently practicing in the field.[2] In the chapter, there are embedded case studies and career trajectories of three prominent educational anthropologists. Anthropologists' relationships with the following topics of concern are discussed: (1) educational change; (2) cultural acquisition, social capital, and empowerment of culturally diverse parents; (3) equity, empowerment, and social justice in school systems and communities; (4) the impact on education for culturally and linguistically diverse populations; and finally, (5) application of anthropological methods to education, with examples of how practicing anthropologists use them. Ethnographic evaluation is included in this section about methods.

What Is Anthropology and Education?

The domain of anthropology applied to education is referred to variously as anthropology and education, anthropology of education, educational anthropology, and education in anthropology. Anthropologists generally prefer anthropology and education, but they do use the term educational anthropology as well. Anthropology and education includes the study of anthropology in educational settings at all levels. Anthropology of education describes the anthropological study of education, but it implies a hierarchical relationship. For our purposes, I use the term anthropology and education and the term educational anthropology interchangeably. A great deal of applied educational anthropology currently addresses education in schools and classrooms, but some of the central tenets of all anthropology and education are context, education as enculturation (or acquisition of culture), and the intertwining of formal, nonformal, and informal education.

Exploration of parameters for these types of education might constitute part of the anthropology and education domain. Formal education is what we recognize as schooling. It is systematic and organized, with its procedures, rules, curriculum, and activities developed and imposed from outside the immediate educational context. Accountability in formal education also is imposed by an external authority. Nonformal education, according to Thomas La Belle, "refers to organized out-of-school educational programs designed to provide specific learning experiences for specific target populations" (1984, 80). This might include anything from English lessons for new immigrants to sailing lessons for new boat owners. Informal education is the lifelong acquisition of knowledge, skills, insights, attitudes, and experiences accumulated through a person's interaction with personal, social, cultural, and physical environments. Informal education can take place in formal educational environments if, noted Walter Precourt, "the rules governing educational activities and processes are generated from *within* the immediate context" (1982, 447).

Educational anthropologists apply anthropological constructs and methods to education in all of its contexts. Anthropologists generally consider educational anthropology as inherently applied, perhaps because education is such a complex institution, with its schooling dimension largely anchored in psychology, and because most educational anthropologists, even those in academe, are employed in educational rather than anthropological settings. Thus, educational anthropologists may be considered applied anthropologists simply by virtue of *being* educational anthropologists (Schensul, Borrero, and Garcia 1985). Harry Wolcott affirmed this status in his reflection on the field: "I guess I have never (or seldom, at least) thought of myself as an applied anthropologist. My anthropological colleagues do, of course, but my educator ones see my work as basic, except when I take on a specific assignment, and even there my work is summative" (2002a). John van Willigen provided the field with a broad definition in the statement, "applied anthropology is anthropology put to use" (2002, 7). He delineated domains of application as including information: raw data to general theory (providing information, making recommendations); policy (usually providing information to policymakers); and action (interventions carried out by anthropologists) (11). Given this breadth of definition, anthropology and education is inherently an applied field.

Educational anthropology has made a great deal of progress as a field of anthropology. Its importance is recognized, at the very least, for a focus on recontextualization of education and on the importance of culture, yet it still struggles with aspects of the same issues it did in its early history.

Historical Perspective

The historical roots of anthropology and education reach back to the late nineteenth century: "It was then that the potential contributions of anthropology to pedagogy, the school curriculum, and an understanding of the culture of childhood were first recognized" (Eddy 1985, 83–4). In 1898, an article by Nina Vandewalker was published in *The American Journal of Sociology* stressing the significance of anthropology for education and the importance of creating a linkage between them (cited in Ford 1997, 27–8). At the turn of the twentieth century, according to Ford, anthropologist Edgar Hewett and educator/physician/anthropologist Maria Montessori also were advocates for connecting anthropology and education. Areas of focus were pedagogy and cultural influence on learning styles. Montessori, a professor of anthropology at the University of Rome, developed the concept of *pedagogical anthropology*. Pedagogy involves the science of teaching. Drawing from the contextual learning of children in their cultural milieu, she developed the Montessori method, advocating teaching through modeling and using planned interactive environments to foster learning by hands-on exploration and imitation. Montessori also initiated teaching lower-class children the cultural and social capital necessary to integrate into society. At the same time, philosopher and educator John Dewey was playing with some of these same concepts in American education.

Historically, when educational issues were considered and teachers were trained, culture and context were relegated to the periphery by the grounding of education in psychology. In 1957, Theodore Brameld noted:

> Educational sociology, philosophy, and similar fields are still regarded as of subordinate importance [to psychology in teacher training] if they are studied directly at all. . . . Without question, the new field of educational anthropology is ignored by a still larger number. One may doubt whether the average prospective teacher, through no fault of his own, could clearly define anthropology, much less demonstrate familiarity with its subject matter or its significance for his professional work. (Cited in Ford 1997, 38)

In the years between 1925 and 1954, anthropologists such as Bronislaw Malinowski, A. R. Radcliff-Brown, Jules Henry, Solon Kimball, and Margaret Mead applied anthropology to developing educational policy and administration as well as to finding solutions for other educational problems, especially where indigenous populations were colonized or oppressed by a dominant culture. The psychological orientation of the culture and personality movement in anthropology and, later, in cognitive anthropology appeared to have direct relevance to educational issues and child development, or at least to find kindred spirits in educational psychology. This opened another door for applied anthropology.

Each time the eugenics movement surfaced, anthropologists entered the debates about the nature of intelligence, the relationship of nature and nurture, and how children learn and develop, all of which have important implications for education, policy development, and attention to diversity in education. Eugenics is the practice of controlling human reproduction with the intent to refine and strengthen hereditary factors deemed desirable. It is informed by the belief that the human race would improve if some people were prohibited from mating and others were encouraged to do so. Sterilization of people having physical and character traits considered undesirable is justified by purported altruistic concern for humanity. It perpetuates racism, prejudice, and sexism under the guise of science. Early twentieth century intelligence testing and pseudoscientific experiments differentiating mental capacities of "races" and genders arose in response to the great influx of immigrants at the turn of the century. Franz Boas presented policy research in efforts to dispel the racist sentiments embedded in and proliferated by this pseudoscience.

The racist theories spawned by dissemination of these skewed research study results often inspired well-meaning, though ill-informed, initiatives such as the 1930s and 1940s philanthropic American efforts in Africa to educate the "backward races" by exporting industrial and vocational education.[3] In addition to the work of Boas, applied anthropologists worked on many fronts to rectify damage done through these initiatives and to influence more enlightened foreign policy. Often there was controversy in anthropology as to whether this work effected support of colonial administrations or aided in ameliorating a bad situation (van Willigen 2002, 9). Through various governmental agencies, such as the Bureau of Indian Affairs (BIA), applied anthropologists consistently attempted to influence policy surrounding issues affecting indigenous and immigrant populations in America, especially with fluctuating political attitudes toward immigration and toward the rights and survival of indigenous nations. Depending on the larger historical contexts, anthropologists applied their specialized knowledge and insight to various dimensions of educational issues and policy, defining the relationship of anthropology to education and loosely shaping the parameters of educational anthropology.

The post–World War II influx of diverse veterans into higher education sharpened a focus on culture and education. An apparent turning point in the development of anthropology and education as a professional field was the 1954 Stanford-Carmel Valley Conference, organized by George and Louise Spindler. This conference was a gathering of 22 scholars—anthropologists, educationists, sociologists, and psychologists—presenting and discussing papers about the benefits of anthropology and education. Four concerns emerged as themes of the conference: (1) the search for a rationale and encompassing philosophy for the anthropology and education relationship, (2) sociocultural contextualization of the learner, (3) education—teaching and learning—in relation to the life cycle, and (4) intercultural learning and understanding involving the affective as well as the cognitive realms (Spindler 1984, 4). These themes became strands in the fabric of the newly forged field of anthropology and education. Annette Rosenstiel, an anthropologist at the Stanford meeting, "not only proposed a linkage between the two fields but suggested that they be used as a new interdisciplinary approach in the analysis of culture. She called this approach educational anthropology and was the first to coin this term" (Ford 1997, 32). Educational philosopher Theodore Brameld, who also attended the Stanford symposium, published widely (including in the first Spindler *Education and Culture: Anthropological Approaches* volume in 1963), urging recognition of the mutual benefits of collaboration between anthropology and education.

Another major turning point in educational anthropology was the formation, in 1968, of the Council on Anthropology and Education (CAE), which became a section of the American Anthropological Association (AAA). The evolution of its newsletter, initiated in 1970, into a scholarly journal contributed credibility to the field. John Singleton, the first editor of the newsletter, explained of the publication: "Originally a device for the encouragement of a network of anthropological interests in education, it has become a scholarly and, sometimes, respectable journal" (Singleton 1984, 11). The editorial focus changed through the years, but John Chilcott, the editor who brought the publication from a newsletter to the journal *Anthropology and Education Quarterly* (*AEQ*) emphasized that, at least from 1973 to 1976, the editorial focus "sought to meet the requirements of professionals in *both* anthropology and education" (Chilcott 1984, 69). That balance has shifted in various directions through the years—sometimes with controversy—as more educators have joined the CAE and more educational anthropologists have graduated from anthropology and education university programs.

The 1960s and 1970s brought a shift in approaches to anthropology and education. Identification of a "culture of poverty" and the subsequent funding for "War on Poverty" programs and research were buoyed by cultural and linguistic deprivation theories, identifying those who were different as being deficient in some way. The educational cure was perceived as a middle-class white education (Ward 1986, v). In 1964, Murray and Rosalie Wax and Robert Dumont Jr. published a critical ethnography revealing the insensitivity to an educational pluralism that could exist. In the reissue of this volume, Murray Wax stated:

> In my observations and analysis, I pondered what might be authentic as education for the Oglala. . . . As I looked at the reservation schools, I saw them as preaching a single mythical and homogenized version of America, whereas the Sioux had every right to ask that their children be socialized into their own unique ethos. This is what gave to this report a cutting edge too often lacking in other ethnographic studies, and—to be honest—it is why the reviewer in the *American Anthropologist* perceived our report as "hysterical." (Wax, Wax, and Dumont 1989, x)

Alan Howard's 1970 ethnography, *Learning to be Rotuman*, was one of the first general ethnographies to have education at its core. Martha Ward's study (1986) in language learning in a rural African American community in 1971 looked outside the schools, focusing on learning in the home and community. Gerry Rosenfeld's 1971 ethnography focused on an inner-city school. These ethnographies represented a significant historical shift in approach and focus as well as an opening of domestic sites for study in educational anthropology.

At times there is a tension surrounding differing perceptions of where the CAE and the *AEQ* should focus, be it domestic or international, in school or community, on research or direct application. Sometimes that tension is between what is considered important from an educator's point of view and what may be considered important from the point of view of an anthropologist. At other times the tension may be between what is considered the role of an anthropologist and the place of applied anthropology and advocacy. The focus of study for educational anthropologists is reflected in the editorial focus of the *AEQ*, which shifts among schooling within institutions and in classrooms, education within and encompassing communities, education in nonmainstream and international cultures, and research studies emphasizing the theoretical and the applied. Recent efforts are inclusive of the multiple interests and the diversity of focus in the CAE and the *AEQ*.

The CAE currently has 12 standing committees that allow for the differences in focus and that define some of the broad arenas of concern to educational anthropologists. Committee members have changed the names of their committees when they have an internal shift of focus, a broadened mission, or when the sociopolitical context changes. For example, Committee 3 used to be called Teaching of Anthropology, and Committee 6 was the Joint CAE/Society for Applied Anthropology Policy Committee on Culture and Bilingual Education. According to *AEQ* (2003), current committees are:

1. Anthropological Studies of Schools and Culture
2. Language, Literacy, and Cognition
3. Anthropology of Post-Secondary Education
4. Ethnographic Approaches to Evaluation in Education
5. Transnational Issues in Education and Change
6. Multicultural and Multilingual Education
7. Blacks in Education
8. Spanish-Speaking Concerns
9. Gender in Schools and Society
10. Culture, Ecology, and Education
11. Study of Cultural and Educational Futures
12. Study of Cultural Transmission/Acquisition

These lay out the terrain. There is applied work in each of these arenas, as well as in territory shared with other anthropological applications, such as education in museum anthropology or medical anthropology. Additionally, some issues tie committees together for various periods of time. Some committees have more consistently encouraged advocacy.

Advocacy in the History of Applied Educational Anthropology

The ebb and flow of applied educational anthropology's popularity may be tied to sources of funding and to fluctuations in the job market, but entrenched attitudes toward the relative respectability of applied anthropology, as well as the subfield's trend toward advocacy, have contributed to its status and the consequent nature of its popularity.

Advocacy is the championing of a cause, perspective, position, or people; it is speaking or writing in favor or support of something. Because advocacy implies making a choice based on some criterion or criteria, it also implies bias. Advocacy in itself may be considered a positive thing, usually guided by a moral imperative and ethical choice, but we attach a negative value to it in our society when we associate it with bias because we associate bias with a lack of objectivity and with the nonscientific. The fact that physicists have for several decades been telling us that true objectivity is an illusion seems to have little deterrent impact on the defining and redefining of what is objective—and therefore scientific. A prime example is the recent determination of what qualifies as "scientific" for funding educational research, which has severe negative implications for ethnography and other qualitative research methods that are often erroneously considered anecdotal and unscientific.

The impetus for advocacy may grow from an immediate need for protection and survival, or it may evolve from working with the complexity and embeddedness of education. For example, we recognize the acquisition of culture, primary in notions of education, as occurring everywhere—including in schools. One cannot assume that critical thinking, empowerment, and individuality are believed healthier than acceptance and conformity. Joe Tobin and colleagues (Tobin, Wu, and Davidson 1989) noted in their study of preschool in three cultures that when confronted with the concept of "giftedness," Japanese teachers defined it as "fitting in" rather than "standing out." The extremes on the continuum of connectedness, for which we educate members of society, might be like the one-minded Borg of *Star Trek* on one end and individualism to the point of anarchy on the other.

Educational anthropologists know that beliefs about what is best for "the good society" and what is envisioned as "the good society" vary between and within cultures. Are social justice, equity, and unity-in-diversity integral to that vision, or are other conceptions supported by embedded assumptions foremost? One cannot live in these times without realizing that notions of good or effective education are disparate. The choices for educational policy usually reflect the assumptions and perceptions of the powerful and do not necessarily benefit all.

Educational anthropologists address the full spectrum of educational issues, and, like all human beings, however much they may believe everyone has a right to her or his own perspective, they perceive some approaches and outcomes as better than others. Selecting one perspective as more valued—indicating the desirable path—is advocacy.

For example, in the case of children whose culture and first language are different from those of the dominant group, or in the case of immigrants in new host cultures with new languages, there is a range of responses perceived as most advantageous for the children. There are educational anthropologists who advocate a "maintenance" bilingual and multicultural education program, others who advocate for "transitional" bilingual education programs and cultural accommodation, and yet others who believe it is in the best interest of the culturally different immigrant families to be required to learn the dominant language so that the children can assimilate and be able to navigate their host culture with ease and little or no stigma.[4]

Each of these advocacy positions is based on the interpretation of specialized knowledge. We have learned from history and experience that just offering the "facts" does not ensure that everyone will come to what may be considered the wise conclusion. Our specialized knowledge is a referent for assumptions about what should be the position of advocacy.

The degree of our advocacy—whether implicit or explicit—might depend on the context, our position in it, and the surrounding political climate, but there is always an agenda, even if it is simply to empower a community to have its own agenda or evaluate a program or policy in light of goals and assumptions. Concha Delgado-Gaitan said:

> The way that I work with community is applied. Through my role as a participant-observer, I have become actively engaged with the communities where I research to act as a "facilitator." By doing so I am able to act as an advocate for the families, using research data to inform and develop agency for the people as they shape policies and practices in the schools and the community at large to improve their living conditions. (2002)

Donna Deyhle noted, "Applied anthropologists, by the very nature of their work, attempt to put into action their research findings to assist the informants and the communities in which they work" (1998, 44).

Most teachers believe they are advocates for children. Most educational anthropologists, some of whom also are teachers, believe their specialized knowledge makes them potentially more effective advocates for children—and for amelioration of the issues having an impact on their success within their micro- and macro-sociocultural contexts. Advocacy is virtually embedded in anthropology and education.

The tradition of advocacy in work with education of culturally diverse and indigenous groups is quite strong. Contemporary educational anthropologists build on the foundation of earlier applied anthropologists. Theresa McCarty, advocate for Navajo indigenous education, community empowerment, voice, and identity on the path to social justice, explained:

> I long ago stepped "over the line" between researcher, writer, and friend, a line that is, I believe, artificial and obstructive to long-term ethnographic and applied research and that, at any rate, would have been impossible to sustain with this small, kin-centered community. (2002, 3)

McCarty's comment is more than a statement of method; it is a declaration of connectedness that holds within it embedded advocacy. Donna Deyhle also assumed an advocate's role through her research. In 1998 she explained the path of multiple roles in her years of research with Navajos in a Mormon community school district.

> After I had been in the field for 2 years, listening, observing, and learning, I moved into an informed advocacy role. At first my efforts started with writing a dropout prevention grant and providing in-service training for teachers and parents. Four years later, my role has moved to the position of expert witness for the Office for Civil Rights, the Justice Department, and a Navajo civil case. (44)

However much advocacy is an integral part of applied anthropology, historically it has held a tenuous, if not subordinate, role in general anthropology. Entrenched attitudes toward the relative respectability of applied anthropology and the commitment to advocacy contributed to its variable status and consequent popularity. Spindler (1984) explained that there was a distancing from offering advice and a striving toward objectivity. He suggested that "Kroeber would try to avoid personal biases and moral judgments but would agree that an analysis of the effectiveness of an educational program in light of its declared goals and in comparison to alternative procedures would be acceptable anthropological behavior" (1984, 4). Advocacy, however, was discouraged because it was considered to be outside the parameters of proper anthropological behavior. Spindler summed up the Stanford Conference participants' strong feelings, indicating that "anthropologists could study and report on educative process and systems, but they should refrain from advocating specific policy decisions, since these are essentially political and administrative domains" (1984, 4).

Historically, however, the CAE has taken a stand on controversial issues and advocated for equity, diversity, and amelioration of problems threatening education. Inspired variously by the CAE Committee on Spanish-Speaking Concerns and collaboration between the CAE and the Society for Applied Anthropology (SfAA) Policy Committee on Culture and Bilingual Education, the CAE passed resolutions in 1974, 1978, and 1981, advocating for equity in education and the rights of culturally diverse students in education. Of the resolutions, Marietta Saravia-Shore and Steven Arvizu indicated:

> They are succinct summaries of anthropologists' suggestions to educators concerning the significance of becoming aware of and taking into account their own cultural expectations, perspective, and interaction patterns and those of their students. The resolutions also state clearly . . . concern for respecting and attending to cultural and linguistic differences in educating students of diverse ethnolinguistic backgrounds and

ensuring that members of the community participate in decision making concerning the education of their children. (1992, xvii)

These issues continue to be in the forefront of educational policy debates.

The 1980s brought more explicit pleas for direct application of anthropological research to educational practice and policy. Courtney Cazden
recalled only "two clear examples . . . where ethnographers . . . not only
described problems but . . . stayed to collaborate with teachers in designs for
change" (1983, 35). Jean J. Schensul shared her belief that "the cutting edge
in our field lies in the expansion of educational anthropology from the university into local communities, school systems, and other learning settings"
(1985, 64). Yet she noted that

> [i]n educational anthropology, the tradition of research and demon-
> stration, of testing theory through practice, is limited. Most accounts
> of application in education presented by anthropologists focus on
> evaluation, the uses of ethnographic research methods in the class-
> room, or ways of teaching teachers to use ethnography to understand
> their students. (66)

Schensul suggested that the questions educational anthropologists need to
address, such as those involving equity, race, and location of power, were considered outside the boundaries of what was acceptable because they required
intervention or advocacy, rendering them controversial and biased.

Current official attitude toward advocacy, reflected in American Anthropological Association policy, provides more professional comfort for those
educational anthropologists who have, especially since the 1970s, urged
advocacy in shaping policy and programs to reflect anthropological insight
and to foster equity and social justice. The rhetoric has changed, and there
certainly are many more anthropologists advocating change, but there still
exists ambivalence toward application and advocacy. Providing a historical
perspective, Donna Deyhle, herself committed to advocacy, warned, "Advocacy work . . . can have negative repercussions on both the work of the
anthropologist and on the local participants" (1998, 44). Issues surrounding
advocacy are themselves complex. Reflecting on advocacy in her work with
the Navajo Nation and Mormon school community, Deyhle posed:

> From the advocacy position of critical theory, critique and transforma-
> tion are goals of research. But what voice does one listen to in complex
> communities? What does *transformation* mean when one group's core
> religious beliefs require the transformation of the other group against
> its will? Ethically, what does taking sides, or advocacy, mean in com-

plex communities? What happens when research results are used by the powerful to serve their own means, rather than to empower the powerless, as the researcher intended? (1998, 46)

Advocacy, precarious in the field, also remains precarious in the academy. Rosemary Henze (2003) warned that "One has to be willing to risk academic marginalization because one is doing something very *applied,* and this is still not well accepted or valued in the higher education industry."

Advocacy has moved to a larger arena within the AAA. Contemporary advocacy against eugenics issues focuses on recognition of race as a socially constructed concept. Educational anthropologist Yolanda Moses brought this issue to the fore during her 1995 to 1997 tenure as AAA president-elect and president. Education of the general public and of teachers and students through videos to be used in schools and on television grew from initiatives throughout the AAA.

The public policy segment on the AAA's Web site has a section specifically addressing *Culture and Diversity in Education.* This site delineates such areas of concern as the improvement of schooling, policies surrounding standardized testing (and its uses and meaning), the *culture* of schools, equity, the relationship of violence in media to violence in the schools, demographic shifts and the impact of immigrant influx on education, policies surrounding bilingual and multicultural education, affirmative action, and learning technology in cultural context. The Web site lists three education-related goals of the Committee on Public Policy:

1. To identify anthropologists who are studying culture and diversity in education;
2. To determine the state of knowledge and to identify gaps in knowledge that need to be filled; and
3. To assist policymakers and those engaged in related research in understanding the social and cultural factors affecting education policies. (AAA Committee on Public Policy 2004)

It is the third of these that has potential for direct application. The policy committee is in the process of forging an administrative structure among the AAA, the National Association for the Practice of Anthropology (NAPA), and the SfAA in establishing a Center for Public Policy, the very core of which will be advocacy and direct impact on specific issues, including educational issues (Thu 2004).

The CAE continues to be a strong voice for the field. It sponsors a large block of sessions at annual AAA meetings, and it raises issues of concern for discussion and resolutions on its Listserv and other forums. In 2004 the CAE took a firm stand to support locked out workers at the proposed AAA

San Francisco meeting by holding its own meeting at another San Francisco hotel and inviting other AAA sections to join it.

Because the majority of educational anthropologists work in educational contexts, they maintain their viability by linking with special interest groups (SIGs) in the American Educational Research Association. Members of the Council on Anthropology and Education are prominent members of the Anthropology Education Commission, which was established in 1999 by the American Anthropological Association. The charge of the commission is to integrate anthropology–issues, concepts, and methods–into all levels of education, pre-kindergarten through adult education. The thought is that public understanding of anthropology will increase, and anthropology will help improve education (AAA 2004). Thus, advocacy in educational anthropology has moved beyond its traditional boundaries and promises to build momentum toward making a difference in education.

For those of us who are proponents of advocacy, it is good news that explicit advocacy is developing in educational anthropology–though in some venues political awareness shapes the nature of that advocacy. After navigating advocacy with varying degrees of efficacy, educational anthropologists seek ways to participate in shaping public policy and public debate that invite connection rather than instigate–however inadvertently–reaction. This may occur in the arena of systemic school reform or diverse student success in an era of widespread standards-based, culture-bound, test-driven pseudoreform that appears to reinforce inequity rather than ameliorate it.

But, advocacy-inspired change is occurring in pockets. Hugh Mehan has shifted to primarily applied work such as the CREATE (Center for Research on Educational Equity, Assessment and Teaching Excellence) program in San Diego. Rosemary Henze's Leading for Diversity program is gaining momentum in the schools. Other pockets of change exist due to passionate advocacy by educational anthropologists.

All of the areas discussed in the remainder of this chapter involve such transformation of education in schools and communities. All of the work looks toward understanding cultural and interactional dynamics and creating a shift toward equity, empowerment, and social justice. Some of the areas overlap, but for the purpose of discussion, they are identified as discrete entities.

Educational Change

Systemic educational reform and restructuring is an issue that, since the late 1970s, has gained increasing attention among educational anthropologists. Initially, the term restructuring, as applied in education, meant substantial change in how we conceive of and do education; it encompassed reinvention and deep structural change. However, the term has been appropriated, and its meaning has become variable, and it is at times synonymous with downsizing. The nature of the issues also has changed through the years, and the issues vary depending on whether the focus is international or domestic. On the international front, Susan Jungck's extensive unpublished work in fostering and facilitating change and restructuring of education in Thailand is disseminated within Thai educational systems and continually has a direct impact on Thai educational policy. Jungck often shares her work with other educational anthropologists at professional meetings. Some educational anthropologists working internationally may address educational changes imported from Western education. Anthropologists take a contextualized look at the impact of imported child-centered philosophy and pedagogy and engaged learning on various differently structured cultures; these constructs are thought to be inherently superior and ideal by many Western educators. Other educational anthropologists work in various capacities for government agencies, the United Nations, or nongovernmental organizations (NGOs).

For American education, the 1970s seemed to provide a window of opportunity to address significant changes in educational organizational structure, with profound shifts in approaches to leadership, accompanied by empowerment of teachers, students, and parents. My own work in this area grew out of frustration from encountering rigid barriers in my efforts to create emergent, interdisciplinary, and multicultural curricula in a culturally diverse Southwestern community. Using several small grants from the Cultural Awareness Center of the University of New Mexico, I developed and implemented innovative elementary education programs addressing cultural diversity in New Mexico. For the Education Division of the Museum of New Mexico, I developed a videotape about using traveling museum kits to integrate culture into an interactive, interdisciplinary curriculum. Eventually, my doctoral dissertation addressed sociocultural and philosophical barriers to educational change. I focused on the entrenchment of worldview in educational structures (Greenman 1994). As a consultant to the superintendent of the district where I had taught, I analyzed plans for restructuring and wrote the preliminary report for the school district's first yearly School Improvement Plan efforts.

Educational anthropologists involved in educational change are employed in a wide range of venues such as school districts, universities, privately funded centers for change, and think tanks. G. Alfred Hess, Jr. was, for many years, executive director of the Chicago Panel on Public School Policy and Finance, where he had direct input to school policy. The Chicago Panel was made up of 20 nonprofit agencies comprising a multiethnic, multiracial coalition with a focus on Chicago public education improvement (Hess 1991, xvii). Even before he was hired by the Chicago Panel, Hess was directly involved in policy development and implementation in the Chicago Public Schools (CPS). He engaged in planning for Mayor Harold Washington's Educational Summit in the fall of 1986. Hess was instrumental in crafting legislation that created the Chicago School Reform Act in 1988. According to Hess, "The act fundamentally changed the structure of public education by creating Local School Councils consisting of two teachers, six parents, two community representatives, the principal, and, in high schools, a nonvoting student" (Hess 1991, 1). One of the central tenets of the restructured CPS governance was participatory decisionmaking and decentralized authority, intended to empower the community. Unfortunately, the full promise of the Chicago school restructuring for improvement has not yet come to fruition. Currently, Pauline Lipman, who has written extensively about inequity in school restructuring—and, more specifically, Chicago school reform (2002, 1998)—is advocating against the most recent privatization initiative in Chicago.

For urban educational change, concerns about inequity and location of power in decisionmaking fuel educational anthropologists' focus. In an e-mail communication, Patrick McQuillan elucidated how this focus might translate to the work of an educational anthropologist working in academe.

[A]s long as we remain ignorant of the enormity and complexity of the challenges that confront urban schools, we will never create a truly equitable educational system.

With this overarching concern in mind, I consider . . . interrelated areas [e.g., the "achievement gap," low income, native language, race/ ethnicity] to be of tremendous importance. . . . [T]oo often we treat schools as though "all students are created equal" and distribute resources accordingly.

Research is therefore needed in two areas, at least. First, to assess which programs and policies work effectively in situations of concentrated poverty. And second, to provide data on the impact these populations have on schools. This information could then be used in a court of law to argue that such schools, because they face additional challenges, should receive disproportionate funding. (This has already occurred in some states.) As funding systems are currently structured, relying so extensively on property taxes, those schools with the least need tend to have the most resources.

A final focus for me is that of involving students in school governance and in shaping their education. In most instances, educational opportunity is defined for students, not by them. . . . When I began research with CES [Coalition of Essential Schools] . . . my colleague and I took a decidedly theoretical, rather than applied, stance toward our work, in part because that is what CES wanted. . . . We did not offer any specific recommendations. We mainly tried to create a rich description of what was happening in member schools. Nonetheless, our descriptions were, to varying degrees, used by CES schools and staff members. . . . Thus, our research had an impact, albeit indirect.

I am about to embark on a study of a Boston public high school. This time, I intend to have a more direct impact on the school, although I consider it presumptuous to state this goal. Schools are not easy places to change, especially for someone with no formal authority working from outside the school system. However, at this point in my career I think I know enough about research, schools, and educational reform to be explicitly applied. . . . (2002)

Educational anthropologists conduct research to understand how change in educational institutions can occur, and they are persistent in seeking ways to have an impact on improving education. Lisa Rosen's current work at the University of Chicago's Center for School Improvement examines how anthropological research can contribute to innovative institutions that support urban school improvement. She works with a recursive model to have an ongoing impact on changes in professional roles, norms, and practices, that is, to examine how individual and organizational learning, as well as shifts in professional culture, occur (2002).

Educational change, reform, and restructuring may focus on institutional and structural changes but, as was evident in the above examples, include concerns about the locus of power in conceptualizing and implementing those changes. Empowerment of teachers, students, parents, and invested community members is hotly debated. These are areas that lend themselves to advocacy for educational anthropologists.

Cultural Acquisition, Social Capital, and Empowerment of Culturally Diverse Parents

Cultural acquisition is a fundamental anthropological construct that quite naturally falls into the domain of anthropology and education. Anthropological study of cultural acquisition has been approached from many perspectives, including linguistic (Hymes 1964; Ward 1986) and the perspective of mothers' relationships with their children in the sociocultural context (Babcock 1991; Mead 1960; Bateson 1994). Mary Anne Pitman, Rivka A. Eisikovits, and Marion Lundy Dobbert (1989) described cultural acquisition as a "holistic approach to human learning" with a focus on the processes of learning in cultural context. As they so succinctly explained, cultural acquisition is a concept much broader than schooling, than informal teaching and learning, than childraising, or even than cultural transmission. Certainly in many societies parents and other adults do a considerable amount of directing, teaching, and shaping, all of which is designed to transform children into desirable adults. But for humans, as for other primates, instructive and formative activity constitutes a very minute part of the learning process. Instead, the major forces "shaping" children and young people in the process of culture acquisition are the same as those that shape or direct all learners, namely, the structures and processes of the entire sociocultural life going on around them. In addition, the process of culture acquisition by which children and young people learn to be fully functioning adults is a holistic one. One does not become a mature adult by sequentially learning the separate elements of adult life and then putting them together to form a whole, nor does one survive as a competent old person through that process. Rather, the junior members of a society or a social group learn whole patterns within the context of everyday life and then in personal action they individualize and adapt these patterns by varying some of the elements or creating new ones. (3)

Harry Wolcott said that he believes cultural acquisition to be *the* central construct in educational anthropology.

The [primary] aspect of my work, encompassing the other [aspects] as well, is cultural acquisition, including cultural transmission but focusing more on the learner than on the transmitter. I have been writing about this theme in articles over the years and have now completed a book that draws some of this work together in a case study that begins with an ethnographic autobiography of an out-of-school youth. The book, *Sneaky Kid and Its Aftermath*, incorporates the title of an article originally published in 1983 and brings the story up to the present, with its subtitle, *Ethics and Intimacy in Fieldwork*.

Cultural acquisition is the banner that I have proposed as the core topic for our efforts in anthropology and education: a focus on how individuals acquire and act out their unique versions of culture. The topic does not preclude all the other things that go on in anthropology and education, including studies of the social organization of schools or the enactment of formal educator roles. But it is a far broader charter: a focus on what and how as individuals we learn from the cultural influences surrounding us. It takes a broader look, to study not only what educators are doing, and what children are learning in schools, but inquiring into what [each] of us learns in our out-of-school lives as well. It is not school-focused; it is person-focused. It is not focused on school-age students or professionally trained teachers but on all human beings, anywhere, and how they have come to act, and more or less want to act, as their fellow participants want and expect them to act. This is not "applied" work per se; rather, it is a broad issue that guides the particular questions we pursue and gives the anthropological perspective we want to bring.

> Educational researchers do a thorough job of assessing what is learned in school—almost too thorough a job from an anthropological point of view, since they can and do ignore what else is learned, or what is not learned, or what is learned that negates the formal learning taking place. But far more important is to place the learner in a broader context so that school itself—even when achieving its stated purposes—is never more than part of the entire picture. That charter provides an endless assignment. Educational anthropologists need to confine their purposes to the questions being asked and the assistance they can offer, but they must stay tuned to their orientation of what *is* while others concern themselves with what might be. Thus even the most applied of educational projects will find its anthropologist asking about, or at least wondering aloud, how the system works now, what may be gained or lost in the proposed change, and whether what people are learning—everyone involved, not just the so-called target group—will be different, and "better." (2002a)

Mary Catherine Bateson poetically described the learning process as an improvisational dance, warning that we cannot trip over ambiguity or uncertainty.

> Improvisation and new learning are not private processes; they are shared with others at every age. The multiple layers of attention involved cannot safely be brushed aside or subordinated to the completion of tasks. We are called to join in a dance whose steps must be learned along the way, so it is important to attend and respond. Even in our uncertainty, we are responsible for our steps. (1994, 9–10)

Bateson provided examples of cultural acquisition and learning in cultural context where the dance takes place.

To acquire an operational knowledge of a culture is to acquire cultural or social capital within that culture. That social capital gives one the power to navigate the culture in question. Children may gain cultural and social capital implicitly as part of their enculturation process. Adults, however, must take a more explicit approach to gain cultural capital. They may acquire it through consciously learning about another culture and using that knowledge to function well in their secondary culture while maintaining their

primary culture (accommodation), or through adopting the secondary culture as primary and infusing it into their lives (acculturation). They may gain
social capital by consciously learning how to attain resources and how social
organizations, such as bureaucracy, operate. Consciously gaining cultural or
social capital is a form of empowerment.

Empowerment of immigrant, poor, and culturally diverse parents and
communities has been a focus of educational anthropologists since the late
1960s and early 1970s, accompanying the focus on culturally relevant curricula and education. Steven Arvizu's early work with the Cross Cultural
Resources Center at California State University in Sacramento focused on
parent participation and home-school linkages with an eye toward empowering parents (Arvizu 1992). His demystifying the concept of culture for parents helped provide them with an understanding of themselves in
multicultural contexts, which led to gaining the cultural and social capital
needed to help their children navigate their world.

When educational anthropologists see the difference this empowerment
makes in the lives of people who had been disenfranchised, they may
develop a sense of satisfaction from their work and advocate further for
facilitating the acquisition of social capital. Kathryn M. Borman has done
extensive work on projects addressing educational reform on a national
scale, such as the National Science Foundation's Urban Systemic Initiative, a
reform that directed resources to schools in the highest poverty urban districts in the United States. However, in terms of direct impact on educational change, the one project that stands out for her is one that related the
parental gain of social capital to the education of their children.

> I believe that the effort with the largest impact was the work I carried
> out with colleagues at the Urban Appalachian Council in Cincinnati.
> At the UAC during the 10 years I worked with the dedicated staff
> members of that organization (many of whom were of Appalachian
> origin), we were able to provide training for parents of children who
> were students in the public schools of the city. The training was aimed
> at providing parents the tools they needed to get the services and assis-
> tance they needed for their children. (2004)

Some educational anthropologists work with parents of very young children, in both community settings and preschool environments. Cultural
acquisition is a focus in this work, and, when there are dual cultures, multicultural acquisition often becomes an issue. Progress of children in complex
cultural environments is followed during formal schooling years. Parents of
those children tend to lack the social capital needed to effectively advocate
for their children. Lotty Eldering, working with immigrant families in the

Netherlands, tried to influence immigration policy with an eye toward acquisition of social capital for immigrant mothers. She described her career-long efforts to this end:

> In my view family education should be a substantial part of research being done by anthropologists focusing on formal school education. In my work I have studied amongst others preschool intervention programs and risk factors for children growing up in *female-headed* immigrant families (Moroccan and Hindustani families in the Netherlands). Family education studies are essential for a good understanding of the impact of schools and other formal educational settings on school success.
>
> As to the application of research outcomes, that is a complicated matter. . . . Sometimes research outcomes are too new to be applied (politicians always are far behind social reality). One of the conclusions of my PhD study for instance was that the Moroccan families would permanently stay in the Netherlands and I recommended [that it be policy for] them to learn Dutch. Only in 1998, 20 years after the publication of my book on Moroccan families, are new immigrants compelled to learn Dutch. Most of the earlier generations of immigrants speak no or very little Dutch, particularly mothers, who are the main educators of the children. These examples show, in my view, that processes within the family, in the broadest sense, have great impact on school achievement and social mobility of immigrant children. (2002)

Policy and power surrounding the education of preschool children was a focus of Sally Lubeck's work. She studied, internationally, the social processes through which women socialize young children to particular ways of life, how governments support the care and education of young children, and the implications for policy support of institutional structures. Lubeck posed the following questions that evolved from her research and drove subsequent work:

1. How can public policy be formulated to address the strengths and challenges that exist within local communities?
2. How do power, social relations, language, and material practices effectively serve to "construct" particular kinds of services and organizations within communities and nation states?
3. How does discourse function to constrain what is seen as necessary or desirable within a particular policy context?
4. What are the possibilities for creating self-conscious, democratic communities willing and able to dialogue across difference? (2002)

Three interrelated areas formed the core of Lubeck's work: (1) Cross-national policy research regarding early childhood education and care (ECEC), (2) ECEC policy research within the United States, and (3) "cultural politics," dealing with issues of diversity, power, and voice in political decisionmaking. She explained the nature of some of her research and work:

> In my early work I used data from the International Labour Office (ILO) to compare parental leave and child care policies and provisions cross-nationally (e.g., Lubeck, 1989). Later, I did fieldwork in the former German Democratic Republic (GDR) when, prior to unification, the GDR had the most extensive publicly supported child care system in the world. I was responsible for interviewing American teachers for the TIMSS Case Study Project (which compared the American educational system with those of Germany and Japan). More recently, I served as a member of the review team and Rapporteur for the Country Note on the United Kingdom, in conjunction with the OECD *Thematic Review of Early Childhood Education and Care Policies* in 12 countries. (2002)

The levels of influence here are from the details of everyday practice to the broad scope of policy. All of the examples support equitable education by recognizing the part that parents play in the education of their children.

Equity, Empowerment, and Social Justice in School Systems and Communities

Educational anthropologists address many dimensions of equity, as well as success and failure in education (Erickson 1987; Mehan, Hubbard, and Villanueva 1994; Trueba 1988; Voght, Jordan, and Tharp 1987). John Ogbu's (1982, 1990; Gibson and Ogbu 1991) controversial theories about differential achievement of *immigrant* and *involuntary* minorities and cultural discontinuity have generated spirited and continuous debate. His theories have been used in the development of educational policy. Margaret Eisenhart's extensive work with gender equity in education and in the scientific community identified the illusion of gender neutrality in policies. The concept of gender neutrality addresses assumptions that a policy is considered objective and gender neutral if it is framed in the male voice. When asked to reflect on her current work, she said:

> I think that the challenges to traditional ways of conceptualizing culture that are posed by phenomena such as youth culture, popular culture,

transnational movements, globalization, etc. and their resolutions bear directly on how we use "culture" in schools and other educational settings.

The core of my work right now is to design, implement, and study an after-school program in science and technology for low-income African American and Latino middle-school girls. These girls live in an inner city environment that includes the phenomena referred to above. They do poorly in poor schools, and they have little or no interest in science and technology as presented in school. What I am trying to do is: (1) learn about the "culture" of these girls; (2) learn what science and technology experts consider good curriculum for girls; (3) join 1 and 2 in an attempt to create a sci/tech curriculum that motivates the girls and develops their skills; (4) study the girls' responses to the curriculum, modify it, and re-study it. I see this as similar to a "design experiment" or "design study" as described by Ann Brown and others.

In addition to my own use of my research findings to improve the after-school program, the findings are also being used to redesign programs for high school girls in engineering, precollegiate preparation programs for high school students and their parents, and academic support groups for minority students. (2002)

Social justice, equity, and diversity-embedded change also are goals of advocates, such as Rosemary Henze, who focus on change within the school system. Like so many educational anthropologists, Henze works with pre-service and in-service teachers as well as educational administrators in efforts to create change and embed diversity. She seeks ways to have greater impact on teachers, students, and school systems. Henze discussed some of her problem-solving approach and initiatives.

I'm very interested in seeing if I can have an impact on practice by "translating" some key concepts of educational anthropology into terms that teachers can use. One concept I am trying to translate, currently, is the notion of the social construction of race. I find it amazing that with so much written about this in the past century, it still has not made its way into the public consciousness.

The other thing that is "core" to what I'm doing now is what we call the "Leading for Diversity Project." Together with colleagues, I have been working on researching, describing, and disseminating what it is school leaders can do to improve ethnic relations in schools. It's a workbook format, for pre-service or in-service school leaders, so very "practical" in an effort to [have an impact on teachers, students, and school systems]. We're also working on a video to accompany . . . the book. . . .

I'm trying to enfold what I know of important educational anthropology concepts and practices in what I teach my students. (2003)

The role of the family and community in effecting educational change, especially for immigrant populations, is central to the work of many educational anthropologists. In her long-term research and advocacy relationship with a California Latino community, Concha Delgado-Gaitan learned new dimensions of community self-determination. Reflection on her work began with the question, "How can research in anthropology and education be used to inform local community change?"

> [Anthropologists] know so much about the "problems" that oppress communities where we work and we need to look at how all of this research can directly impact the people who need it most. Through long-term ethnographic methodology in poor and immigrant communities, my research has shown that meaningful change and empowerment is possible from the grassroots level through family and community literacy. It gives a model for other communities' self-empowerment.
>
> In addition to academics who work in my home field of anthropology and education, I am contacted on a regular basis by [practitioners and scholars] . . . that use my work for its methodological paradigm as well as the theoretical premises that culturally acknowledge the people's potential for changing the power relations of the conditions in which they live involving language learning, literacy practices, accessing family resources, and building sociopolitical organization. (2002)

Educational change in communities includes education in informal settings that engage and empower urban youths to be agents of change through informed social action. Jean J. Schensul reflected on the variety of ways she applies educational anthropology to urban education and social justice initiatives. Schensul champions education as an open construct; taking place in the community and envelopes other-than-traditional school curricula. Her reflection summarizes her career trajectory as an educational anthropologist and the range of her work.

Career Trajectory of Jean J. Schensul

I have viewed myself as an educational anthropologist from the moment that I understood, under the mentorship of a critical sociologist, that I had the power, as a teacher/instructor, to reverse power relationships in the classroom. I learned as a college anthropology instructor that I could put aside didactic instruction and engage students in a dialogic exploration of critical questions relating to race, ethnicity, culture, difference, language, intelligence, interpretations of history, power and control simply by raising questions and exposing them to sources of information and the opportunity to engage in facilitated discussion. For me this was a dual revelation. First, I saw that I could bring about educational change–that I could, as an anthropologist, function as an interventionist. Second, I saw that I could study these issues and that I was interested in testing interventions that reversed the established power structure and studying factors that prevented such reversals in settings where the students were not heard, in contrast to settings in which they believed, because of wealth and social status and the privilege of race, that they had the right to be heard.

My burning questions in educational anthropology have been directed toward understanding the circumstances that stimulate, support, and encourage urban American children and youth to pursue knowledge and social action, to see that they have the right to know and to promote their civic engagement as active and critically involved citizens. Further, I do not see that educational anthropology's purview is in the classroom only. For me, education occurs in multiple formal and informal settings. For this reason, I have a passionate commitment to creating the informal settings that support both youth and adults in a process of engaged learning, critical analysis, and social action. Questions that are central to my work have to do with how such settings vary across provinces, states, countries and class; how, for example, critical inquiry can occur in national settings where active conflict and confrontation are not acceptable; how gender, ethnicity, race, and power restrict, enhance, empower, and restructure learning processes.

I believe that the concept of education is interdisciplinary and intersectoral–addressing art, intelligence, social and emotional learning, sexuality and AIDS, substance use and abuse, and a vast range of other social phenomena. Educational anthropology should not limit itself to the subject matter of classrooms. A burning question has to do with why the field has restricted itself to an analysis of school-based phenomena, when learning qua education takes place in multiple settings in multiple ways. I have been proud of my discipline's perspective on formal education and, at the same time, frustrated with the limitations the discipline has placed on the way we conceptualize, address, intervene in, and study/evaluate educational processes.

The core of my work in educational anthropology has been theorizing about developing, describing, and evaluating alternative learning environments for adults and youth. My first piece of research addressed individual, institutional, and structural changes in the Mexican education system as a response to industrialization. This was not applied research, but the research was published in Mexico in Spanish and may have had some effect on the country's perception of the limited role of education in promoting upward mobility and the ways in which worksites used educational degrees to promote or restrict entry to work and occupational mobility.

A second thrust of my work has been the creation of alternative community-based work environments, in which applied research for social action has played a major role. The two main settings where I have used this approach have been the Hispanic Health Council (1978–1987) and the Institute for Community Research (1987–present). [The Institute consists of] a multiethnic group of 65 full-time, 12 part-time, and 41 youth researchers. I was a co-founder of the first organization and the founder of the second. Each of these environments has involved dedicated applied research. Each has integrated university-trained researchers with a political commitment to community change, with community educators and activists who see the opportunity to use research as a tool for change. My role has been to develop and implement projects that permit these two radically different sectors, with a common goal, to come together, to learn from one another, and to integrate their experience and knowledge in the context of a formal research project directed toward social change. The organizational environments I favor and promote are communal learning environments. Principles include good facilitation that supports equally valued input from all participants, sharing popular and academic knowledge, providing good social and cultural supports, and directing work toward an accomplishable goal with community importance.

Probably the most significant focus of my formal applied educational anthropology work has been the development of a popular action research training model that the Institute for Community Research (and prior organizations) have used with low income community residents—men, women, older adults, adolescents, pre-adolescents, gay and lesbian youth of color, and other groups. This model is driven by a constellation of integrated theories of identity, multiple intelligences, personal and social empowerment, social learning and social construction, critical analysis, gender and power, and more recently queer theory. It begins with the development of close working and personal relationships between adult facilitators and participants. These relationships provide the foundation for broadening interactions and trust among members of the group or learning community. The group then engages in the traditional steps of participatory action research—identifying an issue, developing a conceptual and action model, learning about and utilizing multiple interactive approaches to data collection, using the relationships derived through data collection to build a power base, jointly analyzing and presenting data, and using data as a means to rally and organize support for desired action. This process seems simple, but it is indeed very complicated. It requires dedicated, experienced, and politicized research staff, a supportive learning environment, appropriate creative and flexible research technology, rules and regulations that are suitable for different target populations (by age, ethnicity, sexual preference, or other factors), proper analytic procedures and technology, and a variety of means of disseminating and utilizing research results over time. We have conducted at least twelve demonstration programs that use this fundamental model, most of which have been funded with public sector money and some private funds . . . ; we are currently evaluating this model for risk prevention with funding for a three-year Center for Substance Abuse.

Another approach to the development of alternative educational environments involves the introduction of cooperative learning and the social construction of problem solving knowledge to middle school children. This project, funded for almost five years by the National Institute on Drug Abuse, is really intended to change the instructional relationship between students and teachers, between teachers and principals, and between schools and the Social Development Department of an urban school district. The use of cooperative learning and social constructivist techniques engages students in building on their own realities and knowledge base, learning from other students, and obtaining new information from guided informational sources. Students construct and co-construct new narratives of situations related to addressing social problems, drug use, and sexual risk—situations more closely culturally and socially related to their own realities. As they co-construct alternative pathways to risk avoidance and harm reduction, which they discuss and agree on, they create safer options for themselves when they confront these social risks. The most important underlying message of the curriculum, however, is not that there is a right or wrong way of approaching these social problems. It is that youth, working together and utilizing their knowledge base and social and informational resources, can emerge with a variety of social options that work for them, while reducing their exposure to drug, social, and sexual harm. Our team of anthropologists and psychologists . . . is delighted that this approach is now being integrated into our partnership school district, with the intention of utilizing the model instructional program in years to come. We are especially delighted, since the objective of the curriculum is inherently subversive—it is explicitly designed to enhance the power of the teacher AND the student together, in generating new solutions to both new and ongoing social and educational problems. (2002)

Education for the Culturally Diverse and Multicultural Education

Educational anthropologists perhaps are best known for their work with culturally diverse and indigenous groups. The tradition of advocacy in this arena is quite strong. Cathie Jordan's (1985) applied work with the Kamehameha Project is a classic example of how ethnographic information demonstrating cultural discontinuity was directly applied to create culturally relevant educational structure and pedagogy. Jerry Lipka's (1991) work with the Yup'ik also had direct impact on creating indigenous programs, curricula, and pedagogy. Theresa McCarty (2002) worked with the Dine/Navajo, advocating for indigenous education, particularly at Rough Rock. She supported community members' redefinition of identity, finding their voice, and empowerment to attain social justice. Donna Deyhle, who has been working with Dine/Navajo in a Mormon community school district for many years, indicated that there is evidence of recent profound change.

> One issue that has changed, and is very exciting, is that the district seems to be coming full circle—moving from a racially based decision— no Navajo language or culture—to using Navajo language and culture in the school curriculum to enhance student success. Rather than ignoring the ethnographic research . . . they are trying to "come on board." Most amazing is that they have asked me to come back into the district and do research for the next three years looking at what they are calling "pockets of excellence"—successful teachers working with Navajo youth. I think it is exciting! It also speaks to the some-times roller coaster ride I've had with the district and Navajo communities over the past twenty years. First [I] started as the ethnographer, then "Indian lover," lawsuit enemy, etc., etc., and now, back to ethnographer. What a wild path. And I am flattered that the district trusts me, even though I was super critical of them. So a team [of educational anthropologists and graduate students] will be working in and out of there. (2002)

Although culturally relevant education, education for cultural understanding and multicultural, cross-cultural, and intercultural education have longevity among educational anthropologists, the concept of multicultural education, since its emergence in the late 1960s, has also been an area of concern. There are frequent complaints that the concept has been appropriated, trivialized, packaged, or otherwise applied in ways contrary to intent (Greenman and Greenbaum 1996). Margaret Gibson developed the first typology of multicultural education in 1976. Shane Martin and Magaly

Lavadenz (1998) developed one of the most recent typological models of educational response to diversity. Christine Sleeter and Carl Grant's typology presented in their book, *Making Choices for Multicultural Education* (2003), now in its fourth edition, is one of the most widely used. Though they tried to present different approaches to multicultural education and the implications of each in an objective, nonhierarchical way, Sleeter and Grant include a chapter in which they articulated strong advocacy for the transformational/ social reconstructionist types of multicultural education.

These typologies and others clearly reveal the philosophical assumptions implicit in each approach. Work with preservice teachers and educators in the schools reveals a lack of openness to assumptions different from those held personally, which results in resistance to diversity (Greenman and Kimmel 1995). Educational anthropologists consistently seek new ways to create bridges to understanding and acceptance of difference. Linda Levine (2002) stated

> I'm still concerned with the need to move beyond essentialist notions of culture while acknowledging the persistent power and politics and impact of difference in this society. . . . I've been trying to help preservice and practicing teachers move beyond popular assumptions and their own sedimented histories by creating (and guiding) opportunities for the [discussions] across differences that are so crucial today.

Mary Hauser (2002) assessed the core of her educator work as a need "to help students to understand the influence of culture (the culture of the students, the teacher, and the larger American culture) on what happens in schools."

Heewon Chang, who shares some of the same concerns, advocates vigorously for multicultural education. She struggles with ways to be most effective in her work with educators. Chang stated that the following questions are ever present:

1. How can I safeguard (at the same time, critically examine) the anthropologically sound understanding of culture in multicultural educational research and writing?
2. How can I keep educators from essentializing culture (ascribing a set of characteristics to a certain cultural group and reducing all distinctive characteristics as cultural differences) and help them develop functional cultural sensitivity toward their students of diverse cultural backgrounds?
3. How can we bring more global perspectives (and comparison) to the understanding of educational issues in the United States? (2002)

Chang's focus on multicultural education is intertwined with her work in educational anthropology. In her advocacy work, she returns to these questions to disengage trivialized notions of culture and multicultural education. One solution she initiated is a journal dedicated to issues surrounding multicultural education. She stated: "To bring more anthropological and global approaches to multicultural education I have been editing and publishing the Electronic Magazine of Multicultural Education for the last 4 years, which reaches scholars and practitioners of multicultural education in 40 different countries" (2002). The journal can be found at http://www.eastern.edu/publications/emme.

Educational anthropologists working with cultural diversity issues can have an impact on education by working outside of the schools. For example, I work with the Cultural Connections Program of the Center for Cultural Understanding and Change at the Chicago Field Museum. For the 2003–2004 program year, there were 23 core partners that are ethnic museums or cultural centers. The program uses anthropological concepts as its core, in efforts to help teachers, parents, and community members understand culture and diversity and the rich traditions in Chicago neighborhoods. The program also intends to have direct impact on curriculum design and culturally relevant teaching through the teacher component. A theme, such as *Traditions of Transition: Understanding Rites of Passage*, is selected each program year, and the core partners have events for the parent programs and the teacher and community member programs.

Chicago anthropologists, many of whom are members of the Chicago Association for the Practice of Anthropology (CAPA), are an integral part of the program development and implementation. CAPA provides resources and expertise. Members participate as volunteers and consultants. They facilitate discussions for the Cultural Connection teacher and community program events, guide neighborhood and cultural center visits, conduct workshops for Cultural Connection parent group program events, provide feedback and guidance in program development, and conduct ethnographic program evaluation.

As an educational anthropologist, I am able to create bridges between the anthropological constructs and the teachers and parents. I have contributed unique insight to designing and conducting evaluations, creating workshops for ethnically diverse parents and to developing and facilitating programs. The first year I worked with the Cultural Connections Program, I became part of the program evaluation team, focusing on the program's teacher component. I developed the protocol for a teacher focus group to augment their written evaluation questionnaires, conducted the focus group, and analyzed the data gathered from the focus group and participant observation of teacher events. The Center for Cultural Understanding and Change uses evaluations to inform content and to structure changes for further program development. Other anthropologist work includes facilitation of discussions at the program events.

The anthropological perspective brought to the Center for Cultural Understanding and Change is invaluable in the Center's diversity work, and it adds depth to understanding for program participants. Data from teacher focus groups and ethnographic program evaluations affirm that the quality and focus of discussions were greatly improved when anthropologists were facilitators. I also worked in the parent program component. A group of Spanish-speaking parents from one school attended two cultural events and participated in a follow-up workshop. At the ethnic museum and cultural organization events, I presented content about life transitions and rites of passage, grounding it in their own life experiences. Also, I developed and facilitated for parents a capstone workshop at their children's school. The facilitator team developed a final event for all parent groups. In the program evaluation, parents said they developed a broader perspective and learned a great deal that would benefit them in educating their children about their own culture and in being open and appreciative of difference and diversity. The anthropological theory and methods infused in the Cultural Connections Program has made such an obvious and profound contribution that the relationship to the Chicago Association for the Practice of Anthropology is becoming increasingly formalized.

Methods Used in Educational Anthropology— Including Ethnographic Evaluation

Though recent studies more frequently weave in quantitative methods, ethnography, in its many incarnations, is the heart of the methodology used in anthropology and education. Basically, ethnography is the description of a culture or group. In educational anthropology, this may be education in a community, in an ethnic neighborhood, on a reservation, in a foreign country, in an urban area, in a suburban development, in a village, or in the rural countryside. It may encompass a school district, a playground, a bus route, a school, or a classroom. Ideally, the initial approach is broad, and the foci and subsequent methods emerge from observation; however, in applied anthropology, an existing predefined problem may guide the research and intervention.

The foundation of ethnography is *participant observation*, which David Fetterman suggested is necessary for fieldwork to be effective: "Participant observation combines participation in the lives of the people under study with maintenance of a professional distance that allows adequate observation and recording of data" (1989, 45). As the research progresses, the educational anthropologists develop or bring in additional methods and tools. The methods may include formally structured, semistructured, or informal interviews; focus groups; questionnaires with open-ended questions; life histories; review of records, documents, or other written material; discourse analysis; or projective techniques. To validate information, data are derived from at least three different sources. This is called *triangulation.* Multimethod research has become quite common for educational anthropologists. Given the current climate overshadowing credibility for what is considered "scientific" and valid, statistics often are infused in largely ethnographic studies. These may be descriptive statistics derived from thematic analysis or other statistical analyses generated from surveys or forced-choice questionnaires. To facilitate observation, educational anthropologists may use classroom observation forms, protocols or topical checklists, sociograms to graph movement and interaction, and predetermined codes for actions or incidents. Time frames for observation and recording may be blocked out. Educational anthropologists also may use audio or video recording devices and still photography. Analysis of data includes sorting and coding, looking for patterns, and identifying themes. This can be done in many ways, perhaps employing color-coding or index card organization. There also are computer programs that facilitate analysis. Reflection is integral to the process.

Traditional ethnographic studies have long been used to inform policy and program development. Ethnographic studies of school districts, schools, and classrooms are a mainstay of educational anthropology. Margaret D. LeCompte and Jean J. Schensul (1999) developed a seven-volume *Ethnographer's Toolkit* as a guide for the increasing number of people using ethnography for educational research. These volumes take the researcher from design and methods through analysis, interpretation, and application. Harry Wolcott (1990) offers guidance on organizing and writing about the results from qualitative research.

Patrick McQuillan described the importance of ethnography to his work.

As an educational anthropologist I try to spend as much time as possible in schools working with a wide range of school personnel over extended periods of time so I have an holistic sense for what is happening in the real world of schools and classrooms, with the concomitant responsibility of writing up this work for relevant audiences. . . . I believe the ethnographic method helped me understand the micropolitical dimensions of an educational reform endeavor that many viewed as mainly academic in nature. (2002)

Ethnography also has spawned and inspired other forms of qualitative methods. Michele Foster (1997) employed oral life history to learn about African American teachers' teaching. Joseph A. Maxwell (1996) developed a model for an interactive approach to qualitative research design. Judith Preissle also has been innovative in qualitative research design: "The broadest application of my work has been in qualitative research methods and design where it is used by other researchers in planning their own inquiries and by methodologists in ongoing discussions in the field" (2002).

Many variations of ethnography have evolved, largely from attending to the context in which research is being done. For example, Lisa Rosen's current project uses a recursive ethnographic loop. She described the method as follows:

> My project is explicitly conceptualized as ethnographic "design research," which means that my findings regularly feed back into the design of the charter school and the work that surrounds it. Likewise, I regularly present findings to the participants in my study, who are also my colleagues, and facilitate reflective dialogue about both progress and challenges. My research thus has both immediate and long-term application. (2002)

The sociolinguistic ethnography of communication research conducted by Susan Urmston Philips (1993) is considered microethnographic within the context of traditional ethnography. Microethnography usually is associated with focused study in one location, such as a classroom. Philips examined communication structures in classrooms and community. Her work inspired further study of participation structures, using a variety of methods for gathering data. Frederick Erickson and Gerald Mohatt (1982) were early proponents of videotaping in schools and classrooms as part of ethnographic study. They used videotape to gather data in their study of participant structures and activity transitions in an Odwa school. The unit of analysis was determined by studying the tapes. Taping of any kind in schools, however, has become more cumbersome with the extensive permission-granting process.

Discourse analysis is used in studying interaction dynamics in schools, classrooms, school board meetings, and policy development. Educational anthropologists incorporate different methods as called for within a single study. For example, Sally Lubeck described her use of multiple methods:

> My research group recently completed a three-year study of four Head Start programs using ethnography and discourse analysis as tools for understanding how Head Start takes shape in a diversity of

communities. In conjunction with this work, we assisted one program in creating a "community of practice" among staff members, who now provide half of their own professional development. (2002)

Lubeck also used deconstruction to illuminate taken-for-granted assumptions about particular social groups, practices, and policies (e.g., Swadener and Lubeck 1995).

Policy- and program-driven ethnographic work within the parameters and time restraints of international agencies may inspire innovative adaptations and means of rapid assessment while maintaining ethnographic integrity (e.g., Handwerker 2001) and resisting what may look like "drive-by ethnography." In developing anthropological methods for the application of anthropological wisdom, Robert Textor sought the path less traveled. He developed "anticipatory anthropology" (1985) for use in educational and community planning. Textor was one of the organizers of the Educational Futures Committee in the CAE. Currently he is advocating for ethics education in business.

Harry Wolcott writes extensively about using ethnographic methods in education, with an emphasis on trying to maintain the integrity of ethnography. His ethnography of a school principal (1984) has been used to make decisions about the leadership role in schools. Reflecting on his work in educational anthropology, he shed light on his career path.

Career Trajectory of Harry Wolcott

I "grew up" with anthropology and education; my respective "careers" are intertwined. My dissertation was a study of a Kwakiutl Indian village and its school, a study that satisfied professors in both fields and helped to form the link between them. Fieldwork was in 1962–63, the dissertation completed the following year, and a book, *A Kwakiutl Village and School,* in 1967. My next study was done closer to home—across town, as a matter of fact—as I assumed a faculty position at the University of Oregon. That was a study of an elementary school principal; not what he should do, or what the literature said about him, but of one real live human being and how he actually went about doing it. *The Man in the Principal's Office: An Ethnography* was published in 1973. Another study looked at a school district working through a district-wide and grand scale (but not otherwise so grand) educational innovation, an innovation that I put in anthropological perspective by comparing the social organization of the school district to a moiety organization. *Teachers Versus Technocrats* was published in 1977.

From my perspective, none of these studies was "applied" in its intent, but each of them could be reviewed for its lessons for the future as well as its observations on how things were at present. And they heralded a new turn in educational research in which it became okay to examine single cases in depth of what was actually occurring in schools. So for a second thrust, I began writing what became a quartet of books dealing with aspects of qualitative research in general and ethnographic research in particular. My intent was to keep ethnography distinguishable as a particular kind of research at the same time that its fieldwork techniques were made more widely available to all. *Transforming Qualitative Data, The Art of Fieldwork, Ethnography: A Way of Seeing,* and *Writing Up Qualitative Research,* now in a second edition, are the result of that line of work. . . .

My studies have helped prepare teachers going into similar assignments like the village school, or administrators to find a broader perspective, or researchers to employ a wider assortment of field techniques in addressing their problems. More often I think my work has led to a softening of objectives, a less heavy-handed approach toward a "recalcitrant" group, more patience on the part of the official transmitters of cultures, more appreciation for what people already *are* than what they can become. It is "work in progress" in a constantly shifting ethnoscape. (2002a)

Building on Wolcott's seminal work in developing educational anthropological methodology and the tradition of action research in applied anthropology, action research has become a popular method in educational anthropology. According to Geoffrey E. Mills,

Action research is any systematic inquiry [using qualitative methods] conducted by teacher researchers, principals, school counselors, or other stakeholders in the teaching/learning environment to gather information about the ways that their particular schools operate, how they teach, and how well their students learn. This information is gathered with the goals of gaining insight, developing reflective practice, effecting positive changes in the school environment (and on educational practices in general), and improving student outcomes and the lives of those involved. (2000, 6)

Application of research resulting in action or intervention is key in the commitment to bringing about educational change. In applied educational anthropology or in action research, how can one increase the odds of being effective? Kathryn M. Borman shared what she believes ensures success.

In my experience, the best way to ensure some impact is to get as close as possible to the folks whose lives you are most invested in. . . . I am now convinced that the best results attend efforts that (1) are close to the community, (2) are carried out over a long period of time, and (3)

become institutionalized in both the target organization (in this case, the schools) and the facilitating organization (in this case, the UAC). (2004)

One of the first applied uses of ethnography in education was in evaluation. Judith Preissle Goetz and Margaret LeCompte (who at the time worked in the Department of Planning, Research, and Evaluation of the Houston Independent School District) not only fostered use of ethnography in educational research (e.g., Preissle Goetz and LeCompte 1984) but also in educational evaluation (e.g., LeCompte and Preissle Goetz 1984).

Whether applying ethnography to evaluation through school district employment, academic research, independent consulting, or, like Jolley Bruce Christman (with Elaine Simon and Eva Gold), starting a dedicated business like their Research for Action, educational anthropologists ensured that this approach became more widely known and accepted in both educational and anthropological circles. David Fetterman, known for his innovative evaluation work (e.g., Fetterman 1984; Fetterman, Kaftarian, and Wandersman 1996), talked about his inspirations and the path of his career.

Career Trajectory of David Fetterman

There are questions that have stayed with me over time that seem to have great meaning for me, questions that continue to preoccupy me, capture my imagination, and make me think.

1. Questions of equity—How can it be that groups are systematically disenfranchised from the society because of the color of their skin or their socioeconomic status?
2. Questions of fairness—Why are good people often treated so badly while those with little regard for others often prosper?
3. Questions of hope—How can we help others help themselves to improve their lives and the lives of others?

The core of my work is soliciting the insider's or emic perspective of reality and allowing it to guide the construction of theory and meaning. My book *Ethnography: Step by Step* (1989) highlights ethnographic concepts such as . . . contextualization (placing data in context to meaningfully interpret data), nonjudgmental, triangulation, and culture. These have been guiding forces in my life and my work as I do my best to unravel the grand mystery before us each day. I have taken this core tradition and applied it to evaluation in my books (e.g., 1984). . . .

Traditional ethnographic concepts and techniques applied to evaluation enable the insider's voice to be heard and have an impact on policy decisionmaking. In addition, an ethnographic approach to evaluation allows for a more meaningful and fair evaluation of a situation, classroom, or event. Shifting gears yet again, I have moved into a new domain fusing ethnography, evaluation, and empowerment. I developed a new approach to evaluation called "Empowerment Evaluation" (e.g., 1996). This approach has stirred the imaginations and emotions of many evaluators. It is designed to help people learn how to evaluate their own program, instead of relying on an external evaluator. It is built on the premise that the insider's view or emic perspective matters. More to the point it is similar to action anthropology, since the group is in charge, not the ethnographer or evaluator. The evaluator in this case is a facilitator helping the group determine their mission, take stock of where they are as a group/program, and plan for the future. . . .

My approaches have been adopted in higher education, government, inner-city public education, rural education, nonprofit organizations, corporations, and foundations throughout the United States and abroad. A wide range of program and policy sectors use these approaches, including substance abuse prevention, HIV prevention, crime prevention, environmental protection, welfare reform, battered woman's shelters, agriculture and rural development, adult probation, adolescent pregnancy prevention, tribal partnerships, individuals with disabilities, doctoral programs, and educational reform movements such as the Accelerated Schools Project.

A final note: Although my mom was not sure how I would get a job as an anthropologist, she always encouraged me to follow what I believed in. I have done that and for the most part the money has followed. I recommend the same to anyone as they contemplate their future—follow your heart; it will bring you where you really want to go or at least where you belong. Educational anthropology has done that for me. (2002)

Conclusion

This chapter barely scratches the surface of the anthropology and education domain. I defined the concept of educational anthropology as the anthropological study of education in all of its contexts, including early enculturation, formal, informal, and nonformal education. The rich history of anthropology and education was discussed, along with the evolving strength in advocacy for issues supported by ethnographic data and other research. Examples were offered of how educational anthropologists approach advocacy in questions of equity, of empowerment, of facilitating understanding of culture in a complex multicultural society, of creating educational change, and of providing teachers with knowledge and understanding to teach and help attain social justice.

The ways in which educational anthropologists work to achieve educational change were explored. How educational anthropologists have an impact on empowerment of culturally diverse parents and communities and the acquisition of social capital also was discussed. Cultural acquisition was reviewed as a fundamental construct in anthropology and education, and education of culturally diverse students was examined. Obviously, there is exciting and important territory to be explored. The field of educational anthropology is constantly evolving, seeking new ways to address persistent educational problems and rising to the challenges of new educational issues. Educational anthropology is ripe with possibilities to apply anthropological knowledge and methods in transforming society. This is an era of increased standardized testing, where testing itself under the rubric of accountability is perceived as educational reform, and where standardized testing induces reification of racial and class categories, where inequity persists, and where legislatures are influenced by fundamentalist segments of society. Doing applied anthropology in these conditions raises its own new challenges. Work is needed in learning and teaching how to navigate the new "culture" created by standardization so students can succeed in the ways deemed essential. One of the wonderful things about educational anthropology is that it provides the context so often lacking in other educational research. Because we look at the whole picture, we include important information that might reframe the problem. We examine what is left out as well as what is included.

There is increased interest among educational anthropologists in the way policy is framed, developed, and implemented, and in the impact it has. A simple policy may be ineffectively implemented or may have unintended impact. In efforts to "leave no child behind," letters sent home to notify parents that a teacher "is not qualified to teach" their child may intend to empower the parents to seek the best education for their child, but may actually undermine the teacher and what learning may be occurring. Educational anthropologists often pose the questions people do not think to ask, and perceive interactions and ramifications that are so embedded that they are invisible to the untrained eye. It is exciting to be part of the insightful efforts in applying anthropology to various dimensions of education.

Notes

1. E. D. Hirsch Jr. (1988) constructed a list of 5,000 "essential names, phrases, dates, and concepts" that he suggested every American must know to be culturally literate. He followed this with a series of books detailing

which of these items should be known by each grade level. The content of Hirsch's list was widely criticized for being ignorant of the diversity that characterizes America, and for being culture, gender, and time bound. Anthropologists, however, also criticized the very conceptualization of cultural literacy as a list of things.

2. To get a pulse on the current thoughts of some active educational anthropologists, I posed three questions to a group: (1) What are your burning questions in educational anthropology? (2) What is the core of your work? and (3) How has your work been applied? I weave throughout the chapter responses from 20 professionals to these questions.

3. The most recent forays into this territory include published responses to the "Cultural Literacy" movement and the challenge to the construct of "race" as physiologically based. Educational anthropologist Yolanda Moses, during her tenure as AAA president, spearheaded the initiative to share understanding of race as a social construct. This initiative resulted in publicly disseminated information, including a series of programs for PBS and schools.

4. For purposes of discussion, delineation of the various positions here is somewhat essentialist. Actual responses to the issue constitute a far richer fabric with subtle variations.

References

American Anthropological Association. 2004. *Anthropology in education: Anthropology Education Commission.* Retrieved November 11, 2004, from http://www.aaanet.org/

Anthropology & Education Quarterly (AEQ). 2003. 34: inside back cover.American Anthropological Association Committee on Public Policy. 2004. Retrieved November 11, 2004, from http://www.aaanet.org/committees/ppc/brief.htm

Arvizu, Steven F. 1992. Home-school linkages: A cross-cultural approach to parent participation. In *Cross-cultural literacy: Ethnographies of communication in multiethnic classrooms,* edited by Marietta Saravia-Shore and Steven F. Arvizu. New York: Garland Publishing.

Babcock, Barbara B., ed. 1991. *Pueblo mothers and children: Essays by Elsie Clews Parsons, 1915–1924.* Santa Fe: Ancient City Press.

Bateson, Mary Catherine. 1994. *Peripheral visions: Learning along the way.* New York: Harper Collins.

Bloomfield, Leonard. 1964. Literate and illiterate speech. In *Language in culture and society: A reader in linguistics and anthropology,* edited by Dell Hymes. New York: Harper & Row.

Borman, Kathryn M. 2004. E-mail communication from the David C. Anchin Center, University of South Florida, Tampa. Feb. 29.

Bull, William E. 1964. The use of vernacular languages in education. In *Language in culture and society: A reader in linguistics and anthropology,* edited by Dell Hymes. New York: Harper & Row.

Cazden, Courtney. 1983. Can ethnographic research go beyond the status quo? *Anthropology & Education Quarterly* 14 (1):33–41.

Chang, Heewon. 2002. E-mail communication from Eastern University, St. Davids, Penn. June 15.

Chilcott, John H. 1984. The *CAE Quarterly*, 1973–1976: From newsletter to quarterly. *Anthropology & Education Quarterly* 15 (1):67–9.

Delgado-Gaitan, Concha. 2002. E-mail communication from El Cerrito, Calif. June 24.

———. 1990. *Literacy for empowerment: The role of parents in children's education*. New York: The Falmer Press.

Deyhle, Donna. 2002. E-mail communication from University of Utah, Salt Lake City. July 8.

———. 1998. The role of the applied anthropologist: Between schools and the Navajo nation. In *Qualitative research reflections: Inside stories*, edited by Kathleen Bennett deMarrais. Mahwah, N.J.: Lawrence Erlbaum Associates.

Eddy, Elizabeth M. 1985. Theory, research, and application in educational anthropology. *Anthropology & Education Quarterly* 16 (2): 83–104.

Eisenhart, Margaret. 2002. E-mail communication from the University of Colorado, Boulder. July 5.

Eldering, Lotty. 2002. E-mail communication from Leiden University, the Netherlands. June 18.

Erickson, Frederick. 1987. Transformation and school success: The politics and culture of educational achievement. Anthropology & Education Quarterly 18 (4): 335–6.

Erickson, Frederick, and Gerald Mohatt. 1982. Cultural organization of participation structures in two classrooms of Indian students. In *Doing the ethnography of schooling: Educational anthropology in action*, edited by George Spindler. New York: Holt, Rinehart and Winston.

Fetterman, David M. 2002. E-mail communication from Stanford University, Stanford, Calif. July 2.

———. 1989. *Ethnography step by step*. Applied Social Research Method Series, vol. 17. Newbury Park, Calif.: Sage Publications.

———, ed. 1984. *Ethnography in educational evaluation*. Beverly Hills, Calif.: Sage Publications.

Fetterman, David M., Shakeh J. Kaftarian, and Abraham Wandersman, eds. 1996. *Empowerment evaluation: Knowledge and tools for self-assessment and accountability*. Thousand Oaks, Calif.: Sage Publications.

Ford, Rosalee. 1997. Educational anthropology: Early history and educationist contributions. In *Education and cultural process: Anthropological approaches*, edited by George D. Spindler. 3rd ed. Prospect Heights, Ill.: Waveland Press.

Foster, Michele. 1997. *Black teachers on teaching*. New York: The New Press.

Gibson, Margaret. 1976. Approaches to multicultural education in the U.S. *Anthropology & Education Quarterly* 7 (4):7–8.

Gibson, Margaret A., and John U. Ogbu. 1991. *Minority status and schooling: A comparative study of immigrant and involuntary minorities*. New York: Garland Publishing.

Greenman, Nancy P. 1994. Not all caterpillars become butterflies: Reform and restructuring as educational change. In *Changing American education: Recapturing the past or inventing the future?*, edited by Kathryn M. Borman and Nancy P. Greenman. Albany: SUNY Press.

Greenman, Nancy P., and Susan D. Greenbaum. 1996. Multicultural education. In *The encyclopedia of cultural anthropology*, edited by David Levinson and Melvin Ember. Lakeville, Conn.: American Reference Publishing.

Greenman, Nancy P., and Ellen B. Kimmel. 1995. The road to multicultural education: Potholes of resistance. *Journal of Teacher Education* 46 (5): 360–8.

Handwerker, W. Penn. 2001. *Quick ethnography.* Walnut Creek, Calif.: AltaMira Press.

Hauser, Mary. 2002. E-mail communication from Carlton College, Northfield, Minn. July 8.

Henze, Rosemary. 2003. E-mail communication from San Jose State University, Dept. of Linguistics and Language Development. July 4.

Hess, G. Alfred, Jr. 1991. *School restructuring, Chicago style.* Newbury Park, Calif.: Corwin Press.

Hirsch, E. D., Jr. 1988. *Cultural literacy: What every American needs to know.* Updated and expanded. New York: Vintage Books.

Howard, Alan. 1970. *Learning to be Rotuman.* New York: Teachers College Press.

Hymes, Dell. 1964. General introduction and section introductions. In *Language in culture and society: A reader in linguistics and anthropology*, edited by Dell Hymes. New York: Harper & Row.

Jordan, Cathie. 1985. Translating culture: From ethnographic information to educational program. *Anthropology & Education Quarterly* 19 (2): 105–23.

La Belle, Thomas J. 1984. Liberation, development, and rural nonformal education. *Anthropology & Education Quarterly* 15 (1): 80–93.

LeCompte, Margaret D., and Judith P[reissle] Goetz. 1984. Ethnographic data collection in evaluation research. In *Ethnography in educational evaluation*, edited by David M. Fetterman. Beverly Hills, Calif.: Sage Publications.

LeCompte, Margaret D., and Jean J. Schensul. 1999. *Ethnographer's toolkit.* 7 vols. Walnut Creek, Calif.: AltaMira Press.

Lee, Dorothy. 1986. What price literacy? In *Valuing the self: What we can learn from other cultures.* Prospect Heights, Ill.: Waveland Press. Originally published in 1976 by Prentice Hall.

Levine, Linda. 2002. E-mail communication from Bank Street College, New York. July 2.

Lipka, Jerry. 1991. Toward a culturally based pedagogy: A case study of one Yup'ik Eskimo teacher. *Anthropology & Education Quarterly* 22 (3): 203–23.

Lipman, Pauline. 2002. Making the global city, making inequality: The political economy and cultural politics of Chicago school policy. *American Educational Research Journal* 39 (2): 379–419.

———. 1998. *Race, class, and power in school restructuring.* Albany: SUNY Press.

Lubeck, Sally. 2002. E-mail communication from the University of Michigan, Ann Arbor. July 2.

———. 1989. A world of difference: American child care policy in cross-national perspective. *Educational Policy* 3 (4): 331–54.

Martin, Shane P., and Magaly Lavadenz. 1998. Beyond multicultural education: A framework for understanding responses to cultural diversity in teacher education. Presented at the Annual Meeting of the American Anthropological Association, Philadelphia, Penn. December 5.

Maxwell, Joseph A. 1996. *Qualitative research design: An interactive approach*. Applied Social Research Methods Series, vol. 41. Thousand Oaks, Calif.: Sage Publications.

McCarty, Theresa L. 2002. *A place to be Navajo: Rough Rock and the struggle for self-determination in indigenous schooling*. Mahwah, N.J.: Lawrence Erlbaum Associates.

McQuillan, Patrick J. 2002. E-mail communication from Boston College. June 27.

————. 1998. *Educational opportunity in an urban American high school: A cultural analysis*. Albany: SUNY Press.

Mead, Margaret. 1960. *Four families*. National Film Board of Canada. 1–800–542–2164.

————. 1954. *Bathing babies in three cultures*. University Park, Penn.: Penn State Audio-Visual Services. Retrieved from http://www.medianet.libraries.psu.edu

Mehan, Hugh, Lea Hubbard, and Irene Villanueva. 1994. Forming academic identities: Accommodation without assimilation among involuntary minorities. *Anthropology & Education Quarterly* 25 (2): 91–117.

Mills, Geoffrey E. 2000. *Action research: A guide for the teacher researcher*. Upper Saddle River, N.J.: Merrill of Prentice Hall.

Muncey, Donna E., and P. J. McQuillan. 1996. *Reform and resistance in schools and classrooms: An ethnographic view of the coalition of essential schools*. New Haven, Conn.: Yale University Press.

Ogbu, John U. 1990. Minority education in comparative perspective. *Journal of Negro Education* 59 (10): 45–57.

————. 1982. Cultural discontinuities and schooling. *Anthropology & Education Quarterly* 13 (4): 290–307.

Philips, Susan Urmston. 1993. *Invisible culture: Communication in classroom and community on the Warm Springs Indian Reservation*. Prospect Heights, Ill.: Waveland Press. Originally published in 1983 by Susan Urmston Philips and the Warm Springs Confederated Tribes.

Pitman, Mary Anne, Rivka A. Eisikovits, and Marion Lundy Dobbert. 1989. *Culture acquisition: A holistic approach to human learning*. New York: Praeger.

Precourt, Walter. 1982. Ethnohistorical analysis of an Appalachian settlement school. In *Doing the ethnography of schooling*, edited by George Spindler. New York: Holt, Rinehart and Winston.

Preissle, Judith. 2002. E-mail communication from the University of Georgia, Athens.

Preissle Goetz, Judith, and Margaret D. LeCompte. 1984. *Ethnography and qualitative design in educational research*. Orlando: Academic Press.

Rosen, Lisa. 2002. E-mail communication from the Center for School Improvement, the University of Chicago. June 24.

Rosenfeld, Gerry. 1971. *"Shut those thick lips!": A study of slum school failure*. Prospect Heights, Ill.: Waveland Press.

Saravia-Shore, Marietta, and Steven F. Arvizu. 1992. Cross-cultural literacy: An anthropological approach to dealing with diversity. In *Cross-cultural literacy: Ethnographies of communication in multiethnic classrooms*, edited by Marietta Saravia-Shore and Steven F. Arvizu. New York: Garland Publishing.

Schensul, Jean J. 2002. E-mail communication from the Institute for Community Research, Hartford, Conn. September 3.

————. 1985. Cultural maintenance and cultural transformation: Educational anthropology in the eighties. *Anthropology & Education Quarterly* 16 (1): 63–8.

Schensul, Jean J., Maria Gonzales Borrero, and Robert Garcia. 1985. Applying ethnography in educational change. *Anthropology & Education Quarterly* 16 (2):149–64.

Shor, Ira, and Paulo Freire. 1987. *A pedagogy for liberation: Dialogues on transforming education.* New York: Bergin & Garvey.

Singleton, John 1984. The CAE Newsletter, 1970–1973, Origins of the *AEQ*: Rituals, myths, and cultural transmission. *Anthropology & Education Quarterly* 15 (1): 11–16.

Sleeter, Christine E., and Carl A. Grant. 2003. *Making choices for multicultural education.* 4th ed. New York: J. Wiley Publishers.

Spindler, George D. 1984. Roots revisited: Three decades of perspective. *Anthropology & Education Quarterly* 15 (1): 3–10.

————. 1963. *Education and culture: Anthropological approaches.* New York: Holt, Rinehart, and Winston.

Swadener, Elizabeth B., and Sally Lubeck, eds. 1995. *Families and children "at promise": Deconstructing the discourse of risk.* Albany: SUNY Press.

Textor, Robert B. 1985. Anticipatory anthropology and the telemicroelectronic revolution: A preliminary report from Silicon Valley. *Anthropology & Education Quarterly* 16 (1): 3–30.

Thu, Kendell. 2004. Presentation by the Chair of AAA Committee on Public Policy to the Chicago Association for the Practice of Anthropology, Chicago. February 29.

Tobin, Joseph J., David Y. H. Wu, and Dana H. Davidson. 1989. *Preschool in three cultures: Japan, China, and the United States.* New Haven, Conn.: Yale University Press.

Trueba, Henry T. 1988. Culturally based explanations of minority students' academic achievement. *Anthropology & Education Quarterly* 19 (3): 270–87.

van Willigen, John. 2002. *Applied anthropology: An introduction.* 3rd ed. Westport, Conn.: Bergin and Garvey.

Voght, Lynn A., Cathie Jordan, and Roland G. Tharp. 1987. Explaining school failure, producing school success: Two cases. *Anthropology & Education Quarterly* 18 (4): 276–86.

Ward, Martha C. 1986. *Them children: A study in language learning.* Prospect Heights, Ill.: Waveland Press. Originally published in 1971 by Holt, Rinehart and Winston.

Wax, Murray L., Rosalie H. Wax, and Robert V. Dumont Jr. 1989. *Formal education in an American Indian community: Peer society and the failure of minority education.* Prospect Heights, Ill.: Waveland Press. Originally published in 1964 by the Society for the Study of Social Problems.

Wolcott, Harry F. 2002a. E-mail communication from the University of Oregon. June 28.

————. 2002b. *Sneaky kid and its aftermath: Ethics and intimacy in fieldwork.* Walnut Creek, Calif.: AltaMira Press.

————. 2001. *Writing up qualitative research.* 2nd ed. Thousand Oaks, Calif.: Sage Publications.

————. 1999. *Ethnography: A way of seeing.* Walnut Creek, Calif.: AltaMira Press.

————. 1995. *The art of fieldwork.* Walnut Creek, Calif.: AltaMira Press.

————. 1994. *Transforming qualitative data: Description, analysis, and interpretation.* Thousand Oaks, Calif.: Sage Publications.

————. 1984. *The man in the principal's office: An ethnography.* Prospect Heights, Ill.: Waveland Press. Originally published in 1973 by the University of Oregon.

————. 1977. *Teachers versus technocrats: An educational innovation in anthropological perspective.* Eugene: Center for the Advanced Study of Educational Administration, University of Oregon.

————. 1967. *A Kwakiutl village and school.* New York: Holt, Rinehart, and Winston.

10 Applied Anthropology and the Aged

Robert C. Harman

Why should applied anthropology students be interested in gerontology, the study of the aged? There are a number of reasons; the most obvious, and perhaps the most important, is that the world's population is rapidly aging. Approximately 420 million people worldwide were 65 or over at the turn of the century. Population experts estimate that the number of older persons will more than double within a generation (U.S. Census Bureau 2004a). In 25 years, one out of every nine people on this planet will be 65 or older. In light of the social and economic effects associated with an older world, we must consider that developing societies are aging the most rapidly (Kinsella 1997, 18).

This global trend is impacting the United States as well. Although the American population is aging at a slower rate than many nations, the 2000 census showed that older Americans, the 35 million people age 65 or over, comprised 12.4 percent of the country's population compared to only 4 percent in 1900. The aging of the population in the first third of the twenty-first century will dwarf the pace at which it occurred previously. By 2030, one of five Americans will be 65 or over (U.S. Census Bureau 2004b).

The rapid growth in the number of older people has major implications for the workforce. The emergence of new policies and programs for the aged worldwide is unprecedented, and infrastructure for older persons is continually growing. Anthropologists offer knowledge, skills, and experience that augment the effectiveness of understanding and improving the late years of life. Anthropology's contributions to the study of the aged are holistic, comparative, and emic. They go beyond approaches that exhibit less concern for the meaning of life experiences (Savishinsky 1991, 239).

Larger numbers of aged people translate into more work opportunities for anthropologists as well as for other professionals in the field of gerontology. This chapter addresses several areas of research and service where applied anthropologists are contributing toward a better quality of life for the aged. Anthropologists are working, often in multidisciplinary teams, with physicians, social workers, psychologists, statisticians, and others on gerontological issues. Anthropologists bring a unique perspective to their work with older persons, a perspective that is broader and more in touch with older people than that of physicians who currently dominate the service sector of what sociologist Carroll Estes calls the aging enterprise (1979). Estes coined that term in reference to the "programs, organizations, bureaucracies, interest groups, trade associations, providers, industries, and professionals that serve the aged in one capacity or another [and not always well]" (1979, 2). The size of the aging enterprise is continually growing, and necessarily so, to meet the needs of older persons; anthropologists are among the legitimate contributors.

Old age is defined in several different ways according to cultural and individual perspectives, and it is clear that world demographics are changing dramatically as the aged become more numerous. Older individuals throughout the world are living very differently than their predecessors, by choice and by necessity. Many experiences of present-day older persons are unprecedented in human history (Keith 1994, 105). This phenomenon provides gerontological anthropologists a fertile ground to conduct applied research, that is, to collect data to benefit the aged and, ideally, to influence policy pertaining to the aged.

In this chapter, I discuss the contributions that applied anthropologists have made toward improving the lives of older persons in the United States. There is a description of the methods applied anthropologists use in their research. The chapter's coverage is limited to the work of sociocultural anthropologists; contributions by biological anthropologists are addressed elsewhere (see Ikels and Beall 2001, 126). Part of this chapter will introduce some of the legislation and policies that determine privileges and constraints affecting older Americans. Following the introduction, I begin with a section on the historical development of anthropology's involvement with aging and the aged. It describes the trends in gerontological anthropology that began in the past century. The second section of the chapter identifies several major concerns of the aged that anthropologists address: long-term care, health and short-term health care, community, and family. A third section identifies a broad range of strategies, methods, and techniques that anthropologists use in their research with older people. The excellent qualitative research by anthropologists has high validity and reliability, which has been acknowledged by policymakers (Caplan, Morrison, and Stambaugh 1975, 30). These methods are usually designed for older people to uncover the meanings of phenomena impacting their lives. The third section summarizes much of the work carried out by applied anthropologists on behalf of the aged. The fourth section of the chapter provides three case studies of gerontological anthropologists who have conducted outstanding research and service with distinction on behalf of older persons. The final two sections address the value of applied anthropology work with the aged and future directions of applied anthropology in gerontology.

A Historic Perspective on Anthropology and the Aged

Ethnographies written by anthropologists over the past century are testimony to the fact that the aged have always been crucial to anthropological research. In most traditional societies studied by anthropologists, the older people were repositories of knowledge about the local culture and served as the ultimate authorities in family and community. Older informants were able to provide ethnographers with an abundance of specific cultural knowledge that quite often was not known by, and was inaccessible to, younger societal members.

The older members of traditional societies were, and continue to be, highly visible residents of houses and house compounds that are shared with adult children (usually sons), children's spouses (usually daughters-in-law) and grandchildren. The nuclear family, a norm in Western cultures, was seldom found in traditional societies, or even in complex societies, outside the Western world. Due to very recent Western influences, however, and internal pressures from industrialization and urbanization, the aged of some complex societies outside the Western cultural sphere are beginning to live apart from close family members. That has become an alternative also in some traditional societies, although the rural villagers of most countries continue to have households where the older people reside with at least some of their grown children (cf. Sokolovsky 1997, 202).

Despite the high profile of older people in societies researched, anthropologists did not begin to conduct systematic studies of the aged until the mid-1900s. Christine Fry (1999, 273) has identified three generations of focused anthropological contributions to gerontology. In the first generation, Leo Simmons (1945), a sociologist working with an anthropological database, conducted the initial social science study of the aged. His quantitative research utilized a worldwide sample of nonindustrial societies for a cross-cultural study. The second generation of anthropological work on aging was notable for its involvement with gerontological issues using qualitative methods, primarily emphasizing participant observation and in-depth interviewing; it demonstrated that the concepts and approaches of anthropology were applicable to the domain of old age. Some large-scale theorizing, similar to that of Simmons, marked the second generation, which covered a period from the mid-1960s to the late 1970s. In the third generation, dating from 1980 to the present, gerontological anthropologists have combined qualitative and quantitative methods to explore many areas of meaning in the lives of older persons. Fry (1999, 273–74) considers the third generation to be characterized by complexity, diversity, context specificity, and cultural understanding. Anthropologists of this generation have also become involved in applied anthropology by contributing to policies and programs that affect the lives of older persons.

Simmons analyzed secondary data with a sample of 71 traditional societies, using the Human Relations Area Files (HRAF), an instrument developed by anthropologists at Yale University in 1949 that is still being updated today. Most of the data in the HRAF are collected by anthropologists who have conducted field research in traditional societies. Simmons's objective was to find cross-cultural regularities that might predict favorable or unfavorable cultural conditions for older people. He correlated 112 variables pertaining to the treatment of older people with more than 100 other sociocultural variables (Fry 1980, 2). He did not discover highly predictable regularities, but he did document many social characteristics of older people's involvement in activities (Fry 1999, 272). Simmons also found that old age itself does not bring respect from others and that the senile, decrepit, older person is not respected in any society (Boyer 1980, 200).

Margaret Clark was the most influential anthropologist of the second generation of anthropological researchers on the aged. She was instrumental in the development within anthropology of a gerontological focus. Some 22 years after Simmons's work, Clark and Anderson (1967) addressed concerns of the aged in contemporary urban United States. Their book brought gerontology to anthropology and vice versa. The authors, using a distinctly anthropological approach, contributed to a scientific and humanistic understanding of the aged in a San Francisco sample. They utilized standard qualitative methods of anthropology, namely, interviews, and participant observation. Original data were collected from subsamples of 365 older San Francisco Bay area residents. One subsample was of "disturbed" older residents who had spent time in a psychiatric hospital, and a control subsample consisted of "normal" older persons who had not been hospitalized.

Clark and Anderson (1967) studied the older subjects ethnographically as they carried on their daily lives. The main research instrument, however, was an interview schedule. The anthropologists analyzed their data to understand how the older subjects fit, or did not fit, according to their mental and physical health, into the prevailing social system. Their book was anthropological with explicit attention to theories and concepts of those times, such as structural-functional analysis and kinship. They looked at dyadic kinship relations between husbands and wives, parents and children, and grandparents and grandchildren. Outside the kinship realm, Clark and Anderson analyzed broader aspects of their aged subjects' social network such as relations with friends, neighbors, and voluntary association cohorts. They also examined American values that influenced the lives of the older Americans.

Clark and Anderson found that high morale for the residents was associated with good physical health and financial security (1967, 118). They found that good physical and mental health was necessary to maintain a high level of social involvement (1967, 169). Clark and Anderson were impressed with the emphasis that older Americans place on independence, which they seek to maintain even at the expense of foregoing many other satisfactions of life (1967, 390–91). They were also concerned with the adaptation of Americans as they grow older. Clark and Anderson (398–433) found that individuals who adhered rigidly to American values in old age, and those who were psychiatrically impaired, did poorly on five adaptive tasks of aging for the older person: (1) perception of aging and definition of instrumental limitations, (2) redefinition of physical and social life space, (3) substitution of alternative sources of need-satisfaction, (4) reassessment of criteria for self-evaluation, and (5) reintegration of values and life goals.

When the Association of Anthropology and Gerontology (AAGE) was formed in 1978, Clark was an inspiration for some of the AAGE founders. The AAGE had the purpose of serving as a hub for the integration of anthropologists working in gerontology. The organization publishes a directory of members to facilitate communication for the membership, and a teaching primer that promotes excellence in the classroom for anthropologists teaching about the aged. The AAGE holds an annual meeting for members to exchange ideas. At the American Anthropological Association annual meeting, the AAGE sponsors paper sessions for research on the aged and holds a business meeting. AAGE sessions on the aged are also held at the annual meeting of the Society for Applied Anthropology and sometimes at the conference of the Gerontological Society of America.

Early in the third generation of anthropological research on gerontological issues, Fry (1980, 1981), an AAGE founder, edited two volumes on the work anthropologists had conducted with the aged. Thirty anthropologists contributed chapters to those volumes on a number of topics pertaining to old age. One examined biological factors in aging, whereas others covered sociocultural issues. Some described their gerontological research in peasant communities, and one wrote on a middle-class American town. Among the selections were comparative studies of older Americans and old people of other cultural backgrounds. Most of the contributors wrote on lives of the aged in a specific country or community, focusing on one or more of the key characteristics that distinguish anthropology from other disciplines: shared culture, holism, insider perspective, and cross-cultural comparison.

Eleven of the chapters (in Fry 1980, 1981) addressed health issues that older people confront on a more frequent basis than do younger people. The contributions set the stage for most of the topics that gerontological anthropologists would address over the following two decades: methods, activities of the aged, life satisfaction, life course, culture change effects, family kinship, networks, voluntary associations, status in community, community formation, intergenerational relations, ethnicity, death and dying, institutions for the aged, and a multitude of health concerns. Many of the authors for Fry's volumes became leading figures in anthropological research on, and practice with, the aged. In assessing the contributions to Fry's 1980 collection of anthropological studies, Lowell Holmes (1980, 281–84) expressed a vision for applied anthropology and gerontology that bore fruition before the end of the century. Holmes asserted, unequivocally, that the research of anthropologists on the aged should be considered applied anthropology by indicating that, "Nearly every one of the studies [in the book] . . . has its practical applications" (1980, 281).

Gerontology is an interdisciplinary field that dates back to 1945 (Estes and Linkins 2000, 156). That year marked the formation of the Gerontological Society of America and the start of the *Journal of Gerontology*. These events coincided with the publication of Simmons's cross-cultural research. Anthropologists have contributed to gerontological theory and methods since the 1960s, and they have added considerably to its practice in more recent years. Theories on aging are diverse. They are divided, generally, into those from biology and clinical medicine, which are biologically based, and those from the social and behavioral sciences, which are socially and psychologically based. The biological theories of aging have had considerable influence on American policy for the aged, but recent social science theories raise new concerns that critique the applicability of earlier thought and practice. Anthropological research, along with that from other social and behavioral sciences, has influenced the direction of recent innovations in gerontological theory and practice.

Anthropologist Ralph Linton (1936) is acknowledged by social scientists for his classic writings on the concept of status, including age status, which contributed to the development of the "life course" perspective in sociology (Settersten 1999, 7). Life course is a theoretical perspective that addresses the aging of individuals within historical context, and it refers to "the successive statuses held by individuals as they age" (Pavalko 2002, 777). The life course perspective in sociology and psychology dates back to the 1960s. By the early 1980s, a number of anthropologists who were working with the aged had adopted the life course perspective. Keith and Kertzer indicated that "The emphasis is not on the product [old age] of the aging process, but on the process itself and its relationships to social, cultural, and historical context" (1984, 19–20). Fry (2003) recently wrote, from the perspective of an academic anthropologist, an intriguing essay on the complexities of life course as a cultural construct.

Sharon Kaufman (1986), an anthropologist influenced by the life course approach, collected life stories from 60 aged Americans in an attempt to understand how they found meaning in late life. She discovered that her subjects retained a meaningful sense of self throughout the life span—a self that integrates a broad range of personal experiences within a particular cultural and historical context (1986, 187–88). Joel Savishinsky (2000) used a similar life course perspective to find out what meanings are associated with retirement for older Americans. To learn about those meanings, he conducted in-depth interviews of 26 retiring men and women in a town in upstate New York over a period of several years. Savishinsky identified several specific retirement issues within the chapters and concluded his book with "lessons" and "cautions" for the reader (2000, 338–45). The life course approach in anthropology has produced outstanding ethnographies of older people, such as those by Kaufman and Savishinsky, although the life course perspective has not yet contributed substantially to the empirical solutions of problems faced by older persons.

In contrast to academic endeavors, applied anthropology addresses older persons' present needs. Much of the work by applied anthropologists in gerontology is funded by corporations or government agencies that are seeking solutions to existing gerontological problems. Applied anthropological research is usually conducted with the understanding that the results will be used to benefit the research subjects. Thus, in gerontological anthropology, nearly all of the ethnographers become involved in advocacy on behalf of their subjects. Due to the intimate nature of data offered to the anthropologists by their older informants, special bonds usually develop between the researcher and informant. More often than not, the anthropologist working with older people is of the same societal background, sometimes sharing identity with the same city, state, and country as his or her subjects. The sense of responsibility a gerontological anthropologist has for protecting and nurturing older informants often lasts a lifetime. Some of these special anthropologist-older person relationships are reported in publications (Savishinsky 2000; Sokolovsky 1997; Stafford 2003), but most are spread by word of mouth among anthropologists in other informal settings.

Applied anthropology, of course, has a conceptual linkage with gerontology; thus it is surprising to find that the two overlapping fields are not closer in terms of research collaboration and practice. Several conditions may inhibit a closer alliance. Many of the jobs in gerontology have been co-opted by social work because of limiting federal legislation that excludes anthropologists from some positions that they might be able to perform as well or better than their counterparts from other disciplines. This exclusion is being challenged (Slorah 2003b). Another concern is that applied anthropology textbooks and supplementary readers seldom cover gerontological topics as a legitimate substantive area of applied anthropology. That curious phenomenon, particularly when an anthropology department offering an applied course does not have a faculty member interested in gerontology, has probably dissuaded some applied students who might otherwise have pursued work with the aged.

Areas of Anthropological Interest in the Aged

Anthropologists have contributed considerably over the past generation toward understanding the aged, and their work has provided an impetus for program improvements and policy implementation affecting older persons. Contributions of applied anthropology generally fall into four categories: long-term care, health and short-term health care, community, and family.

Long-Term Care

Long-term care consists of a broad range of services offered to people who require assistance in order to perform essential daily activities (Wright 2002, 826). When most people think of long-term care, they think of nursing homes, and, in fact, approximately half of the seriously impaired aged Americans reside in that type of institution. The majority of long-term care residents are older persons who occupied nearly 1.5 million nursing home beds and over one million home care beds in 1999. Nursing homes are a major part of the aging enterprise, with more than one million full-time equivalent employees as of 1999 (2002, 826). Yet long-term care is more than just nursing homes, and programs have recently been created in the United States that provide professional support for the needs of many frail older persons, at different levels of disability, without having to remove them from their homes and communities (Eckert and Morgan 2001). Informal caregivers, such as family and friends, do the largest share of caring for millions of other frail elderly who are confined to their homes.

Long-term care is an area in which anthropologists have made substantial contributions to gerontology over the past 30 years (Ikels and Beall 2001, 126). Anthropologists who have completed ethnographies of nursing homes include Jeanie Kayser-Jones, Joel Savishinsky, and Renee Rose Shield. Those anthropologists have used their research data to advocate on behalf of nursing home clients. Kayser-Jones (1981) conducted fieldwork in nursing homes in Scotland and California, and she later presented her cross-cultural findings, and those from subsequent research, before a U.S. Senate Special Committee on Aging. Savishinsky (1991) delved deeply into the meanings of institutional living for residents, as well as for staff and volunteers, at a nursing home in upstate New York. Shield (1998) was responsible for policy changes at the facility she studied in-depth, and she later went on to serve the state of Rhode Island as a staff member of Aging 2000. The message from those anthropologists and others (Henderson and Vesperi 1995; Stafford 2003) is that nursing home treatment is frequently unsatisfactory and sometimes inhumane. Documented failures of many nursing homes to meet residents' needs occurred at a time when the federal government was taking measures to remove itself from directly supporting individual nursing home resident payments through Medicaid. Federal and state legislation in 1987 enacted support for community and home care arrangements. As a result, the number of occupied nursing home beds has been declining for more than a decade and a half.

Shield had a good reputation for solid ethnographic research in a Rhode Island nursing home, and she had a proven ability to get her findings used for policy changes that improved residents' quality of life (1997). She was hired, subsequently, to carry out research and program development at another nursing home in the same state. At that facility, Shield (1998, 11) introduced new perspectives to the staff, residents, families, and community. She developed staff workshops on, among other topics, death and bereavement and restraint-free care. She also ran a one-year workshop on the physical environment of nursing homes, with attention to the special needs of sensory impaired residents, and raised individuality and privacy concerns related to space as those play out in the context of nursing home regulations. Shield challenged the staff to consider existing occupational boundaries as a deterrent to the best care for residents and used strategies to foster more respect for aged residents and nursing assistants (1998, 12).

Margaret Perkinson (2002) wrote a guide, which was published simultaneously in English and Spanish, for home care aides who work with

Alzheimer's patients. The manual is designed to clarify what the patient and family need beyond the basics and how the aide can address those needs. The manual is based on findings from ten focus groups conducted with family caregivers, home care aides, and agency personnel on how to provide quality care for people with dementia. The guide answers relevant questions for home care aides in their interaction with family members. It is written for the aide in a style that is supportive, and it is published in an attractive format. The guide utilizes an empathic approach that motivates the aide to understand patient and family concerns on a broad range of topics that aides might not have previously considered.

Health and Short-Term Health Care

Apart from long-term care, gerontological anthropologists are concerned with other aspects of day-to-day health and health care of the aged. In California, for example, researchers found that physicians of home health care for older persons tend to underestimate the physical impairment of their patients. As advocates of older people with functional impairments, the research anthropologists proposed that physicians treating the aged need to have more accurate knowledge of their patients' functional capabilities. They found that the physicians most frequently overlooked the difficulties their patients were having with stair-climbing and urinary incontinence (Barker, Mitteness, and Muller 1998).

Rosemarie Lamm works in central Florida on projects designed to determine the health-related needs of the aged and how the health care system can help to meet those needs. Since 1998, she has been affiliated with the Coalition on Aging Think Tank, which has similar concerns. Lamm (2003b) became involved in a coalition project for caregivers of the elderly, most of whom are elderly themselves. In focus group settings, she conducted a needs assessment of the older local caregivers. Results indicated that a high proportion of those caregivers had unmet chronic medical conditions.

Subsequently, Lamm (2003a) used the research results to write a brochure and a manual. She also produced a video that assists elderly caregivers with their own self-care and decisionmaking for treatment. By early 2003, Lamm had already offered a series of educational seminars to 1,100 elderly caregivers, at which they utilized the video and information from the manual. Audience feedback was overwhelmingly positive, with 98 percent of those in attendance indicating, in an evaluation survey, that they received benefits. All participants received a copy of the manual, and additional copies were distributed throughout the community (Lamm 2003b).

Neil Henderson (1997, 430) initiated the development of ethnic-specific Alzheimer's support groups for Hispanics and for African Americans in two cities of the American South. Those were among the first ethnic-specific groups in the nation for dementia caregivers. The cultural problems that plagued African American caregivers were of a different nature than those in the Hispanic community (Henderson 1994, 41). African Americans who were not integrated into previous Alzheimer's support groups, dominated by Anglo Americans, were able to benefit from the ethnic-specific organization. The applied anthropologist, who moderated the groups, was well accepted by African Americans of the community.

Hispanic caregivers met monthly at a local Hispanic hospital in Tampa with a Spanish-speaking support group leader and the help of local professionals. Certain culturally specific dynamics pervaded the Hispanic home caregiver settings, and the local support group helped individuals with those problems. The vast majority of Hispanic primary caretakers, for example, are female, and they seldom get assistance from males in the family. Hispanics bear a stigma of family "craziness" when members, including those with Alzheimer's, behave in an erratic manner. Older people, such as wives of Alzheimer's patients, tend to be reluctant to attend support group meetings, but they can often be persuaded to attend by adult children (Henderson 1994, 437). Caregivers participating in the support group found an outlet for sharing experiences with other caregivers, and they became more willing to use formal sector services. Those benefits helped considerably to lessen their burdens and decrease their stress levels. Despite its success, the support group existed for only two years because the caregivers were unable to carry on the organizational duties after funding was terminated.

Shield, who was mentioned earlier for her nursing home work, served as an anthropologist on the initial staff of the Aging 2000 program to reform health care for the older people of Rhode Island (Shield and Zesk 1997). That program, conceived in 1989, was created in response to the rising costs of health care in the nation and the state. Rhode Island was to become a model for the nation with its less expensive and more effective approach to care for the aged. Shield (1998, 12) exerted considerable influence on the initial direction of Aging 2000 because the philosophy and research were to be guided by anthropological principles.

Shield designed the research project that followed a participatory model and an insider approach for eliciting subjects' views. Research focused on obtaining and utilizing the ideas elicited from local older persons on the shortcomings of existing health care delivery to the aged and how those problems should be overcome (Shield and Zesk 1997). That needs assessment was essential to the project, and it utilized open-ended interviews. The approach was consistent with the bottom-up, grassroots movement desired by the program leaders (1997, 4). Here was an opportunity for Shield, using anthropological knowledge, to affect health care for the aged throughout the entire state of Rhode Island. Much of the anthropological contribution, unfortunately, was lessened due to management and political issues that arose as the program developed. Aging 2000 survives, but it has been unable to institute many of the reforms envisioned back in 1989. According to the current executive director of Aging 2000, the organization is now limited to training retired, older volunteers to become workshop leaders in order to help their peers with health care issues and concerns (Cimini 2003).

Thomas Arcury and Sara Quandt are the authors of a number of papers on the health and health care of rural elderly people in the American Southeast. They found that informal sector care by spouses, children, friends, and neighbors, as well as voluntary organizations, plays a larger role in rural settings than it does in urban ones (Quandt and Arcury 2001, 129). Arcury and Quandt concluded that rural areas require unique formal sector policy to meet the transportation, nutrition, health promotion and prevention, and mental health needs of the elderly. They offered several suggestions for improving public health services for the aged in rural locations (141). Arcury and others (2002, 180) also found that large numbers of Southern elders rely on specific forms of complementary and alternative medicine (CAM), treatment, and prevention, namely, home and folk remedies, as well as vitamin and mineral supplements. They concluded that health and social service providers in the region should utilize this knowledge about high rates of CAM utilization by asking patients about their CAM use and providing advice to individuals about the risks of certain CAM therapies (2002, 183).

Community

Several anthropologists have been involved in research and practice with older immigrants and refugees over the past two decades. Elzbieta Gozdziak has worked with refugees in the eastern United States. She wrote on social problems specific to older refugees and programs that were attempting to address them (1988). Her ethnographic work revealed several health, housing, transportation, intergenerational, community, and religious problems that afflicted older people of different national origins. The problems were so severe that some of the older refugees returned to their countries of origin (1988, 34). In California, Patricia Omidian (1996) conducted intergenerational research with a community of refugees who fled Afghanistan during the Soviet occupation in the 1980s. Omidian and Lipson (1992) found that older people lament a lack of respect from younger refugee family members who expect them to work more. Lack of respect is also a concern for older Mayan refugees who fled Guatemala due to violence and now live in California (Harman 1996).

Older persons from Afghanistan, Guatemala, and Southeast Asia used to be sought for knowledge and advice in their countries of origin (Omidian 1996, 116; Harman 1996, 167; Yee 1997, 297), but in the United States, they are perceived as having little practical advice to offer on most affairs, even within the family. Elderly immigrant Afghan women in this country are expected to stay at home, where they clean the house and care for grandchildren. These older women are unhappy in the United States, with problems beyond those afflicting other Afghan refugees, due to loneliness, physical ailments, and extreme dependence on other family members for transportation. Omidian (1996, 177–78) engaged a group of older Afghan women in a participatory project that came to be called "Ladies Day." Every Tuesday, she transported from 7 to 15 older women to a location of their choice, such as a local park, where they could interact with peers. The program helped some women overcome depression and led to a linkage with the local senior center that introduced the women to additional recreational and religious activities.

Family

Some anthropologists working with issues of the aged have focused on family and kinship. The problems include financial and emotional support, companionship, guardianship, transportation, and housing. Colleen Johnson has researched family matters for most of her career, and much of her recent work analyzes data from a longitudinal study of the oldest old (85 and older). Her findings show that a large proportion of the oldest old are profoundly prone to injury but that they live independently. Johnson (2002) concluded that the medical community needs to be sensitive to the frailty of the oldest old and become aware of their greater acceptance of dependency and assistance in some areas of their lives when compared to the younger old.

The rapid increase in the number of oldest old persons in the United States makes their protection an important issue. Many who are impaired have no family members; therefore, they need formal sector protection. Guardianship is one way to provide protective intervention for impaired older persons who are still capable of remaining in the community. Guardianship may be granted to a relative, another person, or an organization when an aged individual needs binding legal and financial protection (Iris 1990, 58). In one study, only a small percentage of the petitions for guardianship in Chicago involved family (Iris 1989, 225). The vast majority of petitioners were not family members.

Madelyn Iris (1989, 219) was the principal investigator on a research team that evaluated the impact of the three-year Guardianship Project in Chicago. Iris, who eventually became a consultant to the project as well as researcher

(1989, 230), provided useful feedback to the agency, subjects, guardianship workers, and administrators who benefited from the Guardianship Project. After the official project ended, she continued to disseminate the findings widely to policymakers and program planners in Illinois and throughout the nation. The beneficiaries of the research comprise a broad range of older Americans:

> Although no one individual will benefit . . . the research has contributed to the development of better service systems and more humane approaches to guardianship for elderly persons. For example, project findings are now being used to help shape recommendations for national standards of guardianship practice and reform of the guardianship process. . . . It is anticipated that some form of federal legislation regulating guardianship will emerge from these efforts. (Iris 1989, 226)

Patricia Slorah has used her anthropological knowledge for successful advocacy in Florida on behalf of the grandparents of children at risk. In 1989, Slorah (1998, 4–6) founded a grassroots support group for grandparents seeking court-ordered visitation rights. The main concern of those grandparents was the protection of grandchildren who were not receiving adequate child care and protection. According to Slorah (2003b), older people will mobilize quickly on two issues: social security and visitation rights with grandchildren.

Slorah utilized her political knowledge and skills to collaborate with and, in some instances, convince Florida state legislators to act (1994a). Slorah gave testimony before the State Judicial Committee on Family Law about the need for new laws supporting grandparents' visitation rights. In 1991, she testified before the U.S. House Select Committee on Aging, Subcommittee on Human Services (Slorah 1994a, 26). Slorah and fellow senior activists advocated relentlessly for grandparents' visitation rights at the state legislature level. Data from her research with Florida grandparents were submitted to the legislature. When those who opposed the bill for visitation rights threatened to block its passage, older activists took to the streets to make other Florida citizens aware of the issues. They were very assertive in communicating their concerns, posting information notices on parked cars and entering restaurants to speak to patrons, one table at a time, to explain their plight and seek support. A Florida state bill supporting grandparents' rights passed in 1990, and a subsequent bill, three years later, broadened those rights (Slorah 1998, 6).

Slorah uses her communication skills strategically and effectively. She has published a very helpful handbook for grandparents, which gives advice to those who are seeking visitation privileges on how to protect endangered grandchildren without resorting to the courts (Slorah 1994b). In the late

1990s, Slorah wrote a shorter pamphlet for grandparents on the history of Florida's Grandparents' Rights Laws that details the benefits of the 1990 and 1993 laws for which Slorah and her group Grandparents' Rights Advocacy Movement (GRAM) advocated so vigorously (Slorah 1994a, 24). Slorah (2003a) more recently wrote *Grandparents' Rights: What Every Grandparent Needs to Know*, which contains legal information and places the issue of grandparents' rights in the context of family changes in this country over the past half century, from nuclear families to numerous alternative forms.

Methods and Strategies of Scholars and Practitioners in Gerontology

Anthropologists have contributed their best thoughts on methods for studying the aged in three volumes of essays on research methods. Anthropologists wrote 12 chapters on methods from their work with older people in a volume edited by Fry and Keith (1986). Jaber Gubrium, a sociologist, and Andrea Sankar, an anthropologist, have edited another book that has a number of chapters on methods that were written by anthropologists and sociologists (1994). In a third volume, which Gubrium edited with James Holstein, anthropologist Claire Wenger (2001) contributed an important essay on how to interview older persons.

The strategies, methods, and techniques used by applied anthropologists for studying the aged are numerous and predominately qualitative. Some anthropologists working with the aged also use quantitative methods, and many applied anthropologists now believe that most projects can best be served by a combination of qualitative and quantitative methods. Participant observation, in-depth interviewing, and focus groups are examples of frequently used qualitative data collection methods. Techniques associated with those particular methods include taking community censuses, making maps, recording audio and visual tapes, taking photos, recording fieldnotes, and managing computers. Portable computers now facilitate entry, storage, and analysis of fieldnotes, and they have enabled the use of new field techniques such as free-recall listing, pile sorting, and triad questionnaires. Probably no anthropologist uses all of these methods and techniques for a single project, but all anthropologists use some combination of them. Specific methods and related issues are addressed in the following sections.

Qualitative and Quantitative Methods

Some general research methodologies described for old age research in Fry and Keith (1986) include cognitive methods and network methodology. Other modes of data collection include participant observation, measurement of functional capacity, life course, life satisfaction, ethnic measurement, and treatment of the aged cross-culturally. Project Age, led by Jennie Keith and Christine Fry, is perhaps the only long-term, comparative qualitative project to be conducted by American anthropologists. Keith and her collaborators were concerned with using methods that would obtain valid cultural data at each site. They utilized systematic research techniques at seven sites in four countries (Keith 1994, 110; Keith et al. 1994). The applied anthropology student today is fortunate to have several excellent sources to consult for an understanding of highly productive qualitative methods that apply to aging and other cultural domains (Weller 1998; Weller and Romney 1988; Schensul, Schensul, and LeCompte 1999).

Project Age participants relied primarily on qualitative data collection. Yet they also used quantitative approaches for such tasks as sampling the populations. John van Willigen, Narender Chadha, and Satish Kedia combined qualitative and quantitative research in their work in a neighborhood of Delhi, India (van Willigen and Chadha 1999; van Willigen, Chadha, and Kedia 1995). Project Age ethnographers switched from qualitative to quantitative and back again throughout the project in order to structure their systematic data collection. They proceeded with coding and interpretation that took into consideration their holistic ethnographic knowledge of each community. The Project Age anthropologists frequently converted their verbal data into numbers during their analysis of data. H. Russell Bernard, an expert in anthropology methods, encourages ethnographers to quantify their qualitative data (2002).

Insider View

Keith suggested that what is most lacking in gerontological research is the point of view of older persons (1994, 105). She echoes the main concern of many gerontological anthropologists when she calls for methods that discover the meaning of older persons' experiences. Keith stated that "the consequences of qualitative data collection for research design span the entire process from application for funding to the interpretation and presentation of data" (106). She urges proposal writers to be very explicit in stating what they will do in each stage of the research process. She also points out that qualitative research is less of a linear process and more of a holistic activity, in contrast to most quantitative data collection and analysis.

Kaufman (1986) and Savishinsky (1991) have written award-winning books on the aged that are based on data that were carefully collected using qualitative methodology. Kaufman (1994, 123) provides guidelines for in-depth interviewing of older people, in which the objective is to elicit what is meaningful to the individuals. The ethnographer must explore topics of interest through open-ended questions that enable the subject to talk easily about the topic during in-depth interviews.

Ethics

Within the field of applied anthropology, the highest ethical standards are required. The Society for Applied Anthropology provides professional and ethical responsibilities that serve as guidelines for applied anthropologists (1983). This statement on ethics covers responsibility to individual subjects, communities, colleagues, students, employers, and society (van Willigen 2002, 59–61). Those anthropologists who are working with the aged are obligated to take the extra step to protect them from any kind of harm because of the vulnerability of older persons. The anthropologist has to be absolutely certain that no confidential information pertaining to older subjects becomes public. It is essential to make certain that no physical or mental harm befalls older informants as a result of action on the part of the anthropologist. Likewise, the social position of older people should not be compromised in any way. And because anthropologists sometimes develop very close friendships with older subjects, it is necessary to be honest with those subjects about everything, which includes keeping them abreast of intentions to maintain contact after the project is completed.

In conducting ethnographic work with the aged, an ethnographer should anticipate questions about the nature of the project and more personal topics. The anthropologist must answer those questions as thoroughly as possible. It is also important to be a good listener, which is part of the reciprocal nature of the interview process. Patience and respect for the elderly subject are essential. The interviewer should not be deterred from projecting an interested, humane demeanor even if an aged subject engages in seemingly irrelevant musings or tires quickly during the interview (Kaufman 1994).

Jeanie Kayser-Jones and Barbara Koenig (1994) have provided strong statements on ethical issues in research situations with the old and the oldest old. Applied anthropologists are bound to protect the anonymity of those subjects, including that of their caregivers and facilities. Kayser-Jones and Koenig summarize a number of the ethical issues that an anthropologist may encounter in gerontological research. Ethnographers conducting applied research might find themselves in the difficult position of deciding whether to intervene in dangerous situations. Sometimes conflicting obligations arise that involve two or more subjects, and the anthropologist has to make a decision about how to act. To illustrate, Kayser-Jones and Koenig (1994, 21–28), who are nurse anthropologists, encountered a situation when an 85-year-old nursing home resident became ill with an acute infection and her life was endangered. Although her condition was treatable, the attending physician and the patient's grown child refused to move her to an acute hospital for appropriate care until six days after the onset of a severe upper respiratory infection with symptoms of a sore throat, fever, difficulty swallowing, and difficulty talking (1994, 21). The anthropologists considered the physician's decision to be a wrong one, and they tried to get available staff personnel to obtain revised orders. On the sixth day of the patient's suffering, the anthropologists successfully urged a staff nurse to call the patient's doctor for an order of intravenous fluids. The patient died, however, two hours after the fluids began to be administered (1994, 23).

Most applied anthropologists have experienced, at least once, the dilemma of conflicting obligations to different individuals or groups. Slorah (1994a), advocating for grandparent visitation rights in Florida, used the media effectively in her efforts to educate the public about antiquated state laws that failed to protect children whose parents were unable to fulfill their parenting role. Yet she turned down invited contributions to *Family Circle* magazine and a national television show when those media giants injected stipulations that would have compromised the privacy of specific older grandparents. By disengaging from those specific commitments, Slorah protected her subjects and their families from probing questions in very public settings about highly personal information.

Collaboration

Collaboration between anthropologists and their subjects is the most important factor in putting knowledge to use (van Willigen 2002, 170). In a somewhat different vein, Kaufman (1994, 128) describes the in-depth interview process as one of collaboration between researcher and informant. Both the ethnographer and the subject bring to the interview their stereotypes and attitudes. In the collaboration, the interviewer takes on the roles of friend, confidant, counselor, and pupil (Kaufman 1994).

Multidisciplinary teams frequently include an applied anthropologist who must be able to collaborate with other team members. Madelyn Iris and Rebecca Berman (1998) were the ethnographers for an early 1990s multidisciplinary project aimed at a better understanding of the lives of elderly residents in Chicago. The overall project became known as Aging in Chicago. The anthropologists emphasized collaboration as they related to the other team members on the project, who were conducting quantitative research and who had little knowledge of anthropology and its approach. One part of Iris and Berman's work was the education of other team members about anthropology. They had to explain, for example, why it is necessary to elicit a working definition of community from the subjects rather than use one imposed by the team, which the other researchers had begun to do.

Applied anthropologists are increasingly conducting research in teams, which are often multidisciplinary, that require collaboration with colleagues and good coordination of the researchers' data collection and analysis. Philip Stafford has used multiple research strategies to ensure successful participatory action among staff researchers, older residents, university students, diverse ethnic components, and other constituencies in the Evergreen Project of Bloomington, Indiana. Among the usual methods of applied anthropology used for the project are participant observation, in-depth interviews, focus groups, and young children's drawings (Stafford 2001b, 558). The Evergreen Project is covered in detail later in this chapter.

Communication

Applied anthropologists working in gerontology need to be good communicators. The anthropologists' part in the Aging in Chicago Project utilized the strategies of communication in particularly effective ways. They met on a regular basis with the interdisciplinary team members for the first year of the project, and when those meetings were discontinued, they maintained regular face-to-face contact with a representative of the funding organization to ensure no departure from the funder's goals through any misunderstanding. Also, they sent out frequent reports to the funder.

Iris and Berman were effective in communicating with the public during the course of their research. They sent out announcements of preliminary findings to the media, which included public television, public radio, and the *Chicago Tribune*. Those media sources featured some of Iris and Berman's findings on the richly diverse aged people of Chicago. The anthropologists provided information and direction for a multisegment (more than 40 parts) television and radio series on aging issues that was presented in 1992.

The communication was quite successful, judging from the way that it has influenced the way that the people of Chicago now look at the aged. Policymakers in Chicago were affected, and the Chicago Department on Aging used the researchers' findings in developing a long-range plan. Other service providers and agency personnel, including local funding organizations, were influenced by the ethnographic findings. The work of Iris and Berman clearly benefited the aged of Chicago.

Themes

Several ethnographers of a past generation sought to develop concepts that would capture the basic organizing principle of a culture (Benedict 1934; Linton 1936; Kluckhohn and Kelly 1945; Herskovits 1955). Anthropologist Morris Opler put forth the theme to "denote a postulate or position, declared or implied, and usually controlling behavior or stimulating activity, which is tacitly approved or openly promoted in a society" (1945, 198). He provided ethnographic examples from two diverse cultures (Opler 1945, 1968). One of the themes he identified for the Chiricahua Apache was "[l]ong life and old age are important goals." Opler (1945, 203–204) described numerous customs of the Chiricahua that demonstrate a high degree of respect for the aged.

Mark Luborsky works with thematic analysis in older populations as a way to get at the insider view of their experiences. Themes can be rich, contextual, and culturally based, and there are a limited number of themes in a culture. Luborsky (1994, 195) considers themes to be explicit and meaningful to the subject. Themes are identified during interviews and from careful reading of fieldnotes and texts; later, at the time of coding, they can become quantified. Luborsky and Rubinstein (1997) found that ethnic identity and practices for Irish, Italian, and Jewish widowers brought about different modes of adaptation in response to grief over the loss of a spouse in old age. Anthropologists may be able to assist psychotherapists and program planners for groups of aged survivors based on their knowledge of themes found to be prominent in adaptive and nonadaptive, self-destructive behavior after a significant loss.

Funding

Applied research on concerns of the aged requires financial support in order to become a reality. Some sources of funding are federal agencies, like the National Institute on Aging. Private foundations have funded some of the most productive research and practice involving applied anthropologists. Those include the American Association of Retired Persons (AARP), which enabled Margaret Perkinson to research and write a manual for caretakers of older people with Alzheimer's disease (2002). Research for the Aging in Chicago Project was funded by the Chicago Community Trust, and the large-scale, long-term Evergreen Project in Bloomington, Indiana, was funded largely by the Retirement Research Foundation of Chicago.

Robert L. Rubinstein (1994) wrote a helpful essay on how to author funding proposals. He provided information on what to include on the topics of sampling, project design, and hypotheses. Quantitative research is still the norm in gerontology, as evidenced by examining the table of contents of most gerontology journals (1994, 68). Rubinstein suggested that a preferred approach for the anthropologist is first to acknowledge that a wide range of research perspectives exist and then to indicate the advantages of qualitative methods for certain purposes, such as capturing meaning and natural categorizations. Rubinstein suggested ways that qualitative researchers can write their research proposals with an approach that is likely to enhance the probability of funding by piquing the interest of quantitatively oriented review board members.

Case Studies of Applied Anthropologists Working for the Aged

This section presents three case studies of applied anthropologists working on behalf of older people in the United States: the first addresses the work of a nurse anthropologist specializing in malnutrition among the aged; the second is about the Evergreen Project, led by an applied anthropologist, which promotes better communities for older people; and the third is a series of projects conceived and conducted by an applied anthropologist for older native people in Alaska. The three anthropologists have been working on projects to empower and assist the aged for several years.

Malnutrition among Older Americans

Kayser-Jones's work in nursing homes demonstrates how research that may appear to be academic can later lead to strong advocacy on behalf of the aged. In the late 1970s, Kayser-Jones (1981) compared the quality of care in an American nursing home with that in a Scottish nursing home. She found that, on every criterion, the Scottish residents were more content with institutional living, even though the American institution selected for study was considered the finest in its city. One area Kayser-Jones explored was the availability and meaning of satisfactory food consumption. On a scale of 1 to 5, the Scottish residents rated their satisfaction with meals a highly commending 4.8. The American residents, in contrast, rated their food with a poor 2.5. Kayser-Jones gave examples of several American residents losing weight and being hungry as a result of being unable to eat the food due to some form of disability. None of those disabilities would have precluded food consumption had proper care been available.

Kayser-Jones found that activities and personal care at the American facility were also lacking in comparison to those in the Scottish facility. She found instances of American staff victimizing residents by theft of personal belongings (1981, 54). In general, she found medical care and nursing care in the American facility to be substantially inferior. From these findings, she offered a critique of the American medical system's failure to provide adequate gerontological care (1981, 122). Residents, family members, and staff of two American nursing homes were the subjects of another, albeit similar, dietary research project in the 1990s. Kayser-Jones again found numerous problems associated with food and eating, not unlike what she had observed years earlier.

In 1997 Kayser-Jones testified before the U.S. Senate Special Committee on Aging as a member of a panel on the "Risk of Malnutrition in Nursing Homes." Kayser-Jones indicated, in her report, the importance of several variables that often contribute to an inadequate diet in long-term care settings. In addition to the poor quality of food, residents objected to the environment in which the food was presented. Some residents, for example, who required assistance at mealtimes did not get any help and had to eat with their fingers (1997, 4). Kayser-Jones presented the senators with graphic descriptions of residents in the process of starving to death due to preventable problems of feeding. In addition, she cited cases of dehydration as a result of insufficient fluid intake.

Kayser-Jones told the senators that analysis showed four factors were negatively associated with nutritional intake in American nursing homes: lack of attention to individual and ethnic food preferences, unrecognized swallowing disorders, oral health problems (for example, few or no teeth), and inadequate staffing. She presented both qualitative and quantitative research data on the opinions of residents, family members, physicians, nurses, and certified nurse aides. All categories of respondents agreed that, because of understaffing, nurse aides lack sufficient time to properly feed the many residents who were unable to leave their rooms for meals. In advocacy of long-term care patients, Kayser-Jones presented a strong case for the need to improve low-cost, low-tech nursing home care to benefit residents throughout the country. She did not explicitly mention "policy," but, considering that her audience was a Senate committee, she was clearly using her anthropological knowledge in an appeal for those policymakers to act.

The Evergreen Institute on Elder Environments

Philip Stafford is director of the Evergreen Institute on Elder Environments in Bloomington, Indiana. He has served Bloomington in that capacity since 1995. The Evergreen Project is an outstanding example of participatory action research that occurs "when individuals of a community join together with a professional researcher to study and transform their community in ways that they mutually value" (van Willigen 2002, 77). Stafford considers the Evergreen Project to be "a community development model for the creation of healthy environments for older adults" (2001a, 137). The project is based upon the propositions that empowerment of older persons to design their communities is essential and that young persons should also be empowered to help create healthy environments for the aged (2001a, 152).

Stafford (2003) is a strong advocate of aging in place. He interacts with and chats with older and younger people in Bloomington with an eye toward enhancing the environment for older persons in particular. Stafford is dedicated to enabling people to create home and to re-create home through memories. He opposes most nursing homes for older people because they erase rather than rekindle memories. He asserts that home and self are intertwined, and his career is devoted to helping older persons live better at home.

Evergreen is a multifaceted, intergenerational program led by Stafford. Various groups and facilities in Bloomington are stakeholders. The project puts an emphasis upon place. Stafford seeks community input at every stage of the project in order to find out what community members want next and how they wish to undertake those ventures. More than a thousand local people have become involved. The research methods employed include, but are not limited to, standard ethnographic procedures of participant observation, focus groups, and a randomized household survey of 200 older persons. The project is designed to promote multigenerational participation in planning a community at the same time that the research data are collected. Research procedures have tapped the vision of all age groups within Bloomington. Input from hundreds of Bloomington households led Stafford and his colleagues to infer that certain community principles were of concern in Bloomington: neighborliness; an environment for growth, learning, and autonomy; a positive image of the environment; diverse and affordable housing options; and an intergenerational retirement community (Stafford 2003, 142).

The Evergreen staff recognized that housing equity, social capital, and principles of cooperation and communitarianism were basic assets in Bloomington. This led to a community-based aging-in-place project that includes five components: a reverse-equity mortgage counseling program, an expanded range of home modification resources and services, a home-sharing clearinghouse, a health and home care program based on principles of cooperation, and new housing options in core neighborhoods (Stafford 2003, 143). Those five project components operate in Bloomington in a community context, with the residents interacting cooperatively and for the mutual benefit of all. The action derived from the design principles established during the first phase of the research by the citizens of Bloomington. Those principles revolve around the idea of aging in place, which was interpreted locally to mean that "the concept of *home* entailed not merely the house, but also the neighborhood and the larger community of Bloomington" (Stafford 2003, 142).

The reverse-mortgage program began with community education on the subject using an AARP video and face-to-face contacts. A local lending institution committed itself to the program. Home modifications also got started with education measures in the form of a full-day seminar. The home-share clearinghouse started off very successfully, with four matches established in the initial half-year between elderly women homeowners and university students. Evergreen Project staff expected that, within the near future, there would be a dozen matches per year. A health cooperative was established, and within three years it had 150 members who pay a membership fee in exchange for health care and health product discounts, health education, and volunteer services in their homes. New housing options were underway by 2001. One option is a 51-unit affordable, intergenerational housing project that will have numerous innovative features, such as ground floor shops and services providing support to the elderly residents. Another project involves the building of small accessible houses, architecturally compatible with the neighborhood, on empty lots in existing neighborhoods.

Stafford is committed to improving the environment in which older persons reside. His philosophy, research, and practice are consistent and effective. Through the Evergreen Project, the elderly people of Bloomington have gained a strong voice for influencing policy decisions within their neighborhoods. Their lives are undoubtedly richer for the experience.

Participatory Research and Communication in Alaska

Several master's degree training programs in applied anthropology are graduating dozens of students every year (Harman, Hess, and Shafe 2001). Erve Chambers (1989, 216), advocating confidence in applied anthropology practitioners with only a master's degree, asserted that it does not require a PhD to fulfill one's duties in most positions for anthropologists outside academia. Kay Branch is practicing with a master's degree in applied anthropology. Her success in serving the native people of Alaska is testimony to the capability of master's level practitioners in applied anthropology.

Branch is the Elder Rural Health Services Planner for the Alaska Native Tribal Health Consortium. Her involvement with aged Alaskans goes back to the mid-1990s. She has worked for several programs funded by the Alaska Commission on Aging, in managerial positions for native elderly nonprofit service programs, and in the evaluation of a program for the Alzheimer's Association (Branch 1998, 14–16). Branch works at the grassroots level in Alaska, a state that is largely inaccessible by road throughout much of the year, making it difficult to visit native villages. She has primarily used participant observation, interviews, and focus groups to understand the perspectives of service recipients and agency personnel. Her anthropology background ensures that she gets a holistic understanding of issues. Branch has communicated successfully to service agency administrators that they must accommodate the native culture in order to get local elders and their caretakers to adopt their agencies' services.

In one of her roles, Branch was manager of a native nonprofit elder services program. The agency provides services to 7,000 individuals in 31 villages located over an area of 40,000 square miles. Eskimos, Athapascans, Aleuts, and Anglos live in the area. One major objective is to provide support services that enable elders to live at home. The work requires cultural knowledge and vigilant overseeing to keep recipients satisfied. The Alaskan Native elders wanted, and now get, for example, more traditional foods, like caribou, among the five weekly meals that are served through the Older Americans Act nutrition program (Branch and Heyano 2002, 87).

Branch is helping develop program training for village caregivers of elders needing assistance in performing activities of daily living. Personal care attendants in rural Alaska help frail elders to live at home instead of in a nursing home. The attendants go into an elder's home and assist with all the person's activities of daily living and other tasks. Their work is valuable for maintaining elders in the home setting. A high turnover of Alaskan Native attendants, who care for those elders whose villages are far from roads, led Branch to invite current and former attendants to Anchorage to discuss in a focus group setting what they liked about the job, what they did not like, and their suggestions on how to retain workers in the future (Branch and Johnson Shearer 2003, 27).

The Native attendants have a strong commitment to keeping the elders at home, and all indicated that they receive emotional satisfaction from caring for the elders. Part of that satisfaction derives from the positive cultural value placed on elder care. In the focus group and during the meal break, the attendants indicated, however, that they experienced a high level of stress, which gets exacerbated by an unfulfilled need for peer support and a lack of respect by physicians and elders' families (Branch and Johnson Shearer 2003, 28–29). The past and present employees suggested pay raises, a benefits package, and continued training as incentives to keep attendants on the job. Branch submitted the research findings to the state with a request to the Alaskan policymakers to change the policy on attendant salary limitations and to provide a benefits package. Branch advocated for agencies to provide meetings and peer support for their workers, and she is on a statewide planning committee, formed in April 2002, to hold an annual conference for direct service workers.

Branch's work involves ongoing advocacy in a state where she is a permanent resident. Through Branch's work, Alaska received funding from the Robert Wood Johnson Foundation to begin plans for assisted living quarters as an alternative to nursing homes in outlying native areas. The unique cultural, geographical, and financial conditions in Alaska pose interesting challenges to assisted-living development that can be overcome with community support and creativity (Branch and Heyano 2002).

Applied Value of Anthropological Work with the Aged

Applied anthropology contributes to policy development for the aged in both direct and indirect ways. Sometimes the association of anthropological data and their input to improve policies and programs is quite obvious. In other instances, the research conducted by anthropologists has no immediate effect on policy or programs, although it is influential in the long term. Some find it tempting to label such work academic rather than applied. Yet in matters pertaining to the aged, the boundary between applied and academic is not as clear as it is in other cultural domains.

Applied anthropology research in association with the aged sometimes entails studying the agencies that provide services. Medical anthropologist George Foster (1969) identified several issues and fallacies that sometimes characterize bureaucratic service organizations. He may have been the first to refer to "bureaucratic [agency] cultures" that impede the delivery of services (1969, 96–106). Foster and Anderson (1978, 233–41) described several ways in which Western medical bureaucracies failed the people they were serving. Some gerontological anthropologists have contributed toward the functioning of bureaucracies or agencies that assist the aged. Usually that is done through program evaluation.

Applied anthropologists often engage in program evaluation. Some research by anthropologists for long-term care facilities involves evaluation that is a step toward policy change. In the course of program evaluation, leaders of a project under review by Iris began to use her as a consultant before the evaluation was completed because her data and interpretations were so helpful. That flexibility on the part of the evaluator which enabled Iris's "useful information" to be utilized while the policy research continued would be rated high by evaluation expert Michael Patton (1990, 491). Renee Rose Shield had considerable impact, described earlier, on the operations of a nursing home she researched in Rhode Island.

A number of applied anthropologists have suggested ways that the federal government should allocate dollars directed toward the care of older people. Stafford (2001a) and Kayser-Jones (1997) have done that while appealing to the humanistic side of caregiving for elders without sacrificing a scientific model. Anthropologists, who take a holistic view of quality of life of the aged, are critical of the government for overreliance on a medical model based upon disease. Kayser-Jones requested that sufficient federal monies be spent on necessary, empathic caring from institution personnel who have long-term residents in their charge.

Jay Sokolovsky (1997) is the editor of a book that is on the must-read bibliography for applied anthropology students interested in gerontology. Contributors to the volume include many leading anthropology figures who work with the aged. All of the chapter authors are advocates for the elderly. Sokolovsky has provided the student and the practitioner with a wealth of resources, in print and on the Internet, in his general introduction and subsequent introductions to the book's six parts.

Future Directions of Applied Anthropology in Gerontology

Applied anthropology has matured considerably over the past 30 years. As anthropology has aged, so has the population, and a situation exists for the short- and long-term future that calls for anthropological resources to help meet the needs of an aging society. The future of anthropology depends largely on its success in making practical contributions to humanity, a growing proportion of which is elderly.

The fact that additional applied anthropologists work with the aged holds promise for improving elders' lives and for the future employment of anthropologists. Gerontological research is, generally, not carried out in short-term contract positions like those that exist in other domains of applied anthropology. Rapport with aged subjects is usually based upon long-term friendship and intimacy. Anthropologists excel at such an approach. Longer periods are necessary for data collection, and for the anthropologist, subjects, and other collaborators to formulate solid plans of action based on good ethnographic research.

Ikels and Beall indicate that anthropologists of the aged were conducting much of their research in the 1980s and 1990s in new settings,

> struggling to justify their research methodology and objectives in terms that non-anthropologist service providers, policymakers, and funders would find acceptable. In the abstract, bringing the anthropological message to people working outside of the discipline is essential and desirable if anthropologists believe in the intrinsic value of an anthropological perspective. In the concrete, it should result in greater understanding of the experience of aging within our own society and in the development of programs and policies that are sensitive to the needs of their intended beneficiaries. (2001, 136)

New opportunities for anthropologist practitioners will likely increase as the recent national trend to support aging-in-place gains momentum. Because anthropologists are well trained in matters relating to community and family, our expertise in those areas fits well with current research and administrative needs. Applied anthropologists are proving that they have the skills to lead community programs, and we will see more such involvement in the future. Stafford and Branch are among the pioneers in bringing benefits to older people through an integrative community-based approach.

After a period of favorable federal policy toward the aged from 1965 to 1980, the government retracted much of its support (Atchley 1991, 63). As responsibility for the care and administration of older people shifts to the 50 states, some have implemented cost-saving programs to treat elders at home and in the community. Older people prefer long-term care options that keep them out of nursing homes, and a number of states are finding it cost-effective to offer alternatives. Long-term care encompasses a number of different programs and services. Among those are special care units within nursing homes, adult foster homes, assisted living, and other models that blend housing and services (Kane, Kane, and Ladd 1998, 159–88). A U.S. Senate Special Committee on Aging (2002, 6–16) report is highly critical of the existing long-term care structure, which still relies heavily on nursing homes, for economic and humanitarian reasons. The average annual cost to care for an individual in a nursing home is $50,000 per year, whereas the cost to provide an elder with home and community-based care is approximately $20,000 per year (16).

We may look forward to more government support for assisted living, where 90 percent of current funding is private. Adult day care is a growing industry, and the government will be under some pressure to devote a larger percentage of the payments to the care of daytime residents (U.S. Senate 2002, 14). This decade, approximately 76 million baby boomers start reaching age 65, the bureaucratically defined threshold of old age (Altman and Shactman 2002, 5). That number is equal to the total population of our country in 1900. As government spending on the aged increases, the amount of taxation is decreasing (88). A shortage in the workforce could compound the difficulty of providing care for the growing number of older persons, and that includes a shortage of professionals (U.S. Senate 2002, 17). In connection with these changes, applied anthropologists, possessing a broad understanding of issues pertaining to the aged, have the potential to become much more prominent in making contributions toward better service for the nation's older population.

Anthropology contributions to family and kinship studies are likely to grow considerably as the societal need to cut costs requires ways to better utilize family members as care providers in conjunction with formal sector services. Anthropologists' knowledge of kinship is the most expansive in the sciences. Anthropologists may assume a more visible role in working with older immigrants and refugees, whose challenges in the United States revolve to a great extent around kin and disruption of traditional kinship roles.

Anthropologists have served effectively for many years as expert witnesses in the nation's courts and before policymaking bodies. Future advocacy for the aged is likely to take the direction of more association with attorneys and lawmakers as litigation in the United States expands and contesting parties seek the knowledge of anthropologists to support their claims. Knowledge utilization factors or strategies interweave with methods and techniques. Barbara Rylko-Bauer and others (1989) as well as van Willigen (2002) have written comprehensive statements on the factors. The strategies for getting one's work utilized by policymakers are associated with factors pertaining to collaboration, agency, community and politics, research process, communication, time, advocacy, and ethical issues.

In future anthropological work with the aged, greater numbers of multidisciplinary projects can be anticipated. Today, anthropologists, from researchers to administrators, are collaborating with people from other disciplines. This contrasts with the "lone ethnographer" approach that was dominant in anthropology a generation ago. The collaborative trend, with researchers working in teams, will continue in gerontology. Applied anthropologists have become well established because of their excellent qualitative research. Anthropologists are also increasingly competent in the quantitative work necessary to provide statistical reports that are familiar to policymakers, physicians, and others who look favorably on quantitative research results. Anthropologists in the gerontology field already have begun to utilize quantitative methods alongside qualitative ones.

Anthropologists have been on the cutting edge in developing qualitative research techniques that satisfy requirements for the validity of data within a specific culture and the reliability for cross-cultural comparisons (Weller 1998; Weller and Romney 1988). Qualitative research, which encompasses the component of meaning, is, without a doubt, essential for successful policymaking. Future applied anthropology research promises to continue to use innovative and high-quality research techniques. Keith aptly summarizes the expectation that "[q]ualitative researchers in gerontology should be leaders in creating research about aging that is both reliable and culturally valid, and both rigorous and humane" (1994, 118). Much has been accomplished, and much more remains to be done.

References

Altman, Stuart H., and David I. Shactman. 2002. *Policies for an aging society.* Baltimore, MD: Johns Hopkins University Press.

Arcury, Thomas A., Sara A. Quandt, Ronny A. Bell, and Mara Z. Vitolins. 2002. Complementary and alternative medicine use among rural older adults. *Complementary Health Practice Review* 7: 167–86.

Atchley, Robert C. 1991. *Social forces and aging: An introduction to social gerontology.* Belmont, Calif.: Wadsworth.

Barker, Judith C., Linda S. Mitteness, and Hayyah B. Muller. 1998. Older home health care patients and their physicians: Assessment of functional ability. *Home Health Care Services Quarterly* 17 (2): 21–39.

Benedict, Ruth. 1934. *Patterns of culture.* Boston: Houghton Mifflin.

———, ed. 1998. *Handbook of methods in cultural anthropology.* Walnut Creek, Calif.: AltaMira.

Bernard, H. Russell. 2002. *Research methods in anthropology: Qualitative and quantitative approaches.* 3rd ed. Walnut Creek, Calif.: AltaMira.

Boyer, Eunice. 1980. Health perception in the elderly: Its cultural and social aspects. In *Aging in culture and society: Comparative viewpoints and strategies,* edited by Christine L. Fry. New York: Praeger.

Branch, P. Kay. 1998. Aging and anthropology in Alaska. *Practicing Anthropology* 20 (2): 14–16.

Branch, P. Kay, and Rose Heyano. 2002. Rural, affordable assisted living in Dillingham, Alaska. *The HIS Primary Care Provider* 27 (5): 85–89.

Branch, P. Kay, and Amanda Johnson Shearer. 2003. Maintaining a long-term care workforce: Ideas from front line workers. *Practicing Anthropology* 25 (2): 27–30.

Caplan, Nathan, Andrea Morrison, and Russell J. Stambaugh. 1975. *The use of social science knowledge in policy decisions at the national level.* Center for Research on Utilization of Scientific Knowledge. Ann Arbor: University of Michigan Institute for Social Research.

Chambers, Erve. 1989. *Applied anthropology: A practical guide.* Prospect Heights, Ill.: Waveland Press.

Cimini, Mary. 2003. Personal communication. Providence, R.I. October 7.

Clark, Margaret, and Barbara Gallatin Anderson. 1967. *Culture and aging: An anthropological study of older Americans.* Springfield, Ill.: Charles C. Thomas.

Eckert, J. Kevin, and Leslie A. Morgan. 2001. Quality in small residential settings. In *Linking quality of long-term care and quality of life,* edited by Linda S. Noelker and Zev Harel. New York: Springer.

Estes, Carroll L. 1979. *The aging enterprise: A critical examination of social policies and services for the aged.* San Francisco: Jossey-Bass.

Estes, Carroll L., and Karen W. Linkins. 2000. Critical perspectives on health and aging. In *Handbook of social studies in health and medicine,* edited by Gary Albrecht and Ray Fitzpatrick. Thousand Oaks, Calif.: Sage Publications.

Foster, George M. 1969. *Applied anthropology.* Boston: Little, Brown.

Foster, George M., and Barbara Gallatin Anderson. 1978. *Medical anthropology.* New York: John Wiley & Sons.

Fry, Christine L. 2003. The life course as a cultural construct. In *Invitation to the life course: Toward a new understanding of later life*, edited by Richard A. Settersten. Amityville, N.Y.: Baywood.

―――. 1999. Anthropological theories of age and aging. In *Handbook of theories of aging*, edited by Vern L. Bengtson and K. Warner Schaie. New York: Springer.

―――, ed. 1981. *Dimensions: Aging, culture, and health.* New York: Praeger.

―――.1980. Toward an anthropology of aging. In *Aging in culture and society: Comparative viewpoints and strategies*, edited by Christine L. Fry. New York: Praeger.

Fry, Christine L., and Jennie Keith, eds. 1986. *New methods for old-age research: Strategies for studying diversity.* New York: Bergin and Garvey.

Gozdziak, Elzbieta. 1988. *Older refugees in the United States: From dignity to despair.* Washington, D.C.: Refugee Policy Group.

Gubrium, Jaber F., and Andrea Sankar, eds. 1994. In *Qualitative methods in aging research.* Thousand Oaks, Calif.: Sage Publications.

Harman, Robert C. 1996. Intergenerational relations among Maya in Los Angeles. In *Selected papers on refugee issues*, vol. 4, edited by Ann Rynearson and James Phillips. Arlington, Va.: American Anthropological Association.

Harman, Robert C., Jim Hess, and Amir Shafe. 2001. Masters of applied anthropology alumni survey. *Anthropology News* 42 (5): 25.

Henderson, J. Neil. 1997. Dementia in cultural context: Development and decline of a caregiver support group in a Latin population. In *The cultural context of aging: worldwide perspectives*, edited by Jay Sokolovsky. Westport, Conn.: Bergin and Garvey.

―――. 1994. Ethnic and racial issues. In *Qualitative methods in aging research*, edited by Jaber F. Gubrium and Andrea Sankar. Thousand Oaks, Calif.: Sage Publications.

Henderson, J. Neil, and Maria D. Vesperi, eds. 1995. *The culture of long-term care: Nursing home ethnography.* Westport, Conn.: Bergin and Garvey.

Herskovits, Melville. 1955. *Cultural anthropology.* New York: Alfred A. Knopf.

Heumann, Leonard F., Mary E. McCall, and Duncan P. Boldy, eds. *Empowering frail elderly people: Opportunities and impediments in housing, health, and support service delivery.* Westport, Conn.: Praeger.

Holmes, Lowell D. 1980. Anthropology and age: An assessment. In *Aging in culture and society: Comparative viewpoints and strategies*, edited by Christine L. Fry. New York: Praeger.

Ikels, Charlotte, and Cynthia Beall. 2001. Age, aging, and anthropology. In *Handbook of aging and the social sciences*, edited by Robert H. Binstock and Linda K. George. San Diego: Academic Press.

Iris, Madelyn A. 1990. Uses of guardianship as a protective intervention for frail, older adults. *Journal of Elder Abuse and Neglect* 2 (3–4): 57–71.

―――. 1989. The use of feedback in a model project: Guardianship for the impaired elderly. In *Making our research useful: Case studies in the utilization of anthropological knowledge*, edited by John van Willigen, Barbara Rylko-Bauer and Ann McElroy. Boulder, Colo.: Westview.

Iris, Madelyn, and Rebecca Berman. 1998. Developing an aging services agenda: Applied anthropology's contribution to planning and development in a community foundation. *Practicing Anthropology* 20 (2): 7–10.

Johnson, Colleen. 2002. http://www.ucsf.edu/dahsm/pages/faculty/johnson.html

Kane, Rosalie A., Robert L. Kane, and Richard C. Ladd. 1998. *The heart of long-term care.* New York: Oxford University Press.

Kaufman, Sharon R. 1994. In-depth interviewing. In *Qualitative methods in aging research*, edited by Jaber F. Gubrium and Andrea Sankar. Thousand Oaks, Calif.: Sage Publications.

———. 1986. *The ageless self: Sources of meaning in late life.* Madison: University of Wisconsin Press.

Kayser-Jones, Jeanie. 1997. Nutritional care in nursing homes: Eating problems, weight loss, and malnutrition. *Risk of malnutrition in nursing homes.* Testimony before the U.S. Senate Special Committee on Aging, October 22. Washington, D.C.: Congressional Forum.

———. 1981. *Old, alone, and neglected: Care of the aged in Scotland and the U.S.* Berkeley: University of California Press.

Kayser-Jones, Jeanie, and Barbara A. Koenig. 1994. Ethical issues. In *Qualitative methods in aging research*, edited by Jaber F. Gubrium and Andrea Sankar. Thousand Oaks, Calif.: Sage Publications.

Keith, Jennie. 1994. Consequences for research procedure. In *Qualitative methods in aging research*, edited by Jaber F. Gubrium and Andrea Sankar. Thousand Oaks, Calif.: Sage Publications.

Keith, Jennie, Christine L. Fry, Anthony P. Glascock, Charlotte Ikels, Jeanette Dickerson-Putnam, Henry C. Harpending, and Patricia Draper. 1994. *The aging experience: Diversity and commonality across cultures.* Thousand Oaks, Calif.: Sage Publications.

Keith, Jennie, and David I. Kertzer. 1984. Introduction. In *Age and anthropological theory*, edited by David I. Kertzer and Jennie Keith. Ithaca, N.Y.: Cornell University Press.

Kinsella, Kevin. 1997. The demography of an aging world. In *The cultural context of aging: Worldwide perspectives*, edited by Jay Sokolovsky. 2nd ed. Westport, Conn.: Bergin and Garvey.

Kluckhohn, Clyde, and William H. Kelly. 1945. The concept of culture. In *The science of man in the world crisis*, edited by Ralph Linton. New York: Columbia University.

Lamm, Rosemarie Santora. 2003a. Seamless and accessible: Action anthropology for the aging. Paper presented at the Society for Applied Anthropology 63rd annual meeting. Portland, Oregon.

———. 2003b. *Who am I? The caregiver.* Lakeland: University of South Florida.

Linton, Ralph. 1936. *The study of man: An introduction.* New York: D. Appleton-Century.

Luborsky, Mark R. 1994. The identification and analysis of themes and patterns. In *Qualitative methods in aging research*, edited by Jaber F. Gubrium and Andrea Sankar. Thousand Oaks, Calif.: Sage Publications.

Luborsky, Mark R., and Robert L. Rubinstein. 1997. The dynamics of ethnic identity and bereavement among older widowers. In *The cultural context of aging: Worldwide perspectives*, edited by Jay Sokolovsky. 2nd ed. Westport, Conn.: Bergin and Garvey.

Omidian, Patricia A. 1996. *Aging and family in an Afghan refugee community.* New York: Garland.

Omidian, Patricia A., and Julience G. Lipson. 1992. Elderly Afghan refugees: Traditions and transitions in northern California. In *Selected papers on refugee issues*, vol. 1, edited by Pamela A. DeVoe. Washington, D.C.: American Anthropological Association.

Opler, Morris E. 1968. The themal approach in cultural anthropology and its application to north Indian data. *Southwestern Journal of Anthropology* 24 (3): 215–27.

———. 1945. Themes as dynamic forces in culture. *American Journal of Sociology* 51 (3): 198–206.

Patton, Michael Quinn. 1990. *Qualitative evaluation and research methods*. Newbury Park, Calif.: Sage Publications.

Pavalko, Eliza. 2002. Life course. In *Encyclopedia of aging*, edited by David J. Ekerdt. New York: Macmillan, Thompson, Gale.

Perkinson, Margaret A. 2002. *Nurturing a family partnership: Alzheimer's home care guide*. Washington, D.C.: AARP Andrus Foundation.

Quandt, Sara A., and Thomas A. Arcury. 2001. The rural elderly. In *Aging and public health*, edited by G. Lesnoff-Caravaglia. Springfield, Ill.: Charles C. Thomas.

Rubinstein, Robert L. 1994. Proposal writing. In *Qualitative methods in aging research*, edited by Jaber F. Gubrium and Andrea Sankar. Thousand Oaks, Calif.: Sage Publications.

Rylko-Bauer, Barbara, John van Willigen, and Ann McElroy. 1989. Strategies for increasing the use of anthropological research in the policy process: A cross-disciplinary analysis. In *Making our research useful: Cases studies in the utilization of anthropological knowledge*, edited by John van Willigen, Barbara Rylko-Bauer and Ann McElroy. Boulder, Colo.: Westview.

Savishinsky, Joel. 2000. *Breaking the watch: The meanings of retirement in America*. Ithaca, N.Y.: Cornell University Press.

———. 1991. *The ends of time: Life and work in a nursing home*. New York: Bergin and Garvey.

Schensul, Stephen L., Jean J. Schensul, and Margaret D. LeCompte. 1999. *Essential ethnographic methods: Observations, interviews and questionnaires*. Walnut Creek, Calif.: AltaMira.

Settersten, Richard A. 1999. *Lives in time and place: The problems and promises of developmental science*. Amityville, N.Y.: Baywood.

Shield, Renee Rose. 1998. Real world anthropology in two settings: A nursing home and a health care policy project. *Practicing Anthropology* 20 (2): 10–13.

———. 1997. Liminality in an American nursing home: The endless transition. In *The cultural context of aging: Worldwide perspectives*, edited by Jay Sokolovsky. 2nd ed. Westport, Conn.: Bergin and Garvey.

Shield, Renee Rose, and Edward Zesk. 1997. *Aging 2000: Case study*. Report for the Health Care Financing Administration.

Simmons, Leo W. 1945. *The role of the aged in primitive society*. New Haven, Conn.: Yale University.

Slorah, Patricia P. 2003a. *Grandparents' rights: What every grandparent needs to know*. Bloomington, Ind.: 1st Books [electronic publication].

———. 2003b. Personal communication, February 6, 2003. Tarpon Springs, Florida.

———. 1998. Grandparents, gray power and grassroots organizing: Implications for anthropologists. *Practicing Anthropology* 20 (2): 4–6.

———. 1994a. Grandparents of children at risk for abuse and neglect: A policy analysis. Unpublished dissertation, University of South Florida.

———. 1994b. *Grandparent talk*. Tarpon Springs, Fla.

Society for Applied Anthropology. 1983. *Professional and ethical responsibilities.* Revised from 1949. Washington, D.C.: SFAA.

Sokolovsky, Jay. 1997. Aging, family and community development in a Mexican peasant village. In *The cultural context of aging: Worldwide perspectives*, edited by Jay Sokolovsky. 2nd ed. Westport, Conn: Bergin and Garvey.

Stafford, Philip B. 2003. *Gray areas: Ethnographic encounters with nursing home culture.* Santa Fe: School of American Research.

———, ed. 2001a. When community planning becomes community building: Place-based activism and the creation of good places to grow old. In *Empowering frail elderly people: Opportunities and impediments in housing, health, and support service delivery*, edited by Leonard F. Heumann, Mary E. McCall, and Duncan P. Boldy. Westport, Conn.: Praeger.

———. 2001b. Teaching the ethnography of aging. *Educational Gerontology* 27 (7): 557–67.

U.S. Census Bureau. 2004a. Table 94. International database. Retrieved from http://www.census.gov/ipc/www/idbagg.html

———. 2004b. Table 2a. Projected population of the United States, by age and sex: 2000 to 2050. Retrieved from http://www.census.gov/ipc/www/usinterimproj

U.S. Senate. 2002. Special Committee on Aging. *Long-term care report: Findings from Committee hearings.* 107th Cong., 2nd Sess.

van Willigen, John. 2002. *Applied anthropology: An introduction.* 3rd ed. Westport, Conn.: Bergin and Garvey.

van Willigen, John, and Narender K. Chadha. 1999. *Social aging in a Delhi neighborhood.* Westport, Conn.: Bergin and Garvey.

van Willigen, John, Narender K. Chadha, and Satish Kedia. 1995. Personal networks and sacred texts: Social aging in Delhi, India. *Journal of Cross-Cultural Gerontology* 10 (3): 175–98.

Weller, Susan C. 1998. Structured interviewing and questionnaire construction. In *Handbook of methods in cultural anthropology*, edited by H. Russell Bernard. Walnut Creek, Calif.: AltaMira.

Weller, Susan C., and A. Kimball Romney. 1988. *Systematic data collection.* Qualitative research methods series, vol. 10. Thousand Oaks, Calif.: Sage Publications.

Wenger, G. Claire. 2001. Interviewing older people. In *Handbook of interview research: Context and methods*, edited by Jaber F. Gubrium and James A. Holstein. Thousand Oaks, Calif.: Sage Publications.

Wright, Bernadette M. 2002. Long-term care. In *Encyclopedia of aging*, vol. 2, edited by David J. Ekerdt. New York: Macmillan, Thompson, Gale.

Yee, Barbara W. K. 1997. The social and cultural context of adaptive aging by Southeast Asian elders. In *The cultural context of aging: Worldwide perspectives*, edited by Jay Sokolovsky. 2nd ed. Westport, Conn.: Bergin and Garvey.

11 Emerging Trends in Applied Anthropology

John van Willigen and Satish Kedia

As substantiated by the essays of this collection, applied anthropologists today are engaged in a variety of diverse settings, which we have called domains of application. They work for domestic and international organizations; municipal, state, and federal agencies; philanthropic and consumer groups; grassroots and advocacy groups; and private consulting firms and corporations. In the future, the scope of settings in which applied anthropologists work is likely to expand even further as the discipline continues to evolve. Although much of this growth comes from within the community of applied anthropologists, external forces have had and will continue to have a significant influence on the discipline's future as well. This concluding chapter briefly summarizes some of the key trends in the field: demographic shifts affecting employment opportunities, creative adaptation to new work contexts, interdisciplinary exchange in applied work, the changing relationships with study subjects, and contributions of applied work to basic anthropology. Additional perspectives on the topic are discussed in a special issue of *Human Organization* entitled "The Future Lies Ahead: Applied Anthropology in Century XXI" (Hackenberg and Hackenberg 2004).

Demographic Shifts Affecting Employment Opportunities

Demographic changes have long affected anthropologists' employment opportunities. World wars, migration, and globalization have resulted in population fluxes that have most indelibly marked contemporary anthropology. About 50 years ago, a number of key interlocking academic employment and demographic trends in the United States began having a significant impact on anthropology, which in turn altered the possibilities for applied work—most notably, the rapid expansion of the college population following the flood of servicemen returning from World War II. In 1944, the U.S. government started providing veterans with education subsidies through the GI Bill, leading to an influx of college students and a greater need for university professors. Returning GIs also led to the baby boom, the unprecedented surge of births in the United States from 1946 to 1964. When the children born in this era reached college age, the need for professors once again expanded the academic market for anthropologists.

Ultimately, as this population bulge passed into subsequent life stages, the need for faculty decreased, leading to a decline in the academic job market in the early 1970s, when the annual production of anthropologists with graduate degrees became greater than the employment needs of university departments. As a result, in the last 20 years, almost half of new anthropology PhDs, and the majority of those with master's degrees, have moved into careers outside of academia. Although these conditions have been tempered somewhat by the imminent retirement of the baby boom generation of academic anthropologists, other economic and social changes in postsecondary education have mandated increased use of part-time personnel rather than full-time, tenure-track faculty. At the same time, many anthropologists have chosen careers outside academia of their own volition rather than by necessity because work in the private sector has many attractive features not characteristic of a university post, including higher pay, limited or no teaching, and less pressure to publish.

In the last 30 years, the rapid rise of immigrants to the United States has also greatly affected anthropology, calling attention to the expanding local immigrant and ethnic communities at home instead of those in Third World nations. The ensuing backyard anthropology addresses the newer issues of ethnic communities, such as first-generation Americans' relationships with their immigrant parents and relatives and their sociocultural ties to the countries of their ancestors. For example, the growing Hispanic-American immigrant community has impacted U.S. society, economics, and politics by compelling change in education, language, welfare, health care, trade, legislation, and even election of public officials, who now clamor to garner the votes of this expanding minority group.

Simultaneously, the landscape of traditional anthropological work has been drastically altered by the expanding influence of globalization in business, government, and national and international commerce. Large multinational corporations and international aid organizations now conduct business in multiple countries, requiring personnel with an understanding of many cultures, societies, and economies to be successful in their endeavors. Thus, these demographic shifts, as well as the forces of globalization, have not only led to new types of employment for anthropologists but have also altered the face of much anthropological work and the discipline through the growing domains of application. The domains discussed in this anthology reflect, in part, the effects of the demographic shifts mentioned here. Gerontology and anthropology's contribution to understanding aging as a sociocultural phenomenon as well as a biological one is gaining focus partly because the baby boomers are reaching retirement age. The education, nutrition, and health and medicine domains also are growing in scope as a result of the baby boomers, migrations, and economic development. The scope of research and practice in agriculture, environment, business and industry, development, and involuntary resettlement are all advancing, at least in part due to economic globalization, which continues to expand the opportunities for applied anthropologists. In addition, there are many other domains, such as substance abuse, criminal justice, forensic science, human rights, cultural resource management, fisheries, forestry and wildlife, urban development and housing, and mass media where a significant number of applied anthropologists are engaged and are making critical contributions.

Creative Adaptation to New Work Contexts

The economic and professional incentives that motivate graduate education and structure opportunities in the job market are core forces that determine the basic nature of any discipline. Because these incentives may be slow to develop, there is a lag between what anthropology professionals actually do in the field and what is considered mainstream academic anthropology. However, it is clear that the newly emerging work opportunities have profoundly affected anthropology in general. Applied anthropologists have responded in innovative ways to the challenges in these new work contexts, generating new knowledge and methodologies. These responses have stimulated change in anthropology as a discipline, although in ways that may not be immediately evident.

Social programs and policy requirements frequently generate resources for research, which, in turn, have led to new work opportunities for anthropologists. Although anthropological work is not just a response to the market or based solely on opportunism, it is nevertheless useful to consider those forces that motivate our work at any given time. Some practitioners have suggested redefining our enterprise as "public anthropology," in order to move "our frame of reference to beyond the discipline: start with the world's problems—as they come to us—rather than focusing on the discipline's traditional formulations that do little more than perpetuate the status quo" (Borofsky 2002, 474). Peggy Reeves Sanday, working with Paula Sabloff, has suggested the conceptual framework of public interest anthropology (PIA) be employed, an approach that merges theory, analysis, and problem solving in a commitment to positively impact human lifeways, with a focus on conveying the anthropological perspective to the masses for consumption and debate (Sanday 2004). There is no doubt that applied anthropologists' skills in employing cultural knowledge, grounded in sound ethnographic method, to solve real-life problems is highly relevant, but one of the future goals must be to move anthropology into the sphere of public discourse and to do so in ways that the layperson can comprehend.

Although globalization is not univocally positive and comes with its own set of problems, it has nonetheless created opportunities for applied anthropologists, as illustrated by the contributors to this anthology. Robert Rhoades describes how anthropologists have been and continue to be in demand to identify and advocate local cultural, environmental, and economic factors that promote well-being and sustainability in response to global large-scale transnational agribusiness. The broad resurgence of ethnic identity movements and religious fundamentalism, as well as the periodic onslaught of large-scale natural disasters, continues to give rise to areas where applied anthropologists can contribute as part of established organizations in the development field. Peter Little points out that a number of these employment opportunities are now being created on the institutional level, through the World Bank, the International Monetary Fund, and a proliferation of nongovernmental organizations, such as Oxfam-UK and World Vision International. In such settings, practitioners assess the regional impact of these organizations' economic reform and investment programs.

Further, Anthony Oliver-Smith explores the key role played by applied anthropologists in mitigating the severe impact of development-induced displacement and resettlement (DIDR) upon communities deprived of both livelihood and human rights. He suggests that in the future, the field will continue to address the challenges presented by DIDR at the local community and project level, in national and international political discourse, and in the policy frameworks of multilateral institutions. The specific knowledge and analytical skills of applied anthropologists will be crucial in critiquing current development models, which assume the necessity of relocation without questioning the scope of initiatives that cause such disruption in individuals' lives and their environment. Similarly, David Himmelgreen and Deborah Crooks predict that in the twenty-first century, nutritional anthropologists will continue to use their expertise to resolve the ongoing concerns of public health officials and policymakers at the local, state, and international levels. Such practitioners will address the problem of malnutrition and nutrient deficiencies, the rise of obesity-related diseases, the connection of food insecurity to under- and overnutrition, the impact of globalization on the consumption of traditional food versus junk food, and the development of culturally competent nutritional programs for diverse populations.

Currently, applied work requires practitioners to leave the legend of the lone anthropologist behind and to become skilled in working collaboratively and with greater diplomacy. Governments are not as willing to allow anthropologists to work wherever and whenever they please, and the nature of applied work increasingly demands that anthropologists be "members of a team of local social scientists" (Wolf 2002, 7). This team may consist of other professionals or scientists, national or regional officials, and members of the community being studied. It is essential for applied anthropologists to effectively act in concert with all of these parties to "share data and cope with the assertion of quite different expectations on what questions are important" (Wolf 2002, 7). For anthropology, collaboration, in particular broader community involvement or outreach, has resulted in the need for broader dissemination of research results, increased skills in communication of findings to new audiences in new formats, and employment of techniques from other fields.

For example, Kedia's evaluation of substance abuse treatment effectiveness in Tennessee, which is used to inform state policy, involves partnerships with many stakeholders. The complex and lengthy tasks of evaluation require not only collaboration with treatment providers (private, nonprofit, and faith-based) but also with funding arms of the government, Tennessee Bureau of Alcohol and Drug Abuse Services officials, regional organizations that deal with substance abuse issues, clients, clients' families and advocates, project staff, information systems specialists, and software and Web developers. As evaluator, he "facilitate[s] stakeholders' active and effective participation in the process" by offering his guidance and expertise in "scientific knowledge, systematic methodology, research rigor, and skills that many stakeholders may not possess" (Kedia 2005). These collaborative efforts only scarcely resemble traditional anthropological pursuits but result in multiple policy reports, bulletins, and other forms of communication that disseminate research results to the stakeholders to facilitate desired changes and to encourage continued partnerships.

Interdisciplinary Exchange in Applied Work

All social science disciplines have been altering their assumptions and procedures as a result of increased interdisciplinary exchange. Although anthropology has had a significant effect on other disciplines, it has also been influenced by them. Probably the most striking changes in anthropology include the addition of more time-effective methodologies, including rapid assessment procedures (RAP) and collective interviewing strategies, such as focus groups (Scrimshaw and Hurtado 1987; van Willigen and Finan 1991). Originally a marketing tool, the use of focus groups to collect data is now commonplace in many of the social sciences.

At the same time, ethnographic approaches and the culture concept of traditional anthropology have been increasingly used outside the discipline. Over the last two decades, ethnographic research practices changed from being a mystery for persons in other fields to being mainstream methodology. For a number of years, van Willigen has given a series of guest lectures on ethnographic methods for a program evaluation course taught in the College of Education at the University of Kentucky. When he first started delivering this talk, many students seemed puzzled by the content of the lecture, often asking whether it was possible to generalize from this kind of data, because their own dominant research technique had always been the random-sample survey with results analyzed using statistical methods. Through the years, however, their awareness and enthusiastic acceptance of an ethnographic approach has become clear. This trend is also evident in the practices of new graduates and professionals in related disciplines, in which ethnographic or qualitative methods have gradually become common. In fact, it is not unusual to find edited volumes on qualitative methods in which virtually all the authors are sociologists or to find textbooks on the subject written by scholars in communication or culture and media studies.

The influence of anthropology's theoretical content, particularly the culture concept, has been extensively used in other disciplines, and it has been recast in the process. One result of this cross-fertilization has been fewer distinctions between the knowledge produced by anthropologists and that produced by those trained in other areas. One could argue that there is a coming together of ideas from various disciplines to form what might be thought of as a new synthesis of concepts, with loose networks of people working in the applied and academic realms that share ideas and influence each other even though they were trained in different fields. This interdisciplinary trend has significant implications for current and future applied anthropologists in many domains of application. Practitioners will need to master methodologies and technical terminology from a variety of fields to be able to work collaboratively. In addition, they shoulder the responsibility to articulate exactly what an anthropologist can bring to the various settings in which they might be employed.

This is particularly true in the contemporary information-driven government and corporate world, where job classifications and requirements are being broadened rather than narrowed to a specific expertise or skill set. In her chapter on the business and industry domain, Marietta Baba argues that anthropologists' fine-grained analysis of carefully recorded qualitative data, informed by knowledge of human biological and cultural systems, is ideally suited to understanding those subcultures reflected in consumer behavior and emergent in corporate organizations. In particular, anthropologists can add tremendous value to modern business operations through their understanding of culture in holistic terms both within society and in specific settings (e.g., the corporation itself), even when the researcher may not have knowledge of that setting. Their holistic perspective integrates a large range of social and behavioral phenomena to explain culture, cultural changes, and the roots of cultural patterns. Baba suggests that anthropologists' knowing how to learn about other cultures is a great asset; their grasp of best practices in ethnographic research, their ability to depict human experience in nuanced and innovative ways, and their commitment to protect the individuals being studied make anthropologists uniquely suited to initiate productive activities and bring humane approaches to (in Baba's case) the corporate work environment.

This is equally applicable to other domains, such as the study of the classroom as a cultural and social space. As educational anthropologist Nancy Greenman demonstrates in her chapter, anthropologists are uniquely trained to meet the pedagogical challenges of an increasingly multicultural and multiracial society via their ability to grasp the complexities of student-teacher relations and, particularly, their understanding of historical inequities and systematic disenfranchisement of minority groups in public education in the United States. In his chapter on the environment, Thomas McGuire argues that anthropologists, with their substantive expertise in ethnographic techniques as well as their understanding of the geopolitical dimensions of environmental change, are increasingly being called upon to ensure that a healthy and productive life—in harmony with nature—is indeed a human entitlement. Whatever the approach and subfield of environmental anthropology, McGuire notes, practitioners should always strive to supplement cultural knowledge at local levels with the specific political economy of the region in mind. His work illustrates how ethnographic practices can be used to take local research beyond the realm of statistics through the creation of regionally placed teams that provide real-time ground-truthing of economic data. In the future, the unique capacities of anthropologists will become more familiar to consumers of research services, especially those that involve humans and their communities.

In policy research today, it is far easier to sell ethnography than ever before, in part because policy work demands a firm knowledge of the empirical realities for which ethnographic methods are most appropriate. The use of this approach in program evaluation is common and, in some cases, virtually required. The particular training of anthropologists has always been well suited to policy work, a conviction echoed by a number of our contributors. In their discussion of anthropology and health care, Linda Whiteford and Linda Bennett contend that applied medical anthropology's understanding of the cultural and biological bases of disease, as well as how unequal distribution of resources can impact epidemiological patterns, will be crucial for effective public health campaigns, such as those addressing the HIV/AIDS pandemic. Similarly, in their chapter, David Himmelgreen and Deborah Crooks emphasize that, because sociocultural and biological factors affect how humans select and consume food, anthropologists' expertise in both makes them especially valuable to public health officials who require reliable and culturally specific research data to formulate nutritional policy. And as Robert Harman explains, anthropologists' skills in conducting ethnographic surveys and employing qualitative methods are very useful in developing the close rapport with informants required for advocacy on behalf of frequently disenfranchised but increasingly sizeable groups in the United States, such as the elderly, racial/ethnic minorities, refugees, and immigrants.

Changing Relationships with Study Subjects

Throughout the development of applied anthropology, the relationship between practitioners and the people they study has changed substantially, paralleling the development of anthropology itself. In some sense, the history of anthropology, both basic and applied, is the history of the power relationships between anthropologists and their study subjects. The fact that anthropology is a product of colonialism, when it was a tool used for the control and domination of subjects, is still central to popular memory of this discipline. Since World War II, these power relationships have changed, and the stance of basic and applied anthropology has adjusted accordingly regarding the communities and individuals studied. As Renato Rosaldo put it, this transformation comprises for the researcher new conceptions of the objects of analysis, the language of analysis, and the position of the analyst (1993, 37).

The mainstream anthropological response to this essentially postmodern dilemma is to refigure ethnographic practice as reflexive. As Marcus and Fischer (1986) argued, ethnography is not only about those studied but is also a kind of cultural critique of the anthropologist's culture. In addition, there currently is a tendency to change the mode of representation in the anthropological narrative in order to highlight the voice(s) of those being studied. Increasingly the path followed in applied anthropology has been to work with study subjects in a more collaborative or participatory way. In this approach, the goals of the anthropologists become aligned with those of the community and individuals being studied through the anthropologists' sharing of their skills and knowledge. Thereby, anthropologists can help empower individuals, transforming the study population from an object to be known to a subject who can control. Applied anthropologists become an auxiliary to the naturally occurring community leadership, and they serve in another capacity, as cultural brokers or, in a more neutral role, as co-culture mediators or liaisons, in order to emphasize the conceptual equality of the anthropologists' and the studied population's cultural systems.

Several of the chapters in this volume identify anthropologists working with the local communities and their cultures as partners, indicating that those studied are not only subjects but also individuals who can have greater impact and control over what is being done in their communities. Robert Rhoades, for example, advocates that agricultural anthropologists develop a professional relationship with a public constituency to the extent seen in other fields like economics, law, or education, as a means to declare its [anthropology's] relevance through action. Thomas McGuire promotes anthropologists' collaboration with local communities to develop an ethno-cartography for use as a tool for political mobilization, to gain state recognition of indigenous rights and to protect biodiversity. Robert Harman notes that ethnographic practices and qualitative methods require long-term commitment and close rapport with informants and that, in aging anthropology, both of these approaches are much easier to achieve if practitioners work on a more equal footing with the study population. In addition, scholars from non-Western countries are often being trained in Western universities, and they are beginning to contribute to the scholarship not only on their own cultures but also on Western cultures. Peter Little foresees development anthropologists as having invaluable opportunities to actively collaborate with Third World scholars, for whom the distinctions among theory, method, and practice may be less clear in light of their direct involvement in the socioeconomic and political changes of their countries. Increasingly, the key relationship is not between the anthropologist and the discipline but between the anthropologist and the partnering community.

Contributions of Applied Work to Basic Anthropology

The actions of the working population of anthropologists—what they publish and teach, which associations they join or professional meetings they attend, as well as their exchanges with peers and personal networks—lead to transformation in the discipline. Policy research needs, a cornerstone of applied work, invariably contribute to innovations in basic anthropology because of the opportunities for employment and research funding that emerge and create further incentives. These developments often challenge orthodoxy within the discipline, which in turn produces gate-keeping behaviors calculated to exclude applied anthropology. It is surprising to discover that topics and methods, now regarded as integral to the discipline as conventional anthropology, were once subject to the question "But is it really anthropology?" and were marginalized. A good example would be the development of medical anthropology, which arose outside of academic departments as a research activity to help inform public health programs after World War II. For a time it did not seem necessary to use the modifier "applied" with medical anthropology. It was thought of as an applied field by definition. Today, medical anthropology has both applied and theoretical advocates.

One factor that limits the impact of applied anthropologists on the discipline is that practitioners have a tendency not to write and publish as much as those who work in academic settings. Often they either do not have time or are simply not confronted with the same publish-or-perish pressure that their academic colleagues face. In many instances, practitioners' written work may be proprietary or confidential and not available for public use or for journal publication. Equally prohibitive is the tendency of journal editors or reviewers to reject manuscripts that are perceived as not being academic. As a result of these factors, many applied anthropologists have given up on publishing in traditional anthropology journals, or they engage in code switching, writing on their applied work for certain stakeholders, then altering the writing to meet the requirements for inclusion in traditional anthropological scholarly venues. Applied practitioners' links to basic anthropology may be quite limited; some find it irrelevant to communicate back to the discipline when much of what is published in core anthropological journals contains little material of immediate use to applied work. Nevertheless, there are periodicals such as *Human Organization, Practicing Anthropology,* and the *High Plains Applied Anthropologist* that provide venues of information exchange for applied anthropologists. Also in recent years, the publication of applied materials on Web sites has greatly increased the opportunity for communicating findings of applied work.

Conclusion

This anthology suggests that key trends in applied anthropology reflect a new synthesis, in which knowledge from a variety of disciplines is combined to address human problems and challenges in myriad settings. At the same time, this synthesis maintains a core of traditional anthropological concepts and methods, including an emphasis on the importance of local knowledge; participation and empowerment of the community; increased critical reflection on the underlying structures causing the problems with which applied anthropologists deal; and ongoing concerns about sustainability of the environment, cultures, programs, and livelihoods. Future trends, as Robert Rhoades notes in this volume, exemplify this kind of synthesis: spatial and socioeconomic complexity of innovations involving multiscalar research, integration of computer-based approaches (e.g., Global Information Systems and simulation modeling) with indigenous knowledge, and a new range of issues arising from the transformation of local actions to large-scale transnational operations.

Increasingly, those in academia are under pressure to demonstrate the applied significance of their intellectual endeavors, for politicians and policymakers are demanding that university personnel engage in more activities benefiting society. At the very least, most funding agencies—the source of nearly all anthropological inquiry—require researchers to document the pertinence, scope, and impact of their proposed activity in practical terms. This will entail more emphasis on equipping graduate students with skills appropriate for the real world (see Lamphere 2004), and it will require the communication of applied anthropologists' skills and abilities to an audience beyond the discipline and its limited community of practitioners.

The future of applied anthropology lies in the growth of theoretical and practical work in various domains and in establishing their relevance for solving societal problems. As the various authors in this book suggest, successful applied anthropological work relies on collaboration and integration of the techniques and vocabularies of other fields, development of the most effective and innovative anthropological methodologies, increased facility in the use of emerging technologies, and mobilization of strong communication skills to best disseminate information to a lay public. Applied practitioners and academicians alike must continue to be active and engaged proponents of the diversity and vitality of human lifeways by forming and advocating culturally appropriate policies, programs, and actions that will alleviate the social, economic, health, and technological problems facing our ever-changing global society.

References

Borofsky, Robert. 2002. The four subfields: Anthropologists as mythmakers. *American Anthropologist* 104 (2): 463–80.

Hackenberg, Robert A., and Beverly H. Hackenberg, eds. 2004. The future lies ahead: Applied anthropology in century XXI. Special issue, *Human Organization* 63 (4).

Kedia, Satish. 2005. Facilitating group communication in empowerment evaluation: A case study of substance abuse treatment effectiveness. In *Facilitating group communication in context: Innovations and applications with natural groups*, vol. 2, *Facilitating group task and team communication*, edited by Lawrence Frey. Cresskill, N.J.: Hampton Press.

Lamphere, Louise. 2004. The convergence of applied, practicing, and public anthropology in the 21st century. *Human Organization* 63 (4): 431–43.

Marcus, George E., and Michael Fischer. 1986. *Anthropology as cultural critique: An experimental moment in the human sciences.* Chicago: University of Chicago Press.

Rosaldo, Renato. 1993. *Culture and truth: The remaking of social analysis.* Boston: Beacon.

Sanday, Peggy Reeves. 2004. *Public interest anthropology: A model for engaged research.* Retrieved February 17, 2005, from http://www.sas.upenn.edu/~psanday/SARdiscussion%20paper.65.html

Scrimshaw, Susan C. M., and Elena Hurtado. 1987. *Rapid assessment procedures for nutrition and primary health care.* Tokyo: United Nations University.

van Willigen, John. 2002. *Applied anthropology: An introduction.* 3rd ed. Westport, Conn.: Bergin and Garvey.

van Willigen, John, and Timothy J. Finan, eds. 1991. *Soundings: Rapid and reliable research methods for practicing anthropologists.* Special issue, National Association for the Practice of Anthropology Bulletin 10.

Wolf, Margery. 2002. Future of anthropology: An ethnographer's perspective. *Anthropology News* 43 (6): 7.

Index

About the Editors and Contributors

Marietta L. Baba is Dean of the College of Social Science and Professor of Anthropology at Michigan State University. She also holds an appointment as Adjunct Professor in the Department of Management at the Eli Broad College of Business. Previously, Dr. Baba was Professor and Chair of the Department of Anthropology and founding director of the Business and Industrial Anthropology program at Wayne State University in Detroit. From 1994 to 1996, Dr. Baba was Program Director of the National Science Foundation's industry-funded research program entitled *Transformations to Quality Organizations*. She is the author of 70 scholarly and technical publications in the fields of organizational culture, technological change, and evolutionary processes. In 1998, she was appointed to serve on Motorola's global advisory Board of Anthropologists, the first of its kind in the United States. Dr. Baba was a founding member and past President of the National Association for the Practice of Anthropology (NAPA, 1986–88), a section of the American Anthropological Association (AAA). She served on the Executive Committee and Board of Directors of the AAA (1986–88). In addition, she was appointed Advisory Editor for Organizational Anthropology for *American Anthropologist* (1990–93). Dr. Baba holds an MBA (with highest distinction) from the Advanced Management Program at Michigan State University's Eli Broad Graduate School of Management, and a PhD in physical anthropology from Wayne State University (doctoral research conducted in the School of Medicine). She is listed in *Who's Who in America* (1992–present).

Linda A. Bennett is a Professor of Anthropology and Associate Dean of the College of Arts and Sciences at The University of Memphis. She completed her PhD in Anthropology at American University in 1976. Past president of the Society for Applied Anthropology, the National Association of Professional Anthropologists, and the Washington Association of Professional Anthropologists, and co-founder of the Alcohol & Drug Study Group of the Society for Medical Anthropology, Dr. Bennett is currently a member of the Executive Board of the American Anthropological Association. In collaboration with other leaders in applied anthropology programs in 2000, Dr. Bennett also founded the Consortium of Practicing and Applied Anthropology (COPAA) Programs. She is co-editor of *The American Experience with Alcohol* (1985), co-author of *The Alcoholic Family* (1987), editor of *A Russian-English Language Guide for Adopting Families*, and author of *Personal Choice in Ethnic Identity Maintenance: Serbs, Croats, and Slovenes in Washington, D.C.* (1978). Dr. Bennett has conducted fieldwork in medical anthropology in the former Yugoslavia, especially Croatia, and in the United States and ethnic identity research in Washington, D.C., and Pittsburgh. Recently she has worked on a collaborative study of neighborhood rituals and routines in Memphis neighborhoods. At The University of Memphis, she has received the Meritorious Faculty Award in the College of Arts and Sciences (1999) and the Board of Visitors' Eminent Faculty Award (2003).

Deborah L. Crooks received her PhD in anthropology from SUNY Buffalo in 1992 and was a National Institutes of Health Public Health Service Fellow at the University of Kentucky from 1992 to 1995. She is currently an Associate Professor of Anthropology and Behavioral Science, as well as an Affiliated Faculty in Women's Studies, at the University of Kentucky. Dr. Crooks's work in nutritional anthropology spans the globe. She has done research with Mopan Maya in Belize on the context of child growth and development and its relation to school achievement; on the political-economic context of nutritional status among schoolchildren in eastern Kentucky; and on the production of child growth and nutrition in a fishing community in the Philippines undergoing significant socioeconomic change (with colleague Francisco A. Datar). Her current research, with UK colleague Lisa Cliggett, takes place in Zambia, where they are focusing on the relationship between livelihood security and health and nutrition security among Gwembe Tonga migrants. Dr. Crooks has published her research in *American Anthropologist, Medical Anthropology Quarterly,* and *American Journal of Physical Anthropology.*

Nancy P. Greenman received her PhD from the University of New Mexico in 1987. She is president of the Chicago Association for the Practice of Anthropology, has served on the Board of Directors for the Council on Anthropology and Education, and is a Fellow in the Society for Applied Anthropology, where she has served on the nominations and program committees. Also, she is on the Pow Wow Committee for the Chicago American Indian Center. Dr. Greenman currently is a consultant in educational anthropology and ethnographic evaluation. She was an Assistant Professor of Social Foundations of Education at the University of South Florida, with an additional appointment in the Department of Anthropology (1989–94), and an Associate Professor of Educational Foundations and Research at the University of Texas at San Antonio (1995–2000) and at National Louis University (2000–2001). Dr. Greenman received a Faculty Excellence Award at the University of Texas at San Antonio (1996), a University of South Florida Library Book Author Award (1995) and a University of South Florida College of Education Development Board Award in Appreciation for Excellent Work (1992). She has been listed in *Who's Who in American Education* and *Who's Who of American Women.* Dr. Greenman has presented and published in national and international forums and journals and has co-edited a book, *Changing American Education: Recapturing the Past or Inventing the Future?*. Her research includes studies about educational change and resistance to change, diversity and multicultural education, transformative teacher education, gender equity and related areas. She also collected oral life histories of Tewa women in the Southwest.

Robert C. Harman received a doctorate from the University of Arizona in 1969. The same year, he joined the faculty at California State University, Long Beach, where he continues to be active in the Applied Anthropology program as Professor Emeritus. Dr. Harman is a former department chair at California State University, Long Beach. He is a past president of the Southwestern Anthropological Association and the Southern California Applied Anthropology Network. He has served on the executive board of the National Association for the Practice of Anthropology and on the board of the Consortium of Practicing and Applied Anthropology Programs. He taught in 1974 as a visiting professor on the World Campus Afloat and in 1994 at Chiang Mai University. Dr. Harman's early fieldwork and publications addressed the contemporary Tzeltal Maya of highland Chiapas, Mexico. In 1990 his Maya focus shifted to Q'anjob'al towns of northwestern Guatemala and a refugee community of Q'anjob'al in Los Angeles, California. For the past 15 years Dr. Harman has advocated for the Los Angeles

Maya community, and for the past ten years he has served as the executive director of the Maya nonprofit organization IXIM. For the past decade he has researched old age among the Karen hill tribe people of northern Thailand as well as the Maya. He continues to research and write on those cultures. In February 2005, Dr. Harman summed up much of his work in a presentation on "Aging in the 21st Century: A View from Anthropology" in the Saddleback College Distinguished Guest Lecture Series. He has an entry on "Older Persons" in the *Encyclopedia of Contemporary U.S. Immigration*, which will be published by Greenwood Publishing.

David A. Himmelgreen received his PhD in anthropology from SUNY Buffalo in 1994 and was a Research Scientist and Associate Director of Research at the Hispanic Health Council from 1994 to 1998. He is currently an Associate Professor of Anthropology at the University of South Florida (USF). Dr. Himmelgreen's interests include maternal and child health, nutritional assessment, food security, obesity, nutrition education, and HIV/AIDS. Dr. Himmelgreen has conducted research in India, Lesotho, the United States, and Costa Rica. He is the USF co-director (with Nancy Romero-Daza) of a field methods course in community health in Monteverde, Costa Rica, which is run in collaboration with the Monteverde Institute and several U.S. universities. In addition to being a Fulbright Scholar, he has received grants from the National Science Foundation, the United States Department of Agriculture, UNICEF, Sigma Xi, and from various state and local agencies in Florida. Recently, he was awarded a Presidential Young Faculty Award and Outstanding Undergraduate Teaching Award from USF. Dr. Himmelgreen has published articles in more than 15 peer-reviewed journals and has contributed chapters to several edited volumes.

Satish Kedia is Associate Professor of Anthropology and Director of the Institute for Substance Abuse Treatment Evaluation at The University of Memphis. He received his PhD with a concentration in applied and medical anthropology from the University of Kentucky in 1997. The same year, he received a certificate in Medical Behavioral Sciences from the Medical School at the University of Kentucky. Dr. Kedia's research interests include the health impacts of development projects, alcohol and drug abuse, caregiving and compliance issues associated with HIV/AIDS and cerebral palsy, and pesticide use and integrated pest management. Over the last 12 years, he has conducted fieldwork in India, Philippines, and the United

States. His research in India focuses on health impacts of involuntary reset-tlement among Garhwalis in the Central Himalayas and was funded by a National Science Foundation grant. In the Philippines, he is collaborating with the social scientists at the International Rice Research Institute to study health impacts of pesticide use among Filipino farmers. Since 1998, he has also been doing extensive applied work with the Bureau of Alcohol and Drug Abuse Services at the Tennessee Department of Health, conduct-ing statewide program evaluation for substance abuse treatment. Dr. Kedia has published over 15 journal articles, book chapters, and encyclopedia entries, and more than 30 evaluation and policy reports. He received the Chancellor's Award for Outstanding Teaching at the University of Ken-tucky and the College of Arts and Sciences Early Career Research Award at The University of Memphis.

Peter D. Little is Professor and Chair in the Department of Anthropology at the University of Kentucky. He received his PhD in anthropology in 1983 from Indiana University and initiated anthropological field research in 1980 among the Maasai-related Il Chamus of Northern Kenya. Dr. Little also has conducted intensive field research among Somali pastoralists of southern Somalia and among the Amhara and Oromo communities of Ethiopia. Since 1980, Dr. Little has directed interdisciplinary research pro-grams on development and globalization, pastoralism, political ecology, and food security in several African countries, but with primary emphasis on East Africa. He has served on advisory committees at the Social Science Research Council, the Fulbright Scholar Program, the Rockefeller Founda-tion, and has been a consultant to the UN Food and Agriculture Organiza-tion, the World Bank, the U.S. Agency for International Development (USAID), the U.S. Congress Office of Technology Assessment, and Oxfam America. Dr. Little has published more than 100 journal articles, book chapters, and research reports, and six books, including *Elusive Granary: Herder, Farmer, and State in Northern Kenya, Lands at Risk in the Third World: Local-Level Perspectives* (with Michael M Horowitz), and *Somalia: Economy without State* (co-winner of the 2003 Amaury Talbot Book Prize from the Royal Anthropological Institute).

Thomas R. McGuire is Research Anthropologist with the Bureau of Applied Research in Anthropology, and Research Professor, Department of Anthropology, University of Arizona. He received a PhD in anthropology from the University of Arizona in 1979 for a dissertation published as

Politics and Ethnicity on the Río Yaqui: Potam Revisited (University of Arizona Press, 1986). After a postdoctoral fellowship in Social Science and Public Policy at Carnegie Mellon University, he returned to Arizona to examine Native American water rights and land issues (Tohono O'odham, Salt River Pima-Maricopa, Gila River, and Ak-Chin reservations), fisheries and biosphere reserves in the upper Gulf of California, and, most recently, the development and impact of the offshore oil and gas industry on communities along the Gulf of Mexico, under contracts with the Minerals Management Service, U.S. Department of the Interior. Dr. McGuire has published in *Human Organization, Journal of the Southwest, Maritime Anthropological Studies, American Indian Culture and Research Journal,* and elsewhere. He is a fellow in the Society for Applied Anthropology and the American Anthropological Association, and a member of the International Association for Society and Natural Resources and the American Society for Environment History, among other professional associations.

Anthony Oliver-Smith is Professor of Anthropology at the University of Florida. He is also affiliated with the Center for Latin American Studies at that institution. Dr. Oliver-Smith received his PhD from Indiana University in 1974. He has done anthropological research and consultation on issues relating to involuntary resettlement as well as the impacts of natural and technological disasters in Peru, Honduras, India, Brazil, Jamaica, Mexico, Japan, and the United States since the 1970s. He has served on the executive boards of the National Association of Practicing Anthropologists and the Society for Applied Anthropology. His work on involuntary resettlement has focused on such issues as the threat and impacts of displacement and the formation of social movements, the policy implications of resistance, and the critiques of development policy and practice articulated by resistance movements. Dr. Oliver-Smith has published extensively and is a prominent scholar on disaster and displacement issues. His recent books include *Catastrophe and Culture: The Anthropology of Disaster* (2002) and *The Angry Earth: Disaster in Anthropological Perspective* (1999), both with Susannah M. Hoffman.

Robert E. Rhoades, Professor of Anthropology at the University of Georgia, is widely regarded as one of the founders of agricultural anthropology. Born on a cattle ranch in Oklahoma, Dr. Rhoades studied agriculture at Oklahoma State. After a Peace Corps experience in Nepal (1962-64), he decided that anthropology offered a refreshing but underutilized perspective on agricultural change. He received his PhD from the University of Oklahoma in 1976. In 1979 he joined the International Potato Center in Lima, Peru, as one of the first anthropologists to work in the Consultative Group for International Agricultural Research (CGIAR). In 1989, he founded the User's Perspective with Agricultural Research and Development (UPWARD), a pan-Asian network focused on participatory research. In 1991, he was hired by the University of Georgia to build a new program in Ecological and Environmental Anthropology. He served two terms on the USDA Secretary of Agriculture's Advisory Council on Genetic Resources, and he is the only anthropologist to have been honored with special awards by the Crop Society of America and the American Society of Horticultural Science. He has published a dozen books and over 130 articles. He has received numerous fellowships, including the Rockefeller Foundation Research Fellowship in Agricultural Development and a Fulbright Scholar award.

John van Willigen is Professor of Anthropology at the University of Kentucky at Lexington, where he is also appointed to the Department of Behavioral Science, College of Medicine, and the Graduate Center on Gerontology. His undergraduate anthropology degree is from the University of Wisconsin, Madison, and his PhD studies were done at the University of Arizona. While at Arizona, he completed training in community development as well as anthropology. He was employed by Papago Tribe of Arizona (now the Tohono O'odham Nation) as Director of Community Development. Dr. van Willigen has published extensively on applied anthropology practice. These publications include the textbook *Applied Anthropology: An Introduction* (now in its third edition), and the edited volumes *Making Our Research Useful: Case Studies in the Utilization of Anthropological Knowledge* (with Barbara Rylko-Bauer and Ann McElroy) and *Soundings: Rapid and Reliable Research Methods for Practicing Anthropologists* (with Timothy J. Finan). He has done field research in India, rural Kentucky, and Indonesia. This work has focused on the social aging process and ethnography of farming and food ways. The products of this work include three research monographs. These are *Gettin' Some Age on Me: Social Organization of Older People in a Rural American Community, Tobacco Culture: Farming Kentucky's Burley Belt* (with Susan C. Eastwood), and *Social Aging in a Delhi Neighborhood* (with N. K. Chadha). He has received the Sol Tax Distinguished Service Award from the Society for Applied Anthropology, the Omer C. Stewart Memorial Award of the High Plains Society for Applied Anthropology, two Fulbright Lectureships (India), and a Chancellor's Award for Outstanding Teaching at the University of Kentucky.

Linda M. Whiteford received her PhD from the University of Wisconsin in 1980 and an MPH from the University of Texas, the same year. She is a Medical Anthropologist and Professor of Anthropology at the University of South Florida. She is also currently the President of the Society for Applied Anthropology, one of the oldest and most prestigious scholarly societies in anthropology. She was Chair of the Department of Anthropology (1997–2003), and Director of Graduate Programs (1994–97). In 2004 she received the President's Award for Excellence, and she was earlier awarded a prize for Outstanding Teaching (1994). In 2002, Santa Clara University named her Outstanding Scholar for the year. Her research focuses on global forces and health such as water scarcity, infectious disease, disasters and recovery, and child/maternal health. Dr. Whiteford has conducted research in Cuba, Ecuador, Bolivia, Nicaragua, Mexico, Costa Rica and the Dominican Republic. Her most recent books are *Globalization, Water and Health: Resource Management in Times of Scarcity* (2005), and *Global Health Policy, Local Realities: The Fallacy of the Level Playing Field* (2000). In addition, Dr. Whiteford consults with international health agencies such as the World Health Organization, the Pan American Health Organization, USAID, the Environmental Health Project, and she and conducts reviews for the National Science Foundation and the Thrasher Fund.